Ordnance Survey

STREET ATLAS
East
Sussex

Contents

III Key to map symbols

IV-V Key to map pages

VI Administrative and post code boundaries

1 Street maps

189 Extra-large-scale map of Brighton town centre

190 Town maps of Chichester and Crawley

191 Town maps of Horsham and Worthing

192 Index of hospitals, railway stations, schools, shopping centres, street names and universities

222 Town and village index

PHILIP'S

D0812961

First edition published 1994
First colour edition published 1997
Reprinted in 1999, 2000 by

George Philip Ltd, a division of
Octopus Publishing Group Ltd
2-4 Heron Quays, London E14 4JP

ISBN 0-540-07312-1 (pocket)

To the best of the Publishers' knowledge, the information in this
atlas was correct at the time of going to press. No responsibility
can be accepted for any errors or their consequences.

The representation in this atlas of a road, track or path is no
evidence of the existence of a right of way.

**The mapping between pages 1 and 191 (inclusive) in this
atlas is derived from Ordnance Survey® OSCAR® and
Land-Line® data, and Landranger® mapping.**

Ordnance Survey, OSCAR, Land-line and Landranger are
registered trade marks of Ordnance Survey, the national
mapping agency of Great Britain.

Printed and bound in Spain by Cayfosa

Digital Data

The exceptionally high-quality mapping
found in this book is available as
digital data in TIFF format, which is
easily convertible to other bit-mapped
(raster) image formats.

The index is also available in digital
form as a standard database table.
It contains all the details found in the
printed index together with the
National Grid reference for the map
square in which each entry is named
and feature codes for places of
interest in eight categories such as
education and health.

For further information and to discuss
your requirements, please contact
Philip's on 020 7531 8440 or
george.philip@philips-maps.co.uk

Key to map symbols

(22a)	**Motorway** (with junction number)		⇌	**British Rail station**
	Primary route (dual carriageway and single)		(railway)	**Private railway station**
	A road (dual carriageway and single)		⬥	**Bus, coach station**
	B road (dual carriageway and single)		◆	**Ambulance station**
	Minor road (dual carriageway and single)		◆	**Coastguard station**
	Other minor road		◆	**Fire station**
- - -	**Road under construction**		◆	**Police station**
	Railway		✚	**Casualty entrance to hospital**
	Tramway, miniature railway		✝	**Church, place of worship**
	Rural track, private road or narrow road in urban area		H	**Hospital**
	Gate or obstruction to traffic (restrictions may not apply at all times or to all vehicles)		i	**Information centre**
- - - - -	**Path, bridleway, byway open to all traffic, road used as a public path**		P	**Parking**
	The representation in this atlas of a road, track or path is no evidence of the existence of a right of way		PO	**Post Office**
160			Bexhill Coll	**Important buildings, schools, colleges, universities and hospitals**
38	**Adjoining page indicators**		·—··—··	**County boundaries**
189	The map area within the pink band is shown at a larger scale on the page indicated by the red block and arrow		River Ouse	**Water name**
				Stream
				River or canal (minor and major)
				Water
				Tidal water
				Woods
				Houses
			Hastings Castle	**Non-Roman antiquity**
			ROMAN FORT	**Roman antiquity**

Acad	**Academy**	Mon	**Monument**
Cemy	**Cemetery**	Mus	**Museum**
C Ctr	**Civic Centre**	Obsy	**Observatory**
CH	**Club House**	Pal	**Royal Palace**
Coll	**College**	PH	**Public House**
Ent	**Enterprise**	Recn Gd	**Recreation Ground**
Ex H	**Exhibition Hall**	Resr	**Reservoir**
Ind Est	**Industrial Estate**	Ret Pk	**Retail Park**
Inst	**Institute**	Sch	**School**
Ct	**Law Court**	Sh Ctr	**Shopping Centre**
L Ctr	**Leisure Centre**	Sta	**Station**
LC	**Level Crossing**	TH	**Town Hall/House**
Liby	**Library**	Trad Est	**Trading Estate**
Mkt	**Market**	Univ	**University**
Meml	**Memorial**	YH	**Youth Hostel**

■ The dark grey border on the inside edge of some pages indicates that the mapping does not continue onto the adjacent page

■ The small numbers around the edges of the maps identify the 1 kilometre National Grid lines

The scale of the maps is 3.92 cm to 1 km (2½ inches to 1 mile)	0 ¼ ½ ¾ 1 mile 0 250m 500m 750m 1 kilometre
The scale of the map on page numbered in red is 7.84 cm to 1 km (5 inches to 1 mile)	0 220 yards 440 yards 660 yards ½ mile 0 125m 250m 375m ½ kilometre

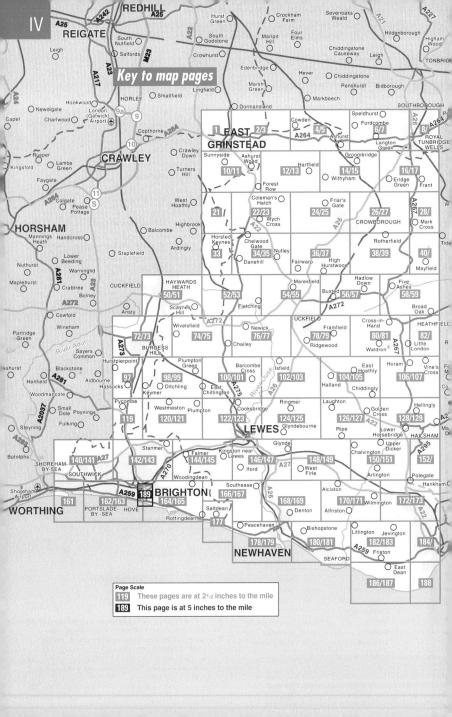

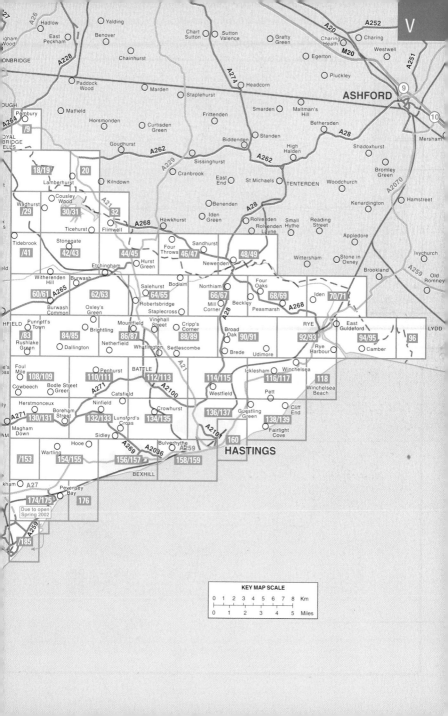

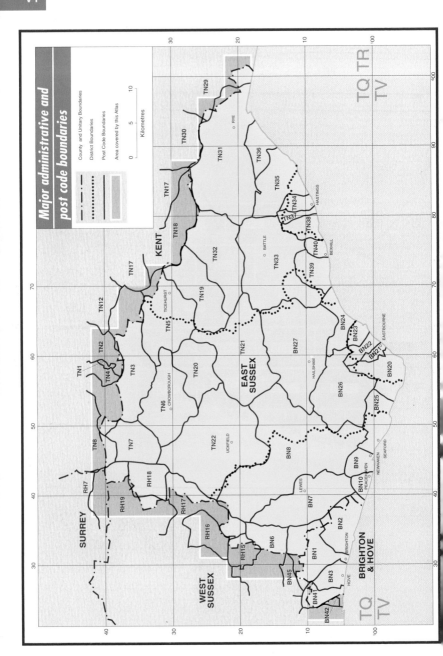

Major administrative and post code boundaries

County and Unitary Boundaries
District Boundaries
Post Code Boundaries
Area covered by this Atlas

Kilometres
0   5   10

A   **B**   **C**   **D**   **E**   **F**

8

7

41

6

5

40

4

39

3

2

1

38

FELCOURT COTTS
FELCOURT LA
Felcourt
Farm
BLACKBERRY RD
Felcourt
PO

High
Wood

Wire Mill
Wood

CHESTNUT WALK

Coll of
St Barnabas

Dormans
Sta
DORMANS STATION RD
STARBOROUGH
COTTS

Yew
Lodge

The
Grange

FELCOURT RD

PARK RD
PARK RD

Stockriding
Wood

Felbridge

Cromwell Hall
Farm

OSMUNDA BANK

ST MARGARET'S
AVE
FURZEFIELD CHASE
THE APPROACH

The
Kennels

Chartham
Park

Dormans
Park

DORMANS
GDNS

Ward's
Farm

Charters
Towers

EDEN VALE

LAKE VIEW RD

EASTBOURNE RD

Chartham
Wood

WADLANDS BROOK RD

EDEN VALE

THE GLEBE

Frith
Manor

Sewage
Works

The
Alders

ITTINGTON
COLL

A264
PTHORNE RD

Lower Barn
Cottage

ROUGH FIELD 1
WELLS MEADOW 2

FURZEFIELD RD

BROWNS WAY

THE NEAL
SPRING
COPSE

Hotel
Baldwins
Hill

THE
ELBRIDGE
CTR

THE
MOORINGS

FURZE LA
HOGARTH CT

FELGWATER
CT

STRATFORD

LOWDELLS DR

KING GEORGE'S AVE

GOODWINS CL
Baldwins
Hill Cty
Prim Sch

HERONTYE DR

WELLS LEA

FRITH PK

BRAMBLETYE

HACKENDEN LA

BEECHFIELDS
The
Queen Victoria

HOLTYE RD
A264

North
End

LONDON RD

NEALE CL
SACKVILLE

SACKVILLE
GDNS

KNOLE GR

Imberhorne
Lower
Sch

WINDMILL LA

DORMANS

HIGHFIELD
RD

HERMITAGE
RD

KENNEDY AVE

ALDERS RD

HACKENDEN CL

H

The
Independent
BSNS PK

BIRCHES
IND EST

HALSFORD LA

Y PK

BUTTESLAND

1 COVERDALE CT
2 TURRET CT
3 ST GEORGES CT
4 DORSET GDNS

KINGSCOTE RD

CHET
NOLE

Blackwell

Blackwell
Cty Prim
Sch

ROBIN
CL

A264 MOAT RD

Imberhorne
Sch

Halsford Park
Cty Prim
Sch

CHANTLERS
CL

ASHDOWN
GATE

SOUTHWICK

New
Life
Sch

THE OLD
CONVENT

EAST
GRINSTEAD

ST AGNES

ST JOHN'S RD

JOHN'S

Cemy

BLACKWELL RD

HOLTYE RD

COLLEGE LA
B2110

Mus

Imberhorne
Farm

IMBERHORNE LA

PO

LINGFIELD

MEADOWCRO

CHAPMAN'S
LA

Moat
Pond

CRANSTON RD

CRANSTON CL

STONELEIGH CL

Worth Way
Sussex Border Path

CHAPMAN LA

CAMPBELL CRES

ST EDWARD'S CL

CROSSWAYS AVE

PARK RD

LODGE CL

BLOUNT RD

STATION RD

WOOD ST

ST JAMES'S

A22

BEECHING WAY

SANDY LA

CHRISTOPHER RD

B2110

GIFFARD

ROCKDENE

COLE

THE BLYTHES

East Grinstead
Sta

SHELLEY RD

THE BRONTES

RAILWAY APP

ORCHARD WAY

QUEENSWAY

WALLIS

PO

A22

ORCHARD

SWITHIN

B2110

A22

SWITHIN

COLE

A   **38**   **B**   **C**   **39**   **D**   **E**   **F**

C1
1 THE BROWNINGS
2 BYRON GR
3 CHAUCER AVE
4 TENNYSON RISE
5 THE SAYERS
6 WORDSWORTH RISE

10

2

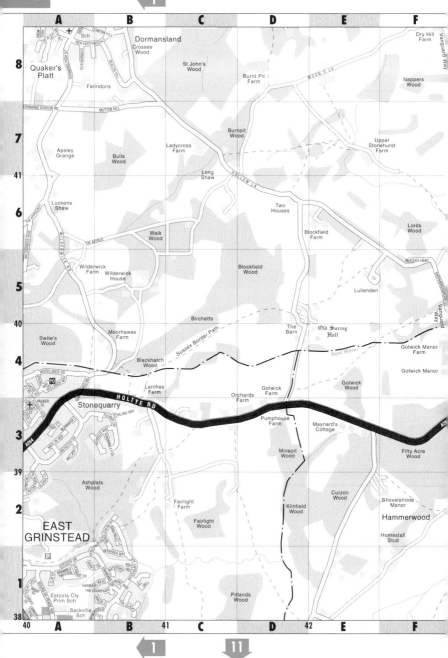

A B C D E F

Jules Wood

Dry Hill

Ten Acre Wood

Minepit Wood

Crippenden Manor

Ludwells Farm

Polefields

8

Willow Bed

Beeches Farm

Old Furzefield Wood

Liveroxhill Wood

Leighton Manor

7

Ravenscroft Farm

41

Woodlands Farm

Clay's Wood

Sussex Border Path

Marlpit Shaw

6

Waystrode Manor

ower nehurst Farm

Basing & Smithers Farm

Drews Rough

Scarletts

5

Pondtail

Furnace Farm

40

GATWICK FARM COTTS

Scarletts Lake

Kent Water

Furnace Pond

Vanguard Way

Mill Wood

Reading's Wood

4

Cleavers Farm

Steadleaze Wood

Bank Farm

Roger's Town

Holtye Common

HOLTYE RD

High Meadows

Home Farm

Cooper's Wood

COUNTESS OF THANET'S ALMSHOUSES

Golf Course

Holtye

Hammerwood

Holtye Golf Club

A264

3

White Horse (PH)

39

Hammerwood Park

Hammer Wood

CANSIRON LA

2

Wet Wood

Cansiron Wood

Little Cansiron Farm

1

Sewage Works

The Grove

DOG COTTS

Water Wood

oklands

38

A B C D E F

44 45

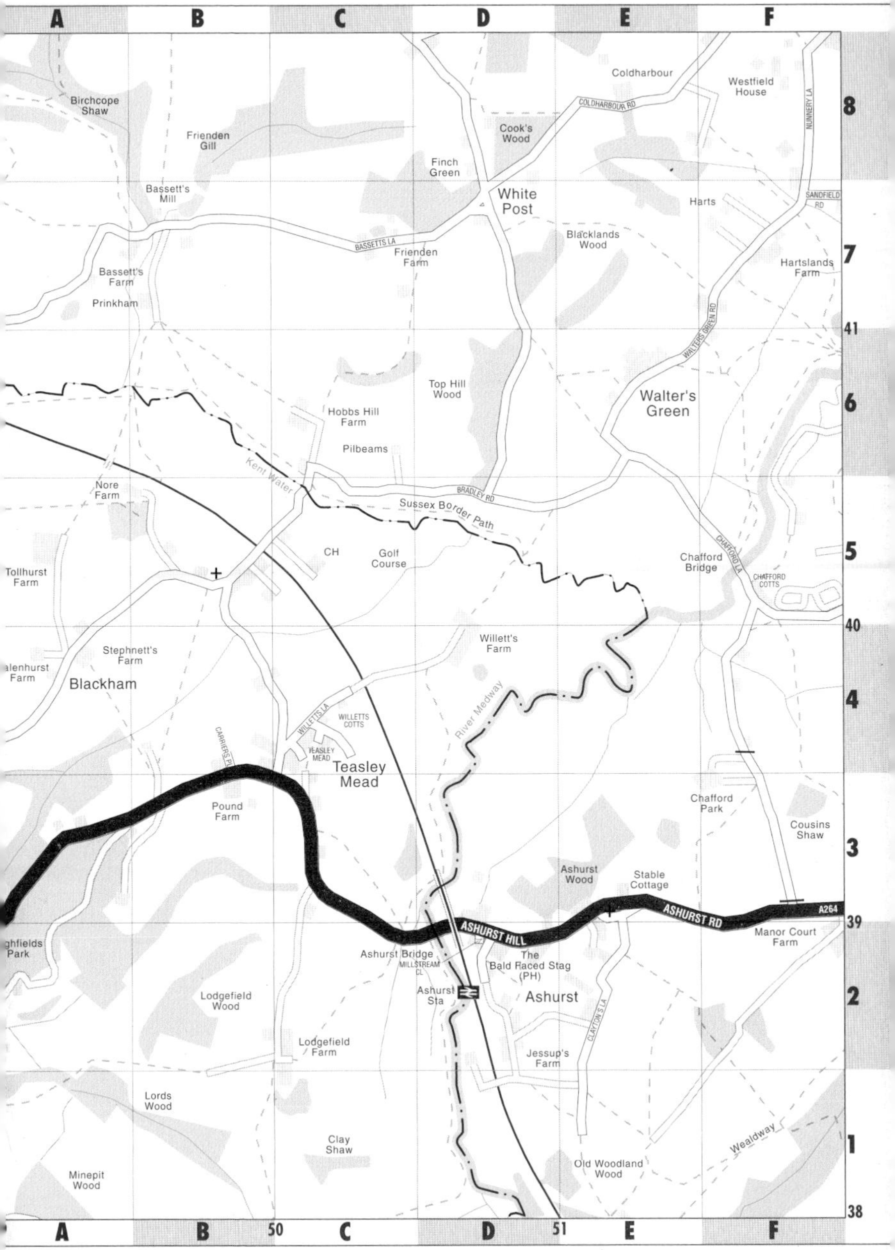
6
A
B
C
D
E
F
Birchcope Shaw
Frienden Gill
Coldharbour
COLDHARBOUR RD
Westfield House
NUNNERY LA
Cook's Wood
Finch Green
White Post
Bassett's Mill
BASSETTS LA
Frienden Farm
Blacklands Wood
Harts
SANDFIELD RD
Bassett's Farm
Prinkham
Hartslands Farm
WALTERS GREEN RD
Top Hill Wood
Hobbs Hill Farm
Walter's Green
Pilbeams
Kent Water
Nore Farm
BRADLEY RD
Sussex Border Path
CH
Golf Course
Tollhurst Farm
Chafford Bridge
CHAFFORD LA
CHAFFORD COTTS
Willett's Farm
Stephnett's Farm
alenhurst Farm
Blackham
River Medway
WILLETTS LA
WILLETTS COTTS
CARRIERS PL
TEASLEY MEAD
Teasley Mead
Pound Farm
Chafford Park
Cousins Shaw
Ashurst Wood
Stable Cottage
ASHURST RD
A264
ASHURST HILL
Manor Court Farm
ghfields Park
Ashurst Bridge
MILLSTREAM CL
The Bald Faced Stag (PH)
Ashurst Sta
Ashurst
Lodgefield Wood
CLAYTON'S LA
Lodgefield Farm
Jessup's Farm
Lords Wood
Wealdway
Clay Shaw
Old Woodland Wood
Minepit Wood
8
7
41
6
5
40
4
3
39
2
1
38
50
51
14
6

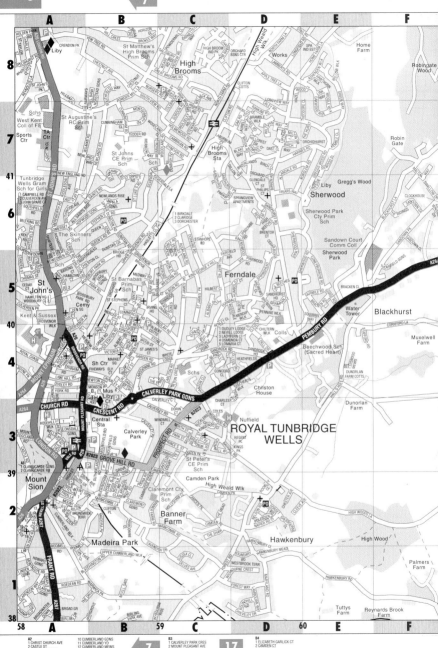

◄ 7   17

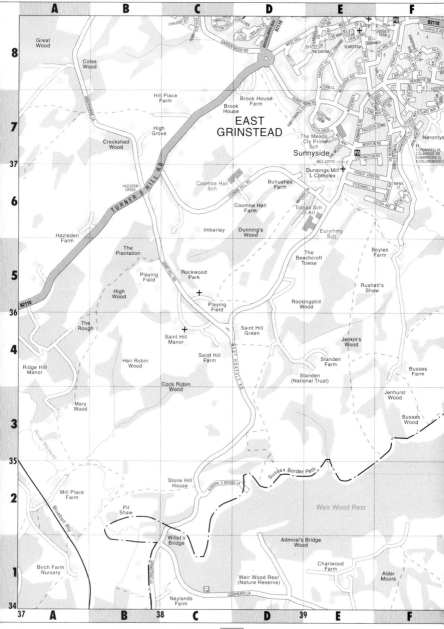

F8
1 MIDDLE ROW
2 FOREST LODGE
3 SACKVILLE CT
4 GREAT HOUSE CT
5 PORTLAND HO
6 CORNWALL GDNS

7 NORMANDY CL
8 WILLOW MEAD
9 KINGS COPSE
10 REGAL DR
11 BECKETT WAY

B2110

| | A | B | C | D | E | F |

8

Great Wood

Coles Wood

Libry

BELL HAMMER

7

Hill Place Farm

Brook House Farm

Brook House

EAST GRINSTEAD

Herontye

High Grove

Crockshed Wood

The Meads Cty Prim Sch

Sunnyside

37

HAZLEDEN CROSS

TURNER'S HILL RD

Dunnings Mill L Complex

MILL COTTS

F7
1 CORNWELL PL
2 CLARENCE DR
3 HARWOODS CL
4 COLLINGWOOD CT

6

Coombe Hall Sch

Bulrushes Farm

Coombe Hall Farm

Tobias Sch of Art

Hazleden Farm

Imberley

Dunning's Wood

Eurythmy Sch

The Plantation

SAINT HILL RD

Rockwood Park

The Beechcroft Towse

Boyles Farm

5

Playing Field

High Wood

Playing Field

Rockingshill Wood

Rushett's Shaw

36

B2110

The Rough

Saint Hill Manor

Saint Hill Green

Jenkin's Wood

4

Ridge Hill Manor

Hen Robin Wood

Saint Hill Farm

WEST HOATHLY RD

Standen Farm

Busses Farm

Cock Robin Wood

Standen (National Trust)

Jenhurst Wood

Mary Wood

Busses Wood

3

River Medway

Sussex Border Path

35

Mill Place Farm

Stone Hill House

ADMIRAL'S BRIDGE LA

Weir Wood Resr

2

Bluebell Rly

Pit Shaw

Admiral's Bridge Wood

Willet's Bridge

Chariwood Farm

Alder Moors

1

Birch Farm Nursery

Weir Wood Resr (Nature Reserve)

Neylands Farm

LEGSHEATH LA

34

| 37 | A | B | 38 | C | D | 39 | E | F |

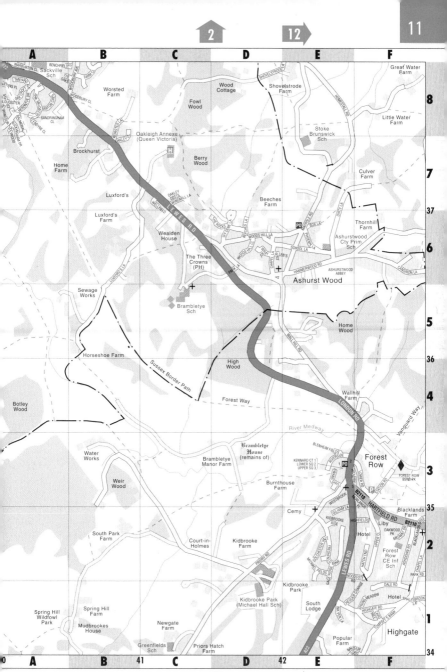

| | A | B | C | D | E | F |

8

Vanguard Way

Owlett's Farm

CANSIRON LA

Church Wood

Great Cansiron Farm

Acre Wood

Holden Wood

BUTCHERFIELD LA

7

Thornhill

Great Surries

Roughfield Wood

Great Surries Farm

37

Little Surries

Pollard Wood

Paupersdale Wood

Marlpit Shaw

6

Grove Farm

Little Surries Farm

North Clays

Vanguard Way

CANSIRON LA

St Ives Farm West

Mast

Collingsbush Wood

Wick Wood

5

Highams Wood

36

Pixton Hill Farm

Ashdown House

Lower Parrock

4

Ashdown Farm

River Medway

Sewage Works

3

Alder Shaw

Sussex Border Path

Gassonsfield Wood

35

BLACKLANDS CRES

MEDWAY DR

B2110

Forest Way

Upper Parrock Farm

PARROCK LA

PARK CRES

STONEPARK DR

STONEDENE CL

Lines Farm

Upper Parrock

CHAPEL LA

HARTFIELD RD

2

Forest Row

PARK RD

BROADSTONE

HIGH ST

LOWER RD

Little Parrock

PRIMROSE LA

RYST WOOD RD

SHALESBROOK

Vanguard Way

Rystwood Farm

Little Parrock Farm

Paternoster Wood

1

Shalesbrook

CH

CAT ST

Royal Ashdown Forest Golf Course

B2110

Quabrook

B2110

34

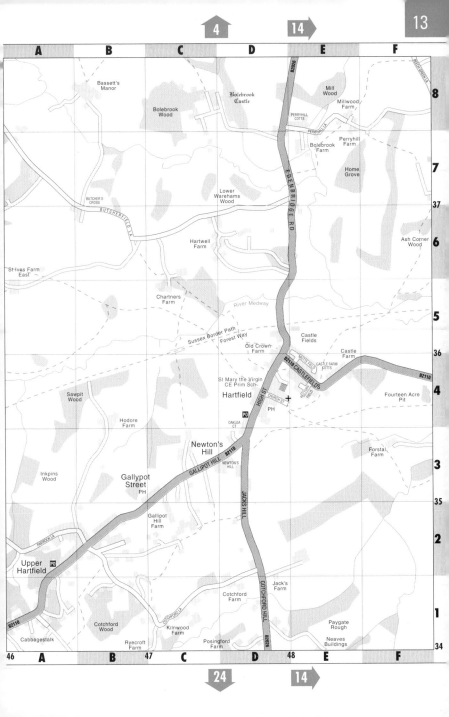

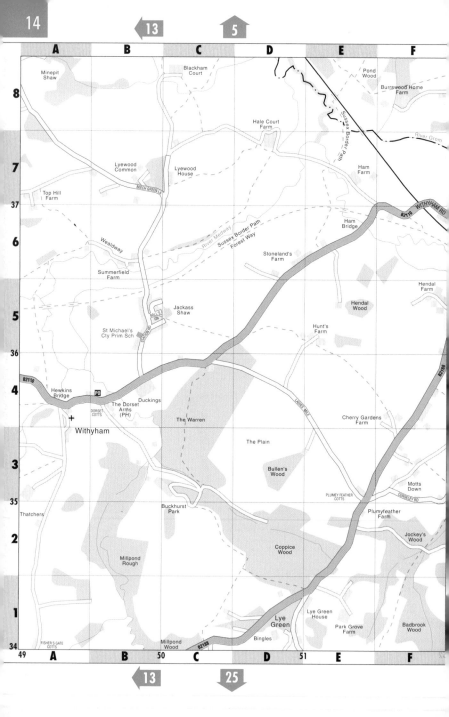

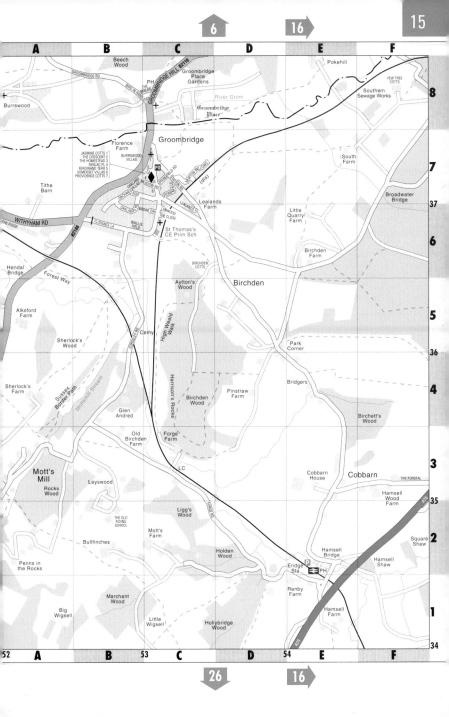

8

Adam's Well (dis)
Crossing

Ramslye
Wood

Ramslye
Farm

EASTLANDS CL.

Strawberry
Hill

7

The Firs

Broadwater
Forest

Ruffet
Wood

Broadwater
Down

Strawberry Hill
Farm

37

Spratsbrook
Farm

Broadwater
Lodge

Firtree
Plantation

Sprat's Brook

Hargate
Forest

6

The
Warren

The Roundabouts

BUNNY LA.

5

Kennels

Bohemia

36

Eridge
Rocks

Whitehill
Wood

Warren
Farm

The Nevill
Crest & Gun
(PH)

4

WARREN FARM LA.

Eridge
Park

Eridge
Park

Eridge
Green

3

Crown
House

Mill
Wood

35

Steel
Bridge

High Weald Wlk

Keepers
Cottages

2

Steel Bridge
Farm

Forge
Wood

Eridge
Old Park

1

Bushy
Wood

Great Robbins
Shaw

Bushy
Shaw

34

17   9

| | A | B | C | D | E | F |

8 Coker's Down
Sunninglye Farmhouse

Rushlye Down
Coneyburrow Wood
Furnace Wood

7 Oxpasture Wood
River Teise
Tollslye
The Bothy

37

Hollow Wood
Bayham Lake

6 Jews Wood
Great Coppice Wood

Rushlye Farmhouse

Highfield
Abbots Down
Diamonds
Forest Lodge

5 MIDDLE RD

B2169
Burnt Wood
Upper Sluice Wood
LITTLE BAYHAM COTTS

36
B216
Little Bayham

Higham Wood
Higham Farm
Bartley Mill Wood

4 Verridge Wood
Bartley Mill

Churchfield Wood
Wickhurst Farmhouse

Little Shoesmiths
Bartley House

3 Sewers Bridge

Brookland Wood

35 Grigg's Wood
Shoesmith's Wood

2 Camden Wood
Brick Kiln Wood

Great Shoesmith Farm
Hewley Wood

Henley Wood
Sussex Border Path

1 TEERIDGE LA
WHITEGATE LA

Down Wood
Sewage Works

34
61   A   B   62   C   D   63   E   F

17   29

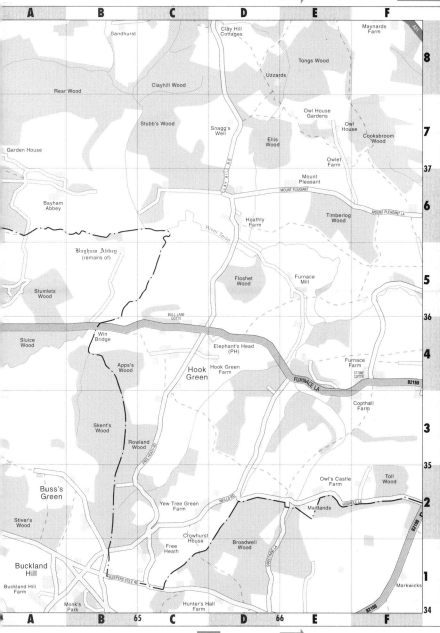

A | B | C | D | E | F

8

Maynards Farm

Clay Hill Cottages

Sandhurst

Tongs Wood

Uzzards

Clayhill Wood

Rear Wood

Owl House Gardens

Owl House

Cooksbroom Wood

7

Stubb's Wood

Snagg's Well

Ellis Wood

Garden House

CLAY HILL RD

Owlet Farm

37

Mount Pleasant

Bayham Abbey

MOUNT PLEASANT

MOUNT PLEASANT LA

6

Hoathly Farm

Timberlog Wood

River Teise

Bagham Abbey (remains of)

Floshet Wood

Furnace Mill

5

Stumlets Wood

BULL LANE COTTS

36

Sluice Wood

Win Bridge

Elephant's Head (PH)

Furnace Farm

STONE COTTS

4

Apps's Wood

Hook Green

Hook Green Farm

FURNACE LA

B2169

Copthall Farm

3

Skent's Wood

Rowland Wood

TREE HEATH RD

35

Buss's Green

Owl's Castle Farm

Toll Wood

2

Stiver's Wood

Yew Tree Green Farm

NEILLS RD

Maitlands

HIGHGATE LA

B2100

Crowhurst House

Broadwell Wood

Free Heath

SHEETING LA

Buckland Hill

Buckland Hill Farm

SLEEPERS STILE RD

Hunter's Hall Farm

1

Markwicks

B2100

Monk's Park

34

A | B | 65 | C | D | 66 | E | F

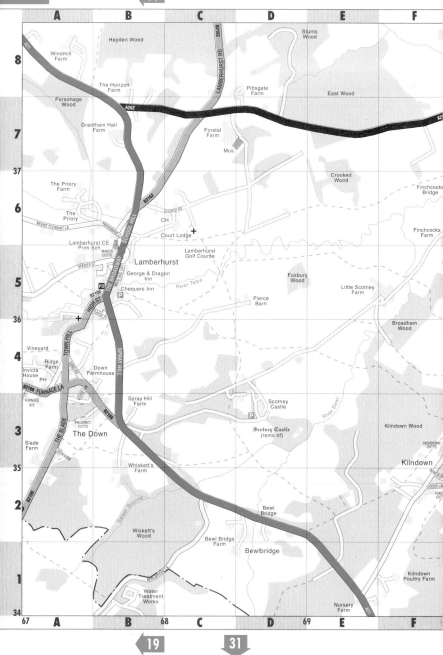

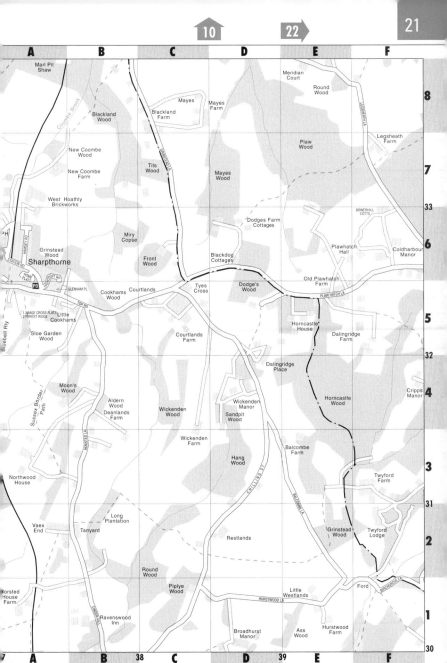

A **B** **C** **D** **E** **F**

8

Kidbrooke
Wood

LEWES RD

A22

BALFOUR RD

TOMPSETS BANK

Tompset's
Bank

Greenhall
Cottage

Royal Ashdown
Forest Golf
Course

Wych
Warren

Fernhill

7

Lavender
Platt

PRIORY RD

Old Cherry
Orchard

33

Hindleap
Warren

Broadstone Warren
Scout Camp

Broadstone
Warren

6

LEGSHEATH LA

PLAW HATCH LA

Hindleap Farm

Hindleap Warren
Activity Ctr

COLEMANS HATCH RD

5

Pillow
Mounds

Eighteen Acre
Wood

32

Wych
Cross

Roebuck
Hotel

Smockfarthing

Wych Cross
Fruit Farm

Half Moon
Copse

4

Wych Cross
Place

A275

Ashdown
Llama Farm

Garde

3

Suttons Farm

Hillsdown
Farm

Press Ridge
Warren

Garde

31

P

Mill Brook

2

Stumblewood
Common

Isle of Thorns
(Univ of Sussex)

Birch Grove
House

The White
House

1

BIRCHGROVE LA

Gosses
Farm

Steel Forge Brook

LEWES RD

A275

Red Lion
(PH)

PO

CHAPEL LA

30

A 40 **B** 41 **C** **D** 42 **E** **F**

	A	B	C	D	E	F

Buckhurst Farm

Fincham Farm

8

Tile Barn Farm

Neaves Farm

Marsh Green

Posingford Wood

Hart's Farm

7

Chuck Hatch

Pimp Barn Cottages

33

Podlea Flock Farm

Jumper's Town

Five Hundred Rough

Five Hundred Acre Wood

Spring Farm

6

Lone Oak Hall

The Rough

Wren's Warren

5

Fagot Stac Corner

P

32

Gills Lap

Wood Eaves

P

Kidd's Hill Farm

KIDD'S HILL

4

Vanguard Way

Wealdway

P

3

Tile Lodge

Jack Daw

Heasman's Lodge Farm

31

Black Hill

Greenwood Gate

The Orcha

2

P

Deerswood Farm

Lodge

The Nursery

P

King's Standing

1

P P

B2188

P

The Old Mill House

B2026

30

46	A		B	47	C		D	48	E		F

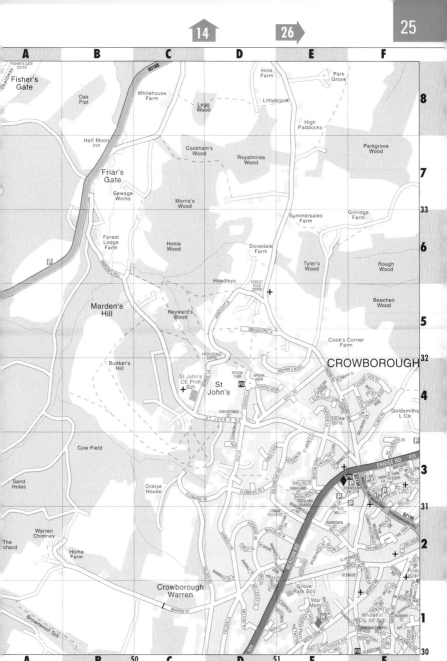

A   **B**   **C**   **D**   **E**   **F**

B2099

Rowden
Farm

Compton
Close

8

Rowden House
Farm

Sewage
Works

B2099

ZOWN LA

Pococksgate
Farm

Furnace
Wood

7

Sussex Border Path

Lightlands

Riverhall

RIVERHALL LA

33

Nap Wood

Colesgrove
Wood

Earlye
Farm

PARTRIDGES LA

6

Saxonbury
Farm

Buckhurst
Place

Ellen Gray

Saxonbury
Farm

TUNBRIDGE WELLS RD

5

Partridges

BUCKHURST LA

32

BRICKYARD LA

Frankham
Wood

Steel
Farm

4

BRICKYARD
COTTS

Strood
Wood

Frankham
Farm

Wessons

Catts Farm

Mark Cross

Strood
House

Frankham

Little
Frankham

Frankham
Dene

Beggars'
Bush

B21

Beechglade
Farm

MILL LA
BELLSPOOL
COTTS
Mark Cross
CE Prim
Sch

WADHURST RD

3

BEECHLANDS
COTTS
Skinner's
Farm

Sandyden
House

Houndsell
Place

Houndsell
Stud

B2100

Marks Cross
Inn (PH)

31

Caravan &
Camping Site

Sandyden
Wood

Earl's
Farm

BASSETTS LA

Bensfield
Farm

2

Renhurst
Farm

Tidle Brook

MAYFIELD RD

Bassetts

Stilehouse
Wood

Rocks
Wood

1

Stile
House

A267

LAKE ST

Little Trodgers
Farm

Devil's
Gill

Highfields
Farm

Badgers'
Hill

30

58   **A**   **B**   **59**   **C**   **D**   **60**   **E**   **F**

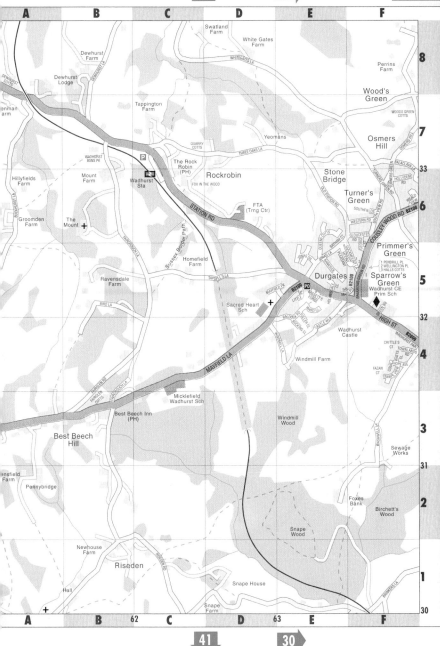

A   B   C   D   E   F

Swatland Farm
White Gates Farm
WHITEGATES LA
Perrins Farm
Dewhurst Farm
DEWHURST LA
Wood's Green
Dewhurst Lodge
WOODS GREEN COTTS
anman arm
Tappington Farm
Osmers Hill
QUARRY COTTS
THREE OAKS LA
Yeomans
WADHURST BSNS PK
The Rock Robin (PH)
Rockrobin
Stone Bridge
BALACLAVA LA
Hillfields Farm
Mount Farm
Wadhurst Sta
FOX IN THE WOOD
Turner's Green
Groomden Farm
STATION RD
FTA (Trng Ctr)
SOUTHFIELDS
COUSLEY WOOD RD B2100
The Mount
WESTERN RD
GLOUCESTER
QUEEN COTTS
1 PENDRILL PL
2 WELLINGTON PL
3 HALLS COTTS
Sussex Border Path
Homefield Farm
Primmer's Green
Ravensdale Farm
TAPSEL STA
B2100
Durgates
Sparrow's Green
Wadhurst CE Prim Sch
BIRD LA
MAYFIELD PK
B2100
PO
Sacred Heart Sch
LITTLE
Windmill Farm
HIGH ST   B2099
Wadhurst Castle
CRITTLES CT
TOWNLANDS RD
HOPE AVE
FAZAN CT
MAYFIELD LA
Micklefield Wadhurst Sch
Best Beech Inn (PH)
Windmill Wood
Best Beech Hill
Sewage Works
ansfield Farm
Pennybridge
Foxes Bank
Birchett's Wood
Snape Wood
Newhouse Farm
Riseden
BISDEN RD
Hall
Snape House
BRINKERS LA
Snape Farm

A   B   62   C   D   63   E   F

29 19

	A	B	C	D	E	F

8

Newbury's

NEWBURY COTTS

NEWBURY LA

The Colleens

B2100

Ladymeads Farm

BEWLBRIDGE LA

Lower Cousley Wood

Gate House Farm

HILLSIDE COTTS

MANOR LA

WINDMILL LA

COUSLEY WOOD RD

PH

7

Pell Green

Cousley Wood

Great Butts

33

BALACLAVA LA

B2100

Little Butts Farm

Bryant's Farm

6

Great Pell Oast

1 FAIR VIEW
2 DEEPDENE
3 THE LEAS
4 PELL CL
5 BIRCH KILN COTTS

Bewl Water

Newbarn

Sussex Border Path

5

Pell Bridge

Wishdow

Vicarage Green

Southfields

32

BLACKSMITHS LA

Little Pell Farm

Foxhole

Little Whiligh

Chesson's Farm

4

B2099

1 THE SQUARE
2 KINGSLEY CT

Wadhurst

P

Uplands Comm Coll

LOWER HIGH ST

Long Wood

WALK

TOTCH LA

BIRCHETTS GREEN LA

3

Stone Cross

Moseham

Whiligh

Birchett's Green

Birchett's Green Farm

31

2

BARDERS LA

Darby's Farm

DARBYS LA

Holbeam Wood

Cattle Breeding Ctr

1

Shover's Green House

HIGH ST

Shover's Green

STONEGATE RD

Upper Wallands Farm

CHURCHSETTLE LA

Normanswood

Bugsey's Farm

B2099

PO

Wallcrouch Farm

Wallcrouch

30

Walland Manor

64	A	65	C	D	66	E	F

29 42

A   B   C   D   E   F

8

Beal Barn
Gardens
P
Visitors
Ctr   Slipway
P
Hook
Farm   Activities
Ctr
Hook
House

River Bewl

Chingley
Wood

Cats
Wood

Chingley
Manor

7

33

Stonecrouch

Beaumans
Oast

Bewl Water

Sussex Border Path

6

Greenwoods

Hazelhurst
Farm

Rosemary
Farmhouse

5

32

LOWER HAZELHURST

Nature
Reserve

Overy's
Farm

Tilehouse
Bungalow

Rowley

Norwoods
Farm

Overy's
Farmhouse

4

LOWER HAZELHURST

Bakers & Strakes
Farm

HUNTLEY MILL

TINTON HILL

Borders
Farm

Walter's
Farm

3

Burnt
Lodge

BORDERS LA

Three Leg
Cross

FINERS LA

31

CORONATION
COTTS

Tolhurst

Broomden

Windmill
Hill

CROSS LA

Landscapes
Farm

Steellands
Farm   PH

Dale
Hill

2

Ticehurst
House

VINEYARD LA

Pickforde

1 FRONT CNTS
2 CHAPEL PL
3 MARLPIT GDNS
4 REEVES TERR
5 LAVENDER GDNS

Ridgeway
Farm

HIGH ST

CROSS LANE GDNS

P

Inn

NEWINGTON
CT

PASTHIS HILL

THE WARREN

Ticehurst

CH

Brick Kiln
Farm

HILLBURY TERR

HAZELWOOD
COTTS

PO

ST MARY'S LA

SPRINGFIELD

ACRES RISE

LOWER PLATTS

HORSEGROVE AVE

Meadowside
Cotts

Upper
Platts

1

30

A   B   68   C   D   69   E   F

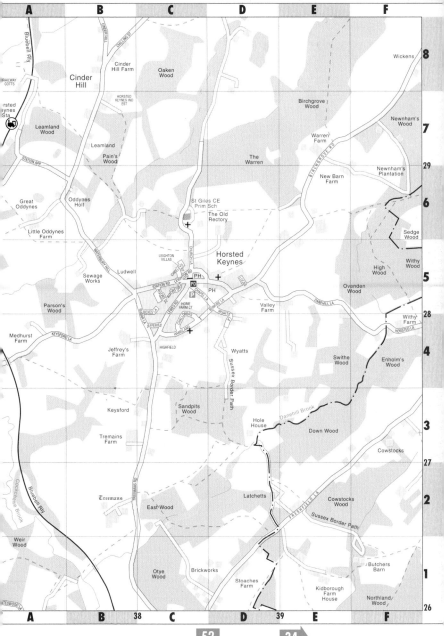

A   B   C   D   E   F

8

Wickens

Cinder
Hill Farm

Oaken
Wood

Cinder
Hill

Birchgrove
Wood

Newnham's
Wood

7

HORSTED
KEYNES IND
EST

rsted
eynes Sta

RAILWAY
COTTS

Leamland
Wood

Warren
Farm

BIRCHGROVE RD

29

STATION APP

Leamland

Pain's
Wood

The
Warren

New Barn
Farm

Newnham's
Plantation

Great
Oddynes

Oddynes
Holt

St Giles CE
Prim Sch

The Old
Rectory

Sedge
Wood

6

Little Oddynes
Farm

Leighton
Villas

Horsted Keynes

High
Wood

Withy
Wood

Ludwell

WATERMILL HILL

CHURCH LA

Sewage
Works

STATION RD

LEIGHTON RD

PH

PO
P

PH

Ovenden
Wood

5

Parson's
Wood

CHELT RD

BROOKE RD

LEWES RD

HOME
FARM CT

DANEHILL LA

Withy
Farm

28

Medhurst
Farm

KEYSFORD LA

JEFFERIE

CHALK

CINDER

HAMSLAND

WYATTS

Valley
Farm

HORSTED LA

Jeffrey's
Farm

HIGHFIELD

Wyatts

Swithe
Wood

Enholm's
Wood

4

Keysford

Sandpits
Wood

Sussex Border Path

Hole
House

Danehill Brook

Down Wood

Cowstocks

3

Tremains
Farm

27

Treemans

East Wood

Latchetts

Cowstocks
Wood

Sussex Border Path

2

Weir
Wood

Bluebell Rly

Cockhaise Brook

TRESFIELD RD

Butchers
Barn

1

Otye
Wood

Brickworks

Stoaches
Farm

Kidborough
Farm House

Northland
Wood

26

A   B   38   C   D   39   E   F

8

Birchgrove

BIRCHGROVE LA

Danehill Brook

A

B

C

D

E

F

Gitlands
Wood

Forest
Farm

Chelworth

A275 LEWES RD

ALDERSEY LA

Chelwood
Gate

BEACONSFIELD RD

P

The
Ridge

Braberry
Hatch

Ford

Beacon
Wood

7

Wheeler's
Wood

Small's
Wood

STONE QUARRY RD

Beaconwood
Farm

Chelwood
Beacon

29

Buttocks Bank
Wood

BOX LA

BAXTERS LA

Chelwood
Common

Streeter's
Rough

CHELWOOD GATE RD

Chelwood
Corner

6

Coach &
Horses
Inn
(PH)

OLD HORSES LA

CHURCH LA

Chelwood
Farm

5

Woodgate
Farm

Cumnor
House
Sch

Avenings
Farm
Cottage

Lambs
Farm

Lamb's
Rough

Maskett's
Wood

28

LONDON RD

SCHOOL LA

Danehill
Lodge

Grindfield
Farm

4

Danehill
Farm

PO

OAK TREE
COTTS

ROSE
COTTS

Danehill CE
Prim Sch

COLLINGFORD LA

Collingford
Farm

TANYARD LA

Burntwood
Farm

NEW COPPICE LA

Allins
Farm

Annwood
Farm

Ann
Wood

Danehill

HORSTED LA

CHURCH LA

LEWES RD

Sewage
Works

FURNERS GREEN LA

Perryman's
Hill

Pollardsland
Wood

3

North
Northlands
Farm

Tanyard
Farm

Colin
Godmans
Farm

Annwood Brook

Mark
Street

27

Moaps
Farm

Dane
Wood

2

Lane
Wood

Wilmshurst

St Raphaels
(Danehurst)

Stephens
Farm

1

Heaven Farm
Mus

A275

Portmansford

Brooker's
Rough

Sheffield
Forest

Woolpack
Farm

Heaven
Wood

Furner's
Green

26

40

A

B

41

C

D

42

E

F

A B C D E F

8

7

29

6

5

28

4

3

27

2

1

26

Old Lodge

Dovecote Farm

Millbrook Farm

Fairplace Farm

Londonderry Farm

Marlpitts Farm
Windmill

Marlpits

Millbrook

Mill Brook

Chapelwood Manor

Mill Wood

CROWBOROUGH RD

Masketts Manor Farm

Sewage Works

Outback Farm

ASHDOWN

Morrisfield

Nutley, CE Prim Sch

RIDGE CL

ASHDOWN CHASE

SCHOOL LA

The Court House

Carr's Wood

OAKING CLO

ST JAMES LA

THE VINTRY

Rough Ground

Juniper Wood

Jessop's Hill

THE LOFTS

CLOCK HOUSE LA

BELL LA

NURSERY LA

Upper Misbourne Farm

Nutley

Yew Tree Farm

Lower Misbourne Farm

Hole & Alchorne Farm

THREE GABLES

THE CROUCH

PO

Chantersell

LITTLEMEAD

HIGH ST

PH

Chestnut Farm

Great Birch Wood

Hollybush Wood

Ford's Green

FOREST VIEW

NETHERELL

Prickett's Hatch

Dodd's Hill

Dodd's Bottom

Hole Farm

Bowyer's Wood

Funnells Farm

COURT MEAD

Dodd's Bank

Cackle Street

A 22

Searles Wood

Wet Wood

Boringwheel Mill Farm

Woodcock Farm

Hunters Farm

TYEHURST LA

Forest Lodge

A 22

CHELWOOD GATE RD

8

Crabtree
Farm

Brown
Knoll

New Pond
Cottages

Vanguard Way

7

Camp
Hill

29

A26

6

The
Doves Nest

P

P

CROWBOROUGH RD

Duddleswell
Manor

Ashdown Forest
Riding Ctr

Ashdown Forest
Gardens

Crest
Farm

Poplar
Farm

5

Barnsgate
Manor

Vineyard

Campfields
Rough

Barnsden

28

Lodge

Vanguard Way

Weald Way

Brown's
Brook

Oldlands
Wood

4

Strood's House
Farm

Duddleswell

OLDLANDS
HALL

Heron's
Ghyll

Putland's
Farm

Payne's Hill
Cottages

3

Temple Grove
Sch

Spring
Garden

Pleasant
Farm

27

Oldlands
Farm

Quarry
Wood

2

Home
Farm

Spring-garden
Wood

PO

Holly
Cottage

PH Fairwarp

Marlpits

PERRYMAN LA

Paddock
Farm

Perryman's
Farm

Beacon

1

Furnace Wood

Claygate
Farm

Cophall

Summerford

Ford's
Bank

A26

26

A **B** **C** **D** **E** **F**

8

Crowborough Training Camp

Birchfield Farm

Little Warren Farm

NEVILL CL 1
NEVILL CT 2
NEW FOREST LODGE 3
FOREST LODGE 4

CH

WHIN CROFT PK

SOUTH VIEW RD

Whitehill

STONECOTT 1
FERMOR ROW 2

Cemy

Herne Cty Jun Sch

7

The Ghyll

Crowborough Common

Crowborough Beacon Golf Course

Brook Farm

Alderbrook Farm

29

Crow & Gate (PH)

Broomhill

High Broom Rd

High Broom

Stone Cross Rd

6

Vanguard Way

Newnham Park Farm

Bartons

Sweethaws

Allfrey's Farm

Stone Cross

Poundgate

Broom

Sweethaws Wood

Redbridge Farm

Perryman's Farm

Rock Farm Cottage

5

Newnham Park Wood

Moulden Wood

Sinnock's Rough

Sweethaws Farm

Redbridge La

Pick Pale

28

Adam's Farm

Piping Wood

Ketches Farm

4

Chillies Farm

Marlpit Wood

Broadfield Wood

Mabb's Farm

Grovehurst Farm

Welchwood Farm

3

Chillies La

Oaky Wood

Oxley Wood

Brook House

Burnt Oak

27

Greystones Farm

Vanguard Way

Burnt Oak

Fordbrook Hill

Shadwell Farm

PO

Burnt Oak Farm

Fordbrook Farm

2

Pickreed Wood

Grey Burchetts Wood

Wilding Wood

Holly Mount

Lodge Wood

High Hurstwood

High Hurstwood CE Prim Sch

Oldhall Farm

Hurstwood Farm

The Rough

Kiln Farm

1

Mount Pleasant Farm

Royal Oak La

Fordy La

26

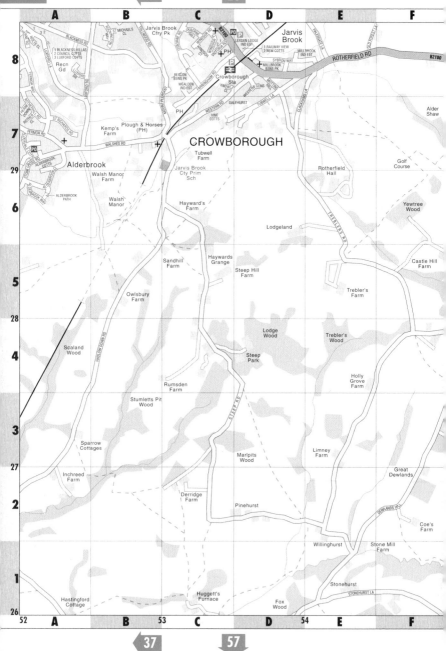

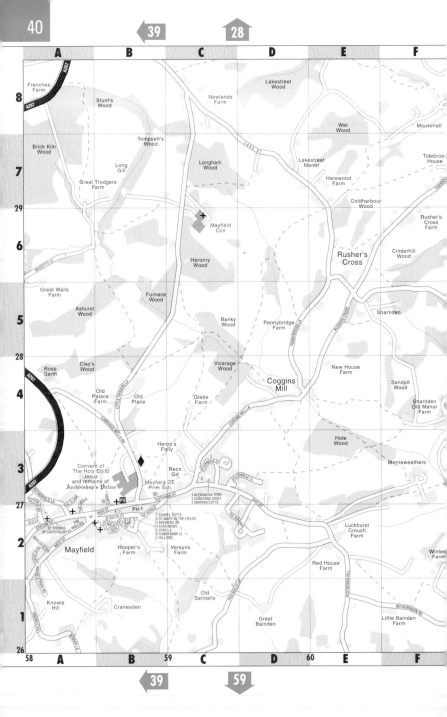

A **B** **C** **D** **E** **F**

8

wngate
Farm

debrook

Snape
Farm

Broad
Shaw

Saxby
Shaw

Scrag
Oak

Tidebrook Manor
Farm

Newland
Wood

Wenbans

Butcher's
Wood

Beals
Oak
Farm

7

Tidebrook Manor

Sinden
Wood

Buttons

Grubbin's
Wood

Chittinghurst

Lodge Hill
Farm

29

COOMBE LA

Tug Brook

Combe Manor
Farm

Railand
Wood

The
Wilderness

6

Cinderhill
Farm

Combe
Farm

Old
Lake

Flattenden
Farm

5

Combe
Wood

Wadhurst
Park

Wadhurst Park
Lake

28

Doozes Gill
Wood

4

Six Acre
Wood

Batt's
Wood

Rolf's
Ghyll

Twelve Acre
Ghyll

Ten Acre
Wood

Clay
Wood

3

Rolf's
Farm

27

Hampden
Lodge

White's
Wood

Golds
Farm

Nine Acre
Shaw

2

Hare
Holt

Bivelham Forge
Bridge

Hawksden Park
Wood

Pound
Bridge

Park
Cottage

Bedlam
Wood

Fair Oak
Cottage

Bivelham
Farm

River Rother

Waterloo
Farm

1

WITHERENDEN RD

Fair Oak
Farm

Gillhope
Farm

Amber
Cottages

26

A **B** **62** **C** **D** **63** **E** **F**

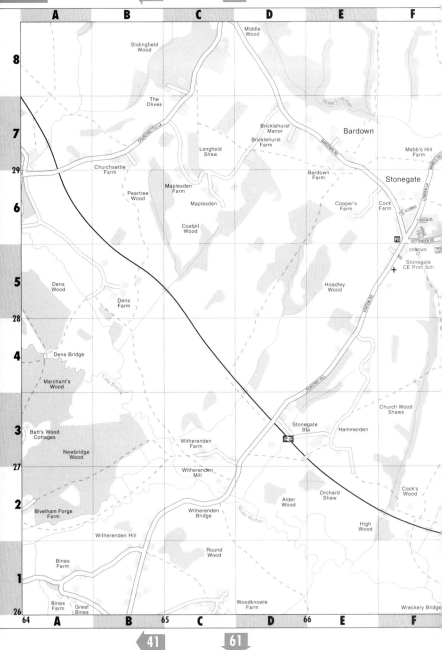

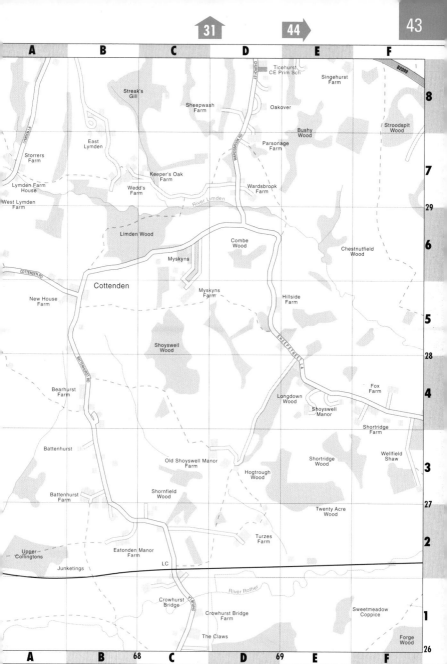

A   B   C   D   E   F

B2099

Devilsden Wood
Birchenwood Farm
Mumpumps
Roughfield
Roughfield Farm
Sussex Border Path
Brookgate Farm
Kent Ditch
Hazelden Wood

8

Cedar Farm
Boundary Farm

Gibbs Reed Farm
Spring Wood
Boarzell Wood

Pashley Farm

7

Pashley Manor
Cox's Wood

29

Pashley Manor Gardens

Conyburrow Wood
Pashleypits Wood
Three Gates Farm
Little Boarszell
Elphicks
Swiftsde

B2099

6

SWIFTSDEN COTTS
Cross Keys (PH)
Swanfield Farm

Swiftsden Farm

5

Quarryfield Wood
London Barn Farm
Bellhurst Wood
We Wo

28

Burgham
Bellhurst

Kitchingham Farm

4

SHEEPSTREET LA
Fleet Wood
Burgham Down Wood
Burgh Wood

Foxhole Wood

River Limden

STATION
A2

3

New House Farm
Fysie Bridge
Burgh Hill

River Rother

CHURCH HILL

Shaw Farm
FYSIE LA

Park Wood
BURGH HILL

27

2

Etchingham CE Prim Sch
HAREMERE HILL
Home Farm

Forge House

Haremere Hall Gardens
Haremere Hall

River Rother

Etchingham Sta
P P
P

1

CHURCH FARM CL
Church House Farm
LC
Grove Wood
Sewage Works

Etchingham
DUDWELL LA

Forge Wood
The Ashes
HORMBLOWER COTTS
PO
A265
HIGH ST
PH
River Dudwell
Houns Woo

26

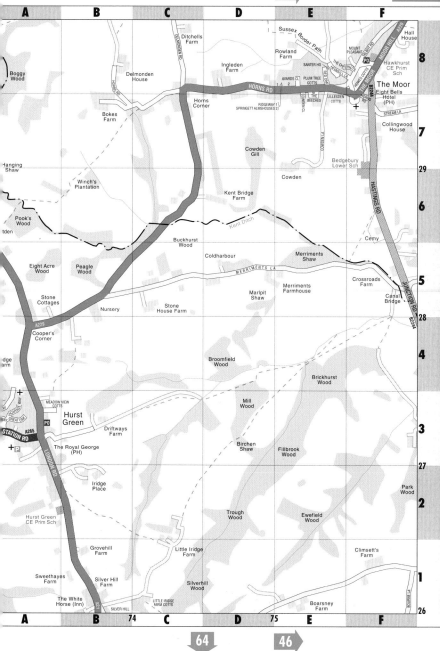

A **B** **C** **D** **E** **F**

Boggy
Wood

Ditchells
Farm

Delmonden
House

Rowland
Farm

Sussex Border Path

Ingleden
Farm

Hall
House

MOOR HILL

Hawkhurst
CE Prim
Sch

MOUNT
PLEASANT

PO

SANTER HO

THE CHESTNUTS

The Moor

Eight Bells
Hotel
(PH)

HORNS RD

Horns
Corner

Bokes
Farm

AVARDS CL

PLUM TREE
COTTS

RED OAK

THE
BEECHES

LILLESDEN
COTTS

Collingwood
House

RIDGEWAY
SPRINGETT ALMSHOUSES

COWDEN LA

STREAM LA

HASTINGS RD

Hanging
Shaw

Winch's
Plantation

Cowden
Gill

Cowden

Bedgebury
Lower Sch

29

Pook's
Wood

Kent Bridge
Farm

6

Kent Ditch

Cemy

Eight Acre
Wood

Peagle
Wood

Buckhurst
Wood

Coldharbour

Merriments
Shaw

Crossroads
Farm

JUNCTION RD

5

Stone
Cottages

Nursery

Stone
House Farm

MERRIMENTS LA

Marlpit
Shaw

Merriments
Farmhouse

Canal
Bridge

B2244

28

A229

Cooper's
Corner

Broomfield
Wood

Brickhurst
Wood

4

dge
rm

MEADOW VIEW
COTTS

PO

Hurst
Green

Driftways
Farm

Mill
Wood

GREAT DIX

3

STATION RD

A265

London Rd

The Royal George
(PH)

Birchen
Shaw

Fillbrook
Wood

27

Iridge
Place

Park
Wood

2

Hurst Green
CE Prim Sch

Trough
Wood

Ewefield
Wood

Climsett's
Farm

Grovehill
Farm

Little Iridge
Farm

Sweethayes
Farm

Silver Hill
Farm

Silverhill
Wood

BOURNE LA

1

The White
Horse (Inn)

SILVER HILL

LITTLE IRIDGE
FARM COTTS

Boarsney
Farm

26

A **B** 74 **C** **D** 75 **E** **F**

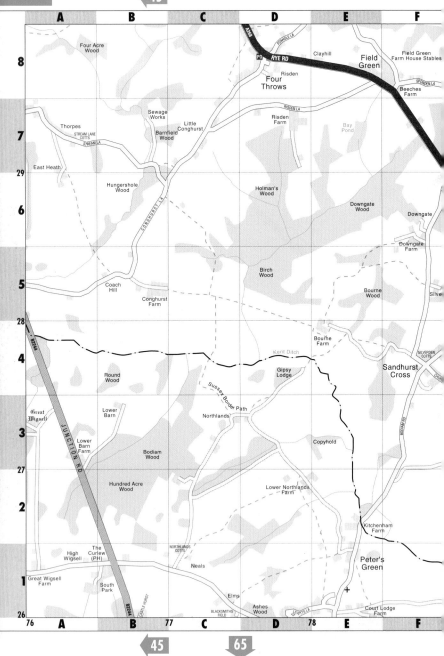

A · **B** · **C** · **D** · **E** · **F**

8

Four Acre Wood

A268 RYE RD

FOXHOLE LA

PO

Clayhill

Field Green

Field Green Farm House Stables

SPONDEN LA

Four Throws

Risden

Beeches Farm

7

Thorpes

STREAM LANE COTTS

STREAM LA

Sewage Works

Barnfield Wood

Little Conghurst

Risden Farm

RISDEN LA

Bay Pond

29

East Heath

Hungershole Wood

Holman's Wood

Downgate Wood

Downgate

6

FOXEHURST LA

Downgate Farm

5

Coach Hill

Conghurst Farm

Birch Wood

Bourne Wood

Silve

28

B2244

Kent Ditch

Bourne Farm

SILVERDEN COTTS

4

Round Wood

Sussex Border Path

Gipsy Lodge

Sandhurst Cross

JUNCTION RD

Lower Barn

Northlands

BODIAM RD

Great Wigsell

3

Lower Barn Farm

Bodiam Wood

Copyhold

27

Hundred Acre Wood

Lower Northlands Farm

2

Kitchenham Farm

NORTHLANDS COTTS

High Wigsell

The Curlew (PH)

Peter's Green

1

Great Wigsell Farm

South Park

Neals

CASTLE HURST

SCOTTS LA

Elms

Ashes Wood

Court Lodge Farm

26

BLACKSMITHS FIELD

76 · **A** · **B** · **77** · **C** · **D** · **78** · **E** · **F**

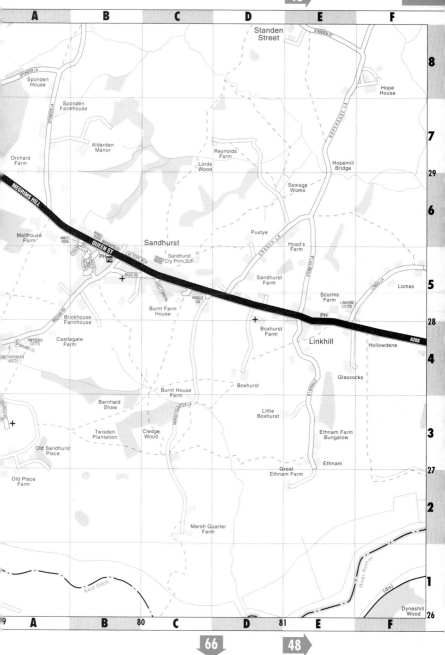

A B C D E F

Standen
Street

STANDEN ST

8

SPONDEN LA
Sponden
House

Hope
House

Sponden
Farmhouse

Alderden
Manor

7

Reynolds
Farm

Orchard
Farm

Lords
Wood

Hopemill
Bridge

29

MEGRINS HILL

Sewage
Works

HOPEMILL LA

6

Puxtye

Malthouse
Farm

CROUCH LA

Hoad's
Farm

ANGEL TERR BROOKFIELD

Sandhurst

ROW
QUEEN ST

STONE PIT LA

Sandhurst
Cty Prim Sch

PH
PO

Sandhurst
Farm

BACK RD

5

LOMAS LA

Lomas

Scurms
Farm

LINKDEN
COTTS

INGHAM RD

LONG TARSTAL

RINGLE
GN

PH

28

Brickhouse
Farmhouse

Burnt Farm
House

Boxhurst
Farm

Linkhill

A268

TWYSDEN
COTTS

Castlegate
Farm

Hollowdene

SILVERHURST CL

4

BETHERINDEN
COTTS

Glassocks

FERRAILL LA

Burnt House
Farm

Boxhurst

Barnfield
Shaw

MARSH QUARTER LA

Little
Boxhurst

3

Twisden
Plantation

Cledge
Wood

Ethnam Farm
Bungalow

Old Sandhurst
Place

Ethnam

27

Old Place
Farm

Great
Ethnam Farm

2

Marsh Quarter
Farm

1

River Rother

Kent Ditch

(dis)

Dyneshill
Wood

26

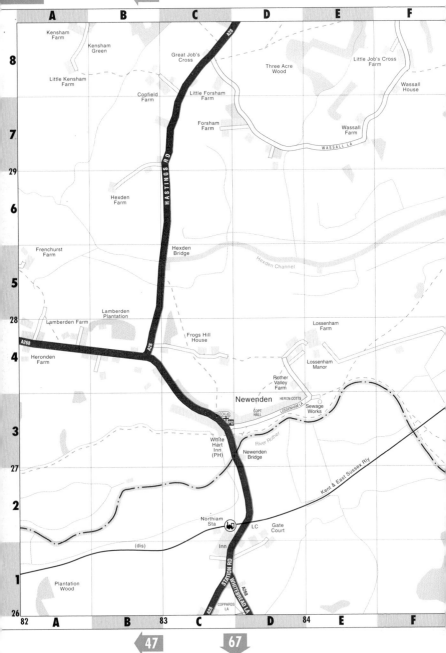

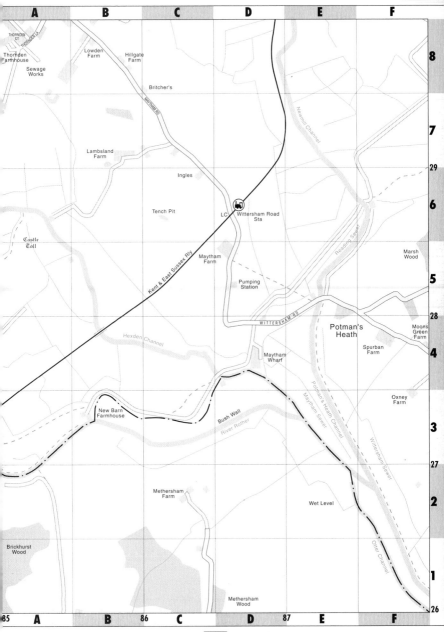

THORNDEN CT

THORNDEN LA

Thornden
Farmhouse

Sewage
Works

Lowden
Farm

Hillgate
Farm

Britcher's

MAYTHAM RD

Lambsland
Farm

Ingles

Tench Pit

LC Wittersham Road
Sta

Castle
Toll

Kent & East Sussex Rly

Maytham
Farm

Pumping
Station

Newmill Channel

Reading Sewer

Marsh
Wood

WITTERSHAM RD

Potman's
Heath

Moons
Green
Farm

Hexden Channel

Maytham
Wharf

Spurban
Farm

Oxney
Farm

New Barn
Farmhouse

Bush Wall

River Rother

Maytham Sewer

Potman's Heath Channel

Wittersham Sewer

Methersham
Farm

Wet Level

Brickhurst
Wood

Otter Channel

Methersham
Wood

8

7

29

6

5

28

4

3

27

2

1

26

85   A   B   86   C   D   87   E   F

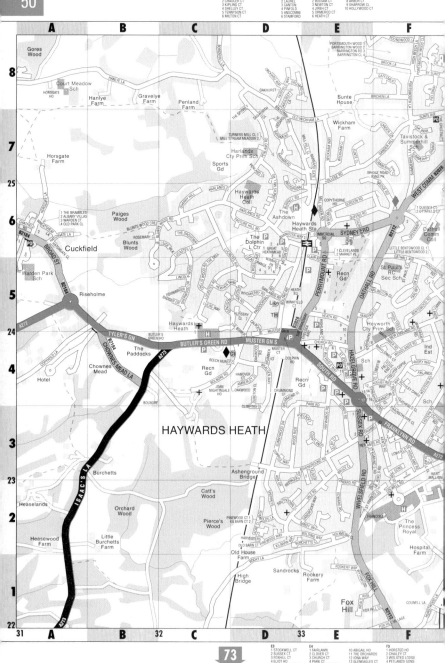

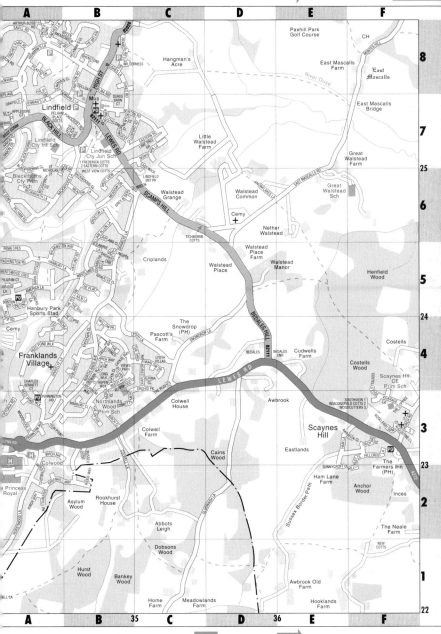

8

COCKHAISE COTTS

Cockhaise Farm

Cockhaise Mill Farm

Wildboar Bridge

Freshfield Halt

Freshfields

Freshfield Crossways

TOWN PLACE FARM COTTS

Town Place

King's Wood

Northland Farm

KETCHE'S LA

7

Town House Farm

Town Place Farm

Sussex Border Path

25

Bluebell Rly

Round Wood

Coneyborou Wood

6

Freshfield Bridges

Freshfield Mill Farm

River Ouse

Old Canal

5

Sewage Works

Home Wood

The Sloop Inn (PH)

Hammer Wood

Cole Wood

24

Nashgill Wood

Pegden House

Wapsbourne Wood

4

Nash Farm

NASH LA

Yew Tree Farm

Butterbox Farm

BUTTERBOX LA

Freshfield Place

Lye Wood

Watlands Farm

Watlands

Massetts

Wapsbourne Farm

3

CLEARWATER

Hammond's Farm

Sussex Border Path

Sennotts

HUNT'S GATE

23

Rock Wood

Blackbrook Bridge

Warr's Wood

ASHBROOK LA

2

LEWES RD

ANCHOR HILL

A272

Lindfield Farm

Clear Water

Lindfield Wood

Warr's Farm

The Plantation

1

Pellingbridge Farm

Great Wood

Broadwater House

Chailey Heritage Craft Sch & Hospl (New Heritage)

MOORE HILL

BANKS RD

A275

22

Springfield Farm

Great Noven Farm

A272

34 54

A B C D E F

8

7

25

6

5

24

4

3

23

2

1

22

Slider's Farm
Glenmore Pig Farm
Sliders
VALLEY VIEW
Pound Wood
Circle Wood
Ketche's Cottages
KETCHE'S LA
Coleham Wood
Bluebell Rly
Coleham Farm
Sheffield Park Sta
Mus
Sheffield Bridge
Wapsbourne Gate
Lane End Farm
River Farm
Lane End Common
WASHGOOD LA
A275

SHEFFIELD MILL LA
Beechy Wood
Sheffield Green
Hotel
Pound Farm
TRICKLAND COTTS
SAWYARD COTTS
Sheffield Park Farm
Sheffield Park
Sheffield Park Gardens
Sheffield Park
Rotherfield Farm House
Rotherfield Wood
Fletching Common

Mill Pond
Sheffield Mill Farm
North Hall Farm
Walk Wood
Ten Foot Pond
Middle Lake
Lower Womans Way Pond
East Park Farm
River Ouse
Great Wet Wood
Netherhall Farm
Goldbridge Wood

Holmesdale Farm
Moyse's Farm
Rigg Wood
Spring Farm
Eastland Wood
Splaynes Green Farm
Manley Wood
Upper Womans Way Pond
Rose & Crown (PH)
Fletching
Fletching CE Prim Sch
CHESTNUT COTTS
Parsonage Farm
Mill Farm
Fletching Mill Bridge
Fletching Mill Farm

41

42

76 54

	A	B	C	D	E	F

8
Searles
Searles Lake
Courtland Wood
Whitehouse Farm
Horney Common
Black Ven Farm
PICKETTS LA

7
Poultry Houses
St Clears Farm
Spring Wood
Marshall's Farm
Kennel Wood

25
Clapwater Farm House
Marshall's Manor

6
Lower Flitteridge Wood
Ruttingham Farm
High Wood
Cave Wood
Flitterbank

Flitteridge Farm

5
Splayne's Green
Down Street
Little Brown's Wood
The Wilderness
Downstreet Farmhouse

24
Knabb Farm
Forge Wood

Atherall's Farm

4
CHERRY COTTS
Downstreet Rough
Batt's Farm

3
Parsonage Farm
White Barn Farm
Mallingdown Farm
Batt's Wood
Sewage Works
Batt's Bridge Stream

23
Hungry Hatch
Grover's Farm
Ruston Wood
Oak Ferrars Farm

2
Park Wood
CH
Pilt Down

1
Moses Farm
Golf Course
Piltdown Pond
Fairhazel Wood
Piltdown
Piltdown Man (PH)

22

A **B** **C** **D** **E** **F**

FORGE LANE COTTS

ampool Farm

Rock Wood

Hendall Manor Farm

Stonehouse Wood

Stonehouse

8

Doma Farm Nursery

BURRELLS LA

Hendall Gate Farm

Stonehouse Farm

Kingsfield Farm

LAMPOOL CNR

Woodlands Farm

Keepers Cottage

Stonehouse Cottage

7

THE DRIVE

NURSERY LA

ROCKS LA

25

Reeding's Farm

Hendall Wood

Dalling

Bevingford

6

Maresfield Park

MIDDLE DR

STRAIGHT HALF MILE

Reeding's Wood

Five Ash Down

Works

Front Wood

THE DRIVE

Gatehouse Wood

Olivespit Wood

5

Maresfield

Chantlers

Strawberry Hall Farm

Olives Wood

24

OAKLANDS

PH

UNDERHILL

COBDOWN LA

The Gate House

COOPERS ROW

Meadway

Firemans Arms (PH)

The Oast Farm

The Old Rectory

4

Maresfield Bonners CE Prim Sch

SCHOOL COTTS

PO

Cooper's Green

Lepham's Bridge House

Harrock House

Park Farm

SCHOOL HILL

Mill House Farm

THE WALLED GARDEN

Lepham's Bridge

Buxted CE Prim Sch

A272

A272

Furnacebank Wood

Shortbridge Stream

A26

Budlett's Common

Vulcan Farm

3

23

Black Down

White House Farm

Buxted Park

Buxted Park Deer Park

2

Shermanreed Wood

Ringles Cross

Cemy

Views Wood

River Uck

Thirty Acre Wood

NEVILL GDN

WEST VIEW

TOWER RISE

CUCKMERE PATH

MICKLEHAM RD

1

47

48

22

A **B** **C** **D** **E** **F**

A B C D E F

8

7

25

6

5

24

4

3

23

2

1

22

49 A B 50 C D 51 E F

Parkhurst

The Maypole Inn (PH)

Coxbrook

Tudor Rocks

The Hermitage

New House Farm

Parsonage Wood

Sewage Works

Buxted

Buxted Sta

White Hart (PH)

Lower Totease Farm

Culver Wood

A272

River Uck

CHELWOOD LA

POUND HOUSE LA

ROYAL OAK LA

CHERRY GDNS

MAYPOLE GDNS

Holders Farm

Nordens Green

FOWLY LA

Huggett's Farm

Coes Rough

Vanguard Way

Littlewood Farm

CHURCH RD

PARK VIEW

NURSERY FIELD

HIGH ST

PARADISE RD

LINCOLN RD

Buxted CT

Potter's Green

Mascalls Farm

TANYARD COTTS

Tanyard Farm

Sleeches

Buxted Wood

Grove Wood

Greenhurst

Stones Rough

Howbourne Farm

Foxhole Farm

Rosemount

BUXTED WOOD LA

HORDENS PARK LA

Dolloways Bank House

Saxon Court

Toll Farm

Pound Green

BRITTS DEAN

TOPM RD

MIDE WELLS

REDWOODS LA

FURNACE LA

LIMES LA

Abbotswood House

NAN TUCKS LA

POUND LA

Popeswood Farm

Stone's Wood

Lower Wood

Bish Wood

Lower Lowlands Farm

Shepherd's Hill

Etchingwood

ROCKS LA

HURSTWOOD RD

A272

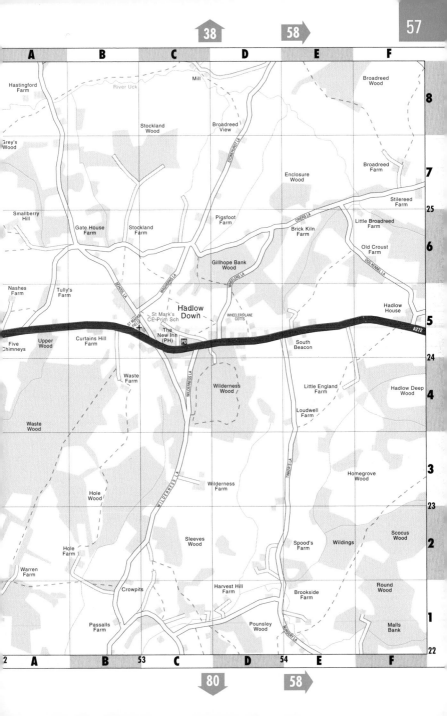

A | B | C | D | E | F

8

Hastingford
Farm

River Uck

Mill

Broadreed
Wood

Stockland
Wood

Broadreed
View

Grey's
Wood

7

Enclosure
Wood

Broadreed
Farm

Smallberry
Hill

Pigsfoot
Farm

Stilereed
Farm

25

Gate House
Farm

Stockland
Farm

Brick Kiln
Farm

FRIERS LA

Little Broadreed
Farm

6

Gillhope Bank
Wood

Old Croust
Farm

DOG KENNEL LA

Nashes
Farm

Tully's
Farm

WHEELERS LA

Hadlow
House

Hadlow
Down

St Mark's
CE Prim Sch

WHEELERS LANE
COTTS

Hadlow
Down

5

A272

Five
Chimneys

Upper
Wood

Curtains Hill
Farm

The
New Inn
(PH)

South
Beacon

24

Waste
Farm

Wilderness
Wood

Little England
Farm

Hadlow Deep
Wood

4

Waste
Wood

Loudwell
Farm

3

Hole
Wood

Wilderness
Farm

Homegrove
Wood

23

Hole
Farm

Sleeves
Wood

Spood's
Farm

Wildings

Scocus
Wood

2

Warren
Farm

Crowpits

Harvest Hill
Farm

Brookside
Farm

Round
Wood

1

Passalls
Farm

Pounsley
Wood

Malls
Bank

22

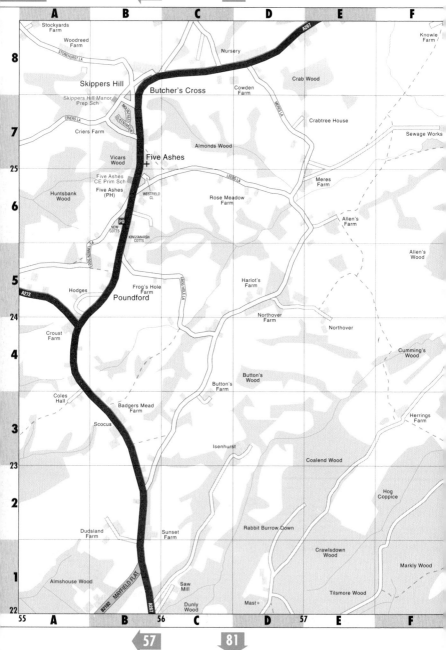

A B C D E F

8 Cookham Shaw

Bainden Wood
Clayland Shaw
Round Wood

Cranesden Farm

Clayton's Farm

7 Scotsford Bridge

River Rother

Moat Farm

Great Pigstrood Farm
25

St Dunstan's Bridge
Moat Mill Farm

Scotsford Farm
6

Old Mill Farm

Little Pigstrood

Spey House

Little Furnace Wood

Bungehurst Farm

Broomhurst Farm
Wet Wood
5

Oxen's Wood
Great Furnace Wood

NEWICK LA

Broomham

St Quentins Farm

24

Oaken Wood
Pheasantry Farm

Coneyburrow Wood

Rock Farm

POTTENS MILL LA
STREET END LA

Street End Farm
4

Quarry Wood

Coneyburrow Wood
Furlong Wood

Newick Wood

Prior's Farm

Holme Chase
3

23

Orchard House
Orchard Farm

Bodell's Farm
Newick Farm

Headrest

Hill Farm
Briway

2

MARKLYE LA

Marklye Farm

Broadoak Cty Prim Sch

North Down Wood
Black Wood

A265

BURWASH RD

Broad Oak
1

Westerns Farm

SOUTH SIDE
A265

HALLEY RD

22

A B C D E F

8

Little Calem
Wood

Great Calem
Wood

Froghole
Farm

Turk's
Bridge

River Rother

Froghole
Bridge

Turk's
Farm

7

Great Broadhurst
Farm

Little Broadhurst
Farm

Holmshurst
Manor Farm

Oaken
Wood

25

6

Little
Stonehurst
Farm

Coxdown
Farm

Great
Stonehurst
Farm

Lakedown
Farm

Nursements
Farm

Shovels
Wood

Great
Bigknowle
Farm

Ashen
Wood

5

Pottens Mill
Farm

Taylor's
Farm

Limberlost
Farm

Marlpit
Shaw

Climshurst
Wood

Knowle
Farm

Broadhurst

SWIFE LA

24

Corner
Farm

Foxhole
Wood

Blackd
Woo

4

Baltham
Wood

PAINE'S CNR

Foxhole
Farm

Oakd
Far

Little Park
Farm

Doel's
Farm

3

Olives
Farm

Barklye
Farm

Burralands

Mill House
Farm

WEST END
COTTS

STOKES
COTTS

MART

Black Sand
Wood

Holban's
Farm

Kingsdown
Farm

23

Swife
Wood

Cedar Swiffe
Farm

Home
Farm

2

Swiffes
Farm

Spinney
Farm House

Poundsford

A265

Poundsford
Farm

Tottingworth
Park

1

Oak Hall
Sch

Milkhurst
Wood

Applebrook
Farm

Stonehole
Wood

Limekiln
Wood

22

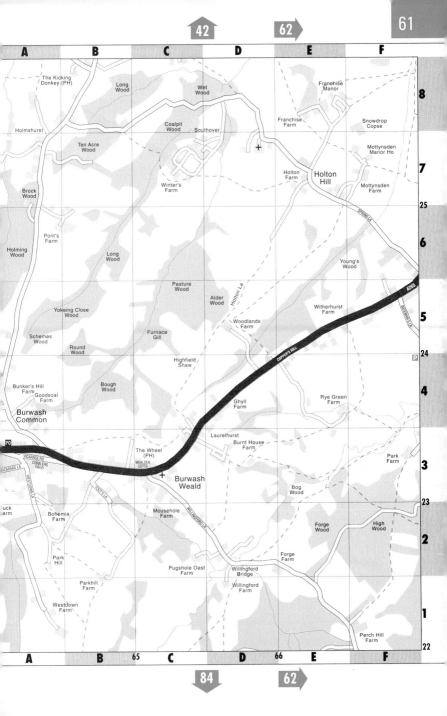

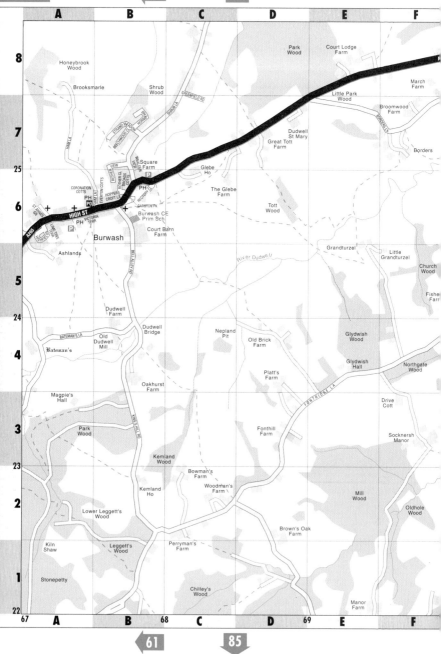

A   B   C   D   E   F

HIGH ST   A265

OAKS CL
PARK ROAD
BROOKSIDE COTTS
BELFAIR CL

8

BORDERS LA

Underwood's
Farm

Church
Wood

Lundsford
Farm

Bugsell Mill
Farm

River Dudwell

Brookside
Farm

DUDWELL LA

Barnfield
Shaw

Gigmore
Wood

Ockham
House

7

Sores
Wood

River Rother

Toll
Wood

25

Athena
Farm

Squibs
Farm

Hutching's
Farm

6

Fontridge
Manor

FONTRIDGE LA

LUDPIT LA

Willard's
Hill

Chambers
Farm

Willards Hill
Farm

Marlpit
Shaw

Hackwoods
Farm

Bugsell
Farm

5

Southside
Farm

Clapson's
Bridge

Bugsell
Wood

Beech
Farm

BUGSELL LA

24

Long
Shaw

Column
Wood

Fair Ridge
Wood

Robertsbridge
Com Coll

4

Burgh
Wood

OAKLANDS DR

HACKWOOD

GREEN
HEDGES

LANGHAM RD

THE SPINN

Park
Wood

Pean's
Wood

COUNCIL
COTTS

3

Furnace
Wood

Little
Peans

Wyland
Wood

Barnfield
Wood

Newhouse
Farm

BRIGHTLING RD

Darvell

23

Middle
Wood

Scalands
Farm

2

Brightling
Hall

Scalands
Wood

Bowden
Wood

Sizzes
Wood

Glottenham Stream

1

Perryfield
Wood

Ladds
Wood

Glottenham
Farm

22

70   A   B   71   C   D   72   E   F

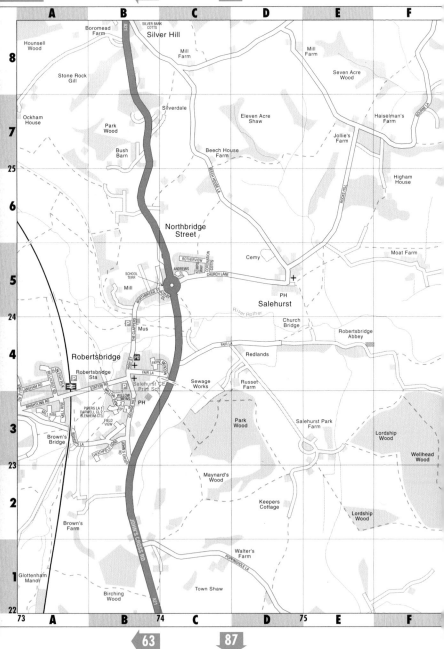

| A | B | C | D | E | F |

8

Hounsell
Wood

Boromead
Farm

SILVER BANK
COTTS

Silver Hill

Mill
Farm

Mill
Farm

Seven Acre
Wood

Stone Rock
Gill

7

Ockham
House

Park
Wood

Silverdale

Eleven Acre
Shaw

Haiselman's
Farm

Bush
Barn

Beech House
Farm

Jollie's
Farm

25

Higham
House

6

Northbridge
Street

Cemy

Moat Farm

5

ROTHERVIEW
COTTS

CHURCH LANE

Salehurst

PH

ANDREWS
CL

SCHOOL
TERR

Mill

24

THE CLAPPERS

Mus

River Rother

Church
Bridge

Robertsbridge
Abbey

4

Robertsbridge

PO

FAIR LA

Redlands

FAIR LA

Robertsbridge
Sta

Salehurst C E
Prim Sch

Sewage
Works

Russet
Farm

STATION RD

WILLOW
MEWS

PH

PIPERS LA

DARWELL CL
BLENHEIM CT

FIELD
VIEW

Park
Wood

Salehurst Park
Farm

Lordship
Wood

3

BRIGHTLING RD

MILL RISE

Brown's
Bridge

Wellhead
Wood

23

Maynard's
Wood

2

Brown's
Farm

Keepers
Cottage

Lordship
Wood

1

Glottenham
Manor

Birching
Wood

Walter's
Farm

POPPINGHOLE LA

Town Shaw

22

| 73 | A | B | 74 | C | D | 75 | E | F |

A B C D E F

8
Mayfield
Farm
Bushyfield
Shaw
Terrace
Wood
CASTLE HIGH ST
B2244
Bodiam Manor Sch
LEVETTS LA
Bodiam CE
Prim Sch
KNOWLE HILL
New House
Court Lodge
Bodiam
Bodiam Castle
(National Trust)

7
Six Acre
Wood
Park
Farm
THE GREEN
Inn
Bodiam
Bridge

25
LC   (dis)
River Rother
Sussex Border Path

6
Quarry
Farm
Ockham
Udiam
Dykes
Farm
West
Wood
Snagshall
B2244

5
Rocks
Farm
JUNCTION RD
UDIAM COTTS
Crainham
Wood
Madame's Farm
Oast
Udiam La
Prawles
Farm

24
Fowlbrook Wood
Holmans
Wood
Ren's Wood
Brasses
Farm

4

3
Eyelids
Farm
Stainsmore
Wood
Hollow Wall
Farm
Crabtree
Wood

23
Wellhead Wood
Bluebell
Farm
Larkins
Hollow
Lordship
Wood
Lordship
Wood

2
Wellhead Wood
West
Staplecross
Methodist
Prim Sch
RIVERSIDE
WALL VIEW
Staplecross
B2165
Collier's
Green

1
Wellhead Wood East
Handsel
Farm
FORGE LA
ICKLESHAM
PO
PH
ROSEFIELD
COTTS
B2244
B2165

22
A B C D E F
77   78

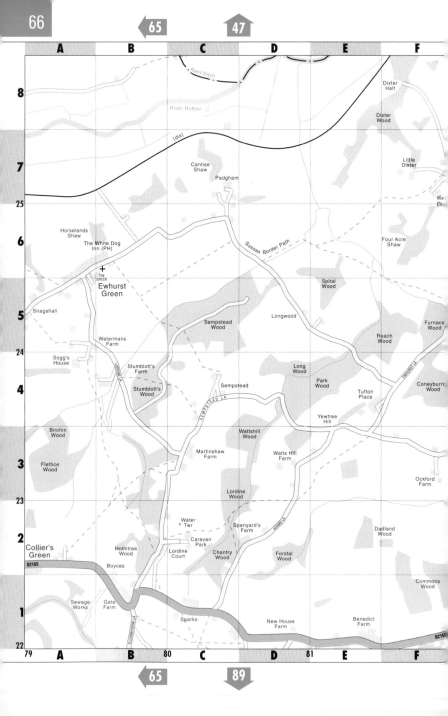

65
47

8

Dixter
Halt

River Rother

Dixter
Wood

(dis)

7

Cantise
Shaw

Padgham

Little
Dixter

25

Gr
Dit

Horselands
Shaw

6

The White Dog
Inn (PH)

Sussex Border Path

Four Acre
Shaw

THE
GREEN

Ewhurst
Green

Spital
Wood

5

Snagshall

Sempstead
Wood

Longwood

Furnace
Wood

Reach
Wood

Watermans
Farm

24

Sogg's
House

Long
Wood

Coneyburro
Wood

Stumblott's
Farm

Sempstead

Park
Wood

Tufton
Place

4

Stumblott's
Wood

Birchin
Wood

Yewtree
Hill

3

Flettice
Wood

Martinshaw
Farm

Wattshill
Wood

Watts Hill
Farm

Ockford
Farm

23

Lordine
Wood

Water
Twr

Dadland
Wood

2

Collier's
Green

Spanyard's
Farm

Holmtree
Wood

Caravan
Park

Lordine
Court

Chantry
Wood

Forstal
Wood

B2165

Boyces

Commons
Wood

1

Sewage
Works

Gate
Farm

Sparks

New House
Farm

Benedict
Farm

B2165

22

79   **A**   **B**   **80**   **C**   **D**   **81**   **E**   **F**

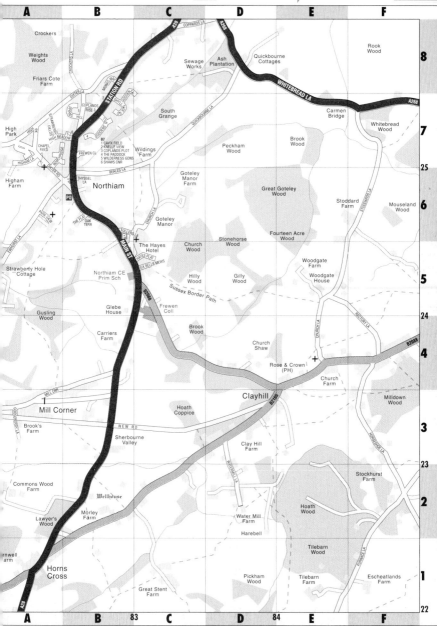

Crockers

Weights Wood

Friars Cote Farm

High Park

Chapel Field

Higham LA

Higham Farm

STATION RD

Coplands Rise

Northiam

PO

OAK TERR

The Hayes Hotel

Northiam CE Prim Sch

Strawberry Hole Cottage

Glebe House

Gusling Wood

Carriers Farm

Mill Corner

Brook's Farm

Commons Wood Farm

Lawyer's Wood

Morley Farm

Sherbourne Valley

Wellhouse

Horns Cross

rnwell arm

DOPPARDS LA

Sewage Works

Ash Plantation

Quickbourne Cottages

Rook Wood

WHITERREAD LA

Carmen Bridge

Whitebread Wood

A268

South Grange

DUCKBOURNE LA

Peckham Wood

Brook Wood

Stoddard Farm

Mouseland Wood

Wildings Farm

Goteley Manor Farm

Great Goteley Wood

Goteley Manor

CHURCH LA

Fourteen Acre Wood

Woodgate Farm

Woodgate House

Church Wood

Stonehorse Wood

Hilly Wood

Gilly Wood

Sussex Border Path

Frewen Coll

Brook Wood

Church Shaw

Rose & Crown (PH)

Church Farm

CHURCH LA

RECTORY LA

B2088

Clayhill

B2165

Milldown Wood

Hoath Coppice

NEW RD

Clay Hill Farm

Stockhurst Farm

Hoath Wood

Water Mill Farm

Harebell

Tilebarn Wood

Pickham Wood

Tilebarn Farm

Escheatlands Farm

Great Stent Farm

A28

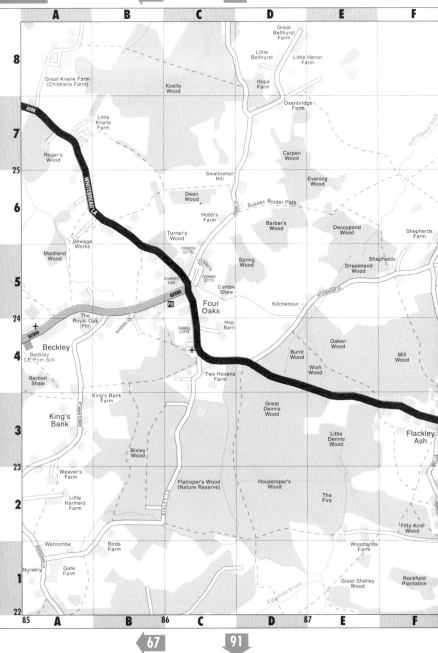

69

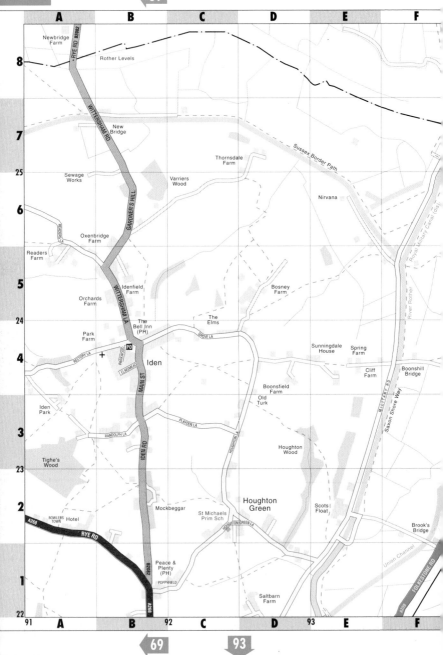

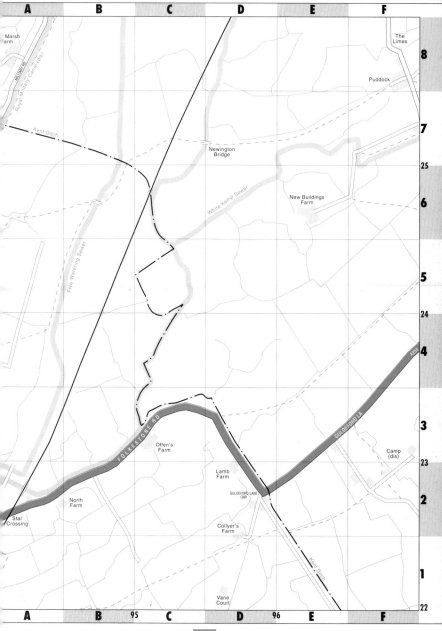

Marsh
Farm

Royal Military Canal (dis)

Kent Ditch

Newington
Bridge

White Kemp Sewer

New Buildings
Farm

Five Watering Sewer

The
Limes

Puddock

FOLKESTONE RD

Offen's
Farm

Lamb
Farm

GUILDEFORD LANE
CNR

Collyer's
Farm

GUILDEFORD LA

A259

Camp
(dis)

North
Farm

Star
Crossing

Kent Ditch

Vane
Court

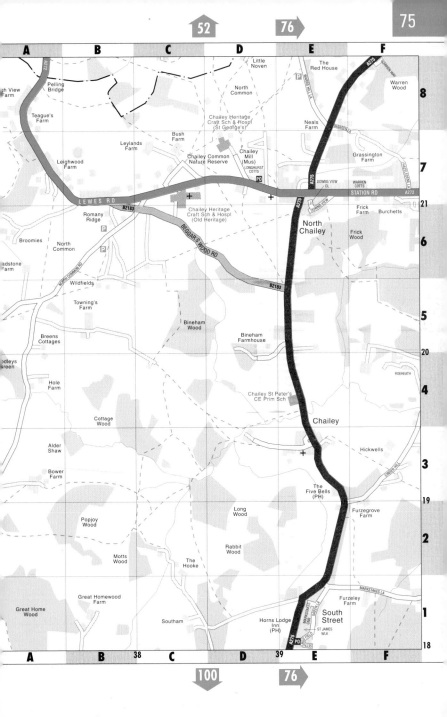

A B C D E F

A275
h View Farm
Pelling Bridge
Teague's Farm
Leighwood Farm
Broomies
North Common
adstone Farm
Wildfields
Breens Cottages
odleys reen
Hole Farm
Alder Shaw
Bower Farm
Popjoy Wood
Motts Wood
Great Home Wood
Great Homewood Farm
Southam

Little Noven
North Common
Leylands Farm
Bush Farm
Chailey Heritage Craft Sch & Hospl (St George's)
Chailey Common Nature Reserve
Chailey Mill (Mus)
LONGHURST COTTS
PO
LEWES RD
B2183
Romany Ridge
Chailey Heritage Craft Sch & Hospl (Old Heritage)
BEGGAR'S WOOD RD
B2183
Bineham Wood
Bineham Farmhouse
Chailey St Peter's CE Prim Sch
Cottage Wood
Long Wood
Rabbit Wood
The Hooke
Horns Lodge Inn (PH)

The Red House
WARREN HILL LA
Neals Farm
WARREN LA
DOWNS VIEW CL
A275
STATION RD
A272
North Chailey
DOWNS VIEW
B2183
Chailey
The Five Bells (PH)
The
A275
MARKSTAKES LA
GREEN LA
South Street
ST JAMES WLK
PO
A275

Warren Wood
TURNERS WAY
Grassington Farm
INHOLMES LA
WARREN COTTS
Frick Farm
Burchetts
Frick Wood
ROEHEATH
Hickwells
CINDER HILL
Furzegrove Farm
Furzeley Farm

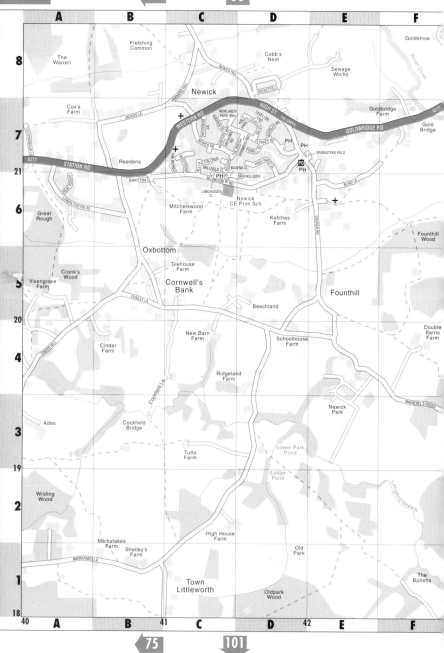

A B C D E F

Grisling
Common

Barkham
Manor
Vineyard

The Old
Farm

Argus
Farm

Golf
Course

Upper
Morgan's
Farm

Shortbridge

Shortbridge Stream

Butcher's
Wood

8

The
Peacock
Inn
(PH)

Lower
Morgan's
Farm

Moon's
Farm

Hanger
Wood

7

Pierpoint's
Wood

Sharpsbridge

21

Eel
Pot

Sharp's
Bridge

Darvel
Wood

Beeches
Farm

Beechen
Wood

Newbarn

6

Sharpsbridge
Farm

Buckham Hill
House

Buckham
Hill

Sharp's
Hanger

Rocky
Wood

oomlye
Wood

Sharps
Farm

Buckham Hill
Farm

River Ouse

5

Broomlye

20

Little
Buckham
Farm

Bunce's
Pit

Bunce's
Farm

Sluggs Eye
Island

Lodge Wood

4

Vuggles
Farm

Foxearth
Wood

p's
m

Parson's
Pit

Constantia
Manor

3

19

Gipp's
Wood

Sutton
Hall

New House
Farm

Lower Barn

2

River Uck

Old Rectory
Farm

Bradness
Wood

Beaks
Farm

Isfield
Place

gford
dge

Lavender Line

1

Longford
Farm

Isfield
Bridge

Isfield
Mill

18

STATION RD

A B 44 C D 45 E F

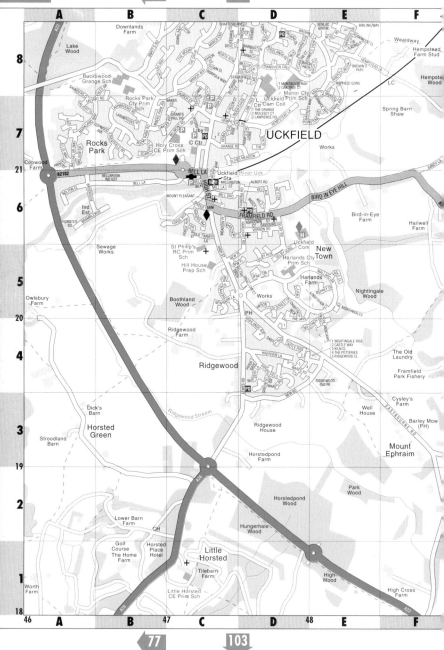

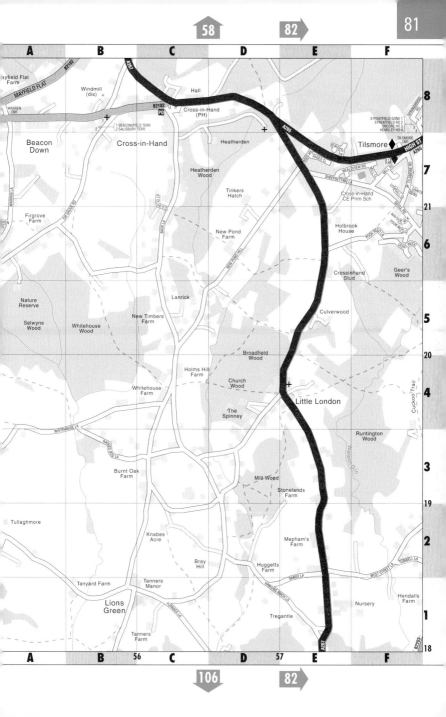

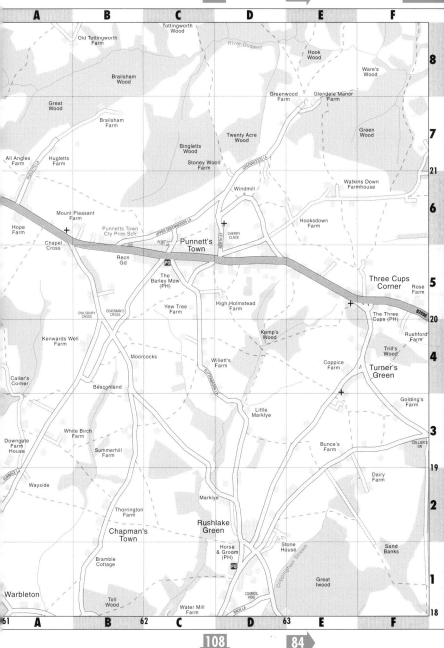

A   **B**   **C**   **D**   **E**   **F**

Old Tottingworth Farm

Tottingworth Wood

River Dudwell

Hook Wood

Ware's Wood

8

Brailsham Wood

Greenwood Farm

Glendale Manor Farm

Great Wood

Brailsham Farm

Green Wood

7

Bingletts Wood

Twenty Acre Wood

All Angles Farm

Hugletts Farm

Stoney Wood Farm

GREENWOODS LA

21

Watkins Down Farmhouse

6

Mount Pleasant Farm

Windmill

UPPER GREENWOODS LA

Hooksdown Farm

Hope Farm

Punnetts Town Cty Prim Sch

PONT LA

CHERRY CLACK

Chapel Cross

Punnett's Town

NORTH ST

Recn Gd

PO

Three Cups Corner

Rose Farm

5

The Barley Mow (PH)

High Holmstead Farm

B2096

The Three Cups (PH)

20

Yew Tree Farm

OWLSBURY CROSS

DEADMAN'S CROSS

Kemp's Wood

Rushford Farm

Kenwards Well Farm

Moorcocks

Willett's Farm

FLITTERBROOK LA

Coppice Farm

Trill's Wood

4

Turner's Green

Caller's Corner

Beaconland

Little Marklye

Golding's Farm

3

White Birch Farm

Bunce's Farm

COLLIER'S GRN

Downgate Farm House

Summerhill Farm

FURNACE LA

19

Wayside

Dairy Farm

2

Thorrington Farm

Marklye

Rushlake Green

Sand Banks

Chapman's Town

Horse & Groom (PH)

PO

Stone House

Clippinghams Stream

Warbleton

Bramble Cottage

Great Iwood

1

Toll Wood

Water Mill Farm

COUNCIL HOS

BACK LA

18

| A | B | C | D | E | F |

8

Blackbrooks

River Dudwell

Coombe
Wood

Stonehouse

Glazier's
Forge
Farm

7

Little Poundsford
Farm

Little Worge
Farm

Long
Wood

Sugarloaf
Wood

Great
Worge

21

Dallington
Forest

6

Forge
Wood

Upper
Plantation

Brightling
Down

Lower
Plantation

5

Cox's
Mill

Highlands
Farm

Rigford
Farm

20

Buckholt
Farm

Oakside

Hook's Farm
House

4

Millars
Farm

Brooklands

Upper
Brooklands
Farm

Carrick's
Hill

Graylings

Earl's Down

Brooklands
Farm

Wolmford Stream

Wyatts
Farm

PO

Rabbetts
Farm

B2096

The
Swan Inn
(PH)

3

Alms
Wood

Dallington CE
Prim Sch

Wood's
Corner

Old Castle

Dallington

19

Northfleet
Farm

Acelands
Farm

High
Wood

2

New Castle
Farm

Hoad's
Wood

HOADSWOOD
CROSS

Uplands
Farm

Highwood Gill

Stream
Farm

Oaklands
Farm

Clayton Gill

1

Grovelye
Farm

Cripps
Farm

Parkfields
Farm

Herring's
Farm

18

| 64 | A | B | 65 | C | D | 66 | E | F |

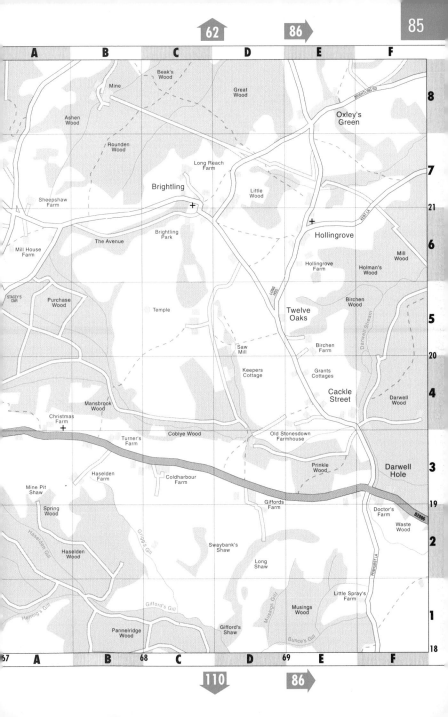

A B C D E F

8

Beak's Wood

Mine

Great Wood

BRIGHTLING RD

Oxley's Green

Ashen Wood

Rounden Wood

7

Long Reach Farm

Brightling

Little Wood

KENT LA

21

Sheepshaw Farm

Hollingrove

Mill House Farm

The Avenue

Brightling Park

6

Hollingrove Farm

Holman's Wood

Mill Wood

STACEY'S CNR

Purchase Wood

Temple

LONG REED

Twelve Oaks

Birchen Wood

5

Darwell Stream

Saw Mill

Birchen Farm

20

Keepers Cottage

Grants Cottages

Darwell Wood

Mansbrook Wood

Cackle Street

4

Christmas Farm

Coblye Wood

Old Stonesdown Farmhouse

Turner's Farm

Prinkle Wood

Darwell Hole

3

Haselden Farm

Coldharbour Farm

Mine Pit Shaw

Giffords Farm

Doctor's Farm

19

B2096

Spring Wood

Waste Wood

2

Haselden Wood

Swaybank's Shaw

Long Shaw

PEKHURST LA

Haselden Gill

Grigg's Gill

Little Spray's Farm

Gifford's Gill

Musings Gill

Musings Wood

1

Herring's Gill

Pannelridge Wood

Gifford's Shaw

Bunce's Gill

18

Brightling Rd

Swallowfield Farm

Mountfield Park Farm

Dens Wood

Glottenham Stream

Dray Shaw

Coalbridge Shaw

Darwell Stream

Park Pale

MOUNTFIELD LA

Coal Bridge

Hunters Farm

KENT LA

Tunstall Farm

Bottonholc Wood

Scaland Wood

Darwell Resr

Taylor's Cottage

Hightree Shaw

Baldwin's Farm

Furnace Shaw

Simmett's Wood

The Banks

Banks Farm

Castle Farm

Collier's Croft Wood

Castle Shaw

Millham Wood

Darwell Wood

LC

Limekiln Wood

Factory

Shep's Wood

Mountfield Mine

River Line

Great Wood

Crowhurst Farm

Darwell Hill

ORCHARD DOWN

Woodlands Farm

The Old Rectory

B2096

Netherfield CE Prim Sch

PO

Netherfield

Netherfield Court

NETHERFIELD WAY

EATENDEN LA

Homestead Farm

White Hart (PH)

KANE HYTHE RD

NETHERFIELD RD

Eatenden Wood

Sandy Wood

Ivyland Farm

Netherfield Down

Kerry Farm

Homestead Shaw

B2096

Ibrook Wood

Toll Wood

8

7

21

6

5

20

4

3

19

2

1

18

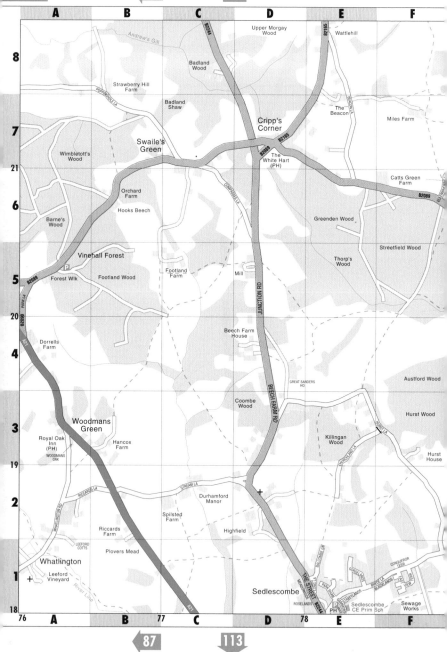

A B C D E F

8

Andrew's Gill

Upper Morgay
Wood

Wattlehill

B2244

B2165

Badland
Wood

Strawberry Hill
Farm

POPPINGHOLE LA

Badland
Shaw

The
Beacon

Miles Farm

7

Swaile's
Green

Cripp's
Corner

21

Wimblefott's
Wood

Orchard
Farm

B2089

The White Hart
(PH)

B2089

Catts Green
Farm

B2089

6

Hooks Beech

COMBWELL LA

Greenden Wood

Barne's
Wood

Streetfield Wood

Vinehall Forest

P

Thorp's
Wood

5

B2089

Forest Wlk

Footland Wood

Footland
Farm

Mill

RABBIT LA

B2089

20

Dorrells
Farm

Beech
Farm
House

JUNCTION RD

Austford Wood

4

GREAT SANDERS
HO

BEECH FARM RD

Hurst Wood

Woodmans
Green

Coombe
Wood

Killingan
Wood

HURST LA

Hurst
House

3

Royal Oak
Inn
(PH)

Hancox
Farm

CHURCH LA

WOODMANS
OAK

19

RICCARDS LA

STREAM LA

Durhamford
Manor

2

Spilsted
Farm

Highfield

Riccards
Farm

WHATLINGTON RD

Plovers Mead

LEEFORD
COTTS

BALCOMBE GRN

CONQUEROR
TERR

Whatlington

THE STREET

GODDENS

BREDE LA

1

Leeford
Vineyard

River Line

Sedlescombe

A21

B2244

PH

Sedlescombe
CE Prim Sch

Sewage
Works

ROSELANDS

NEADLANDS

18

76 A B 77 C D 78 E F

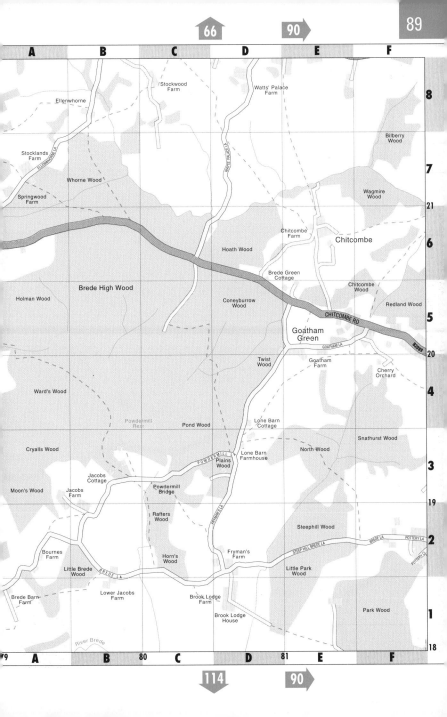

A B C D E F

8

Ellenwhorne

Stockwood Farm

Watts' Palace Farm

Bilberry Wood

Stocklands Farm

ELLENWHORNE LA

7

Whorne Wood

WATTS' PALACE LA

Wagmire Wood

Springwood Farm

21

Chitcombe Farm

Chitcombe

6

Hoath Wood

Brede Green Cottage

Holman Wood

Brede High Wood

Chitcombe Wood

Redland Wood

Coneyburrow Wood

CHITCOMBE RD

5

Goatham Green

B2089

20

Ward's Wood

Twist Wood

Goatham LA

Goatham Farm

Cherry Orchard

4

Powdermill Rear

Pond Wood

Lone Barn Cottage

Cryalls Wood

POWDERMILL

Plains Wood

Lone Barn Farmhouse

North Wood

Snathurst Wood

3

Jacobs Cottage

Powdermill Bridge

Moon's Wood

Jacobs Farm

19

Rafters Wood

Steephill Wood

2

PRIOMILL LA

BREDE LA

POTTERY LA

Bournes Farm

Fryman's Farm

STEEP HILL BREDE LA

Little Park Wood

POTTERY LA

Little Brede Wood

BREDE LA

Horn's Wood

Brede Barn Farm

Lower Jacobs Farm

Brook Lodge Farm

Park Wood

1

Brook Lodge House

River Brede

18

79 A B 80 C D 81 E F

89
67

8

Tanhouse
Farm

Garland
Wood

Doucegrove
Farm

Wharnham
Wood

Little
Doucegrove

Glass Eye
Farm

Moore's
Wood

MOORES LA

Greentiles
Farm

7

Beckley
Furnace

Osier
Gill

Sheepwash
Wood

River Tillingham

Furnace
Wood

21

Maplestone
Farm

NORTHIAM RD

Wagmary
Wood

Furnace
Farm

Arnold Bridge

Conster
Manor

Great Conster
Farm

Burnthouse
Wood

6

Austen's
Wood

West
Wood

Kicker
Wood

Birch
Wood

5

Twist
Wood

Hundredhouse
Bridge

BROAD OAK CL

Granary
Farm

CHESTNUT
CL

Broad Oak

Spring
Wood

Maidlands
Farm

20
B2089

CHITCOMBE RD

PO

4

The
Rainbow Trout
(PH)

THE
CROSSWAYS

Brede
Cty Prim
Sch

Reysons
Farm

Gilly
Wood

Moorsholm
Farm

KINK WOOD HILL

Reysons
Oasts

UDIMORE RD

Broadland Row

Broadlands
Wood

Sowdens
Farm

3

Well
Wood

South Sowdens
Wood

B2089

19

Cackle
Street

Mill
Wood

2

POTTERY LA

CACKLE ST

SPRINGFIELD
COTTS

Brede

Groaning
Bridge

STUBB LA

Alder
Wood

POTTERY CL

Hillyfield

Brede
Place

1

BREDE HILL

The
Red Lion Inn
(PH)

Hare
Cottages

Hare
Farm

Stonelink
Farm

Pickdick
Farm

18
82   A   B   83   C   D   84   E   F

89
115

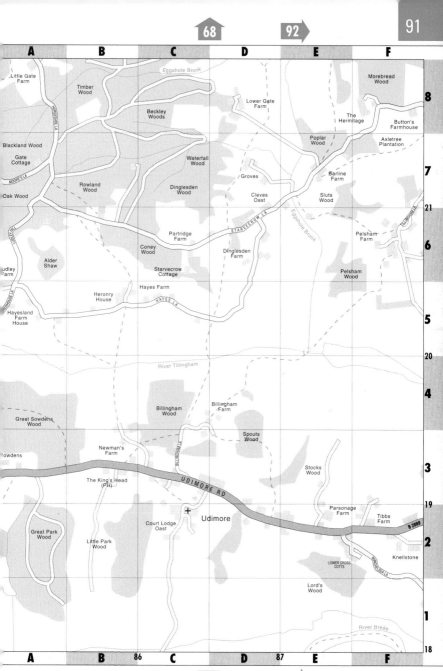

A **B** **C** **D** **E** **F**

Little Gate Farm

Eggshole Brook

Timber Wood

Morebread Wood

Beckley Woods

Lower Gate Farm

8

The Hermitage

Button's Farmhouse

Blackland Wood

Poplar Wood

Axletree Plantation

Gate Cottage

MOORES LA

Waterfall Wood

Groves

Barline Farm

7

Rowland Wood

Dinglesden Wood

Cleves Oast

Sluts Wood

21

Oak Wood

LOSSENHOLE LA

LUCKY HILL

Partridge Farm

STARVECROW LA

Eggshole Brook

Pelsham Farm

TILLINGHAM LA

6

Coney Wood

Dinglesden Farm

Pelsham Wood

udley arm

Alder Shaw

Starvecrow Cottage

WINDMILL LA

Heronry House

Hayes Farm

HAYES LA

5

Hayesland Farm House

River Tillingham

20

Great Sowdens Wood

Billingham Wood

Billingham Farm

Spouts Wood

4

owdens

Newman's Farm

BILLINGHAM LA

Stocks Wood

3

The King's Head (PH)

UDIMORE RD

Parsonage Farm

Tibbs Farm

19

Great Park Wood

Court Lodge Oast

✚ Udimore

B 2089

Little Park Wood

Knellstone

2

WINCHELSEA LA

LOWER CROSS COTTS

Lord's Wood

1

River Brede

18

A **B** 86 **C** **D** 87 **E** **F**

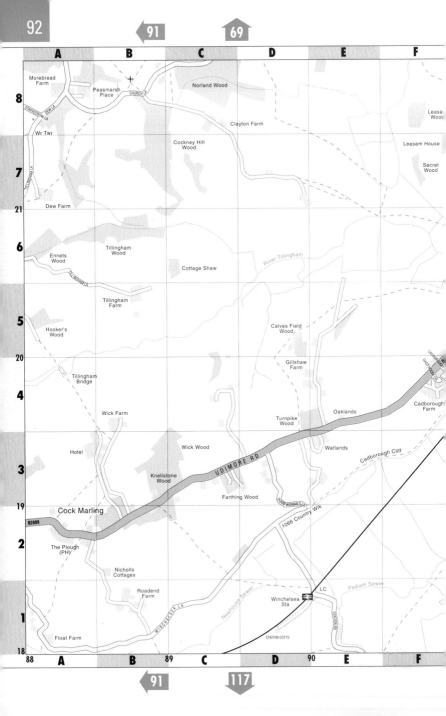

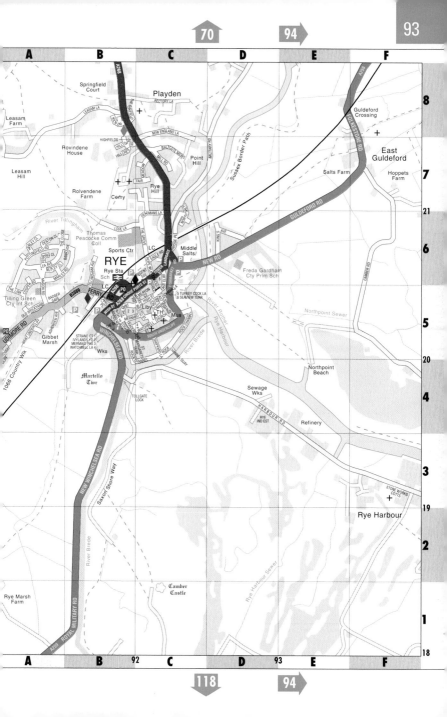

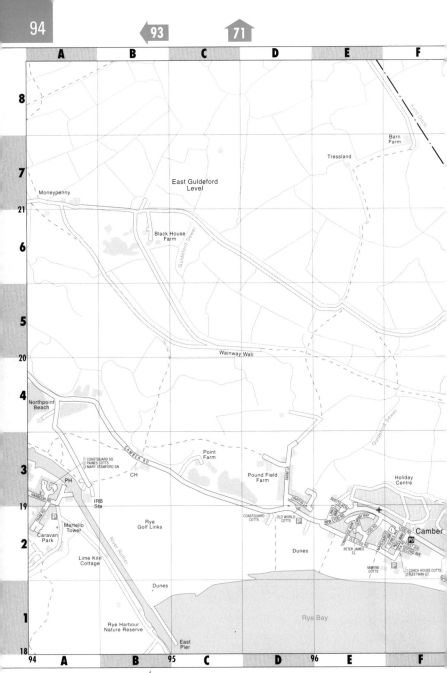

A   **B**   **C**   **D**   **E**   **F**

8

Kent Ditch

Barn Farm

Tressland

7

East Guldeford Level

Moneypenny

21

Black House Farm

6

Guldeford Sewer

5

20

Wainway Wall

4

Northpoint Beach

Guldeford Sewer

CAMBER RD

Point Farm

3

1 COASTGUARD SQ
2 PAINES COTTS
3 MARY STAMFORD GN

CH

Pound Field Farm

HAM LA

Holiday Centre

PH

DRAKIN LA

IRB Sta

COASTGUARD COTTS

OLD WORLD COTTS

19

HARBOUR RD

Rye Golf Links

NEW LYDD RD

Camber

LYDD RD

PO

Caravan Park

Martello Tower

River Rother

Dunes

PETER JAMES CL

FIRST AVE

SECOND AVE

MARINE COTTS

1 COACH HOUSE COTTS
2 FLEETWAY CT

2

Lime Kiln Cottage

1

Dunes

Rye Bay

Rye Harbour Nature Reserve

East Pier

18

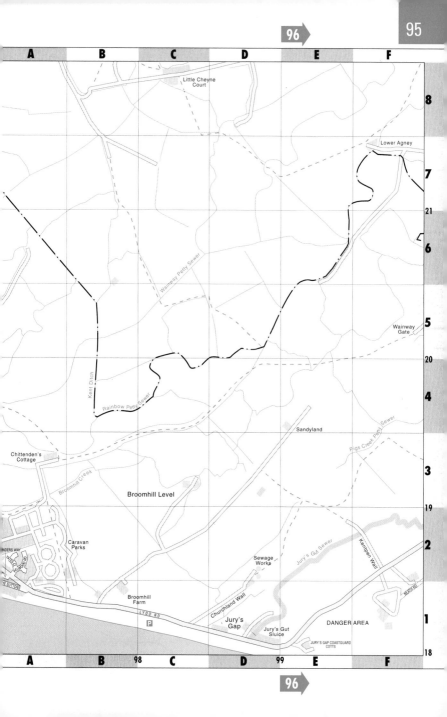

Little Cheyne
Court

Lower Agney

Wainway Petty Sewer

Kent Ditch

Wainway
Gate

Rainbow Petty Sewer

Sandyland

Pigs Creek Petty Sewer

Chittenden's
Cottage

Broomhill Creek

Broomhill Level

Caravan
Parks

FLINDERS WAY

THE SUTHONS

Jury's Gut Sewer

Kentpen Wall

Sewage
Works

Churchland Wall

Broomhill
Farm

LYDD RD

P

Jury's
Gap

Jury's Gut
Sluice

DANGER AREA

NORTH RD

JURY'S GAP COASTGUARD
COTTS

8

7

21

6

5

20

4

3

19

2

1

18

A   B   98   C   D   99   E   F

95

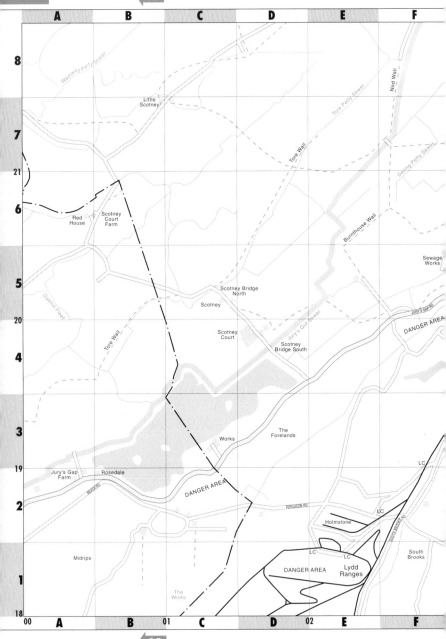

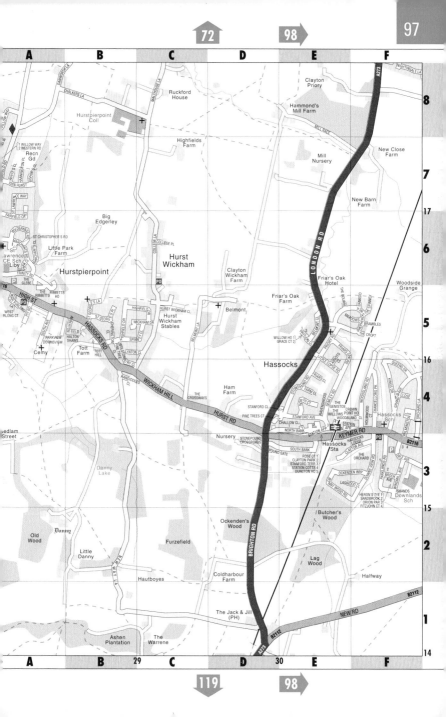

A B C D E F

8

7

17

6

5

16

4

3

15

2

1

14

Gallops

Gallops Farm

Blackbrook Wood

Captains Farm

The Plantation

Malthouse

Shergolds Farm

Golf Course

Blackbrook Farm

Griggs Farm

Elmgrove Farm

The Mid Sussex Golf Club

Marchants Farm

STREAT LA

Jenner's Farm

North Acres

Streat Place

Hayleigh Farm

Streat

Caravan Site

Sedlow Wood

Spinneys

Plumpton Wood

New Barn

Brocks Wood

Middleton Plantation

Middleton Manor (Horticultural Residential Training Centre)

Inholms Farm

Lentridge Farm

COX'S COTTS

The Fountain Inn (PH)

CHAPEL LA

WOOD

SEAMEADOW

STRAWLANDS

WELLS CHASE

Plumpton Green

WEST GATE

THE ODDENS

PO

RIDDENS LA

The Riddens

PH

NORTH BARNES LA

South Downs Cty Prim Sch

Plumpton

The Riddens

EAST VIEW FIELDS

OLD SCHOOL COTTS

Bevern Stream

LC

STATION RD

BARNFIELD

Plumpton Sta

P

LC

Plumpton Race Course

Rylands

Ashurst Farm

PLUMPTON CROSS

The Old Mill House

Chapel Farm

PLUMPTON LA

Upper Mill

Reed Pond

Long Wood

Novington Manor

A B C D E F

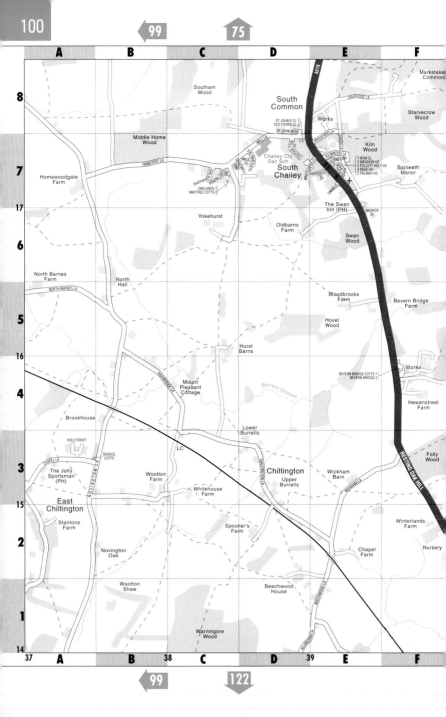

A B C D E F

8

Elms Farm
Tile Barn Farm
TILE BARN CL
NORTHFIELD COTTS
Longfield Stream
Dallas Lane
Down Coppice
Agmond's Wood
White Bridge
Isfield
Oaks Farm
Lavender Line
HORSTED LA

7

Burtenshaw's Wood
PH

17

Birches Farm

6

Scufflings
Gallops Farm
Blunt's La
Iron River
Boathouse Farm
Brook Lodge Farm
Rose Hi
LEWES RD

Delves Farm
ANCHOR LA
The Halfway House (PH)
KILN LA

5

Banks Farm
Anchor Inn
Batchelor's Hall
ISFIELD RD

16

Lower Barn Cottage
River Ouse

Clay Hill Wood
Oaklands Park

4

Bevern Stream
Iron River
Beam Bridge (FB)

Stewards Enquiry (PH)

3

Barcombe Mills
Mill Farm
Barcombe Resr
Upper Clay Hill Farm

15

Barcombe House
BARCOMBE MILLS RD
Pikes Bridge
Ppg Sta

2

Plashett Park Farm

P

Bridge Farm

Lower Clayhill
Clayhill House

Little Norlington
NORLINGTON LA

1

River Ouse
A26
SHELLEYHAM LA

Swingate

14

43 A 44 B C 45 D E F

Pear Tree
Farm

CH

Hunnington's
Farm

Wicklands

Railands
Wood

East Sussex
National Golf Club

Bradford's
Farm

Whitelocks
Pits

Old Farm

Limes
Pit

Bradford's
Bridge

Little Bentley
Farm

South Brockwell's
Farm

Brockwells
Farm

Wind
Pump

Bentley
Wood

CRUMP'S
CNR

Crump's
Wood

Plashshett Park

Moatpark
Farm

Bentley Motor
Mus

HARVEY'S LA

Cooper's
Hatch

Bentley
Farm

Plashett Wood

Mount
Farm

Bentley Wildfowl
Reserve

Harvey's
Gate

Hemsley's
Rough

B2192

Red Barn
Farm

Upper Lodge
Farm

THE BROYLE

Middle Broyle
Farm

Raystede Ctr
for Animal Welfare

B2192

Green Lane
Farm

Gliding
Club

GREEN LA

Ashreed
Wood

B2192

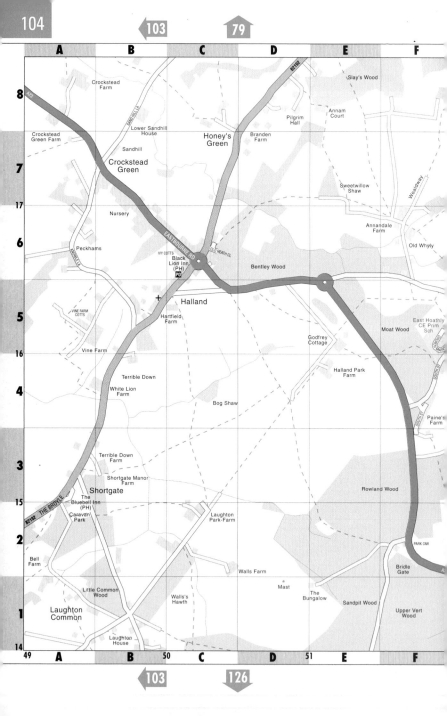

80
106

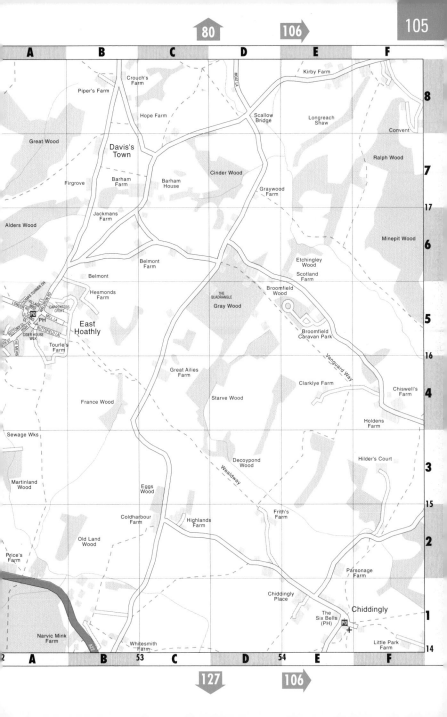

A B C D E F

8

Kirby Farm

Piper's Farm
Crouch's Farm

Hope Farm

Scallow Bridge

Longreach Shaw

Convent

Great Wood

Davis's Town

Cinder Wood

Ralph Wood

7

Firgrove

Barham Farm

Barham House

Graywood Farm

17

Jackmans Farm

Alders Wood

Minepit Wood

6

Belmont Farm

Belmont

Etchingley Wood

Scotland Farm

Hesmonds Farm

THE QUADRANGLE

Gray Wood

Broomfield Wood

THOMAS TURNER DR
CARPENTERS CROFT
LONDON RD
MILL LA
PH
BUTTSFIELD LA
RECTORY GL
CIDER HOUSE WLK
ST. MS WG

East Hoathly

5

Broomfield Caravan Park

Tourle's Farm

16

Great Ailies Farm

Vanguard Way

Clarklye Farm

Chiswell's Farm

4

France Wood

Starve Wood

Holdens Farm

Sewage Wks

Hilder's Court

3

Martinland Wood

Decoypond Wood

Wealdway

Eggs Wood

15

Coldharbour Farm

Highlands Farm

Frith's Farm

Old Land Wood

2

Price's Farm

Parsonage Farm

Chiddingly Place

Chiddingly

1

The Six Bells (PH)
PO

Narvic Mink Farm

Whitesmith Farm

Little Park Farm

14

2 A B 53 C D 54 E F

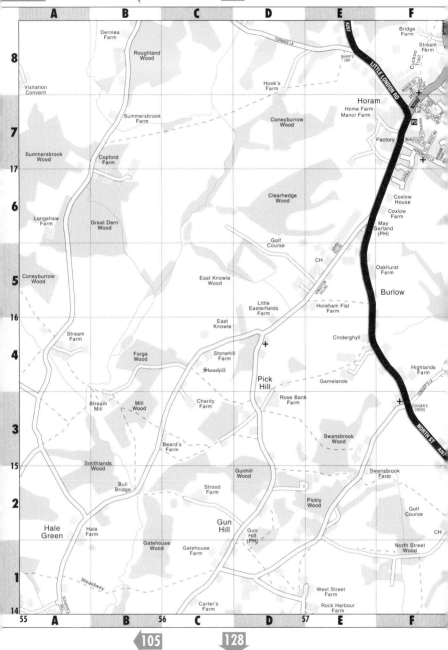

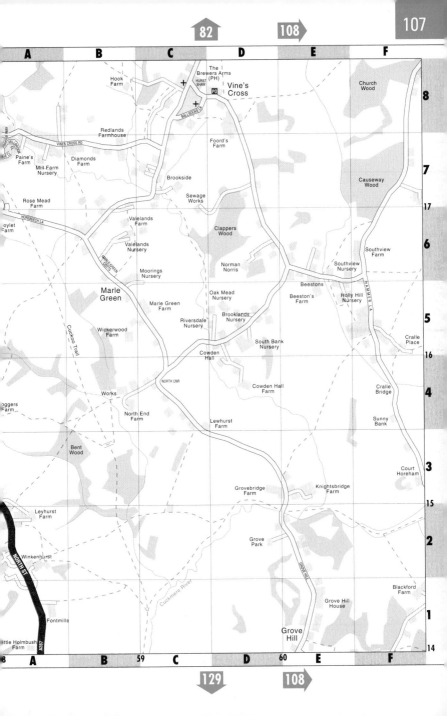

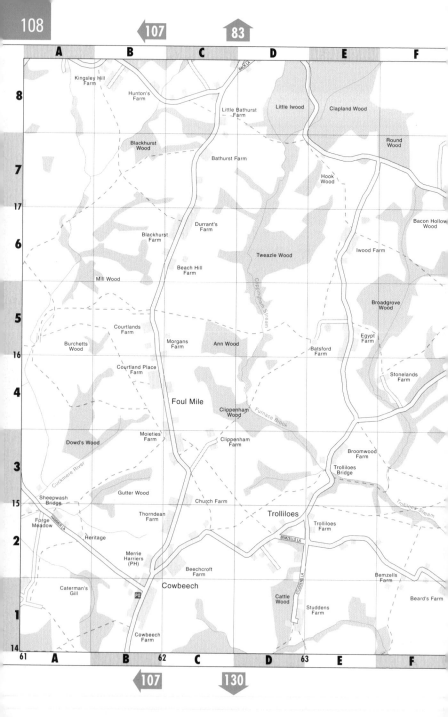

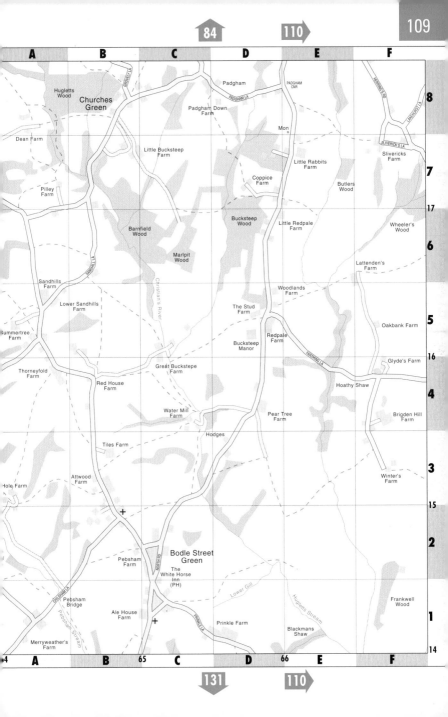

A B C D E F

8 7 17 6 5 16 4 3 15 2 1 14

Hugletts Wood

Churches Green

Padgham

PADGHAM CNR

Dean Farm

Padgham Down Farm

PADGHAM LA

Mon

Little Bucksteep Farm

Little Rabbits Farm

Slivericks Farm

OLIVERICK S LA

LADBROKE LA

HERRING RD

Pilley Farm

Coppice Farm

Bucksteep Wood

Little Redpale Farm

Butlers Wood

Wheeler's Wood

Barnfield Wood

Marlpit Wood

Woodlands Farm

Lattenden's Farm

Sandhills Farm

The Stud Farm

Oakbank Farm

Lower Sandhills Farm

Christian's River

SANDHILL LA

Summertree Farm

Bucksteep Manor

Redpale Farm

HARPIHE LA

Glyde's Farm

Thorneyfold Farm

Great Buckstepe Farm

Red House Farm

Hoathy Shaw

Water Mill Farm

Pear Tree Farm

Brigden Hill Farm

Hodges

Tiles Farm

Attwood Farm

Winter's Farm

Hole Farm

Pebsham Farm

OL FLACK LA

Bodle Street Green

The White Horse Inn (PH)

Lower Gill

Hugtns Stream

Frankwell Wood

OREHAM LA

Pebsham Bridge

Pebsham Stream

Ale House Farm

PRINKE LA

Prinkle Farm

Blackmans Shaw

Merryweather's Farm

A · B · C · D · E · F

8

Pleasure House

Lakehurst

LAKEHURST LA

Pannelridge Wood

Bunce's Farm

Link Wood

Great Spray's Farm

Buckwell Wood

Buckwell Gill

7

Buckwell Farm

Spring Gill

Anderson's Wood

Rocks Farm

Foxearth Wood

17

Furnace Cottage

Thorndale Farm

6

Thornden Farm

Hogstye Wood

Allfrees Wood

Penhurst

Pollyspark Wood

Thornden Cottages

Church Farm

Manor House

5

Court Lodge

Malthouse Wood

1066 Country Walk

Izlebridge Wood

16

PO

Pontsgreen Wood

Forge Cottages

4

Ponts Green

Reedlands Farm

Peens Wood

Tent Hill

Reed Wood

3

Mon

The Bungalow

New Buildings Farm

Ash Bourne

15

Reservoir Pond

Ash Tree Inn (PH)

The Grove

2

Brownbread Street

Brownbread Stud

Pigknoll Farm

Ashburnham Place

Front Water

1066 Country Walk

Linghams

The Pound

A2

1

Lingham's Farm

Walk Wood

Forty Acre Gill

Burrage Wood

Broad Water

14

Bray's Hill

Baker's Wood

A271

67 · A · B · 68 · C · D · 69 · E · F

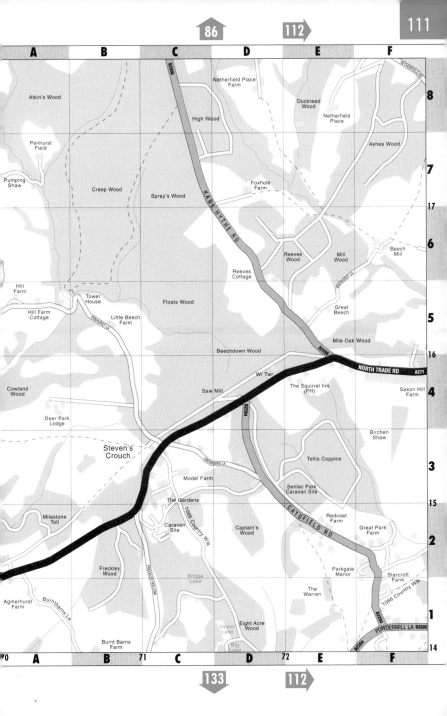

A   B   C   D   E   F

8

Atkin's Wood

Netherfield Place
Farm

Duckreed
Wood

Netherfield
Place

Penhurst
Field

High Wood

Ashes Wood

Pumping
Shaw

7

Creep Wood

Spray's Wood

Foxhole
Farm

17

KANE HYTHE RD

Reeves
Wood

Mill
Wood

Beech
Mill

6

Reeves
Cottage

Hill
Farm

Tower
House

Floats Wood

Great
Beech

Hill Farm
Cottage

Little Beech
Farm

PENHURST LA

5

Beechdown Wood

Mile Oak Wood

16

B2096

B2204

Wr Twr

NORTH TRADE RD   A271

Cowland
Wood

Saw Mill

The Squirrel Inn
(PH)

Saxon Hill
Farm

4

Deer Park
Lodge

Birchen
Shaw

Steven's
Crouch

CROWBERS LA

Tellis Coppice

3

Model Farm

Senlac Park
Caravan Site

CATSFIELD RD

15

The Gardens

Redcoat
Farm

Great Park
Farm

Caravan
Site

1066 Country Wlk

Captain's
Wood

2

Milestone
Toll

Freckley
Wood

Parkgate
Manor

Starcroft
Farm

Agmerhurst
Farm

Burntbarns La

Bridge
Lake

The
Warren

1066 Country Wlk

1

Burnt Barns
Farm

Upper
Lake

Eight Acre
Wood

B2204

POWDERMILL LA   B2095

Big
Lake

14

A   B   71   C   D   72   E   F

0

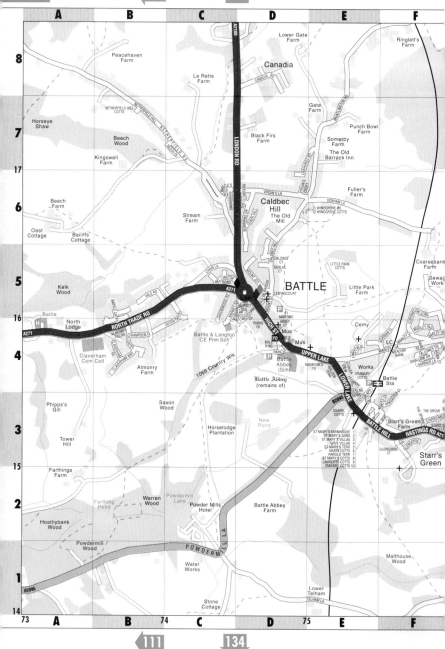

A B C D E F

8
7
17
6
5
16
4
3
15
2
1
14

Riccards Wood

Queen's Head (PH)

Catt's Shaw

THE STREET

GREGORY WY

River Brede

THE BOWLINGS

Sedlescombe Bridge

Petley Wood

Lower Marley Farm

PAYGATE RD

Luff's Farm

Pestolozzi Children's Village

Felon Wood

COTTAGE LA

CHAPEL LA

Magazine Farm

RUTHERFORDS BSNS PK

Cold Spring Shaw

Horsmans Farm
Old Horsmans

Camping & Caravan Site

CRAZY LA

Meadow View

MARLEY LA

Beanford Farm

WHIDDON HILL

NEW ENGLAND LA

Marley Farm

Marley House

Battle Barn Stud Farm

Oak Wood

Whitefield Wood

Fir Wood

CH

1066 Country Wlk

KENT ST

Golf Course

Kent Street

lackfriars

Great Wood

Norton's Farm

LOOSE FARM RD

MERY DREW LA

Burnt Chimney Farm

Upper Morax Wood

Screen Wood

Branshill Farm

Birchin Shaw

Duke's Wood

Little Hemingfold Farm

LOOSE FARM COTTS

Oak Wood

Bishop's Wood

Beauport Park

OOSE FARM BARNS

Loose Farm

Mill Wood

OSE FARM COTTS

Blackhorse Hill

Alder Wood

Golf Course

STONEHOUSE LA

Stonehouse

HASTINGS RD

Bushy Wood

PO

Hemingfold Farm

Ring Wood

Telham

Black Horse (PH)

FELDAM LA

Three Cedar Wood

A2100

6 77 78

A B C D E F

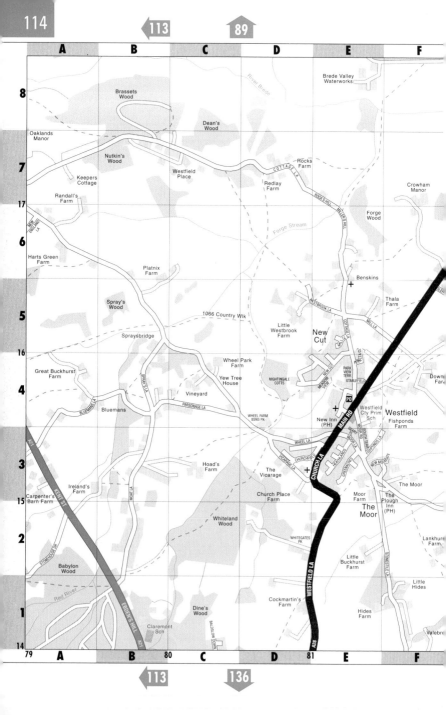

Brede Valley
Waterworks

Brassets
Wood

Dean's
Wood

Oaklands
Manor

Nutkin's
Wood

Rocks
Farm

Westfield
Place

Crowham
Manor

Keepers
Cottage

Redlay
Farm

Randall's
Farm

Forge
Wood

Harts Green
Farm

Forge Stream

Platnix
Farm

Benskins

Spray's
Wood

Thala
Farm

1066 Country Wlk

Little
Westbrook
Farm

New
Cut

Spraysbridge

Great Buckhurst
Farm

Wheel Park
Farm

Down
Farm

Yew Tree
House

NIGHTINGALE
COTTS

PARK
VIEW
TERR

STABLEFIELD

Vineyard

Bluemans

PARSONAGE LA

WHEEL FARM
BSND PK

Westfield
Cty Prim
Sch

Westfield

New Inn
(PH)

Fishponds
Farm

WHEEL LA

Hoad's
Farm

The
Vicarage

The Moor

Ireland's
Farm

Church Place
Farm

Moor
Farm

The
Moor

The
Plough
Inn
(PH)

Carpenter's
Barn Farm

Whiteland
Wood

WHITEGATES
PK

Lankhurst
Farm

Babylon
Wood

Little
Buckhurst
Farm

Little
Hides

Red River

Dine's
Wood

Cockmartin's
Farm

Hides
Farm

Valebr

Claremont
Sch

WESTFIELD LA

A B C D E F

8

7

17

6

5

16

4

3

15

2

1

14

Jubilee Cottages

A28

BREDE HILL

Alder Shaw

River Brede

Brede Bridge

Brede Level

Little Knights

Little Knight's Oast

Gray's Wood

Marlpits Farm

Great Knight's Farm

Doleham Farm

Lidham Hill

Glover's Wood

DOLEHAM LA

Doleham Sta

NORTH LA

DOLEHAM DITCH

DOLEHAM HILL

DOLEHAM COTTS

A259

1066 Country Walk

Ashenden

Smith's Wood

Pattleton's Farm

Luckhurst Wood

SUTTON'S STREAM

FOUR FIELD CROSS LA

Copshall Farm

Oak Wood

Little Maxfield

Great Maxfield

WILLOW STREAM

Plashet Wood

Popland Wood

MAXFIELD LA

MORHA WOOD LA

A259

Eighteen Pounder Wood

LC

Three Oaks (PH)

BUTCHER'S LA

Eighteen Pounder Farm

Three Oaks

Three Oaks & Guestling Halt

Halfhouse Farm

Eastlands Farmhouse

FRONT AVE LA

Blackbrook Farm

Fraysland Farm

Rodger's Farm

IVYHOUSE LA

ROCK LA

A B C 83 D 84 E F

115 91

A B C D E F

8

River Brede

Brede Level

LC

7
Lower Snailham

Snailham Wood

17
Snaylham Farm

Brook Farm

1066 Country Wlk

6
Pond Wood

Broad Street

Icklesham

The Queen's Head I (PH)

FIVE VILLAGES HO

Icklesham CE Prim Sch

PARSONAGE LA

OAST HOUSE FIELD

Toke Farm

HIGH FORGE VIEW

5
Three Corner Wood

Broad Street Wood

BROAD ST

MAIN RD

LITTLE SHERWOOD IND PK

Robin Hood (PH)

SEAVIEW TERR

BREDE VALLEY VIEW

GOLDHURST DR

PO

WELLPLACE COTTS

LAUREL LA

WINGHORSE LA

Stocks Farm

16
THORN COTTS

Bench Wood

Croft Wood

Roughters

Knockbridge

Knockbridge Farm

4
A259

Guestling Thorn

Place Farm

Scrag Oak

Little Pannel Farm

WATERMILL LA

Kitchen Wood

Pannel Sewer

3
Broomham Sch

Pickham Mill

15

Pannel Wood

Factory Wood

2
A259

Church Farm

Pickham Farm

Burnt Wood

PANNEL LA

WINCHELSEA RD

A259

Pound Farm

CHURCH LA

P

Guestling Wood

Nature Reserve

Pett Wood

1

THE GLEBE

ELMS LA

PETT RD

THE OAK FIELD

14
85 A 86 B C 87 D E F

Fairlight Wood

French Court Farm

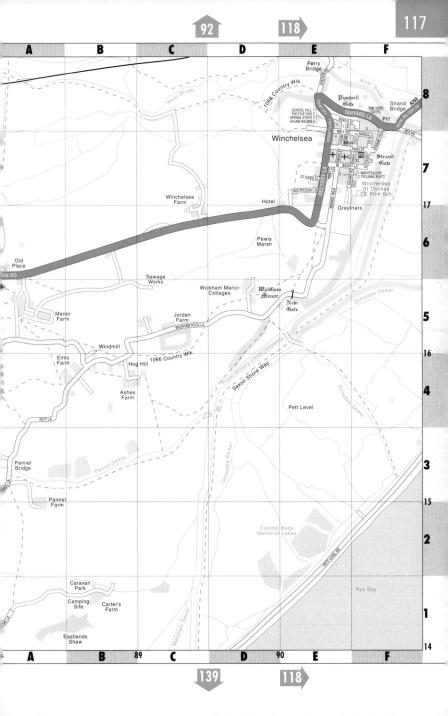

Ferry
Bridge

River Brede

1066 Country Wlk

Pipewell
Gate

TAN YARD
COTTS

Strand
Bridge

A259

SCHOOL HILL 1
THE FIVE HOS 2
SPRING STEPS 3
HIHAM BGLWS 4

TANYARD LA

PH

NORTH ST

MILL RD

BARRA...

Winchelsea

Mus

HIGH ST

PO

Strand
Gate

St GILES CL

1 MARITEAU HO
2 TROJANS PLATT

HOGTROUGH LA

BACK....

Winchelsea
St Thomas
CE Prim Sch

Winchelsea
Farm

Hotel

MONKS WLK

Greyfriars

Pewis
Marsh

Old
Place

...IN RD

Sewage
Works

Wickham Manor
Cottages

Wickham
Manor

New
Gate

Dimsdale Sewer

Manor
Farm

Jordan
Farm

WICKHAM ROCK LA

Windmill

1066 Country Wlk

Elms
Farm

Hog Hill

Royal Military Canal (disused)

Saxon Shore Way

Dimsdale Sewer

Ashes
Farm

Pett Level

PETT LA

Pannel
Bridge

...LA

Pannel Sewer

Dimsdale Sewer

Matsham Sewer

Pannel
Farm

Colonel Body
Memorial Lakes

PETT LEVEL RD

Caravan
Park

Rye Bay

Camping
Site

Carter's
Farm

...LA

Eastlands
Shaw

117
93

Sewage Wks

Nook Beach

The Nook

ROYAL MILITARY RD

River Brede
Farm

Saxon Shore Way

Castle Farm

Nature Reserve

River Brede

SUTTONS
IND PK

Watch
House

Nook Drain

8

SEA RD

OLD RIVER WAY

7

17

WINDMILL WAY

WINDMILL
CT

GREYFRIARS

The Ship
(PH)

HARBOUR
FARM

MONK'S RIDGE

Dimsdale Sewer

WILLOW LA

HARBOUR
BARN

THE RIDGE

6

PO

JACKSON LA

Winchelsea
Beach

Caravan
Park

DOGS HILL RD

5

COOKS WAY

PELHAM WAY

WINDSOR WAY

Caravan
Park

VUE
BRIS NEZ

Rye Bay

Dogs Hill

16

PETTLERS RD

4

3

15

2

1

14

117

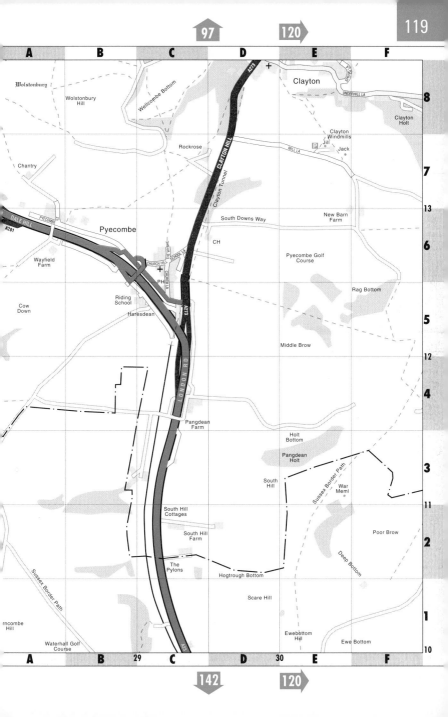

Wolstonbury

Wolstonbury
Hill

Wellcombe Bottom

Clayton

UNDERHILL LA

Clayton
Holt

Rockrose

Clayton
Windmills

P Jill

Jack

MILL LA

Chantry

8

CLAYTON HILL

A273

Clayton Tunnel

New Barn
Farm

7

13

DALE HILL

PYECOMBE RD

Pyecombe

South Downs Way

Pyecombe Golf
Course

A281

CH

6

THE WISH

SCHOOL LA

Wayfield
Farm

CHURCH HILL

CHURCH LA

Rag Bottom

PH

Cow
Down

Riding
School

Haresdean

A273

Middle Brow

5

12

LONDON RD

4

Pangdean
Farm

Holt
Bottom

Pangdean
Holt

3

South
Hill

Sussex Border Path

War
Meml

South Hill
Cottages

South Hill
Farm

Poor Brow

11

The
Pylons

Hogtrough Bottom

Deep Bottom

2

Sussex Border Path

Scare Hill

rncombe
Hill

Waterhall Golf
Course

Ewebottom
Hill

Ewe Bottom

1

10

A **B** **C** **D** **E** **F**

Westmeston Place

Whitelands

UNDERHILL LA

Sailliards

8

Coombe Bottom

Wick Farm

Downview
Westmeston

Westmes Farm

Clayton Holt

Ditchling Beacon Nature Reserve

Westmeston Bostall

7

South Downs Way

13

Ditchling Beacon

Middleton Bosta

Home Bottom

Home Brow

6

Dencher Bottom

Hogtrough Bottom

Big Bottom

5

Heathy Brow

12

North Bottom

4

Highpark Corner

High Park Farm

Lower Standean

Highpark Wood

White Thorn

3

Doddis Plantation

Wonderhill Plantation

New Barn

Green Broom

Moon's Bottom

11

Mid-down House

Millban Wood

2

Piddingworth Plantation

Granny's Belt

Alpha Cottage

Beta Cottage

Flint Heap

1

Tegdown Hill

Upper Lodge Wood

Limekiln Wood

10

31 **A** **B** **32** **C** **D** **33** **E** **F**

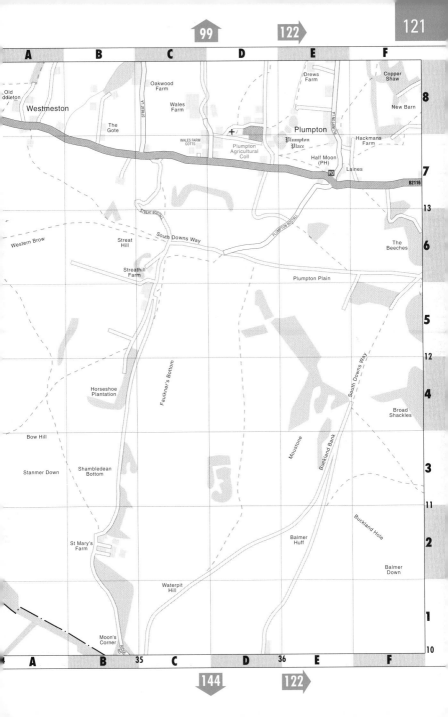

A B C D E F

8 Warningore House

Lower Tulleyswells Farm

BEECHWOOD LA

Warningore Farm

Allington Farm

Russet Shaw

FT KUNINTE

Tulleyswells Farm

7 Newstead Farmhouse

Watershoot Shaw

B2116

13 New Barn

Warningore Bostall

6 Courthouse Farm

Mount Harry House

B2116

Blackcap

Offham Farm

Offham House

Coombe Place

Offham

5 Mount Harry

Coombe Plantation

12 Ashcombe Bottom

4 Offham Hill

3 Training Gallop

Cuckoo Bottom

Landport Bottom

11 HIGHDOWN

2 Training Gallop

EAST WAY

1 Balmer Down

South Downs Way

10

37 A 38 C 39 E F
B D

A B C D E F

Cook's
Bridge

Cooksbridge Sewage
Works

Hamsey Cty Prim
Sch
Cooksbridge
Sta

Cowlease
Farm

North
End

Bushy
Island

Wellingham
Farm

8

7

13

Copyhold
Farm

Hamsey Manor

Hamsey House

Hamsey

River Ouse

Chalkham
Farm

6

Sewage
Works

Drove
House
Hamsey
Crossing

Hamseyplace
Farm

5

12

The Pells

Hamsey
Place

Pay Gate
Cottages

Pellbrook Cut

Upper Stoneham
Farm

4

Chalk Pit
Inn
(PH)

Lower Stoneham
Farm

Landport
Farm

Old Malling
Farm

Malling House
(Sussex Pol HQ)

EARWIG
CNR

B2192

B2192

3

RUSSELL ROW 1
REED CT 2
MEALLA CL 3
PECKHAM CL 4

South Malling
CE Prim Sch

Malling
Hill

Landport

The Martlets

11

Wallands
Cty Prim
Sch

Pells
CE Prim Sch

South
Malling

The Brooks

PH

2

OFFHAM RD

Superstore

Malling
Ind Est

The Spinneys

Wallands
Cres

Pells
CE Prim Sch

Ind
Est

LEWES

Wheatsheaf Gdns

Obelisk

Cuilfail

1

Wallands
Park

WHITE HILL

Castle
Mus

Cliffe

St Anne's

HM Prison Stables

41

A B C D E F

10

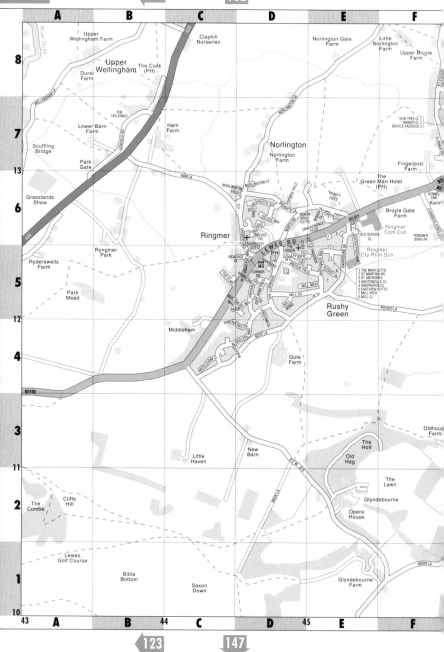

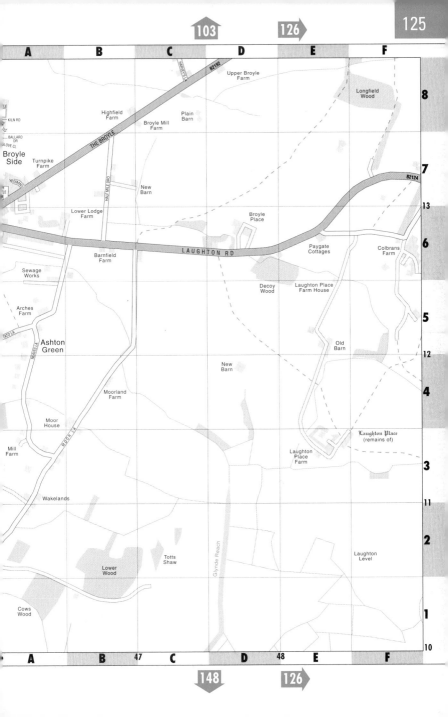

A B C D E F

8

Upper Broyle
Farm

Longfield
Wood

KILN RD

Highfield
Farm

Plain
Barn

BALLARD
DR
GLOVE CL

Broyle Mill
Farm

THE BROYLE

Broyle
Side

Turnpike
Farm

7

B2102

B2124

YEOMANS

New
Barn

HALF MILE DRO

13

Lower Lodge
Farm

Broyle
Place

6

LAUGHTON RD

Paygate
Cottages

Colbrans
Farm

Barnfield
Farm

Sewage
Works

Decoy
Wood

Laughton Place
Farm House

Arches
Farm

5

PARDLA

NEALES LA

Ashton
Green

Old
Barn

12

New
Barn

4

Moorland
Farm

Moor
House

Laughton Place
(remains of)

BROYLE LA

Mill
Farm

Laughton Place
Farm

3

Wakelands

11

Glynde Reach

2

Totts
Shaw

Lower
Wood

Laughton
Level

Cows
Wood

1

10

A B 47 C D 48 E F

| | A | B | C | D | E | F |

8

Brickhurst Wood

Laughton Common Wood

Lower Vert Wood

H

Laughton Lodge

Brickhurst Farm

BRICKHURST LA

Averys Oak Farm

Wood Bungalows

Saw Mill

7

Laughton Manor

The Roebuck (PH)

PO

ELM COTTS

ELM LA

POUND LA

Helouan Farm

Queeake

B2124

LAUGHTON RD

Bowen Wood

13

Home Farm

Laughton

Bowen Farm

6

Laughton Cty Prim Sch

Coopers Farm

B2

Black Shaw

+

Stone Cross Farm

5

New House Farm

Marchants Farm

Milward's Farm

Church Farm

Harben's Farm

12

4

Cleaver's Farm

Muslins Pit

Little Stream Farm

Airfield

3

Mill Farm

Cleggett's Farm

11

2

MARK CROSS

RIPE LA

1

Curl's Farm

Fowler's Barn

Lamb Inn (PH)

PO

Ripe

CHANNERS LA

10

| 49 | A | B | 50 | C | D | 51 | E | F |

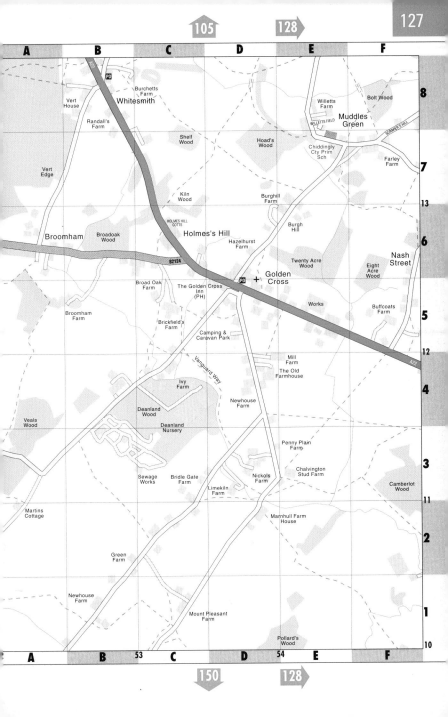

127
106

A **B** **C** **D** **E** **F**

Park Bridge

Popp's Farm

Wealdway

Westen Woo

SCRAPPER'S HILL

Scrapper's Hill Farm

Hamly Bridge

Hawthbush Farm

World's End Farm

Thunder's Hill

Pekes House

Leabrid Farm

Pekes Farm

Nash Street Farm

Nash Street

Perryland Farm

Boggy Wood

Broad Farm

NORTH ST

Marigolds Farm

Hackhurst Farm

HACKHURST LA

Hellingly Cty Prim Sch

B2104

NORTH ST

Cemy

Blackbarn Farm

A22

NORTHFIELDS BSNS PK

THE CROFT

HACKHURST LA IND EST

HACKHURST LA

Caldicott's Wood

Caldicotts Farm

White House

BROOKLANDS TERR

B2104

PO

Nurse

CALDICOTTS LA

Lower Dicker

Knight's Farm

A267

A271

The King's Head (PH)

Lower Horsebridge

A2

Camberlot Farm

MAYNARDS LA

LOWER DICKER

POTTERIES COTTS

Camberlot Wood

Clover Farm

The Mount

Coldharbour Farm

Boship Farm Hotel

Cuckmere River

CAMBERLOT RD

Field House

Hatches Farm

Wealdway

Welbury Farm

The Nurseries

HIDE HALL LA

Starnash

Hempstead Farm

Woodside Farm

Plenties Farm

A22

Malvern House

Bourne Farm

Chicheley Farm

8 7 13 6 5 12 4 3 11 2 1 10

8

Old Barn
Farm

Holmbush

Westenden
Farm

Springham
Farm

Jarvis's
Wood

Mount Pleasant
Cottages

7

Lealands

Blackstock
Farm

Clapsons
Shaw

Nobody's
Wood

13

Shawpits
Farm

Reeves
Land

Ten Acre
Wood

6

Akehurst
Farm

Woodland
Walks
P

Peartree
Shaw

CHURCH
PATH

Hellingly

The Golden
Martlet
(PH)

Danecroft
Nursery

SWINGATE
CROSS

Park
Wood

Carter's Corner
Place

5

Horselunges

STATION RD

Park
Cottage

12

Horselunges
Manor

Wealdway

Cuckoo Way

Nursery

Park
Farm

Amberstone

Nodes
Farm

4

NEW RD

Nursery

Nodes

Magham
Down

Waldernheath

orks

Upper
Horsebridge

1 BECKENHAM CL
2 HAWKSTOWN CL

Amberstone
Bridge

AMBERSTONE

A271

The
Red Lion
(PH)

3

UPPER HORSEBRIDGE RD

CAREW
CT

ASHLEY GDNS

Amberstone Grange
Farm

MANOR
PARK

LANSDOWNE

Hawkes Farm
Cty Prim
Sch

SEAVIEW
COTTS

Amberstone
Nursery

LUNDY
WLK

ARRAN CL

ARUNDEL

11

BEXLEY CL

DOUGLAS CL

1 HAREBEATING CL
2 HAREBEATING GDNS
3 AMBERSTONE VIEW
4 NORTH HEATH CL
5 ABBEY PATH

HAILSHAM

Sewage
Works

2

LONDON RD

LEAP CROSS
SMALL
HOLDINGS

HAWTHYLANDS

HAWTHYLANDS CRES

Longleys
Farm

Spindle
Bridge

PORTLAND
CL

LOWLANDS

HARMERS HAY RD

GREEN WLK

1 CORNFIELD GN
2 HAYLAND GN

Grovelands
Cty Prim Sch

1 ST ANDREWS CL
2 SUNNINGDALE CL
3 WENTWORTH CL
4 WOBURN CL

BLOSSOM WLK

FIELD CL

AVE

MILLAND RD

Hailsham
Com Coll

BATTLE RD

B1
1 FERN GN
2 JASMINE GN
3 ACORN GN
4 ELM GN
5 LABURNHAM GN
6 ILEX GN

Harebeating
Farm

1

GROVELANDS RD

10

A   B   59   C   D   60   E   F

129 108

A B C D E F

8

CINDERFORD LA

Scrip Wood

Kiln Wood

Chilsham

Chilsham Stream

Chilsham Farm

Studdens La

Scripp Farm

Greenway Fruit Farm

Chilsham

CHILSHAM LA

7

Cowbeech Hill Farm

Cowbeech Hill

Stunts Green

Old Court

13

Oaklands

Hollingwood

New Barn Farm

Herstmonceux

Nunningham Farm

6

COUNCIL HOS

Ginger's Green Farm

Ginger's Green

WEST END

JAMES DR
CHURCH RD
MONCEUX RD
FAIRFIELD
HAMMAR LA

Twelveacres

Starvecrow Wood

THE ROCK WAY
BUCKTHORN RD
BELTRING RD

PH

PH PO

GARDNER ST

A271

Squirrel La

HAILSHAM RD

Herstmonceux CE Prim Sch

LIME CROSS

The Welcome Stranger (PH)

5

Deudney's Farm

Cooper's Croft

Buckwell Farm

Lime Park

Chapel Row

12

GILL RD

Upper House Farm

Buckwell Place

CRICKETING LA

Lime End Farm

4

Magham Down Farm

Harkaway

Butler's Farm

BUTLERS LA

Place Farm

A271

Puckridge

UNDER RD

Flowers Green

3

Gilridge Lodge

Willow Farm

Chantler's Farm

LOWER RD

Golden Cross

11

Gildridge Farm

Sackville Farm

Ironcroft Cottage

Cherry Cross Farm

2

Puckridge Stream

Bowley Sewer

Iron Stream

Magham Sewer

Mill Stream

1

Hurst Haven

Whelpley Level

1066 Country Wlk

10

61 A B 62 C D 63 E F

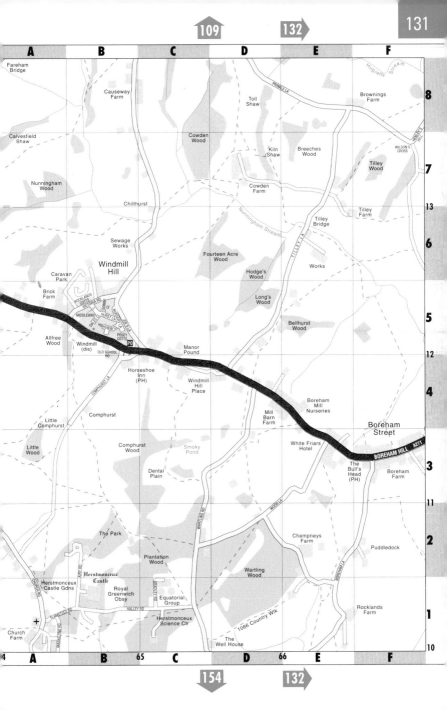

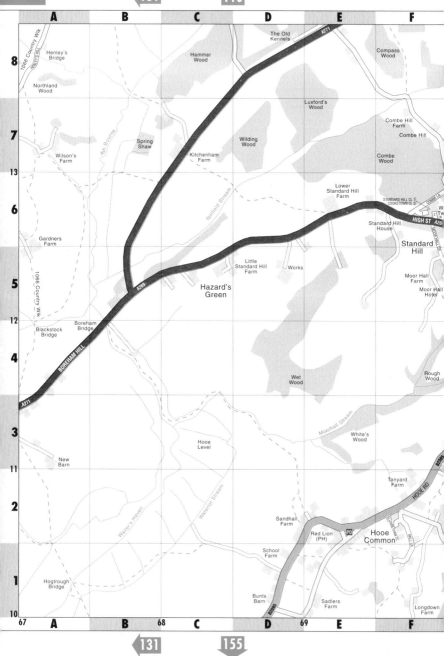

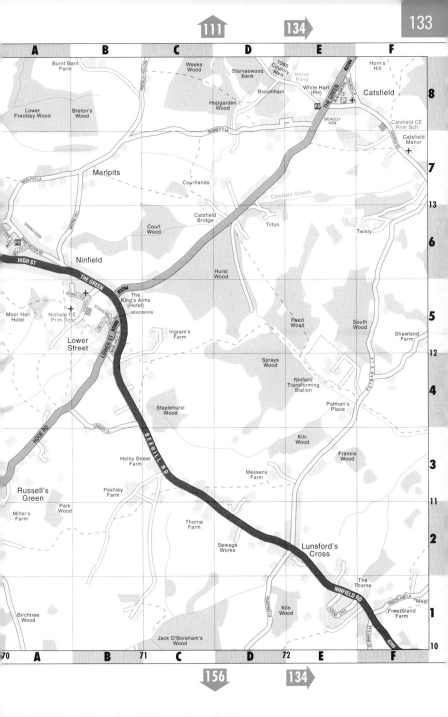

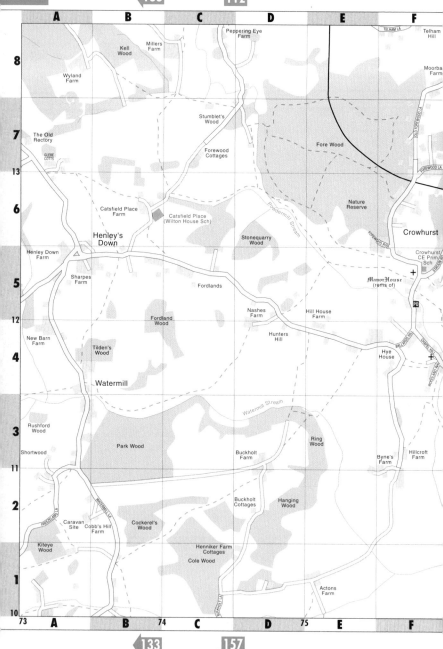

| A | B | C | D | E | F |

8

Peppering Eye Farm

TELHAM LA

Telham Hill

Kell Wood

Millers Farm

Wyland Farm

Moorba Farm

7

The Old Rectory

GLEBE COTTS

Stumblet's Wood

Forewood Cottages

Fore Wood

OLD FOREWOOD LA

FOREWOOD LA

13

6

Catsfield Place Farm

Catsfield Place (Wilton House Sch)

Stonequarry Wood

Powdermill Stream

Nature Reserve

Crowhurst

FOREWOOD RISE

Henley's Down

Henley Down Farm

Crowhurst CE Prim Sch

5

Sharpes Farm

Fordlands

Manor House (rems of)

STREAM

PO

12

Fordland Wood

Nashes Farm

Hill House Farm

New Barn Farm

Hunters Hill

Hye House

FORGE LA

WOODLAND WAY

4

Tilden's Wood

Watermill

3

Rushford Wood

Park Wood

Watermill Stream

Ring Wood

Byne's Farm

Hillcroft Farm

Shortwood

Buckholt Farm

11

2

Caravan Site

Cobb's Hill Farm

Cockerel's Wood

Buckholt Cottages

Hanging Wood

POWDERMILL LA

PRETTY LANE

MOUNTFIELD LA

1

Kiteye Wood

Henniker Farm Cottages

Cole Wood

Actons Farm

10

A B C D E F

8
7
13
6
5
12
4
3
11
2
1
10

Telham Place
TELHAM LA
Pye's Farm
Brakes Coppice Farm
Camping Site
Crowhurst Sta
Rackwell Wood
Sampson's Farm
Green Street
BLACKSMITH'S FIELD
Croucher's Farm
Whitefield Wood
Lower Wilting Farm
CROWHURST RD
Chapel Wood
Little Bog
Upper Wilting Farm
Adam's Farm
Decoy Pond Wood
Monkham Wood
Powdermill Stream
Combe Haven

Wr Twr
Circle Pond
Crowhurst Park
Caravan Site
Crowhurst Park
HASTINGS RD
A2100
Breadsell Farm
Long Plantation
New Wood
Park Farm
Stonebridge Farm
Marline Wood
Park Wood
HARTFIELD MEADOW
Hartfield
SANDRINGHAM HTS
Chapel Wood
Redgeland Wood
CROWHURST RD
Dogkennel Wood

Golf Course
Beauport Wood
Maze Pond
CH
Beauport Park Hotel
Wychnour
BATTLE RD
THE RIDGE W
A2100
B2159
BATTLE RD
TRAFALGAR CL 1
WATERLOO CL 2
Birchen Wood
FALLS CT
THE HIGH BEECH COUNTRY CLUB
CONQUEROR IND EST
COLLETT CL 1
THE KESTRELS 2
NORFOLK DR 3
Ind Est
Inglesea Sch
QUEENSWAY
Superstore
Church Wood Cty Prim Sch
Church Wood
WESTMORELAND CL
SQUIRREL CL
CHAMBERS CRES
HASTINGS
Robsack Wood
DITTONS MEWS
Rocky Shaw
The Grove Sch
BULRUSH PL
HARLEY SHUTE RD
B2093
FERNSIDE AVE

The Inn at Crowhurst (Hotel & PH)
STATION COTTS
CRAIG CL

A B C D E F

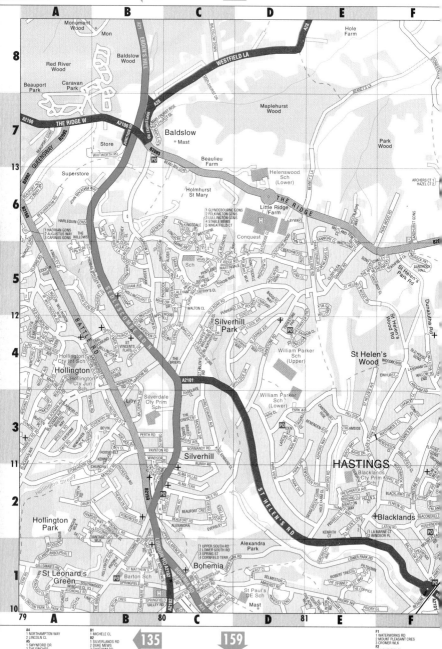

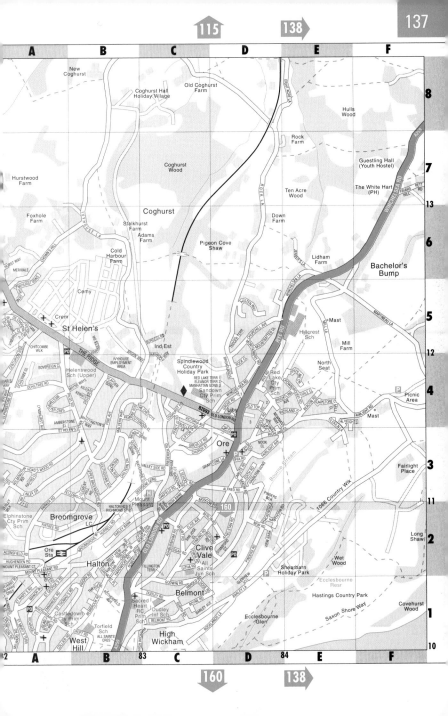

Lunsford

PETT RD

CHICK HILL

COASTGUARDS

Marsham Sewer

CANAL BANK

OLD
COASTGUARDS

IRB Sta

PO

The Smuggler
(PH)

PETT LEVEL

Old Marsham
Farm

CLIFF END

Cliff End

ewage
Wks

Stumblet
Wood

Fairlight
(NT)

Saxon Shore Way

SEA RD

Scabes Castle

Golf Course

DEVIL'S DYKE RD

CH

Golf Farm

Skeleton Hovel

Benfield Valley

Mount Zion

Brighton & Hove Golf Course

Round Hill

West Hove Golf Course

Benfield Hill

Monarch's Way

CH

New Barn

Foredown Hill

West Blatchington Inf Sch

West Blatchington Jun Sch

SHOREHAM BY-PASS

Monarch's Way

PORTSLADE -BY-SEA

Hangleton Park

1 NUTLEY CL
2 MIDHURST WLK

Benfield Valley Golf Course

Foredown Tower

CH

St Helen's Park

Hangleton

Sports Ctr

Portslade Com Coll (Lower)

BUSH TERR

Hillside Sch

Hangleton Cty Inf & Jun Sch

(dis)

Recn Gd

Hangleton

Hove Park Sch (Lower)

Liby

Blatchington Mill Sch

SHANKLIN CT
SANDOWN CT
RYDE CT

Knoll Cty Inf Sch

HOVE

Superstore

Portslade Com Coll

Portslade Village

Easthill Park

ST RICHARD'S

HANGLETON RD

Goldstone Cty Jun Sch

West Blatchington

Allot Gdns

A293

Allot Gdns

CHURCH

Schs

Cemy

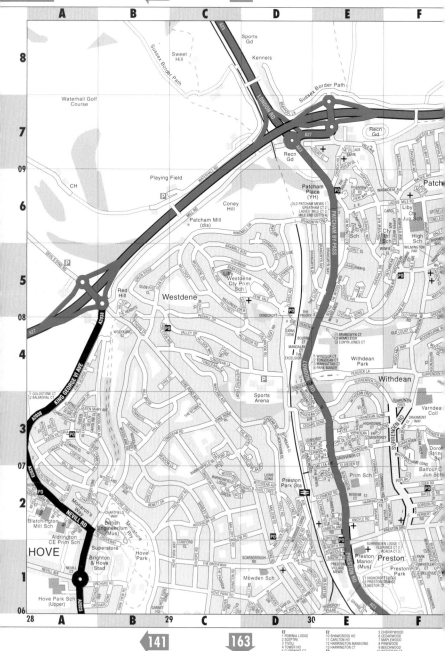

E2
1 ROBINIA LODGE
2 SCEPTRE
3 TIVOLI
4 TOWER HO
5 CLERMONT CT
6 LYNDEN CT
7 STAMFORD LODGE
8 CUMBERLAND LODGE
9 CENTENARY HO

E2
10 SHAWCROSS HO
11 CARLTON HO
12 HARRINGTON MANSIONS
13 HARRINGTON CT
E3
1 THE CEDARS
2 THE APPROACH
3 WITHDEAN HALL
4 LEAHURST CT

5 CHERRYWOOD
6 CEDARWOOD
7 MAPLEWOOD
8 PINEWOOD
9 BEECHWOOD
10 WITHDEAN CT
11 WELLINGTONIA CL

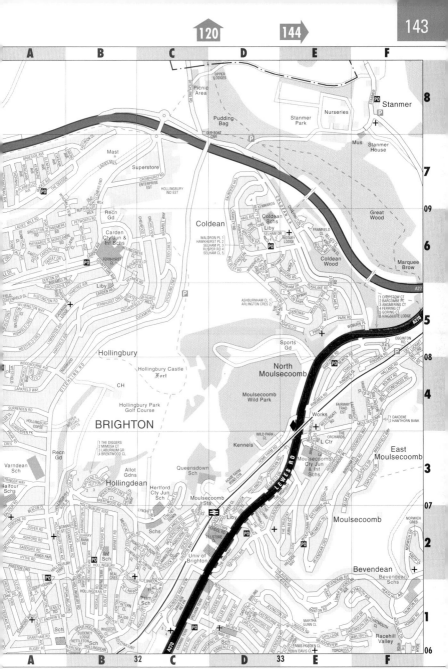

Grubbings

LEWES CT

Stanmore Park

THE PARK VILLAGE

BRIGHTHELM

The Ridge

Ridge Farm

Balmer Farm

Balmer

Richmond Hill

University of Sussex

LANCASTER HOUSE RD

NORWICH HOUSE RD

PO

ARTS RD

GARDNER CENTRE RD

FALMER RD

SPORTCENTRE RD

Old Forge Barn

Upper Housedean Cottages

Housedean Farm

A27

Sports Ctr

Lower Lodges

LEWES RD

FALMER HILL

Pav

Playing Field

Knights Gate

BILL ST

MILL ST

FALMER ST

MIDDLE ST

PO PH

SOUTH DR

THE COURTYARD

Court Farm

Falmer

Cranedean Plantation

New Barn

A27

A270

STATION RD

Falmer Sta

University of Brighton

B2123

VILLAGE WAY

Cemy

Falmer Sch

LOCKET RD

EGGINGTON RD

EGGON RD

Playing Field

GREAT WILKINS

Westlain Plantation

Playing Field

THE DROVE

Loose Bottom

South Downs Way

ASHHURST RD

Hog Plantation

Newmarket Plantation

Falmer Hill

Hogtrough Bottom

Newmarket Hill

Mast

Bevendean

FINCHWORTH GR

NORWICH DR

HAMPDEN CL

ROEDEAN CL

LEYBOURNE PARK

HEATHFIELD AVE

ROEDEAN RD

ST JOHNS CL

PO

HORNBY RD

AUCKLAND DR

LEYBOURNE RD

ROEDEAN RD

WALK

1 TAUNTON GR
2 TAUNTON PL
3 HORNBY PL
4 TAUNTON WAY
5 LEYBOURNE CL

Recn Gd

Upper Bevendean

FALMER RD

SPIPLE AVE

Works

WARREN WAY

DROVE RD

VICTORIA RD

HELENA RD

LARKHURST AVE

Woodingdean

BEXHILL RD

LANGLEY CRES

NORTON DR

Mast

Bullock Hill

BALSDEAN RD

B2123

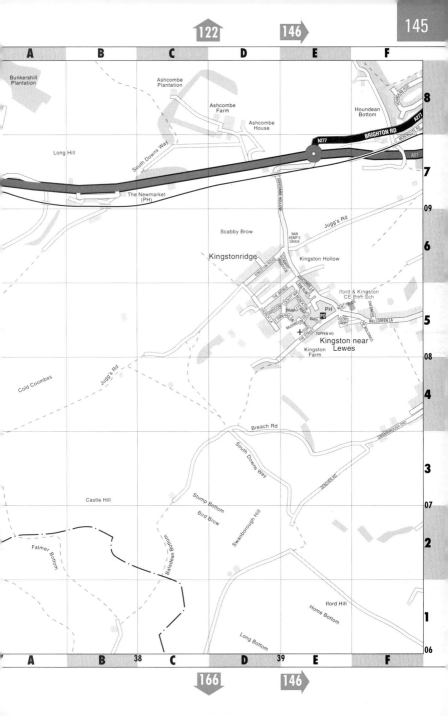

145
123

A B C D E F

8

SOUTHDOWN AVE
Liby
1 CLEVEDOWN
2 BARONS WLK
Cemy
City Hall
Sch
A277 HIGH ST
ANTIOCH
GRANGE RD
RUTTEN ROW
GRANGE RD
Sch
EASTPORT LA
Sch
Sta
B2193
Lewes Sta
Coll

BRIGHTON RD
A277
BERKELEY ROW
DALE RD
VALLEY RD
WINTERBOURNE
BELL LA
HILLYFIELD
ST PANCRAS GDNS
SOUTHOVER HIGH ST
Mus
PRIORY ST

1 DUMBRELL CT
2 GREENE CT
3 BARBER CT
4 THE COURSE
5 CLEVE TERR

1 LANSDOWN PL
2 TANNERS BROOK
3 DORSET RD
4 PRIORY HO
5 PRIORY CT
6 ROYAL SUSSEX CT

MOUNTFIELD RD
Coll
Priory Sch
L Ctr
CLIFFE IND EST

CH

WINTERBOURNE
MORLEY ST
CLUNT ST
B2193

Southover

The Cockshut

Sewage Works

Southerham Farm

7

CANNONDOWN

LEWES

C6
1 ST SWITHUN'S LA
2 BULL LA
3 ST MARTIN'S INN LA
4 ST MARTIN'S LA
5 ST SWITHUN'S TERR
6 FAIRHOLME
7 PRIORY FLATS
8 MONKS LA
9 VERRALL'S WLK
10 ANNE'S PATH
11 ELM GR

River Ouse

09

6

Spring Barn Farm

Rise Farm

Upper Rise

5

WELLGREEN LA

Swanborough Fishing Lake

Celery Sewer

Sewage Works

Rise Barn

08

Swanborough Manor

The Brooks

Lower Rise

4

SWANBOROUGH DRO

SWANBOROUGH HOLLOW

Iford Farm

Celery Sewer

3

Iford

SUTTON COTTS

Iford Farm

07

2

Northease Manor

WHITEWAYS COTTS

Northease Farm

Sewage Works

BARLEY FIELD COTTS

Monk's House

1

Front Hill

WHITE WAY

Rodmell

Rodmell CE Prim Sch

South Farm

MARTENS FIELD

06

40 A 41 B C 41 D 42 E F

145
167

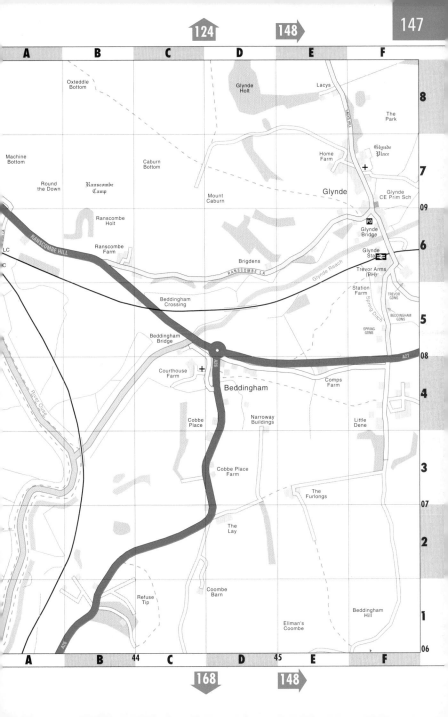

8

Oxteddle
Bottom

Glynde
Holt

Lacys

The
Park

Machine
Bottom

Caburn
Bottom

Home
Farm

Glynde
Place

7

Round
the Down

Ranscombe
Camp

Mount
Caburn

Glynde

Glynde
CE Prim Sch

09

Ranscombe
Holt

RANSCOMBE HILL

LC

Ranscombe
Farm

Brigdens

RANSCOMBE LA

Glynde Reach

PO

Glynde
Bridge

Glynde
Sta

Trevor Arms
(PH)

6

C

Beddingham
Crossing

Station
Farm

TREVOR
GDNS

BEDDINGHAM
GDNS

5

River Ouse

Beddingham
Bridge

A26

SPRING
GDNS

Spring Ditch

08

A27

Courthouse
Farm

Beddingham

Comps
Farm

Little
Dene

4

Cobbe
Place

Narroway
Buildings

Cobbe Place
Farm

The
Furlongs

3

07

The
Lay

2

Refuse
Tip

Coombe
Barn

Ellman's
Coombe

Beddingham
Hill

1

A26

06

147
125

A **B** **C** **D** **E** **F**

New Barn

8 Decoy Wood

Black Shaw

7 Willow Shaw

Glynde Reach

Barber's Wish

09

Burgh Shaw

Middle Barn

LC

6 Burgh Bridge

Bushy Lodge

Loover Shaw

Bushy Lodge Farm

Loover Barn

5 Garage

Wick Street

Newhouse Farm

BURGH LA

Adder Wells

Stamford Buildings

Gibraltar

Mid Fa

08

A27

Preston House

Dairy Farm

Decoy Pond

4 Firle CE Prim Sch

Firle Park

Petland Barn

POSTAL RD

THE STREET

P

Heighton Street

Compton Wood

Ram Inn (PH)

PO THE ROCK

West Firle

3 Newelm

Place Farm

+

Firle Place

Firle Tower

07

Beanstalk

FIRLE BOSTAL

2

Round Hill

1 Beddingham Hill

Firle Plantation

Roundhill Plantation

06

46 **A** **B** **47** **C** **D** **48** **E** **F**

147
169

A B C D E F

8

Yew Tree (PH)

Yew Farm

Selmeston Croft

Clifto Farm

The Ploug (PH)

Diplocks Farm

High Barn

Lovers Farm

Chalvington

Vanguard Way

7

Lower Claverham Farm

Park Wood

Claverham Manor

Parkwood Farm

09

Bungalow Farm

Wickstreet Farm

Wickstreet

6

Batbrooks Farm House

Lower Claverham House

Batbrook Cottages

Sessingham Farm

5

Cobb Court

Cuckmere River

TYE HILL RD

08

Raylands Farm

Ludlay Coppice

4

Vanguard Way

Wealdway

Arlington

Arlington Rest

Ludlay

+

The Yew Tree Inn (PH)

Ludlay Farm

3

Wilbees Farm

PRINCES FIELD

DOWNSWAY

Polhill's Farm

Copyhold Cottages

07

Stapley's

Berwick Sta

Garage

Works

2

Berwick Inn (PH)

LC

PO

Chilverbridge House

Chilver Bridge Farm

Endlewick Cottages

Endlewick Farm

COMMON LA

1

Moors Hill

06

52 A B 53 C D 54 E F

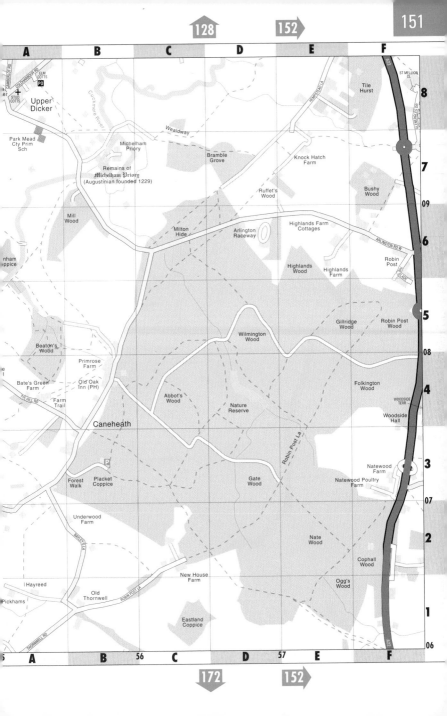

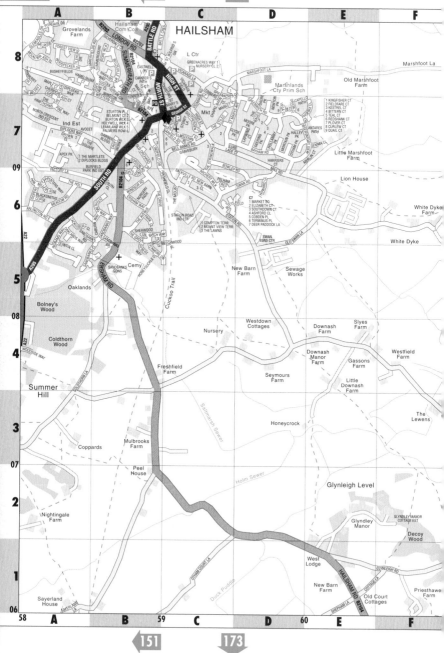

130
154

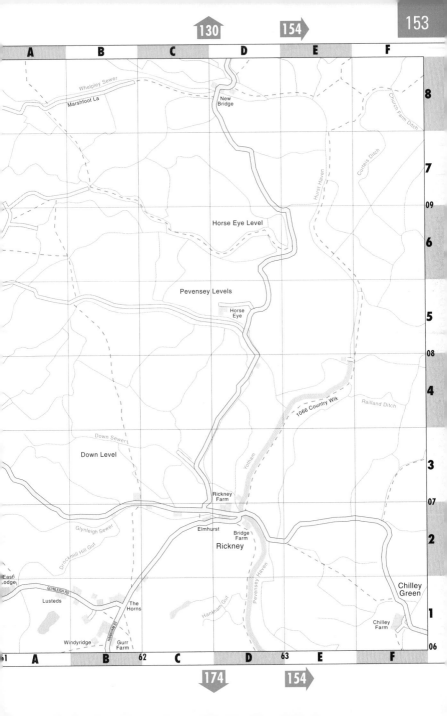

A B C D E F

8

Whelpley Sewer

Marshfoot La

New
Bridge

Church Farm Ditch

7

Hurst Haven

Curteis Ditch

09

Horse Eye Level

6

Pevensey Levels

5

Horse
Eye

08

4

1066 Country Wlk

Railland Ditch

Yotham

Down Sewer

Down Level

3

07

Rickney
Farm

Glynleigh Sewer

Elmhurst

Bridge
Farm

Rickney

2

Drockmill Hill Gut

Pevensey Haven

Chilley
Green

East
Lodge

GLYNLEIGH RD

Lusteds

The
Horns

Hankham Gut

Chilley
Farm

1

Windyridge

Gurr
Farm

HANKHAM ST

06

61 A B 62 C D 63 E F

A B C D E F

8

Royal Greenwich Obsy

Hoads Hill Farm

The Reids

Brooks Farm

Cooper's Farm

7

The Lamb Inn (PH)

Wartling

HORSEWALK

09

Horse Bridge

Court Lodge Farm

6

Lower Barn

Kentland Fleet

Sew Ditch

Marsh Foot Farm

5

08

Dowle Stream

Walter's Haven

4

Mark Dyke

Newhouse Farm

Church Acre Bridge

Pylons Cottages

Buck's Bridge

Lampham Dro

3

Dowle Corner

07

Chilley Stream

Old Haven

2

Middle Bridge

Manxey Level

1

06

64 A B 65 C D 66 E F

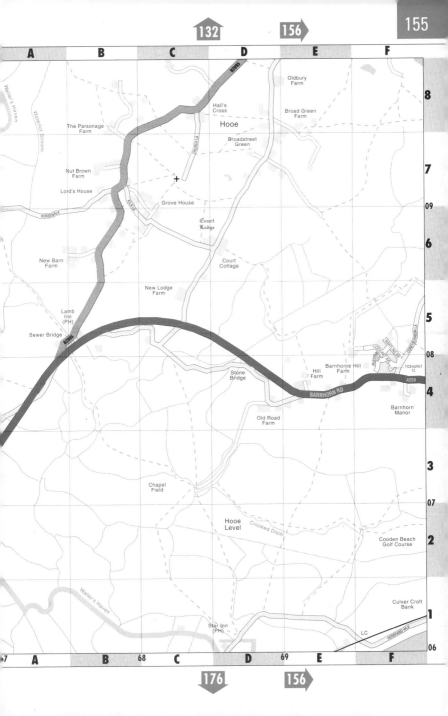

8

7

09

6

5

08

4

3

07

2

1

06

A B C D E F

Waller's Haven

Waterlot Stream

Oldbury Farm

Hall's Cross

Hooe

Broad Green Farm

The Parsonage Farm

Broadstreet Green

Nut Brown Farm

Lord's House

HORSEWALK

CHURCH LA

B2095

+

Grove House

Court Lodge

Court Cottage

New Barn Farm

New Lodge Farm

Lamb Inn (PH)

Sewer Bridge

B2095

Stone Bridge

Hill Farm

Barnhorne Hill Farm

TICEHURST CL

CONISBOROUGH LA

A259

BARNHORN RD

Old Road Farm

Barnhorn Manor

Chapel Field

Hooe Level

Crooked Ditch

Cooden Beach Golf Course

Culver Croft Bank

Waller's Haven

Star Inn (PH)

LC

HERBRAND WLK

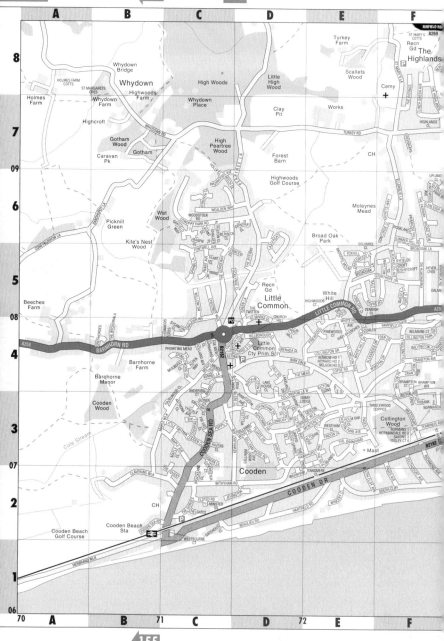

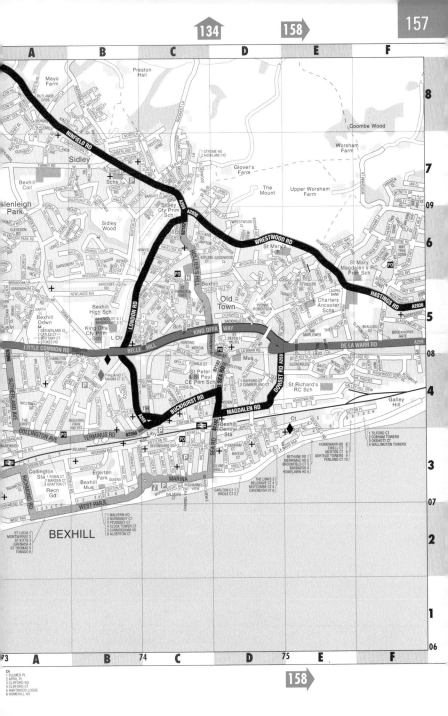

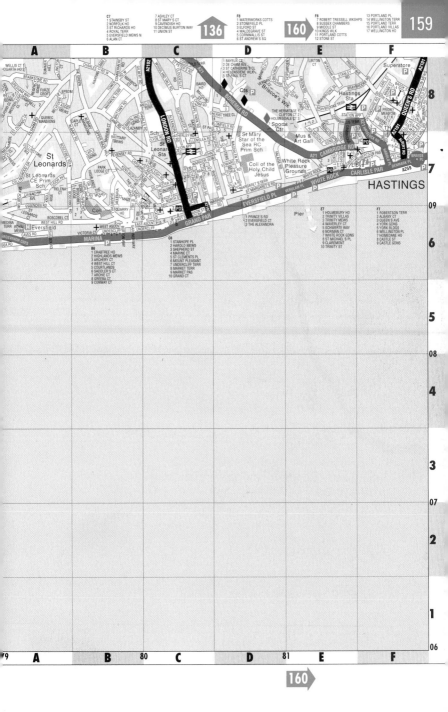

| | | | | | 159 |

C7
1 STAINSBY ST
2 NORFOLK HO
3 ST RICHARDS HO
4 ROYAL TERR
5 EVERSFIELD MEWS N
6 ALAN CT

7 ASHLEY CT
8 ST MARY'S CT
9 CAVENDISH HO
10 DECIMUS BURTON WAY
11 UNION ST

136

F8
1 WATERWORKS COTTS
2 STONEFIELD PL
3 ELFORD ST
4 WALDEGRAVE ST
5 CORNWALLIS ST
6 ST ANDREW'S SQ

160

F8
7 ROBERT TRESSELL WKSHPS
8 SUSSEX CHAMBERS
9 MIDDLE ST
10 KINGS WLK
11 PORTLAND COTTS
12 STONE ST

13 PORTLAND PL
14 WELLINGTON TERR
15 PORTLAND TERR
16 PORTLAND VILLAS
17 WELLINGTON HO

HASTINGS

8

7

11

6

5

10

4

3

09

2

1

08

B2093
Helenswood Sch (Upper)
IVYHOUSE EMPLOYMENT AREA
Spindlewood Country Holiday Park
RED LAKE TERR
ELEANOR TERR
MANHATTAN GDNS
Sandown Cty Prim Sch
North Seat
THE RIDGE
B2093
Picnic Area
Mast
Ore
Mount Pleasant
137
Bourne Stream
Fairlight Place
Broomgrove
Elphinstone Cty Prim Sch
1066 Country Wlk
Long Shaw
Ore Sta
Halton
Clive Vale
All Saints Jun Sch
Wet Wood
Mount Pleasant RD
Shearbarn Holiday Park
Ecclesbourne Resr
Belmont
Sacred Heart RC Prim Sch
Dudley Inf Sch
Hastings Country Park
Covehurst Wood
Castledown Cty Prim Sch
Torfield Sch
High Wickham
Ecclesbourne Glen
Saxon Shore Way
West Hill
Torfield Rd
East Hill
Caves
Mus & Lby
Old Town
Cliff Rly
Hastings Castle
Mus
PELHAM CRES
MARINE PAR
Mus
Sea Life Ctr
A259
LB Sta
Harbour

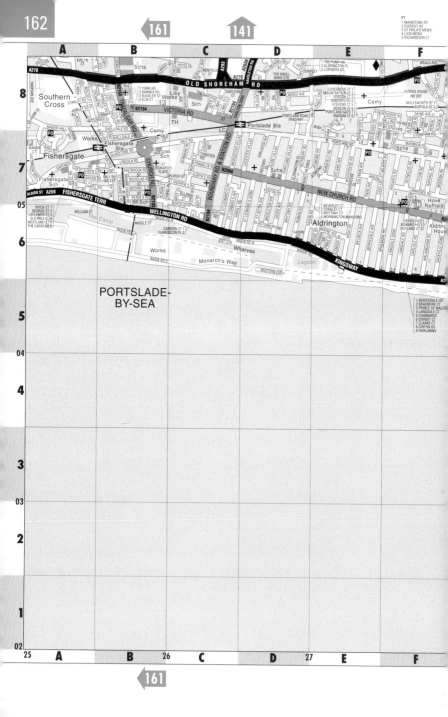

161
141

F7
1 MAINSTONE RD
2 EVEREST HO
3 ST PHILIPS MEWS
4 LION MEWS
5 RICHARDSON CT

A B C D E F

A270

OLD SHOREHAM RD
A270

Southern
Cross

B2194 VICTORIA RD

Portslade Sta

Fishersgate
Sta

Fishersgate

NEW CHURCH RD

ALBION ST A259 FISHERSGATE TERR

WELLINGTON RD

Aldrington

Hove
Nuffield

The Canal

MIDDLE ST

Works

Monarch's Way

Wharves

Lagoon

Kingsway

WESTERN ESP

PORTSLADE-
BY-SEA

1 BERRIEDALE CT
2 BRAEMORE CT
3 PRINCE OF WALES
4 LANGDALE CT
5 CHANNINGS
6 DORSET CT
7 CLARKE CT
8 GIRTON HO
9 FAIRLAWNS

25 A B 26 C D 27 E F

1 KINGS MEWS
2 WINDSOR LODGE
3 DURHAM CT
4 WARNHAM CT
5 ASHLEY CT
6 OLIVER HO
7 HAMILTON MANSIONS
8 THE PRIORY

HOVE

KINGSWAY

Monarch's Way

1 LANSDOWNE SQ
2 BRUNSWICK MEWS
3 DONKEY MEWS
4 UPPER MARKET ST
5 LOWER MARKET ST
6 KERRISON MEWS
7 CHAPEL MEWS
8 EMBASSY CT

BRIGHTON

West Pier (dis)

King Alfred (Swimming Pool & Sports Ctr)

OLD SHOREHAM RD

CROMWELL RD

CHURCH RD

GRAND AVE

WESTERN RD

KING'S RD

For full street detail of the highlighted area see page 189.

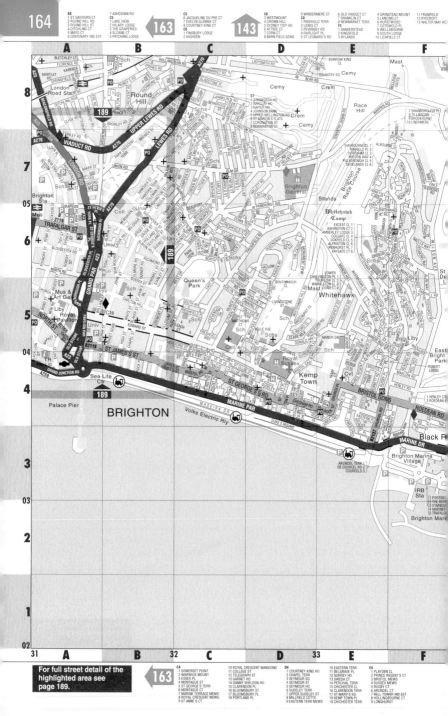

163

143

163

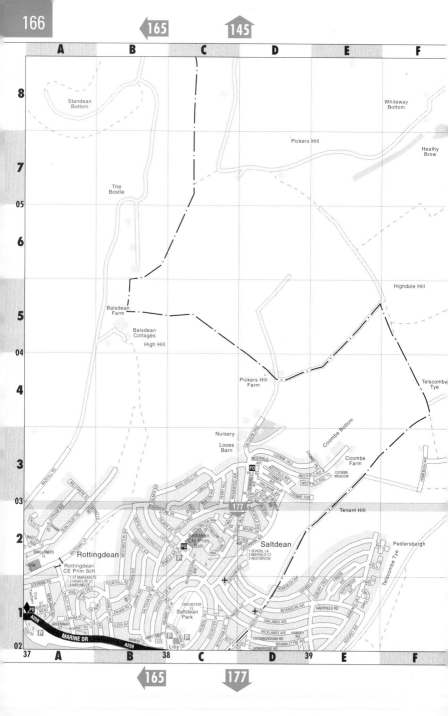

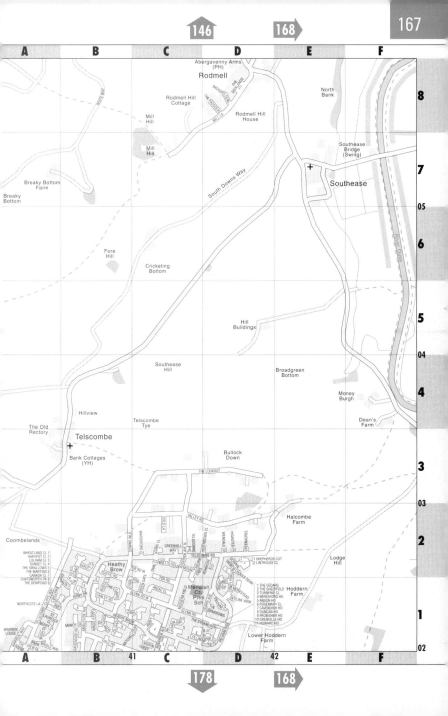

167
147

A **B** **C** **D** **E** **F**

White Lion
Pond

Mast
Radio
Sta

8

Red Lion
Pond

Itford
Farm

Itford
Hill

America
Farm

LC

Southease
Sta

South Downs Way

05

Baydean

Baydean Bottom

Cow Wish Bottom

Well Bottom

6

Itford Bottom

Muggery
Pope

Stock
Cottages

5

Durham
Farm

04

Manor
Farm

Court
Farm

Tarring
Neville

Page's
New Barn

4

LC

Caravan
Park

New
Barn

3

Works

ROCMELL
HO

DOWNS
VILLAS

South
Heighton
Farm

River Ouse

E2
1 SOUTH VIEW
2 ORCHARD MEWS

Royal Oak
(PH)

03

COURT FARM
CL

Piddinghoe

South
Heighton

Der

The
Wish

1 CEDARWELL CL
2 SHEPHERDS CL

PORTLAND TERR 1
FIRLE TERR 2
WEST VIEW TERR 3

2

Nore
Down

Mou
Pleas

Denton
Cty Prim
Sch

Brookside
Farm

Mus

Paradise
Family
L Pk

AVIS RD

1

Cemy

PIDDINGHOE
MEAD

1 MARTELLO
2 COTTAGE CL

Ind
Est

02

43 **A** **B** **44** **C** **D** **45** **E** **F**

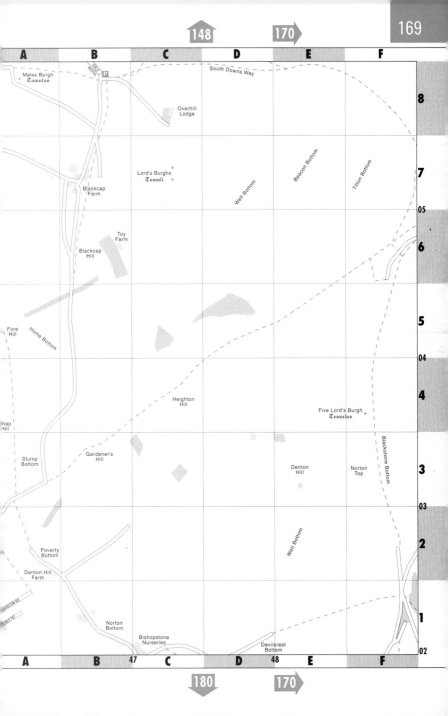

A B C D E F

8

Males Burgh
Tumulus

South Downs Way

Overhill
Lodge

7

Blackcap
Farm

Lord's Burghs
Tumuli

Well Bottom

Beacon Bottom

Tilton Bottom

05

Toy
Farm

6

Blackcap
Hill

Fore
Hill

Home Bottom

5

04

Heighton
Hill

4

Five Lord's Burgh
Tumulus

nap
Hill

Stump
Bottom

Gardener's
Hill

Denton
Hill

Norton
Top

Blackstone Bottom

3

03

Poverty
Bottom

Well Bottom

2

Denton Hill
Farm

LKESTON RD

ORE RD

Norton
Bottom

1

Bishopstone
Nurseries

Devilsrest
Bottom

02

A B 47 C D 48 E F

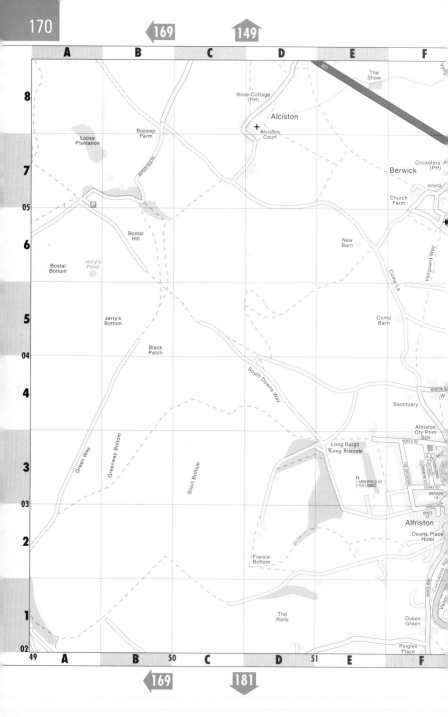

A B C D E F

8

Rose Cottage
(PH)

The
Shaw

A27

Alciston

Alciston
Court

Cricketers'
(PH)

Berwick

BERWICK

Bopeep
Farm

Loose
Plantation

7

Church
Farm

05

P

Bostal
Hill

New
Barn

Vanguard Way

Comp La

6

Bostal
Bottom

Jerry's
Pond

Jerry's
Bottom

Comp
Barn

5

04

Black
Patch

South Downs Way

4

Sanctuary

WINTON S

W

Alfriston
Cty Prim
Sch

NORTH RD

Long Burgh
Long Barrow

WEST

THE BROADWAY

DEANS RD

WEAVERS
LA

KINGS ROAD

WHITE
CT

Alfriston

Deans Place
Hotel

Green Way

Greenway Bottom

3

Short Bottom

F3
1 ABBEYFIELD HO
2 THE LAINES

03

2

France
Bottom

1

The
Rails

Dukes
Green

Cuckmere River

02

49 A B 50 C D 51 E F

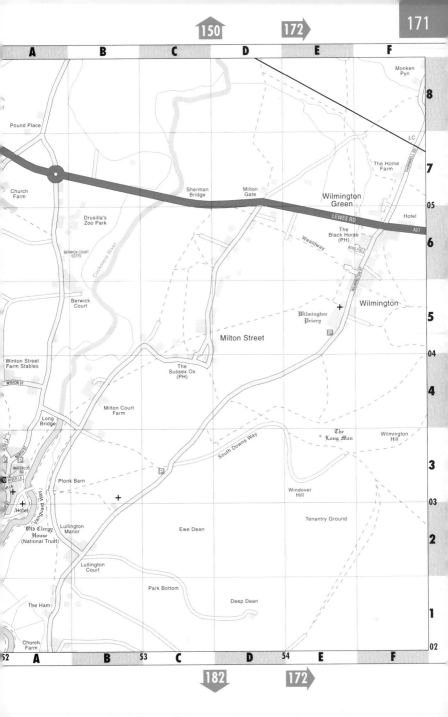

Monken
Pyn

8

Pound Place

LC

The Home
Farm

7

Church
Farm

Sherman
Bridge

Milton
Gate

Wilmington
Green

05

Drusilla's
Zoo Park

LEWES RD

Hotel

A27

The
Black Horse
(PH)

6

Wealdway

ADEE FIELD

BERWICK COURT
COTTS

Berwick
Court

Wilmington

5

Wilmington
Priory

P

Milton Street

Winton Street
Farm Stables

04

The
Sussex Ox
(PH)

WINTON ST

4

Milton Court
Farm

Long
Bridge

The
Long Man

Wilmington
Hill

SOUTH ST

WATERLOO
SQ

RIVER LA

South Downs Way

3

Plonk Barn

P

Windover
Hill

03

Hotel

Old Clergy
House
(National Trust)

Lullington
Manor

Tenantry Ground

Ewe Dean

2

Lullington
Court

Park Bottom

Deep Dean

1

The Ham

02

Church
Farm

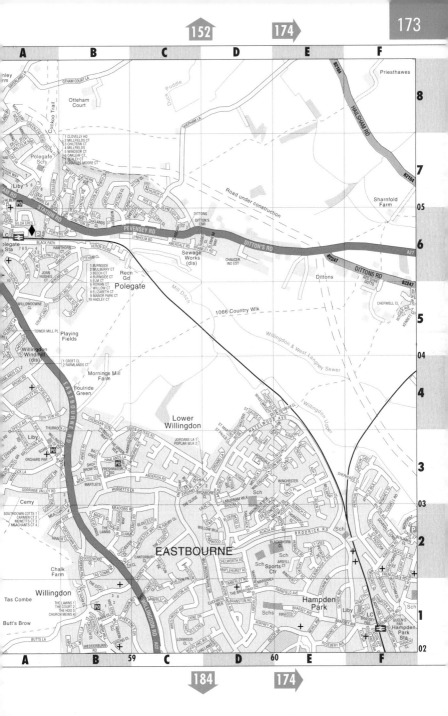

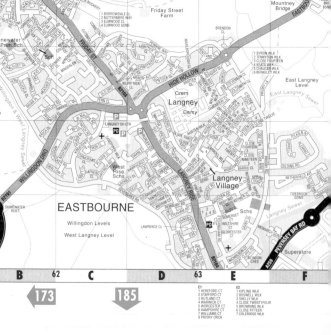

Montague
Wood

Hankham
Nurseries

Montague

Pevensey Haven

1066 Country Wlk

Hankham

Hankham Level

Hankham

1066 Country Wlk

Hankham
Cty Prim Sch

Jenkins' Green

Hankham
Hall

Hankham
Cross

Sharnfold
Cottages

Nurseries

Mill Farm

GALLOWS CL

Milton
Nurseries

Peelings

Mill Hill

KETCHAM
CNR

Castle
Farm

1066 Country Wlk

PEELINGS LA

ROMANS WAY

CASTLE VIEW

PEVENSEY PARK RD

Blackness

Mount Pleasant

LINKWAY

SPRINGFIELD

Stone Cross

Westham

THE CROSSWAYS

DITTONS RD

STONE
CROSS

PH

Windmill
(dis)

Uplands
Farm

Pevens
West
Sta

Stone Cross
Cty Prim Sch

Stone Cross
Junction

Caravan
Park

Mountney Level

LC

Broad Oak Cl

Friday Street
Farm

Mountney
Bridge

Care
Pa

Shinewater
Cty Prim Sch

Friday
Street

1 BORROWDALE CL
2 BUTTERMERE WAY
3 ELMWOOD CL
4 ELMWOOD GDNS

BRENDON
CL

1 BYRON WLK
2 TENNYSON WLK
3 CLOSE FOURTEEN
4 KEATS WLK
5 CHAUCER WLK
6 BERKELEY WLK

East Langney
Level

Shinewater Marsh

Langney

Cemy

East Langney Sewer

LAUGHTON CL 1
FLIMWELL CL 2

EASTBOURNE

West
Rise
Sch

Langney
Village

Willingdon Levels

West Langney Level

1 THE HYDNEYE
2 BARNHAM CL

Highfield
Cty Jun
Sch

LAWRENCE CL

Schs

Superstore

PEVENSEY BAY RD

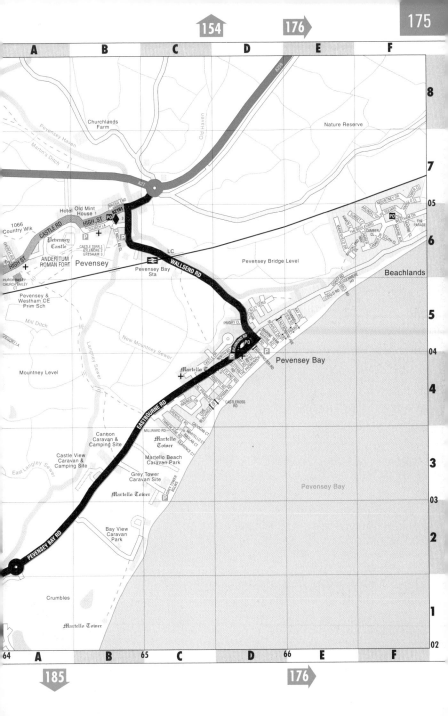

Reman Stream

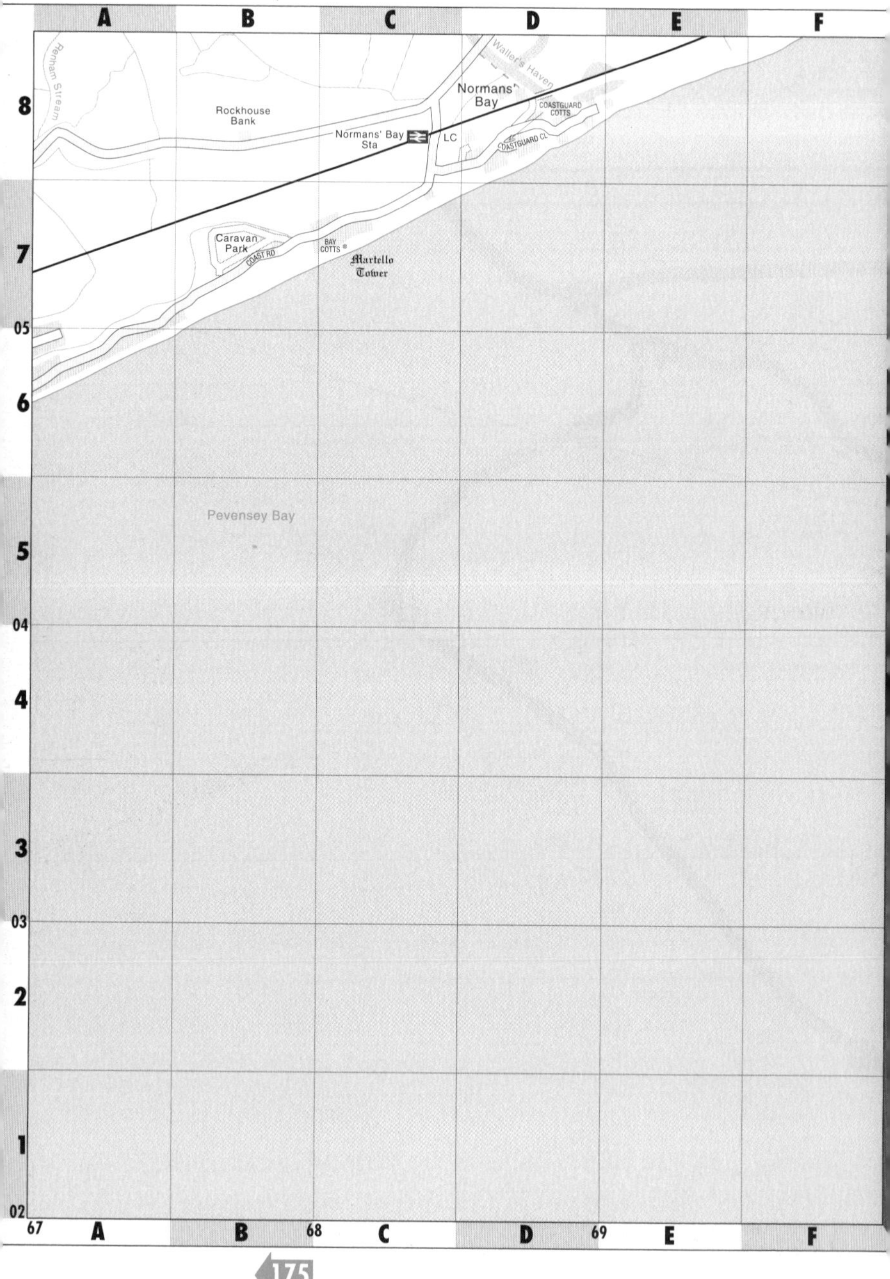

8

Rockhouse
Bank

Normans'
Bay

Normans' Bay
Sta

LC

COASTGUARD
COTTS

COASTGUARD CL

Waller's Haven

05

7

Caravan
Park

COAST RD

BAY
COTTS

Martello
Tower

6

Pevensey Bay

5

04

4

3

03

2

1

02

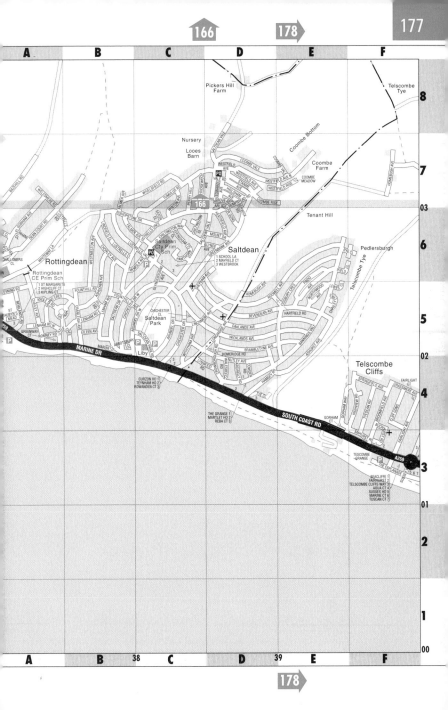

A B C D E F

Pickers Hill
Farm

Telscombe
Tye

Nursery
Looes
Barn

Coombe Bottom

Coombe
Farm

WESTFIELD
AVE
WESTFIELD AVE
WESTFIELD AVE N
WESTFIELD RISE
COOMBE
MEADOW
WESTFIELD RISE
COOMBE RISE

166

Tenant Hill

Saltdean
Cty Prim
Sch

Saltdean

Pedlersburgh

Rottingdean

Rottingdean
CE Prim Sch

1 ST MARGARETS
2 HIGHCLIFF CT
3 KIPLING CT

1 SCHOOL LA
2 MAYFIELD CT
3 WESTBROOK

Telscombe Tye

CHALLONERS
CL

ST
MAURYN'S
MEAD

KNOLL AND CRES

Saltdean
Park

CHICHESTER
OAKLANDS AVE
WICKLANDS AVE
BRAMBLETYNE AVE
HOMERIDGE RD

Telscombe
Cliffs

FAIRLIGHT
CT

GREENWAY
CT
ROMNEY RD

P
Libry

P P

MARINE DR

NUTLEY AVE

SPRINGFIELD AVE
GRASSMERE AVE

GORHAM
CT

CURZON HO 1
TEYNHAM HO 2
ROWANDEN CT 3

THE GRANGE 1
MARTLET HO 2
REBA CT 3

SOUTH COAST RD

TESCOMBE
GRANGE

P A259

THE ESPLANADE

SEACLIFFE 1
FAIRHURST 2
TELSCOMBE CLIFFS WAY 3
AQUA CT 4
SUSSEX HO 5
MARINE CT 6
TUSCAN CT 7

8

Telscombe
Cliffs

Sch
GRASSMERE

St David's CT
Hodden
Sch

Meridian
L Ctr
Liby

1 BALCOMBE CT
2 MERIDIAN CTR
THE MERIDIAN
IND EST

Peacehaven

7

A259
GOLF
THE ESPLANADE
PROMENADE

PO

THIRD RD
SECOND RD

01

1 GREENACRES
2 DANA LODGE
3 AMBLESIDE CT

LURELAND

SOUTH COAST RD

PO

MARGARET CT 1
FAIRFIELD 2
HOMECOAST HO 3

6

PROMENADE

PROMENADE

NEVILLE RD

Friars
Bay

ROUNDHAY AVE

JAY RD

Motel
THE TYES
THE HIGHWAY

Peacehaven
Heights

Chene
Gap

5

Friars' Bay

00

4

3

99

2

1

98

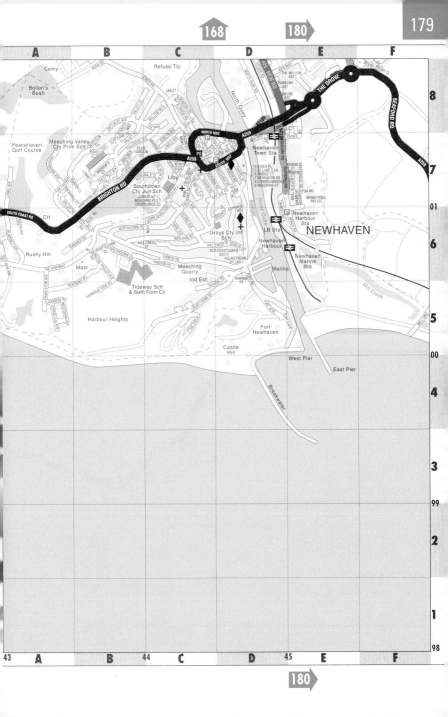

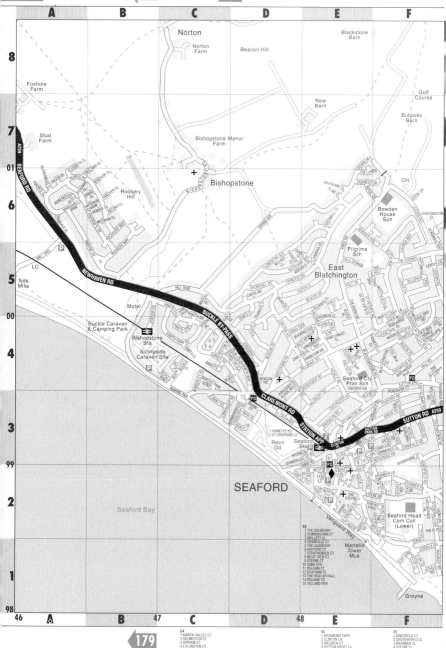

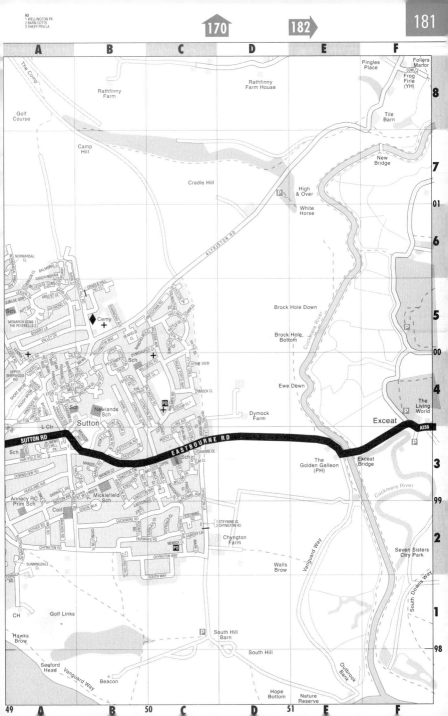

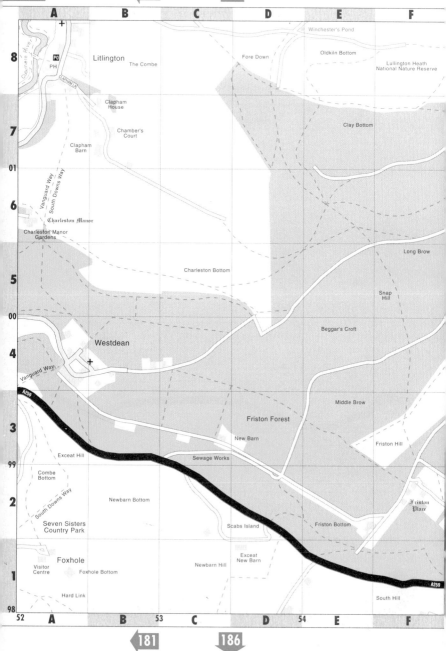

A B C D E F

8

Litlington

Fore Down

Winchester's Pond

Oldkiln Bottom

Lullington Heath
National Nature Reserve

The Combe

Clapham
House

7

Clay Bottom

Chamber's
Court

Clapham
Barn

01

Vanguard Way

South Downs Way

6

Charleston Manor

Charleston Manor
Gardens

Long Brow

5

Charleston Bottom

Snap
Hill

00

Beggar's Croft

4

Westdean

Vanguard Way

A259

Middle Brow

3

Friston Forest

Friston Hill

New Barn

Exceat Hill

Sewage Works

99

Combe
Bottom

2

Newbarn Bottom

Friston
Place

South Downs Way

Scabs Island

Friston Bottom

Seven Sisters
Country Park

Exceat
New Barn

1

Foxhole

Visitor
Centre

Foxhole Bottom

Newbarn Hill

South Hill

A259

Hard Link

98

52 A B 53 C D 54 E F

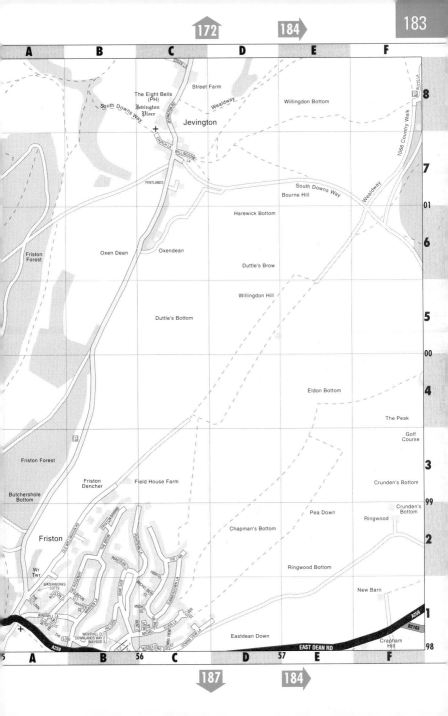

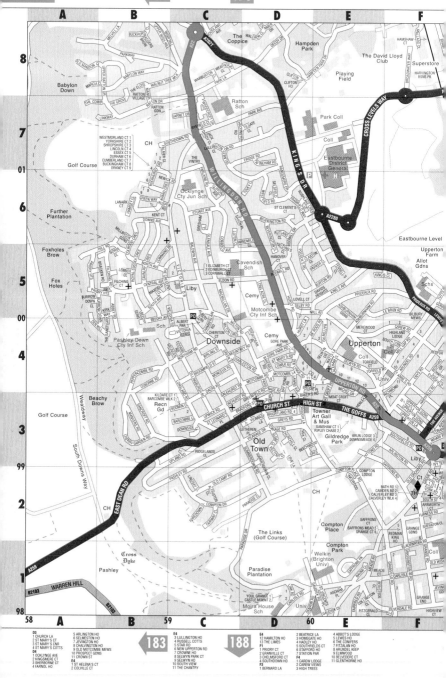

EASTBOURNE

LANGNEY VILLAGE

174

175

181
182

P

8

Gayles

Haven Brow

Crowlink

Cliff
End

Crowlink

Short Bottom

Short Brow

Limekiln Bottom

7

Rough Brow

Rough Bottom

Gap Bottom

Flagstaff Brow

Flagstaff Bottom

97

Brass
Point

South Downs Way

Flat
Hill

Flathill Bottom

Baily's
Hill

Seven Sisters

6

Mon

Flagstaff
Point

Mon Michel Dean

5

96

4

3

95

2

1

94

181

A | **B** | **C** | **D** | **E** | **F**

Crapham Bottom

Warren Hill

B2103 WARREN HILL

Moira House Sch

Warren

Meads

ST GREGORY CT

FAIRFIELD LODGE

ROCHESTER CL

WELLS CL

UPPER CARLISLE RD

CARLISLE RD

THE MOORINGS

WARRIOR SQ

MEADS HO

HOMELANDS HO

MILNTHORPE GDNS

GRANVILLE RD

ST JOHN'S RD

ASCOT CL

SOUTH CLIFFE CRES

LINCOLN CL

DUKENSBROOK AVE

WARREN LA

HYDE TYNINGS CL

BEACHY HEAD RD

SUN LA

DENTON RD

MEADS ST

MATLOCK RD

CHESTERFIELD RD

SOUTH CLIFFE TOWER

JEPHSON CL

ASCOT CL

8

Middle Brow

Black Robin Farm

BEACHY HEAD RD

UPPER DUKE'S DR

Univ

BASLOW RD

HIGHCOMBE

DARLEY RD

MEADS GATE

Aii

Saints

H

KING EDWARD'S PAR

WESTERN CL

B2103

4 ST JOHN'S HO
5 RAVENS CT
6 RUSTINGTON CT
7 WESTCLIFF MANSI
8 REGENCY MEWS

1 MILCHESTER HO
2 ENDCLIFFE CT
3 KEPPLESTONE

EASTBOURNE

7

Black Robin Bottom

Well Combe

Meads CE Prim Sch

St Andrew's Prep Sch

BAGLOW

ROWSLEY RD

EDENSOR RD

SUMMER RD

DUKE'S DR

DOLPHIN CT

Holywell Retreat

St Bede's Prep Sch

97

Holywell

6

South Downs Way

Whitebread Hole

Bullock Down Farm

5

Bullock Down

Sweet Brow

Bulling Dean

Heathy Brow

BEACHY HEAD RD

96

Beachy Head Countryside Ctr

Beachy Head (PH)

Cow Gap

4

West Brow

P

P

Beachy Head

3

95

2

1

94

58 **A** | **B** 59 **C** | **D** 60 **E** | **F**

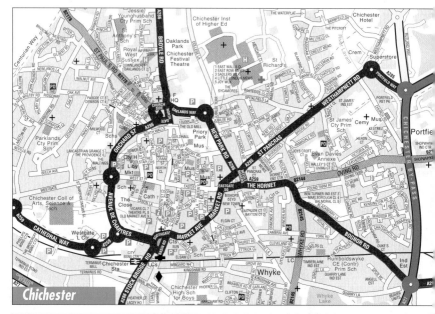

Chichester

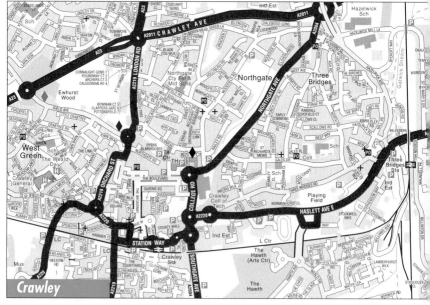

Crawley

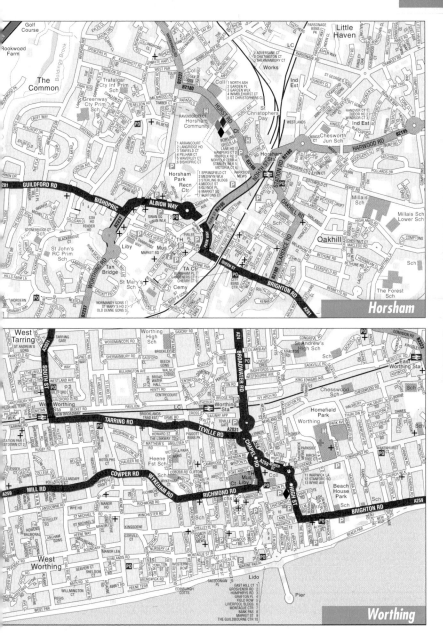

Horsham

Worthing

Index

Street names are listed alphabetically and show the locality, the Postcode District, the page number and a reference to the square in which the name falls on the map page

Neville Rd  **3** Eastbourne BN22 . 185 B4

Full street name
This may have been abbreviated on the map

Location Number
If present, this indicates the street's position on a congested area of the map instead of the name

Town, village or locality in which the street falls.

Postcode District for the street name

Page number of the map on which the street name appears

Grid square in which the centre of the street falls

Schools, hospitals, sports centres, railway stations, shopping centres, industrial estates, public amenities and other places of interest are also listed.

Abbreviations used in the index

App **Approach**	Cl **Close**	Ent **Enterprise**	La **Lane**	Rdbt **Roundabout**
Arc **Arcade**	Comm **Common**	Espl **Esplanade**	N **North**	S **South**
Ave **Avenue**	Cnr **Corner**	Est **Estate**	Orch **Orchard**	Sq **Square**
Bvd **Boulevard**	Cotts **Cottages**	Gdns **Gardens**	Par **Parade**	Strs **Stairs**
Bldgs **Buildings**	Ct **Court**	Gn **Green**	Pk **Park**	Stps **Steps**
Bsns Pk **Business Park**	Ctyd **Courtyard**	Gr **Grove**	Pas **Passage**	St **Street, Saint**
Bsns Ctr **Business Centre**	Cres **Crescent**	Hts **Heights**	Pl **Place**	Terr **Terrace**
Bglws **Bungalows**	Dr **Drive**	Ho **House**	Prec **Precinct**	Trad Est **Trading Estate**
Cswy **Causeway**	Dro **Drove**	Ind Est **Industrial Estate**	Prom **Promenade**	Wlk **Walk**
Ctr **Centre**	E **East**	Intc **Interchange**	Ret Pk **Retail Park**	W **West**
Cir **Circus**	Emb **Embankment**	Junc **Junction**	Rd **Road**	Yd **Yard**

Abberton Field BN6 .... 97 B5
Abbey Cl BN10 .... 167 C1
Abbey Ct TN33 .... 112 C4
Abbey Dr TN38 .... 158 B5
Abbey Path BN27 .... 129 C2
Abbey Rd Brighton BN2 .. 164 C4
 Eastbourne BN20 .... 184 B5
Abbey Way TN33 .... 112 C5
Abbeyfield Ho **1** BN26 .. 170 F3
Abbot's Lodge **4** BN21 ... 184 F4
Abbots Cl Battle TN33 .... 112 F3
 Hassocks BN6 .... 97 E4
Abbotsbury Cl BN2 .... 177 B5
Abbotsfield Cl TN34 .... 136 F3
Abbotsford Sch RH15 .... 72 E6
Abbotts **20** BN21 .... 163 E5
Aberdale Rd BN26 .... 173 C6
Aberdeen Rd BN2 .... 164 C8
Abergavenny Ho **1** BN3 .. 163 D6
Abergavenny Rd BN7 .... 123 B1
Abigail Ho **10** RH16 .... 50 E4
Abinger Pl BN7 .... 123 C1
Abinger Rd
 Portslade-by-Sea BN41 .. 162 B8
 Woodingdean BN2 .... 165 E6
Acacia Ave BN3 .... 141 F1
Acacia Ct BN1 .... 142 F2
Acacia Rd
 Eastbourne BN22 .... 173 D2
 Newhaven BN9 .... 168 E2
Acer Ave TN2 .... 17 C8
Acorn Cl
 East Grinstead RH19 .... 10 E8
 Hastings TN37 .... 136 C4
Acorn Gn **3** BN27 .... 129 B1
Acorn Way TN19 .... 45 A3
Acorns The TN5 .... 42 F6
Acre Cl RH16 .... 50 D2
Acres Rise TN5 .... 31 E1
Adam Cl TN38 .... 135 F4
Adams Cl BN1 .... 143 B2
Adams La TN31 .... 66 C2
Adastra Ave BN6 .... 98 A4
Addingham Rd BN22 .... 185 D4
Addington Cl TN38 .... 158 F7
Addison Rd BN1, BN3 ...... 163 E7
Adelaide Cl BN25 .... 180 E5
Adelaide Cres BN3 .... 163 C5
Adelaide Rd TN37, TN38 .. 136 B3
Adelaide Sq BN43 .... 161 B7
Ades Field BN26 .... 171 F6
Admiral's Bridge La RH19 .. 10 C2

Adur Ct **10** BN43 .... 161 C8
Adur Dr
 Shoreham-by-Sea BN43 .. 161 A7
 Stone Cross BN24 .... 174 A5
Adur Rd RH15 .... 73 C4
Agincourt Cl TN37, TN38 .. 135 F7
Agnes St BN2 .... 164 C7
Ainsworth Ave BN2 .... 165 D3
Ainsworth Cl BN2 .... 165 D3
Ainsworth Ho **1** BN2 .... 164 C7
Air St BN1 .... 189 F5
Airy Rd BN27 .... 131 B2
Alan Cl **6** TN37 .... 159 C7
Alan Way BN2 .... 164 F5
Albany Ct **2** TN34 .... 159 F7
Albany Hill TN2 .... 8 C5
Albany Mansions TN38 ... 159 B8
Albany Mews BN3 .... 163 B6
Albany Rd Bexhill TN40 .. 157 C3
 Hastings TN38 .... 159 B7
 Seaford BN25 .... 180 C3
Albany Villas
 Cuckfield RH17 .... 50 A6
 Hove BN3 .... 163 B6
Albert Cl RH16 .... 51 A4
Albert Cotts TN1 .... 8 B4
Albert Dr RH15 .... 72 E2
Albert Mews **24** BN3 .... 163 C6
Albert Par BN21 .... 184 C4
Albert Pl BN26 .... 173 D7
Albert Rd Bexhill TN40 .. 157 C3
 Brighton BN1 .... 189 F6
 Hastings TN34 .... 159 F7
 Polegate BN26 .... 173 A7
 Southwick BN42 .... 161 D7
 Uckfield TN22 .... 78 D6
Albert St TN1 .... 8 B4
Albert Terr BN21 .... 184 C5
Albion Cl RH15 .... 72 F2
Albion Hill BN2 .... 189 B6
Albion Ho **3** Brighton BN2 189 B6
 Southwick BN42 .... 161 F7
Albion La **4** TN34 .... 160 A3
Albion Rd
 Eastbourne BN22 .... 185 B4
 Royal Tunbridge Wells TN1 . 8 C5
Albion St
 Brighton BN2 .... 189 B6
 Eastbourne BN20 .... 184 C2
Albourne Cl Brighton BN2 . 164 F7
 Hastings TN38 .... 158 F8

Alces Pl BN25 .... 180 E5
Aldborough Rd TN37 .... 136 C1
Alder Cl
 Eastbourne BN23 .... 185 C8
 Hastings TN37 .... 136 C5
 Heathfield TN21 .... 82 A5
Alderbrook Cl TN6 .... 38 A6
Alderbrook Cotts TN6 ...... 38 A7
Alderbrook Path TN6 .... 38 A6
Alderbrook Way TN6 .... 38 A6
Alders Ave RH19 .... 1 E3
Alders View Dr RH19 .... 1 E3
Alderton Cl TN39 .... 157 B3
Aldervale Cotts TN6 .... 38 A7
Aldrich Cl BN2 .... 164 F6
Aldrington Ave BN3 .... 163 A8
Aldrington CE Fst Sch
 BN3 .... 162 F7
Aldrington CE Prim Sch
 BN3 .... 142 A2
Aldrington Cl BN2 .... 162 D7
Aldrington House (Hospl)
 BN3 .... 162 F6
Aldrington Pl BN3 .... 162 D8
Aldrington Sta BN3 .... 163 A8
Alexander Dr TN39 .... 156 E4
Alexandra Cl BN25 .... 180 E5
Alexandra Ct TN37 .... 136 C2
Alexandra Rd
 Burgess Hill RH15 .... 73 C2
 Eastbourne BN22 .... 185 D6
 Hastings TN37 .... 159 C8
 Heathfield TN21 .... 82 B6
 Uckfield TN22 .... 78 B6
Alexandra Terr TN20 .... 40 C3
Alexandra The TN37 .... 159 D7
Alexandra Villas BN1 ...... 189 F6
Alford Way TN40 .... 157 E6
Alfray Rd TN40 .... 158 A5
Alfred Rd Brighton BN1 .. 189 F6
 Eastbourne BN23 .... 185 F8
 Hastings TN35 .... 137 D3
Alfred St TN2 .... 8 C5
Alfriston Cl Bexhill TN39 .. 156 C6
 Brighton BN2 .... 164 F6
 Eastbourne BN20 .... 184 C2
Alfriston Cty Prim Sch
 BN26 .... 170 F4
Alfriston Pk BN25 .... 181 C5
Alfriston Rd BN25, BN26 .. 181 B6
Alice Bright La TN6 .... 37 F7
Alice St BN3 .... 163 D5

All Saint's Cres TN34 ...... 160 B4
All Saints CE Prim Sch
 TN39 .... 157 B7
All Saints Gdns TN21 .... 81 F7
All Saints' Hospl BN20 .... 188 E7
All Saints Jun Sch TN35 .. 160 C6
All Saints La TN39 .... 157 B7
All Saints Rd TN4 .... 8 B6
All Saints Rise TN4 .... 8 A6
All Saints' St TN34 .... 160 B4
Allan Cl TN4 .... 7 C4
Allandale Rd TN2 .... 8 D7
Allards TN35 .... 138 C8
Allegria Ct TN38 .... 159 B7
Allen Rd RH16 .... 51 A4
Allen Way TN40 .... 157 F7
Allen's Cl RH19 .... 11 D6
Allfrey Rd BN22 .... 185 D6
Allfreys La TN6 .... 37 D6
Allington Cres BN8 .... 76 C7
Allington La BN7 .... 122 D7
Allington Rd BN8 .... 76 C6
Allwood Cres RH17 .... 74 C4
Alma Rd RH16 .... 51 B8
Alma Terr TN37 .... 136 C2
Alma Villas TN37 .... 136 C2
Almonry Fields TN33 ...... 112 B4
Alpine Rd Hastings TN34 .. 160 A4
 Hove BN3 .... 162 F8
Alverstone Cl BN23 .... 174 B4
Amanda Cl TN40 .... 157 F7
Ambassadors The **6** BN3 163 C6
Amber Ct **17** Hove BN3 .. 163 C6
 8 Hove BN3 .... 163 D7
Amberleaze Dr TN2 .... 9 D6
Amberley Cl
 Burgess Hill RH15 .... 73 A5
 Haywards Heath RH16 .... 50 D7
 Hove BN3 .... 141 E3
Amberley Ct TN4 .... 8 C8
Amberley Dr BN3 .... 141 E3
Amberley Lodge BN2 ...... 189 A7
Amberley Rd BN22 .... 173 C1
Ambermarle The BN2 ...... 189 A4
Amberstone BN27 .... 129 E3
Amberstone Cl TN34 .... 137 A4
Amberstone Hospl BN27 .. 129 F4
Amberstone View BN27 .. 129 C2
Ambleside Ave BN10 .... 178 A8
Ambleside Cl BN10 .... 178 A7
America La RH16 .... 51 A5
Amesbury Cres BN3 .... 162 E7
Amherst Cl TN37 .... 136 D1

Amherst Cres BN3 .... 162 F8
Amherst Gdns TN34 .... 136 D1
Amherst Rd Bexhill TN40 .. 157 C4
 Hastings TN34, TN37 ..... 136 D1
 Royal Tunbridge Wells TN4 . 8 A5
Amhurst Rd BN10 .... 177 F3
Anchor Field BN8 .... 124 D5
Anchor Hill RH17 .... 52 A2
Anchor La BN8 .... 102 B5
Anderida Ct TN39 .... 156 C4
Anderida Rd BN22 .... 173 C3
Anderson Cl BN9 .... 179 B7
Andrew Rd TN4 .... 8 C8
Andrews Cl
 Northbridge Street TN32 .. 64 C5
 Royal Tunbridge Wells TN2 . 8 D5
Andros Cl BN8 .... 100 E6
Andwell St BN21 .... 185 B2
Angel Row TN18 .... 47 B5
Angel Terr TN18 .... 47 B6
Angela Cl TN40 .... 157 F7
Anglesea Terr TN37, TN38 159 C8
Anglesey Ave BN27 .... 129 A2
Angmering Ct BN1 .... 143 F5
Angus Cl BN20 .... 173 B1
Ann Cl BN6 .... 98 A5
Ann St Brighton BN1 .... 189 A7
 Hastings TN34 .... 160 C6
Anne's Path **10** BN21 ... 146 C8
Annecy RC Prim Sch
 BN25 .... 181 A2
Annington Rd BN2 .... 185 B5
Anscombe **5** RH16 .... 50 D6
Anson Cl BN23 .... 185 E7
Anson Ho BN10 .... 167 C1
Ansty Cl BN2 .... 164 E5
Antares Path BN27 .... 152 E7
Antioch St BN7 .... 146 C8
Antony Cl BN25 .... 180 B6
Antrim Ct BN23 .... 174 D1
Antrona Ct TN39 .... 156 C3
Anvil Cl BN41 .... 141 B2
Anvil Ct TN37 .... 136 C5
Anzac Cl BN10 .... 167 C1
Apex Pk BN27 .... 152 A7
Apple Tree La TN1, TN2 ... 8 D8
Appledene Cnr BN8 .... 100 E7
Appledore Cl BN23 .... 174 D2
Appledore Ct RH16 .... 51 A7
Appledore Gdns RH16 .... 51 A6
Appledore Rd BN2 .... 143 F4
Applesham Ave BN3 .... 141 E2
Applesham Way BN41 .... 141 A1

Applewood Cl TN37 ... 136 B5
Approach The
2 Brighton BN1 ... 142 E3
Dormans Park RH19 ... 1 F6
April Pl 2 TN40 ... 157 C4
Apsley St TN4 ... 7 D4
Aqua Ct BN10 ... 177 F3
Aquarius Cl BN10 ... 178 C6
Aquila Pk BN25 ... 181 A3
Arbor Ct 8 RH16 ... 50 E5
Arbourvale TN38 ... 136 A1
Archers Ct TN34 ... 136 F6
Archery Ct
Eastbourne BN22 ... 185 C6
3 Hastings TN38 ... 159 B6
Archery Rd TN38 ... 159 B7
Archery Wlk BN27 ... 152 C6
Archie Ct 7 TN38 ... 159 B6
Ardingly Ct 10 BN2 ... 189 B5
Ardingly Rd BN2 ... 177 D4
Ardingly St BN2 ... 189 B5
Argent Cl BN25 ... 181 A5
Argos Hill Rd TN20, TN6 ... 39 D4
Argyle Rd BN1 ... 189 F8
Argyll Ct BN22 ... 173 E2
Arkendale RH19 ... 1 A4
Arkwright Rd BN22 ... 174 A1
Arlington Cres BN1 ... 143 E5
Arlington Gdns BN2 ... 177 D6
Arlington Ho 5 BN21 ... 184 D4
Arlington Rd BN21 ... 184 F3
Arlington Rd E BN27 ... 152 A6
Arlington Rd W BN27 ... 151 F6
Arlington Resr BN26 ... 150 C3
Armstrong Cl TN38 ... 135 E4
Arnbury Mews TN38 ... 158 E6
Arndale Ctr BN21 ... 185 A3
Arnold St BN2 ... 164 C7
Arnside Rd TN38 ... 158 E6
Arnworth Ct BN21 ... 184 F2
Arran Cl BN27 ... 129 A2
Arthur Bliss Ho RH16 ... 51 A8
Arthur Rd TN39 ... 157 B4
Arthur St BN3 ... 163 A8
Arts Rd BN1 ... 144 B7
Arun Ct 13 BN43 ... 161 C8
Arun Lodge BN21 ... 184 E3
Arun Path TN22 ... 55 E1
Arun Way BN24, BN26 ... 173 F5
Arundel Cl
Beachlands BN24 ... 175 F6
Hailsham BN27 ... 129 C2
Shoreham-by-Sea BN43 ... 161 C8
Arundel Ct
6 Brighton BN2 ... 164 E4
Burgess Hill RH15 ... 72 F4
14 Shoreham-by-Sea
BN43 ... 161 C8
Arundel Dr E BN2 ... 177 C5
Arundel Dr W BN2 ... 177 C5
Arundel Keep 8 BN21 ... 184 F4
Arundel Mews 10 BN2 ... 164 E4
Arundel Pl BN2 ... 164 E3
Arundel Rd Brighton BN2 ... 164 E4
Eastbourne BN21 ... 184 F4
Newhaven BN9 ... 168 F1
Peacehaven BN10 ... 178 D7
Royal Tunbridge Wells TN1 ... 8 B2
Seaford BN25 ... 181 A3
Arundel Rd W BN10 ... 178 B7
Arundel Road Central
BN10 ... 178 B7
Arundel St BN2 ... 164 E3
Arundel Terr BN2 ... 164 E3
Arundell Gn BN7 ... 123 B2
Ascham Pl BN20 ... 184 E1
Ascot Cl BN20 ... 188 F8
Ascot Mews TN38 ... 159 A8
Ash Cl Eastbourne BN22 ... 173 E3
Hove BN3 ... 142 C3
Royal Tunbridge Wells TN2 17 D7
Ash Ct Hailsham BN27 ... 152 A7
Southwick BN42 ... 140 F1
Ash Dr BN25 ... 181 C3
Ash Gr
Haywards Heath RH16 ... 50 D2
Westham BN24 ... 174 D6
Ash Wlk BN9 ... 179 D7
Ashbourne Ct 13 BN21 ... 185 A2
Ashbrook Rd TN37 ... 136 B4
Ashburnham Cl BN1 ... 143 E5
Ashburnham Dr BN1 ... 143 E5
Ashburnham Gdns BN21 ... 184 E5
Ashburnham Pl BN27 ... 129 A2
Ashburnham Rd
Eastbourne BN21 ... 184 E5
Hastings TN34, TN35 ... 160 C6
Ashby Cl TN39 ... 157 A8
Ashcombe Dr TN39 ... 156 D3
Ashcombe Hollow BN7 ... 145 D7
Ashcombe La BN7 ... 145 E5
Ashcroft 1 BN43 ... 161 D7
Ashcroft Cl Ringmer BN8 ... 124 D5
Shoreham-by-Sea BN43 ... 161 D8
Ashdown 12 BN3 ... 163 C6
Ashdown Ave BN2 ... 177 B5
Ashdown Chase TN22 ... 35 C5
Ashdown Cl
Forest Row RH18 ... 12 A2
Hastings TN38 ... 135 E2
Haywards Heath RH16 ... 51 B4
Royal Tunbridge Wells TN4 ... 7 F4
Ashdown Ct
Crowborough TN6 ... 25 E2
Uckfield TN22 ... 78 D6
Ashdown Forest Riding Ctr
TN22 ... 36 B6
Ashdown Forest Visitors Ctr
RH18 ... 23 A5
Ashdown Gate RH19 ... 1 D2
Ashdown Hospl The RH16 ... 50 D6
Ashdown Llama Farm
RH18 ... 22 E4
Ashdown Pl TN21 ... 82 B6
Ashdown Rd Bexhill TN40 ... 157 E4
7 Brighton BN2 ... 164 B8
Forest Row RH18 ... 11 F2
Ashdown View
East Grinstead RH19 ... 10 E7
Nutley TN22 ... 35 D6
Ashenden Ave TN31 ... 93 A5
Ashenden Wlk TN2 ... 8 E8
Ashenground Cl 5 RH16 ... 50 E3
Ashenground Rd RH16 ... 50 E3
Asher Reeds TN3 ... 7 A4
Ashford Cl 4 BN27 ... 152 C7
Ashford Rd Brighton BN1 ... 143 A2
Eastbourne BN21 ... 185 A3
Hastings TN34 ... 136 E2
Ashford Sq BN21 ... 185 A3
Ashford Way TN34 ... 136 E3
Ashgate Rd BN23 ... 174 E2
Ashington Ct BN2 ... 164 F6
Ashington Gdns BN10 ... 178 F6
Ashington Rd BN22 ... 174 A1
Ashlands TN6 ... 26 B1
Ashleigh Glegg Ho BN25 ... 180 D4
Ashleigh Gdns TN6 ... 25 E4
Ashley Cl BN1 ... 142 E7
Ashley Ct
7 Hastings TN37 ... 159 C7
Hove BN3 ... 163 C5
Ashley Gdns
Hailsham BN27 ... 129 C3
Mayfield TN20 ... 40 A2
Rusthall TN4 ... 7 C5
Ashley Park Cl TN4 ... 7 C5
Ashley Pk TN4 ... 7 C5
Ashley Rd TN6 ... 27 D1
Ashlings Way Hove BN3 ... 141 E2
Shoreham-by-Sea BN43 ... 140 B1
Ashmore Cl BN10 ... 167 D2
Ashtead Towers TN40 ... 157 E4
Ashton Lodge 14 BN2 ... 189 B6
Ashton Rise BN2 ... 189 B6
Ashtonville Cl BN8 ... 124 E5
Ashurst Ave BN2 ... 177 E5
Ashurst Hill TN3 ... 5 D2
Ashurst Rd
Brighton BN1, BN2 ... 143 F5
Seaford BN25 ... 180 F2
Stone Cross TN3 ... 6 B2
Ashurst Sta TN3 ... 5 D2
Ashurstwood Abbey RH19 ... 11 E6
Ashurstwood Cty Prim Sch
RH19 ... 11 E6
Ashway RH15 ... 73 A2
Ashwyn Bsns Ctr RH15 ... 72 F5
Aspen Cl RH16 ... 51 B4
Aspen Rd BN22 ... 173 E2
Aspen Way TN39 ... 156 C4
Aspen Wlk
Haywards Heath RH16 ... 51 B4
Heathfield TN21 ... 82 B5
Astaire Ave BN22 ... 185 B6
Asten Cl TN38 ... 158 E7
Asten Fields TN33 ... 112 C4
Astra Ho 21 BN1 ... 163 E5
Atfield Wlk BN22 ... 173 F3
Athelstan Cl BN23 ... 185 F8
Athelstan Rd TN35 ... 160 D6
Athenaeum The 14 BN3 ... 163 C6
Atlantic Dr BN23 ... 185 F7
Atlingworth St BN2 ... 189 B4
Attree Ct 6 BN2 ... 164 C6
Attree Dr BN2 ... 164 C6
Auckland Dr BN2 ... 143 F1
Auckland Ho TN40 ... 157 C7
Auckland Rd TN1 ... 8 C5
Audrey Cl Brighton BN1 ... 142 E5
Seaford BN25 ... 180 D5
Audrey Sturley Ct TN4 ... 7 D4
Augustines Way RH16 ... 50 F4
Augustus Way
TN38, TN37 ... 135 F6
Austen Cl RH19 ... 1 B1
Austen Way TN35 ... 137 D5
Austen Wlk BN23 ... 174 D2
Avard Cres BN20 ... 184 B6
Avards Cl TN18 ... 45 E8
Avenue Ct 19 BN3 ... 163 C6
Avenue La BN21 ... 184 F3
Avenue The Brighton BN2 ... 143 E1
Dormansland RH19 ... 2 B6
Eastbourne BN21 ... 184 F3
Fairlight Cove TN35 ... 138 F4
Hailsham BN27 ... 152 B6
Heathfield TN21 ... 82 B6
Horam TN21 ... 106 F8
Kingston near Lewes BN7 145 D5
Lewes BN7 ... 123 C1
Mayfield TN20 ... 40 B2
Avery Cl BN41 ... 140 F4
Aviemore Rd TN6 ... 25 D2
Avis Cl BN9 ... 168 E1
Avis Rd BN9 ... 168 E1
Avis Way BN9 ... 168 E1
Avocet BN27 ... 152 A7
Avocet Trad Est RH15 ... 72 F2
Avon St TN1 ... 8 C5
Avondale Rd
Eastbourne BN22 ... 185 B4
Hastings TN38 ... 136 A1
Hove BN3 ... 163 D7
Seaford BN25 ... 180 F3
Avonhurst RH15 ... 73 B3
Awbrook Cl RH17 ... 51 F3
Aylesbury BN3 ... 163 E6
Aylesbury Ave BN23 ... 185 E8
Aymer Ho 4 BN3 ... 163 A6
Aymer Rd BN3 ... 163 A6
Aynsley Ct BN3 ... 163 C8
Ayscue Cl BN23 ... 185 F7

Babylon Way BN20 ... 184 B8
Back La
Cross-in-Hand TN21 ... 81 C6
Fairwarp TN22 ... 36 B2
Rushlake Green TN21 ... 83 D1
Winchelsea TN36 ... 117 E7
Back Rd TN18 ... 47 B5
Backwoods Cl RH16 ... 51 B6
Backwoods La RH16 ... 51 B6
Baden Rd BN2 ... 143 D1
Badens Cl BN8 ... 76 C6
Badger Cl BN41 ... 141 B2
Badger Dr RH16 ... 50 C5
Badger Gate TN31 ... 93 A5
Badger Way BN1 ... 143 E6
Badgers Brow BN20 ... 184 B8
Badgers Cl TN6 ... 25 E3
Badgers Copse BN25 ... 181 C3
Badgers Dene BN7 ... 167 D8
Badgers Field BN10 ... 167 C1
Badgers Mount TN39 ... 156 E5
Badgers Way
East Grinstead RH19 ... 1 F2
Hastings TN34 ... 136 D5
Badgers Wlk RH15 ... 73 D2
Badlesmere Rd BN22 ... 185 B6
Bagham La BN27 ... 130 F6
Bahram Rd BN26 ... 172 F6
Bailey Cres BN22 ... 173 B3
Baillie Ave BN22 ... 185 C5
Bainbridge Cl BN25 ... 180 F3
Bainden Cl TN6 ... 27 D1
Baird Dr TN34 ... 136 E3
Baird Ho TN37 ... 159 C8
Baker Ct TN22 ... 78 C7
Baker St
Brighton BN1, BN2 ... 189 A7
Newhaven BN9 ... 179 E7
Uckfield TN22 ... 78 D6
Baker's Rd BN21 ... 184 D3
Bakewell Rd BN21 ... 184 D4
Bal Edmund TN37 ... 136 B4
Balaclava La TN5 ... 30 A6
Balcombe Ct BN10 ... 178 C8
Balcombe Gn TN33 ... 88 E1
Balcombe La RH17, RH19 ... 21 E2
Balcombe Rd
Haywards Heath
RH16, RH17 ... 50 D7
Peacehaven BN10 ... 178 B8
Baldings Cotts RH17 ... 74 B5
Baldock Rd TN5 ... 29 E4
Baldslow Down TN37 ... 136 C8
Baldslow Rd TN34 ... 136 F1
Baldwin Ave BN20, BN21 ... 184 C5
Baldwins Hill Cty Prim Sch
RH19 ... 1 D3
Bale Cl TN39 ... 156 E5
Balfour Cty Inf Sch BN1 ... 143 A3
Balfour Cty Jun Sch BN1 ... 143 A3
Balfour Gdns RH18 ... 11 E1
Balfour Rd BN1 ... 143 A2
Ball's Gn TN7 ... 14 B5
Ballard Dr BN8 ... 125 A7
Ballards Hill TN33 ... 134 F4
Ballsocks La TN21 ... 107 C8
Balmoral RH19 ... 11 A8
Balmoral Cl BN25 ... 181 A6
Balmoral Ct BN3 ... 142 A3
Balsdean Rd BN2 ... 144 E1
Baltimore Ct 9 BN3 ... 163 C7
Bamford Cl BN2 ... 144 A2
Bampfield St BN41 ... 162 B8
Bancroft Ho TN39 ... 157 B5
Bancroft Rd TN39 ... 157 B5
Bank Rd TN39 ... 157 C7
Banks Rd BN8 ... 52 F1
Bankside Brighton BN1 ... 142 C5
Hassocks BN6 ... 97 F5
Rye TN31 ... 93 B6
Sparrow's Green TN5 ... 29 E5
Banner Cl BN24 ... 174 C6
Banner Farm Rd TN2 ... 8 B2
Banner Way BN24 ... 174 C6
Bannings Vale BN2 ... 177 E5
Bannister Way RH16 ... 50 D6
Bannisters Field BN8 ... 76 D7
Baranscraig Ave BN1 ... 143 A7
Barbados TN40 ... 157 E3
Barber Ct BN7 ... 146 B8
Barclay Ho 2 BN2 ... 164 C7
Barcombe Ave BN25 ... 181 C3
Barcombe CE Prim Sch
BN8 ... 101 D5
Barcombe Cl
Eastbourne BN20 ... 184 C3
Seaford BN25 ... 181 C3
Barcombe Mills Rd BN8 ... 101 E4
Barcombe Pl BN1 ... 143 F5
Barcombe Rd BN1 ... 143 E4
Barcombe Wlk BN20 ... 184 C3
Barden Rd
Eastbourne BN22 ... 185 C4
Speldhurst TN3 ... 7 A8
Bardown Rd TN5 ... 42 E7
Bargate Cl TN39 ... 157 C7
Barham Cl TN34 ... 136 D4
Barkdale RH15 ... 73 D5
Barkham Manor Vineyard
TN22 ... 77 B8
Barley Ave TN35 ... 160 C5
Barley Cl BN10 ... 167 B2
Barley Dr BN6 ... 72 D4
Barley Field Cotts BN7 ... 146 D1
Barley La TN35 ... 160 D5
Barming Cl BN23 ... 174 D2
Barn Cl Hailsham BN27 ... 129 C1
Kingston near Lewes BN7 145 E5
Seaford BN25 ... 181 A6
Stone Cross BN24 ... 174 A6
Barn Cottage La RH16 ... 51 A5
Barn Cotts 2 BN25 ... 181 A3
Barn Ct TN37 ... 136 C5
Barn Field Gdns 8 BN2 ... 164 C6
Barn Hatch Cl BN7 ... 146 A8
Barn Ho The BN25 ... 180 E5
Barn La TN22 ... 79 D8
Barn Rd BN7 ... 123 E3
Barn Rise Brighton BN1 ... 142 D5
Seaford BN25 ... 181 A5
Barn Stables BN7 ... 123 B1
Barnard Gate RH16 ... 50 E7
Barnes Rd BN41 ... 162 B8
Barnet Way BN3 ... 141 E3
Barnett Rd BN1 ... 143 B2
Barnett Way TN22 ... 78 D7
Barnetts Way TN4 ... 8 C8
Barnfield
Crowborough TN6 ... 26 A3
Plumpton Green BN7 ... 99 E5
Royal Tunbridge Wells TN2 16 F7
Barnfield Cl TN34 ... 159 D8
Barnfield Gdns BN6 ... 98 E3
Barnham Cl BN22 ... 174 A2
Barnhams The TN39 ... 156 E3
Barnhorn Cl TN39 ... 156 C4
Barnhorn Rd TN39, TN33 ... 156 B4
Barnmead RH16 ... 50 D7
Barnsgate Manor Vineyard
TN22 ... 36 E5
Barnside Ave RH15 ... 73 D1
Barons Cl BN25 ... 180 C5
Barons Ct
Burgess Hill RH15 ... 73 B2
Royal Tunbridge Wells TN4 ... 8 A5
Barons Down Rd BN7 ... 146 A8
Barons Way BN26 ... 172 F5
Barrack Rd TN40 ... 157 C5
Barrack Sq TN36 ... 117 F7
Barracks Cotts TN32 ... 87 C7
Barrhill Ave BN1 ... 142 F7
Barrie Cl BN23 ... 174 E2
Barrington Cl RH16 ... 50 F8
Barrington Rd RH16 ... 51 A8
Barrington Wood RH16 ... 50 F8
Barrow Cl BN1 ... 143 C2
Barrow Hill BN1 ... 143 C2
Barrow La TN3 ... 6 F1
Barrow Rise TN37 ... 136 C5
Barrowfield Cl BN3 ... 142 C3
Barrowfield Dr BN3 ... 142 D2
Barrowfield Lodge BN3 ... 142 C2
Barry Wlk BN2 ... 164 C6
Bartholomew Sq BN1 ... 189 A5
Bartholomews BN1 ... 189 A5
Bartley Mill TN3 ... 18 E4
Bartley Mill Cl BN24 ... 174 B5
Barton Cres RH19 ... 11 A8
Barton Sch TN38 ... 136 B1
Basin Rd N BN41 ... 162 B6
Basin Rd S BN3, BN41 ... 162 B6
Baslow Ct BN20 ... 188 D7
Baslow Rd BN20 ... 188 D7
Bassett's Forge TN5 ... 29 E5
Bassetts La Argos Hill TN20 ... 39 F5
Mark Cross TN6 ... 28 E2
White Post TN11, TN8 ... 5 C7
Batchelor Way TN22 ... 78 A7
Batchelors TN2 ... 9 E8
Bateman's TN19 ... 62 A4
Bateman's La TN19 ... 62 A4
Batemans Rd BN2 ... 165 E7
Bates Rd BN1 ... 142 F2
Bath Ct BN3 ... 163 A5
Bath Rd BN21 ... 184 F2
Bath St BN1 ... 189 F7
Bathford Cl BN23 ... 174 D2
Battenhurst Rd TN5 ... 43 B4
Battery Hill TN35 ... 138 D5
Battle Abbey TN33 ... 112 D4
Battle Abbey (Sch) TN33 ... 112 D4
Battle Cl BN25 ... 181 C5
Battle Cres
Hailsham BN27 ... 152 B8
Hastings TN37 ... 136 B4
Battle Gates TN33 ... 112 B5
Battle Hill TN33 ... 112 E3
Battle Hospl TN33 ... 112 A4
Battle & Langton
CE Prim Sch TN33 ... 112 C4
Battle Rd Hailsham BN27 ... 129 C1
Hastings TN33,
TN37, TN38 ... 136 A4
Battle Sta TN33 ... 112 E4
Batts Bridge Rd TN22 ... 55 A4
Bavant Rd BN1 ... 142 E2
Baxter Rd BN7 ... 123 B2
Baxter St BN2 ... 164 C7
Baxters La RH17 ... 34 C6
Bay Ave BN24 ... 175 E5
Bay Cotts BN24 ... 176 C7
Bay Pond Rd BN21 ... 184 D4
Bay Rd BN24 ... 175 D4
Bay Tree Cl
Heathfield TN21 ... 82 C5
Shoreham-by-Sea BN43 ... 140 C1
Bay Tree La BN26 ... 172 F8
Bay Vue Rd BN9 ... 179 D7
Bayencourt N TN40 ... 157 C5
Bayencourt S TN40 ... 157 C5
Bayeux Ct Bexhill TN40 ... 157 D3
Hastings TN37 ... 159 D8
Bayhall Rd TN2 ... 8 C3
Bayham Abbey TN3 ... 19 B5
Bayham Ct TN5 ... 29 E6
Bayham Rd
Eastbourne BN22 ... 185 C4
Hailsham BN27 ... 152 D7
Royal Tunbridge Wells
TN2, TN3 ... 17 C7
Bayley's La BN26 ... 151 B2
Baylis Cres RH15 ... 72 D4
Bayview Rd BN10 ... 178 E5
Baywood Gdns BN2 ... 165 C8
Bazehill Rd BN2 ... 165 F2
Beach Cl BN25 ... 180 D3
Beach Ct 10 BN43 ... 161 A6
Beach Mews 6 BN22 ... 185 C5
Beach Rd
Eastbourne BN22 ... 185 C5
Newhaven BN9 ... 179 E6
Beachings The BN24 ... 175 C4
Beachy Head
Countryside Ctr BN20 ... 188 B4
Beachy Head Rd
Beachy Head BN20 ... 188 C4
Eastbourne BN20 ... 188 D8
Beacon Bsns Pk TN6 ... 38 C8

Beacon Cl Brighton BN1 .... 143 A2
Crowborough TN6 .... 25 E2
Seaford BN25 .... 180 D5
Beacon Com Coll
Crowborough TN6 .... 26 A2
Crowborough TN6 .... 26 B3
Beacon Ct BN2 .... 165 D4
Beacon Dr BN25 .... 180 E5
Beacon Gdns TN6 .... 25 E3
Beacon Hill Bexhill TN39 ... 157 A8
Dormansland RH7 .... 2 B8
Ovingdean BN2 .... 165 E3
Beacon Hurst BN6 .... 98 B3
Beacon La TN32 .... 88 E7
Beacon Rd
Crowborough TN6 .... 25 E2
Ditchling BN6 .... 98 D2
Hastings TN35 .... 137 E4
Seaford BN25 .... 180 D4
Beacon Rd W TN6 .... 25 D2
Beaconfield Ho TN6 .... 25 E2
Beaconsfield Cotts RH17 .... 51 F3
Beaconsfield Rd
Bexhill TN40 .... 157 C6
Brighton BN1 .... 164 A8
Chelwood Gate RH17 .... 34 D8
Hastings TN34 .... 136 F2
Portslade-by-Sea BN41 ...... 162 B8
Beaconsfield Terr TN21 .... 81 B8
Beaconsfield Villas BN1 ... 142 F1
Beaconsville Ct BN1 .... 142 F1
Beagles Wood Rd TN22 .... 9 E7
Beal Cres BN1 .... 143 B2
Beale St RH15 .... 72 F1
Beales La TN31 .... 67 B6
Beame Ct BN25 .... 180 D3
Beamsley Rd BN22 .... 185 C4
Beaney's La TN34 .... 136 E6
Bear Rd BN2 .... 164 D8
Bear Yd BN7 .... 123 D1
Beatrice La 2 BN21 .... 184 F3
Beatrice Wlk TN39 .... 157 A6
Beatty Ave BN1 .... 143 D6
Beatty Rd BN23 .... 185 E7
Beauchamp Rd TN38 .... 136 A4
Beauford Rd TN21 .... 106 F7
Beaufort Cres TN37 .... 136 C2
Beaufort Rd TN37 .... 136 C2
Beaufort Terr BN2 .... 164 C6
Beauharrow Rd TN37 .... 136 A6
Beaulieu Ct TN40 .... 157 F5
Beaulieu Gdns TN37 .... 136 C6
Beaulieu Rd TN39 .... 156 D2
Beauport Gdns TN37 .... 136 A7
Beauport Home Farm Cl
TN37 .... 136 A6
Beaver Cl TN6 .... 26 A1
Beckenham Cl BN27 .... 129 B3
Becket Cl TN34 .... 160 A5
Beckets Way TN7 .... 79 B5
Beckett Way
11 East Grinstead RH19 .... 10 F8
Lewes BN7 .... 123 C3
Beckley CE Prim Sch TN31 68 A4
Beckley Cl Brighton BN2 ... 164 E5
Hastings TN38 .... 135 D2
Beckworth Cl RH16 .... 51 A6
Beckworth La RH16 .... 51 A6
Bedales RH16 .... 51 D4
Bedales Cnr RH16 .... 51 D4
Bedales Hill RH16 .... 51 D4
Beddingham Gdns BN8 ...... 147 F5
Bedelands Cl RH15 .... 73 B5
Bedelands Farm
Nature Reserve RH15 .... 73 B6
Bedford Ave TN40 .... 157 D3
Bedford Ct TN22 .... 78 C8
Bedford Gr BN21 .... 184 F4
Bedford Pl BN1 .... 163 E5
Bedford Rd TN35 .... 160 C6
Bedford Sq BN1 .... 163 E5
Bedford St BN2 .... 164 C4
Bedford Terr 1 TN1 .... 8 A2
Bedford Towers 10 BN1 ... 163 E5
Bedfordwell Ct 1 BN22 ... 185 A4
Bedfordwell Rd
BN21, BN22 .... 185 A4
Bedgebury Cl TN38 .... 135 E2
Bedgebury Lower Sch
TN18 .... 45 F7
Bedgebury National Pinetum
TN17 .... 32 E8
Bee Rd BN10 .... 178 C8
Beech Cl Battle TN33 .... 112 C7
Bexhill TN39 .... 156 C6
Portslade-by-Sea BN41 .... 140 F3
Beech Ct BN26 .... 173 A6
Beech Farm Rd TN33 .... 88 D3

Beech Fields RH19 .... 1 F3
Beech Gr BN2 .... 143 E3
Beech Green La TN7 .... 14 B7
Beech Hill RH16 .... 51 B4
Beech House La TN32 .... 64 C6
Beech Hurst TN2 .... 9 D7
Beech Hurst Cl RH16 .... 50 D4
Beech Mews BN9 .... 179 E7
Beech Rd TN18 .... 48 C3
Beech St TN1 .... 8 B4
Beech Villas 1 TN21 .... 82 A6
Beecham Pl TN38 .... 135 F4
Beechers Rd BN41 .... 140 F3
Beeches Cl Heathfield TN21 82 B8
Uckfield TN22 .... 78 D8
Beeches Farm Rd TN6 ...... 26 A1
Beeches Head RH19 .... 2 F5
Beeches La RH19 .... 11 D6
Beeches Rd TN6 .... 26 B2
Beeches The
Brighton BN1, BN3 .... 142 D3
Royal Tunbridge Wells TN2 . 8 D5
The Moor TN18 .... 45 E7
Beechfield Cl BN24 .... 174 B6
Beeching Cl TN39 .... 156 C8
Beeching Park Ind Est
TN39 .... 157 B4
Beeching Rd TN39 .... 157 B4
Beeching Way RH19 .... 1 E1
Beechlands Cotts TN6 ...... 28 F3
Beechwood 9 BN1 .... 142 E3
Beechwood Ave BN1 .... 142 F4
Beechwood Cl
Brighton BN1 .... 142 F4
Burwash TN19 .... 62 B7
Hailsham BN27 .... 152 C5
Beechwood Cres BN20 ..... 184 D3
Beechwood Gdns TN37 ... 136 D5
Beechwood La
Cooksbridge BN7, BN8 ... 122 F8
Heathfield TN21 .... 82 B5
Beechwood Mews TN2 ...... 8 E4
Beechwood Sch
(Sacred Heart) TN2 .... 8 E4
Beechworths RH15 .... 73 A1
Beechy Ave BN20 .... 184 B5
Beechy Gdns BN20 .... 184 B5
Beechy Rd TN22 .... 80 A2
Beeding Ave BN3 .... 141 F3
Beeding Ct 4 BN43 .... 161 B8
Beggar's La BN24 .... 174 B5
Beggar's Wood Rd BN8 ..... 75 C6
Belbourne Ct 5 BN1 .... 189 A6
Belfast St BN3 .... 163 B7
Belfield Rd TN2 .... 9 D6
Belfry Orch TN22 .... 78 D5
Belfry The BN27 .... 152 A8
Belgrave Cres BN25 .... 180 F5
Belgrave Ct TN40 .... 157 D3
Belgrave Pl 1 BN2 .... 164 D4
Belgrave Rd
Royal Tunbridge Wells TN1 .. 8 B4
Seaford BN25 .... 180 E4
Belgrave St BN2 .... 189 B6
Belgrove 5 TN1 .... 8 A2
Bell Alley Rd TN19 .... 62 B5
Bell Banks Rd BN27 .... 152 C7
Bell Hammer RH19 .... 11 E8
Bell La Lewes BN7 .... 146 B8
Nutley TN22 .... 35 A4
Uckfield TN22 .... 78 B6
Uckfield TN22 .... 78 C6
Bell Mead 7 BN3 .... 163 D7
Bell Tower Ind Est 7 BN2 164 E4
Bell Wlk TN22 .... 78 C6
Bellbrook Ind Est TN22 ..... 78 B6
Belle Hill Bexhill TN40 .... 157 B5
Bexhill TN40 .... 157 C5
Belle Vue Ct BN2 .... 164 D5
Belle Vue Rd 4 BN22 ...... 185 C5
Bellevue Cotts BN2 .... 164 F8
Bellevue Ct Brighton BN1 .. 142 F1
2 Eastbourne BN22 .... 185 C5
Bellevue Gdns BN2 .... 164 D4
Bellhurst Rd TN32 .... 64 A4
Bellingham Cl TN37 .... 136 B4
Bellingham Cres BN3 ..... 162 D8
Belmaine Ct TN39 .... 156 F4
Belmont Bexhill TN39 ...... 157 B3
Brighton BN1, BN3 .... 163 E7
Belmont Cl BN6 .... 97 F6
Belmont Ct BN22 .... 152 B7
Belmont St BN1 .... 189 A6
Belmore Rd BN22 .... 185 B4
Belton Rd BN2 .... 164 B8
Beltring Rd
Eastbourne BN22 .... 185 B4
Royal Tunbridge Wells TN4 . 8 A6

Beltring Terr BN22 .... 185 B4
Belvedere Ct 10 BN21 ..... 184 F4
Belvedere Gdns
Crowborough TN6 .... 26 A1
Seaford BN25 .... 181 A5
Belvedere Pk TN38 .... 159 A8
Bembridge Rd BN23 .... 174 B3
Bembridge St BN2 .... 164 C8
Bembrook Rd TN34 .... 160 B5
Bemzells La BN27 .... 108 D2
Benbow Ave BN23 .... 185 E6
Benbow Ho TN39 .... 156 E4
Benchfield Cl RH19 .... 2 E6
Bending Cres TN39, TN40 . 157 C5
Benenden Cl BN25 .... 181 A4
Benenden Rise TN34 ...... 136 E3
Benett Ave BN3 .... 142 B2
Benett Dr BN3 .... 142 B2
Benfield Cl BN41 .... 141 C1
Benfield Cres BN41 .... 141 C1
Benfield Cl BN41 .... 162 C8
Benfield Cty Jun Sch
BN41 .... 162 C8
Benfield Valley Golf Course
BN3 .... 141 C3
Benfield Way BN41 .... 141 C1
Bengairn Ave BN1 .... 143 B1
Benhall Mill Rd TN2, TN3 . 17 D8
Benham Ct BN3 .... 163 B5
Benjamin Cl BN22 .... 173 F2
Benjamin Lodge RH15 .... 73 D3
Bennett Memorial
Diocesan Sch TN4 .... 7 E6
Bennett Rd BN2 .... 164 E4
Benson Ct BN3 .... 162 E7
Bentham Hill TN3 .... 7 D8
Bentham Rd BN2 .... 164 C7
Bentley Motor Mus BN8 .. 103 F5
Bentley Wildfowl Reserve
BN8 .... 103 F4
Bentswood Cres RH16 ..... 51 A5
Bentswood Rd RH16 .... 50 F5
Berberis Cl BN43 .... 140 B1
Beresford Cl TN17 .... 20 F2
Beresford Ct BN3 .... 163 D7
Beresford Ho BN10 .... 167 C1
Beresford Rd Brighton BN2 164 D5
Newhaven BN9 .... 168 E1
Bergamot Cres BN43 ...... 140 C1
Beristede Cl BN20 .... 184 E1
Berkeley Cl TN2 .... 9 E7
Berkeley Ct 2 BN3 .... 163 E7
Berkeley Rd 7 TN1 .... 8 A2
Berkeley Row BN7 .... 146 A8
Berkeley Wlk BN23 .... 174 E3
Berkley Rd TN20 .... 39 E1
Berkshire Ct 7 BN22 ..... 185 B4
Berlin Rd TN35 .... 160 C6
Bernard La 1 BN21 .... 184 F3
Bernard Pl BN2 .... 164 C7
Bernard Rd BN2 .... 164 C7
Bernhard Baron Cottage
Homes The BN2 .... 172 F5
Bernhard Gdns BN26 ...... 172 F5
Berriedale Ave BN3 .... 162 E6
Berriedale Ho BN3 .... 162 E6
Berry Cl Burgess Hill RH15 . 73 A5
Telscombe Cliffs BN10 .... 167 A1
Berwick BN26 .... 170 F7
Berwick CE Bexhill TN39 . 156 C6
Lower Willingdon BN22 ... 173 C3
Seaford BN25 .... 180 E2
Berwick Court Cotts BN26 171 A6
Berwick Rd BN2 .... 166 D3
Berwick Sta BN26 .... 150 B2
Betchley Cl RH19 .... 1 E3
Betherinden Cotts TN18 ... 47 A4
Bethune Rd TN40 .... 157 E3
Bethune Way TN34 .... 136 F1
Beulah Rd TN1 .... 8 C4
Beuzeville Ave BN2 .... 152 B8
Bevendean Ave BN2 .... 177 D5
Bevendean Cres BN2 ...... 143 E2
Bevendean Prim Sch BN2 143 F1
Bevendean Rd BN2 .... 143 D1
Beverington Cl BN21 ...... 184 D6
Beverington Rd BN21 ...... 184 D6
Beverley Cl BN5 .... 162 D7
Beverley Wlk TN34 .... 160 A6
Bevern Bridge BN8 .... 100 F4
Bevern Bridge Cotts BN8 . 100 F4
Beverns The BN7 .... 99 E5
Bevin Ct TN38 .... 136 B3
Bewl Bridge Cl TN5 .... 32 B3
Bewl Water TN5 .... 31 C6
Bewl Water Visitors Ctr
TN5 .... 31 B7
Bewlbridge La
Bewlbridge TN3, TN5 ....·20 B1
Lower Cousley Wood TN5 .. 30 F8

Bexhill Central Sta TN40 . 157 C4
Bexhill Coll TN39 .... 157 A2
Bexhill High Sch TN39 .... 157 B5
Bexhill Hospl TN40 .... 157 C5
Bexhill Mus TN39 .... 157 B3
Bexhill Rd
Eastbourne BN22 .... 185 C5
Hastings TN38, TN40 ...... 158 D6
Lower Street TN33, TN39 133 C3
Woodingdean BN2 .... 144 E1
Bexleigh Ave TN38 .... 158 B5
Bexley Cl BN27 .... 129 B2
Bexley Ct BN26 .... 173 A7
Bicton Gdns TN39 .... 156 E4
Biddenden Cl BN23 .... 174 D2
Bidwell Ave TN39 .... 157 A7
Bigwood Ave BN1 .... 163 D8
Bilbury Mews BN21 .... 184 F5
Billingham La TN31 .... 91 C3
Binstead Cl BN22 .... 173 E1
Biology Rd BN1 .... 144 B6
Birch Ave RH16 .... 51 A3
Birch Cl Eastbourne BN23 . 185 D7
Haywards Heath RH16 ..... 51 B3
Royal Tunbridge Wells TN1 . 8 D7
Uckfield TN22 .... 78 E8
Birch Ct BN22 .... 141 A1
Birch Est The BN23 .... 185 D7
Birch Grove Cres BN1 .... 143 A5
Birch Kiln Cotts TN5 ...... 30 A6
Birch Path TN22 .... 78 D8
Birch Rd BN22, BN23 ..... 185 C7
Birch Rdbt BN22, BN23 ... 185 C7
Birch View TN39 .... 157 C6
Birch Way Hailsham BN27 . 152 B6
Hastings TN34 .... 136 E3
Haywards Heath RH16 ..... 51 A2
Heathfield TN21 .... 82 A5
Royal Tunbridge Wells
TN1, TN2 .... 8 D7
Birchden Cotts TN3 .... 15 C6
Birchen La RH16 .... 50 F8
Birches Cl TN6 .... 25 F4
Birches Ind Est RH19 .... 1 A3
Birchetts Ave TN3 .... 6 E3
Birchetts Green La TN5 ... 31 A2
Birchgrove La RH17 .... 22 A1
Birchgrove Rd RH17 ...... 33 E7
Birchington Cl TN39 .... 156 D4
Birchwood Grove
City Prim Sch RH15 .... 73 C1
Birchwood Grove Rd RH15 73 C1
Bird in Eye Hill TN22 ...... 78 E6
Bird in Hand St TN3 .... 15 B8
Bird La TN5 .... 29 B5
Birdham Pl BN2 .... 143 E3
Birdham Rd BN2 .... 143 F3
Birk Dale TN39 .... 156 D4
Birkdale TN4 .... 8 B6
Birken Rd TN1, TN2 .... 8 D6
Birling Cl Brighton BN2 .. 143 D1
Seaford BN25 .... 180 D4
Birling Dr TN2 .... 8 A1
Birling Gap Rd BN20 .... 187 B6
Birling Park Ave TN2 .... 17 B8
Birling St BN20 .... 184 C4
Birling Way TN22 .... 78 E8
Bishop Bell CE Sch BN23 . 174 E1
Bishop's Cl
Hurstpierpoint BN6 .... 97 A7
Ringmer BN8 .... 124 E6
Bishop's Down
Cty Prim Sch TN4 .... 7 E5
Bishop's Down Park Rd TN4 . 7 F4
Bishop's Down Rd TN4 ...... 7 F3
Bishop's La Ringmer BN8 . 124 D6
Robertsbridge TN32 .... 64 A3
Bishop's Wlk TN40 .... 157 F6
Bishops Cl BN25 .... 180 C4
Bishops Ct TN4 .... 7 F3
Bishops Dr BN7 .... 146 A8
Bishops Rd BN3 .... 142 C1
Bishopstone Dr BN2 .... 177 B6
Bishopstone La BN6, RH17 . 72 A7
Bishopstone Sta BN25 .... 180 B4
Bittern Cl BN27 .... 152 D7
Bixley La TN31 .... 68 B2
Black Hill RH16 .... 51 A7
Black Lion St BN1 .... 189 A4
Black Path BN26 .... 173 A6
Blackberry La RH7 .... 1 E8
Blackberry Rd RH19, RH7 .. 1 D8
Blackbird Cl BN6 .... 72 D3
Blackboys CE Prim Sch
TN22 .... 80 A6
Blackbrook La BN8 .... 52 E2
Blackdon Hill TN3, TN6 ... 27 B6
Blackfields Ave TN39 ..... 156 F5

Blackhouse La RH15 .... 73 B4
Blackhurst La TN2 .... 8 F6
Blacklands TN33 .... 88 F1
Blacklands Cres RH18 ..... 11 F2
Blacklands Cty Prim Sch
TN34 .... 136 C2
Blacklands Dr TN34 .... 136 F2
Blacklands Ave TN34, TN38 136 A3
Blackman St BN1 .... 189 A6
Blackmill Cl TN39 .... 157 A8
Blackness Rd TN6 .... 38 A8
Blacksmith's Field TN33 . 135 A4
Blacksmith's La TN5 .... 30 A5
Blacksmiths Copse BN27 . 152 A6
Blacksmiths Field TN32 .... 46 C1
Blacksmiths La TN33 ...... 133 E8
Blackstone Way RH15 .... 73 A5
Blackthorn Cl
Brighton BN1 .... 142 D3
Eastbourne BN22 .... 173 E2
Hastings TN37 .... 136 C4
Portslade-by-Sea BN41 ... 141 B2
Blackthorn Way TN35 .... 138 F4
Blackthorns RH16 .... 51 A7
Blackthorns Cl RH16 .... 51 A6
Blackthorns The RH15 .... 73 B5
Blackwater Rd BN20, BN21 184 F1
Blackwell Cty Prim Sch
RH19 .... 1 E3
Blackwell Farm Rd RH19 .. 1 F2
Blackwell Hollow RH19 .... 1 F2
Blackwell Rd RH19 .... 1 F2
Blake Ct 2 BN2 .... 189 B6
Blake Way TN1 .... 8 D7
Blakeney Ave BN10, BN9 . 179 A6
Blaker St BN2 .... 189 B5
Blakes Way BN23 .... 185 F6
Blatchington Cl BN25 ..... 180 F4
Blatchington Hill BN25 ... 180 E4
Blatchington Mill Sch BN3 141 F2
Blatchington Rd
Hove BN3 .... 163 B7
Royal Tunbridge Wells TN1 .. 8 B1
Seaford BN25 .... 180 E3
Blenheim Cl RH19 .... 2 A3
Blenheim Ct 1 Hove BN3 163 A6
Robertsbridge TN32 .... 64 B3
Blenheim Fields RH18 .... 11 E3
Blenheim Pl 3 BN1 .... 189 A6
Blenheim Way
Flimwell TN5 .... 32 C3
Polegate BN26 .... 173 D6
Bletchinglye La TN6 .... 27 E1
Bletchley Ct BN1 .... 164 A8
Bletchley Cl BN1 .... 76 E6
Blois Rd BN7 .... 123 B2
Blomfield Rd TN37 .... 159 D8
Bloomsbury Pl 17 BN2 ... 164 C4
Bloomsbury St 16 BN2 ... 164 C4
Blossom Wlk BN27 .... 129 B1
Blount Ave RH19 .... 1 C1
Blowers Hill Cowden TN8 ... 4 D8
Speldhurst TN3 .... 7 B8
Blue Haze Ave BN25 ...... 181 B4
Bluebell Cl
East Grinstead RH19 .... 1 B1
Haywards Heath RH16 .... 50 F4
Bluebell Rly
RH17, RH19, TN22 .... 21 A5
Bluebell Rly Mus TN22 ... 53 A4
Bluebird Ct 10 BN3 .... 163 A6
Bluemans La TN33 .... 114 A4
Bluestone Cl TN38 .... 135 F2
Blytons The RH19 .... 1 A1
Boarders La TN5 .... 31 C3
Boast La BN8 .... 101 F5
Boath Mus of Natural
History BN1 .... 163 E8
Bocking Cl TN5 .... 29 E4
Boddingtons La BN6 ...... 98 D3
Bodiam Ave
Bevendean BN2 .... 144 B1
Bexhill TN40 .... 157 D6
Bodiam Castle (NT) TN32 .. 65 F8
Bodiam CE Prim Sch TN32 . 65 E8
Bodiam Cl
Bevendean BN2 .... 144 B2
Seaford BN25 .... 181 C4
Bodiam Cres BN22 .... 174 A2
Bodiam Ct 2 RH16 .... 50 E5
Bodiam Dr TN38 .... 135 D2
Bodiam Manor Sch TN32 . 65 E8
Bodiam Rd TN18, TN32 .... 46 F1
Bodle Cres TN39 .... 157 B7
Bodmin Cl BN20 .... 184 C3
Bohemia Rd
TN34, TN37, TN38 .... 159 D8

Boiler House Hill BN1 ...... 144 B7
Bolding Way RH16 .... 50 E2
Bolebrooke Rd TN40 ...... 157 D3
Bolney Ave BN10 .... 178 C6
Bolney Rd BN12 .... 143 F4
Bolnore RH16 .... 50 B4
Bolnore Rd RH16 .... 50 C4
Bolsover Rd
  Eastbourne BN20 .... 188 FB
  Hove BN3 .... 162 EB
Bolton Cl TN22 .... 78 A6
Bolton Rd BN21 .... 185 A2
Boltro Rd RH16 .... 50 D5
Bonchurch Rd BN2 .... 164 C7
Bond St BN1 .... 189 A5
Bonfire La RH17 .... 33 D5
Boniface Cl BN24 .... 174 C6
Bonny Wood Rd BN6 .... 97 E3
Booker Cl TN6 .... 26 A1
Bopeep Bostal BN26, BN8 . 170 B7
Borders La TN19 .... 62 F7
Boreham Hill BN27 .... 132 A4
Boreham La BN27 .... 131 E2
Boradales TN39 .... 156 E4
Borough Ave BN20, BN21 .. 184 D3
Borough St BN1 .... 163 E6
Borrow King Cl BN2 .... 164 D8
Borrowdale Cl BN23 .... 174 C4
Boscawen Cl BN23 .... 185 F7
Boscobel Ct TN38 .... 159 A6
Boscobel Lodge TN38 .... 159 B7
Boscobel Rd TN38 .... 159 A7
Boscobel Rd N TN38 .... 159 A7
Boship Cl BN23 .... 174 A4
Bostal Rd BN8 .... 148 B4
Boston Cl BN23 .... 185 F7
Boston Ct RH16 .... 51 A5
Boston St BN1 .... 189 A7
Boswell Wlk 2 BN23 .... 174 F2
Bough Beeches RH15 .... 73 C1
Boughey Pl BN7 .... 123 C3
Boulevard The BN24 .... 175 F6
Boundary Pas 6 BN3 .... 163 E5
Boundary Rd
  Brighton BN2 .... 164 F4
  Portslade-by-Sea
    BN3, BN41 .... 162 C7
  Royal Tunbridge Wells TN2 . 8 D1
Boundary The
  Langton Green TN3, TN4 .... 7 B3
  1 Seaford BN25 .... 180 E2
Bourg-de-Peage Ave RH19 .. 2 A1
Bourne Ct
  Brighton BN1 .... 142 D4
  20 Hastings TN34 .... 160 B4
Bourne Cty Prim Sch
  BN22 .... 185 B3
Bourne La TN32 .... 64 F7
Bourne Pas 12 TN34 .... 160 B4
Bourne St BN21, BN22 .... 185 A2
Bourne The Hassocks BN6 .. 97 E5
  Hastings TN34 .... 160 B4
Bourneside 12 BN22 .... 185 B3
Bowden House Sch BN25 . 180 F6
Bowen Rise BN25 .... 180 D6
Bowen Ct 4 BN3 .... 163 C6
Bowen Rd TN4 .... 7 F4
Bower Cl TN37 .... 136 B4
Bower The RH16 .... 50 D7
Bowerhill Cotts RH19 .... 21 F6
Bowlers Town TN31 .... 70 A2
Bowles Outdoor Ctr TN6 .. 26 E6
Bowley Rd BN27 .... 152 C7
Bowlings The TN33 .... 113 D8
Bowmans Dr TN31 .... 112 D6
Bowood Ave BN22 .... 185 B6
Bowrey Pl TN40 .... 157 C5
Bowring Way BN2 .... 164 D4
Bowsprit Mews TN38 .... 135 E7
Box La RH19 .... 11 E6
Box's La RH17 .... 34 C6
Boxes La RH17 .... 33 C5
Boxgrove Cl TN40 .... 157 F4
Boyce's St BN1 .... 189 F5
Boyne Pk TN4 .... 7 F4
Boyne Rd TN35 .... 160 C5
Bracken Cl
  Crowborough TN6 .... 26 C1
  Royal Tunbridge Wells TN2 . 8 B5
Bracken Rd
  Eastbourne BN20 .... 184 B5
  Royal Tunbridge Wells TN2 . 8 B5
  Seaford BN25 .... 181 A2
Bracken Way TN7 .... 59 E1
Brackenbury Cl BN41 .... 141 B2
Brackendale TN35 .... 160 D6
Brackerne Cl TN39 .... 156 C2
Bradford Cl 9 BN22 .... 185 B4
Bradford Rd BN1 .... 123 B1
Bradford St BN20, BN21 .. 184 D3

Brading Cl
  Eastbourne BN23 .... 174 B4
  Hastings TN34 .... 136 E2
Brading Rd BN2 .... 164 C7
Bradley Rd Wartling BN27 131 C1
  White Post TN3 .... 5 D5
Braemar Ho 5 BN1 .... 163 E6
Braemore Ct BN3 .... 162 E6
Braemore Rd BN3 .... 162 E6
Braeside Ave BN1 .... 143 A7
Bramber Ave Hove BN3 ... 141 F3
  Peacehaven BN10 .... 178 C7
Bramber Ave N BN10 .... 178 C8
Bramber Cl
  Haywards Heath RH16 ..... 50 D4
  Peacehaven BN10 .... 178 C8
  3 Seaford BN25 .... 180 F2
Bramber Ct 8 Hove BN3 .. 163 B7
  2 Shoreham-by-Sea
    BN43 .... 161 B8
Bramber La BN25 .... 180 F2
Bramber Rd BN25 .... 180 F2
Bramber Way RH15 .... 73 A4
Bramble Cl BN23 .... 174 B3
Bramble Croft TN6 .... 26 A2
Bramble Dr BN27 .... 152 A7
Bramble Gdns RH15 .... 72 D4
Bramble Rise BN1 .... 142 C5
Bramble Twitten RH19 ..... 2 A1
Bramble Way
  Brighton BN1 .... 143 C6
  Fairlight Cove TN35 .... 138 F4
Bramble Wlk TN1 .... 8 D7
Brambledean Rd BN41 ..... 162 B7
Brambles BN6 .... 97 F5
Brambles The RH17 .... 50 A6
Brambleside TN22 .... 78 A6
Brambletye Sch RH19 ...... 11 C5
Brambletyne Ave BN2 ...... 177 D5
Bramley Rd BN26 .... 173 D6
Bramleys BN7 .... 145 E5
Brampton Ave TN39 .... 156 F4
Brampton Ct TN39 .... 156 F4
Brampton Rd BN22 .... 184 F8
Brampton Road Trad Est
  BN22 .... 185 A8
Brand Rd BN22 .... 173 E1
Brands Cl BN9 .... 168 E2
Brangwyn Ave BN1 .... 142 E5
Brangwyn Cres BN1 .... 142 E6
Brangwyn Dr BN1 .... 142 E5
Brangwyn Dr BN1 .... 142 E5
Brangwyn Way BN1 .... 142 E6
Branksome Rd TN38 .... 159 A8
Branston Rd BN22 .... 173 D1
Brassey Ave BN22 .... 173 E1
Brassey Par BN22 .... 173 F1
Brassey Rd TN40 .... 157 D3
Brasslands Dr BN41 .... 140 F1
Braybon Ave BN1 .... 142 F4
Braybon Bsns Pk RH15 ..... 72 E2
Braybrooke Cl TN34 .... 159 E8
Braybrooke Rd TN34 .... 159 E8
Braybrooke Terr TN34 ...... 159 E8
Braypool La BN1 .... 142 D7
Brazen Cl BN9 .... 179 C6
Breach Rd BN6 .... 123 A2
Breadsall La TN33, TN38 .. 135 D6
Brecon Cotts TN6 .... 39 A8
Brecon Ct 6 BN3 .... 163 C7
Brede Cl Brighton BN2 .... 164 F5
  Eastbourne BN22 .... 185 D6
  Hastings TN38 .... 135 F7
Brede Cty Prim Sch TN31 .. 90 B4
Brede Hill TN31 .... 115 B8
Brede La
  Cackle Street TN31 .... 89 F2
  Sedlescombe TN31, TN33 .. 89 B2
Brede Valley View TN36 .. 116 E5
Breeds Pl TN34 .... 159 F7
Brendon Cl
  Eastbourne BN23 .... 174 E4
  Royal Tunbridge Wells TN2 . 8 D5
Brendon Rise TN34 .... 137 B3
Brentor Ct TN7 .... 8 D6
Brentwood Cl BN1 .... 143 B3
Brentwood Cres BN1 .... 143 B3
Brentwood Rd BN1 .... 143 B3
Bretland Rd TN4 .... 7 D1
Brett Dr TN40 .... 157 F4
Bretton RH15 .... 72 E5
Bretts Field RH19 .... 167 C2
Brewer St Brighton BN2 .. 189 B7
  Lamberhurst TN3 .... 20 A5
Brewers Gr TN20 .... 40 B2
Brian Cres TN4 .... 8 B8
Briar Cl
  Fairlight Cove TN35 .... 139 A5
  Woodingdean BN2 .... 165 D7
Briar Pl BN23 .... 174 B3
Briarcroft Rd BN2 .... 165 D7

Briary The TN40 .... 157 D5
Brickfield TN31 .... 69 B2
Brickfields TN2 .... 9 E8
Brickhurst La BN8 .... 126 C8
Brickwall TN6 .... 26 A1
Bricky The BN10 .... 178 D8
Brickyard Cotts TN6 .... 28 A4
Brickyard La
  Mark Cross TN6 .... 27 E5
  South Chailey BN8 .... 100 E7
Bridge Cl Burgess Hill RH15 . 72 F4
  Horam TN21 .... 107 A7
Bridge Dr BN9 .... 179 D7
Bridge End BN24 .... 175 B7
Bridge Farm Rd TN22 ...... 78 C6
Bridge Ho TN4 .... 8 B5
Bridge Pl TN31 .... 93 C6
Bridge Rd RH16 .... 50 F6
Bridge Road Bsns Pk RH16 . 50 F7
Bridge St BN9 .... 179 D7
Bridge Way TN38 .... 158 C6
Bridgelands BN8 .... 101 D4
Bridgemere Rd BN22 ...... 185 B6
Bridger Way TN6 .... 26 A1
Bridgersmill RH16 .... 50 D6
Bridgewick Cl BN7 .... 123 D3
Bridle Way BN10 .... 167 A1
Briers Ave TN37 .... 136 C3
Briers Gdns TN37 .... 136 C3
Briers The TN37 .... 136 C4
Brigden St BN1 .... 189 F7
Bright Ridge TN4 .... 7 E8
Brighthelm TN1 .... 144 B8
Brightland Rd BN20 .... 184 D3
Brightling Ave TN35 .... 137 E4
Brightling Rd
  Polegate BN26 .... 173 B5
  Robertsbridge TN32 .... 63 D2
Brighton Coll BN2 .... 164 C5
Brighton Coll of Tech
  Brighton BN1 .... 189 A6
  Brighton BN1 .... 189 B7
  Brighton BN1 .... 189 F8
Brighton Ctr The BN1 ...... 189 E5
Brighton General Hospl
  BN2 .... 164 D7
Brighton & Hove
  Golf Course BN41 .... 141 D6
Brighton & Hove
  High Sch for Girls BN3 .. 163 E6
Brighton & Hove Stad BN3 142 B1
Brighton, Hove & Sussex
  Sixth Form Coll BN3 ...... 163 E8
Brighton Marina BN2 ...... 164 F2
Brighton Marina Village
  BN2 .... 164 F3
Brighton Mus & Art Gall
  BN1 .... 189 A5
Brighton Pl BN1 .... 189 A5
Brighton Race Course
  BN2 .... 165 A8
Brighton Rd Hassocks BN6 . 97 D2
  Lewes BN7 .... 146 A8
  Newhaven BN9 .... 179 B7
Brighton Sea Life Ctr BN1 189 A4
Brighton Sq BN1 .... 189 A5
Brighton Sta BN1 .... 189 A6
Brightwell Ind Est BN9 ... 179 E7
Brills La BN1, BN2 .... 189 A4
Brincliffe TN6 .... 25 E3
Brinkers La TN5 .... 30 A2
Bristol Gate BN2 .... 164 D4
Bristol Gdns BN2 .... 164 E4
Bristol Mews 3 BN2 ...... 164 E4
Bristol Pl BN2 .... 164 E4
Bristol Rd Brighton BN2 .. 164 C4
  Hastings TN38 .... 136 A3
Bristol St BN2 .... 164 E4
Bristol Way TN38 .... 136 A3
British Engineerium (Mus)
  BN3 .... 142 B2
Britland Est BN22 .... 185 C6
Brittany Cl 3 Bexhill TN39 157 A4
  Hove BN3 .... 162 E6
Brittany Mews TN38 ...... 159 B7
Brittany Rd Hastings TN38 159 B8
  Hove BN3, BN41 .... 162 D6
Britten Cl BN23 .... 174 D3
Brittenden La TN21 .... 80 E5
Britts Farm Rd TN22 ...... 56 A1
Britts Orch TN22 .... 56 C3
Broad Gn BN2 .... 165 D8
Broad Gr TN7 .... 8 A1
Broad Green Ave RH15 .... 73 C2
Broad La TN3 .... 6 A4
Broad Oak TN3 .... 15 C6
Broad Oak Cl
  Broad Oak TN31 .... 90 D4
  Eastbourne BN22 .... 174 A4
  Royal Tunbridge Wells TN2 . 7 F1

Broad Rd BN20, BN22 ..... 173 A4
Broad Rig Ave BN21 .... 141 D3
Broad St Brighton BN2 .... 189 A4
  Cuckfield RH17 .... 50 A6
  Icklesham TN36 .... 116 C6
  Seaford BN25 .... 180 E3
Broad View Bexhill TN39 .. 156 F6
  Broad Oak TN21 .... 59 E1
Broad Way TN35 .... 138 F5
Broadcroft TN2 .... 16 F8
Broadfields BN1 .... 143 E3
Broadfields Rd BN2 .... 143 E3
Broadhill Cl TN21 .... 59 E1
Broadlands
  Burgess Hill RH15 .... 98 B8
  Hastings TN35 .... 137 D4
Broadley View TN33 ...... 133 E8
Broadmead TN2 .... 16 F8
Broadmead Ave TN2 ...... 16 F8
Broadoak Cty Prim Sch
  TN21 .... 59 F2
Broadoak La Bexhill TN39 . 156 E5
  Bexhill TN39 .... 156 F5
Broads Cotts TN19 .... 62 B6
Broadstone RH18 .... 12 A2
Broadview Cl BN20 .... 172 F4
Broadwalk The TN39 ...... 156 B4
Broadwater Ct TN2 .... 16 E8
Broadwater Down TN2 ... 16 F8
Broadwater Down
  Cty Prim Sch TN2 .... 16 F8
Broadwater La
  Royal Tunbridge Wells
    TN2, TN4 .... 7 F1
  Royal Tunbridge Wells TN2 16 F8
Broadwater Mews BN26 ... 172 E3
Broadwater Rise TN2 ...... 7 F1
Broadwater Way BN22 ... 184 F8
Broadway 11 BN43 .... 161 C8
Broadway The
  Alfriston BN26 .... 170 F3
  Crowborough TN6 .... 25 F3
  Eastbourne BN21 .... 173 D1
  Hastings TN35 .... 137 D4
  Haywards Heath RH16 .... 50 D4
  Lamberhurst TN3 .... 20 B5
Brockhurst BN2 .... 164 F7
Brockhurst Gate TN40 .... 157 F5
Brockley Rd TN39 .... 157 A3
Brocks Gyhll BN20 .... 173 A3
Brodie Pl BN21 .... 184 D4
Brodrick Cl BN22 .... 173 F1
Brodrick Rd BN22 .... 173 E2
Brokes Way TN4 .... 8 B8
Bromley Cl
  Eastbourne BN23 .... 174 C2
  Keymer BN6 .... 98 A4
Bromley Rd Brighton BN2 . 189 B8
  Pill BN1 .... 189 B8
  Seaford BN25 .... 181 A4
Brompton Cl BN1 .... 142 E6
Brontes The RH19 .... 1 D1
Brook Ave BN6 .... 97 F3
Brook Cl
  Crowborough TN6 .... 26 D1
  East Grinstead RH19 ...... 2 B1
Brook La Beddingham BN8 147 A6
  Haywards Heath RH16 .... 50 FB
Brook Rd TN1 .... 9 A2
Brook St Hastings TN34 ... 159 F8
  Lewes BN7 .... 123 D1
  Polegate BN26 .... 172 F6
Brook Terr TN6 .... 25 D4
Brook View TN6 .... 25 D4
Brook Way TN34 .... 137 B4
Brooker Pl BN3 .... 163 A7
Brooker St BN3 .... 163 A7
Brookfield TN18 .... 47 B5
Brookfield Ct TN40 .... 157 E4
Brookfield Rd TN40 .... 157 E4
Brookhouse Bottom RH17 . 34 D4
Brookhouse Rd TN22 ...... 79 A4
Brookland Cl
  Beachlands BN24 .... 175 E6
  Hastings TN34 .... 136 F2
Brooklands TN1 .... 8 D7
Brooklands Ave TN6 ...... 27 C7
Brooklands Farm Cl TN3 .. 6 A6
Brooklands Terr BN27 .... 128 E3
Brooklands Way RH19 .... 10 DB
Brooklyn Rd BN25 .... 180 E3
Brookmead Cl BN22 ...... 185 B5
Brooks Cl Lewes BN7 ...... 123 D2
  Newhaven BN9 .... 179 D6
Brooks Gdns BN8 .... 76 D6
Brooks Rd BN7 .... 123 D2
Brooks The RH15 .... 72 E5
Brookside
  Piddinghoe BN9 .... 168 B2
  Uckfield TN22 .... 78 A6
Brookside Ave BN26 ...... 172 F7
Brookside Cotts TN19 .... 63 B8

Brookway
  Burgess Hill RH15 .... 73 C3
  Haywards Heath RH16 .... 51 A8
Broom Cl BN22 .... 173 D2
Broom La TN3 .... 6 E2
Broom Pk TN3 .... 6 E3
Brooman's Ct 16 BN7 ..... 123 C1
Broomans La BN7 .... 123 D1
Broomfield Ave BN10 .... 177 F4
Broomfield Dr BN41 .... 141 A3
Broomfield St BN20, BN21 184 C4
Broomgrove Rd TN34 ..... 160 B6
Broomham Sch TN35 ..... 116 A3
Broomhill Bank Sch TN3 ... 7 C6
Broomhill Park Rd TN4 .... 7 F6
Broomhill Rd TN3 .... 7 D7
Bross Est BN9 .... 179 D8
Brow The
  Burgess Hill RH15 .... 73 A2
  Friston BN20 .... 183 A1
  Woodingdean BN2 .... 165 D8
Brown Jack Ave BN26 .... 172 F6
Brown's La TN22 .... 82 A7
Browning Rd 2 TN21 .... 82 A7
Browning Wlk 5 BN23 ... 174 E2
Brownings The 1 RH19 ... 1 C1
Brownleaf Rd BN2 .... 165 E6
Browns Cl TN22 .... 78 D8
Browns Wood RH19 .... 1 E4
Broyle La
  Ringmer BN8 .... 125 A8
  Ringmer BN8 .... 124 F8
Broyle Paddock BN8 ...... 124 F7
Broyle Side BN8 .... 125 A7
Broyle The BN8 .... 125 B7
Bruce Cl RH16 .... 50 E3
Brunel Rd TN38 .... 135 E4
Brunswick Mews BN3 .... 163 D5
Brunswick Pl BN3 .... 163 D6
Brunswick Rd BN3 .... 163 D6
Brunswick Row BN1 ...... 189 A7
Brunswick Sq BN3 .... 163 D5
Brunswick St E BN3 ...... 163 D5
Brunswick St W BN3 ...... 163 D5
Brunswick Terr
  Hove BN3 .... 163 D5
  Royal Tunbridge Wells TN1 . 8 A2
Brushes La RH16 .... 51 B8
Bryants Field TN6 .... 25 E3
Brydges Cl BN22 .... 185 C6
Buchanan Hospl TN38 .... 136 B1
Buci Cres BN43 .... 140 C1
Buckholt Ave TN40 .... 158 A7
Buckholt La TN39 .... 157 C8
Buckhurst Cl
  East Grinstead RH19 ...... 1 C3
  Eastbourne BN20 .... 184 B8
  Lewes BN7 .... 123 C3
Buckhurst La TN5 .... 29 A6
Buckhurst Mead RH19 .... 1 C4
Buckhurst Pl TN39, TN40 . 157 C4
Buckhurst Rd Bexhill TN40 157 C4
  Telscombe Cliffs BN10 .... 177 F3
Buckhurst Way RH19 ...... 1 C3
Buckingham Cl
  4 Brighton BN1 .... 189 F7
  Seaford BN25 .... 180 E4
  Shoreham-by-Sea BN43 ... 161 A8
Buckingham Ct BN20 ..... 184 B6
Buckingham Dr RH19 .... 11 A8
Buckingham Lodge BN1 .. 189 F7
Buckingham Pl BN1 ...... 189 F7
Buckingham Rd
  Brighton BN1 .... 189 F6
  Hastings TN38 .... 136 A4
  Royal Tunbridge Wells TN1 . 8 B2
Buckingham St BN1 ...... 189 F6
Buckland Rd BN25 .... 180 F5
Buckle By-Pass BN25 .... 180 C4
Buckle Cl BN25 .... 180 C4
Buckle Dr BN25 .... 180 C4
Buckle Rise BN25 .... 180 C4
Buckler St BN41 .... 162 B8
Buckley Cl BN3 .... 141 E4
Buckswood Grange Sch
  TN22 .... 78 B8
Buckthorn Cl BN25 .... 181 C3
Buckwell Ct BN7 .... 123 A3
Buckwell Rise BN27 ...... 130 E5
Buddens Gn TN31 .... 68 B5
Bugsell La TN32 .... 63 F4
Bulbeck Cl RH15 .... 72 E1
Bull La 2 BN7 .... 146 C8
Bull Lane Cotts TN3 .... 19 C4
Bull Ring TN3 .... 112 D4
Buller Cl TN6 .... 26 A1
Buller Rd BN2 .... 143 D1
Bulrush Gdns TN22 .... 78 E4

Bullingstone Cotts TN3 .... 6 E7
Bullingstone La TN3 .... 6 F7
Bulls PI TN2 .... 9 D6
Bulrush PI TN38 .... 135 E1
Bulverhythe Rd TN38 .... 158 D6
Bungalows The TN22 .... 79 B5
Bunny La TN3 .... 16 E5
Burchetts CI RH16 .... 50 E2
Burden PI TN38 .... 136 A3
Burdett PI **2** TN34 .... 160 A3
Burdett Rd
  Crowborough TN6 .... 26 C1
  Rusthall TN4 .... 7 B4
Burdocks Dr RH15 .... 73 D1
Burfield Park Ind Est
  BN27 .... 152 B6
Burfield Rd BN22 .... 185 B3
Burgess Hill Sch RH15 ...... 73 B2
Burgess Hill Sta RH15 .... 73 B2
Burgess Rd TN34 .... 137 C5
Burgh Hill TN19 .... 44 E2
Burgh La BN8 .... 148 E5
Burhill Way TN38 .... 158 F7
Burleigh Rd BN22 .... 185 C6
Burlington Gdns BN41 ...... 141 C1
Burlington PI BN21 .... 185 A2
Burlington Rd BN21 .... 185 B2
Burlington St BN2 .... 164 C4
Burlow CI Brighton BN2 .... 164 E5
  Lower Willingdon BN22 .. 173 C3
Burma CI RH16 .... 50 D5
Burners CI RH15 .... 73 D1
Burnham CI BN2 .... 165 F7
Burns Way RH19 .... 1 C1
Burnside BN26 .... 173 A6
Burnside CI BN26 .... 173 A6
Burnt House La TN3 .... 7 A5
Burnt Lodge La TN5 .... 31 B2
Burnt Oak Rd TN22, TN6 ... 37 E2
Burnthouse Bostall BN6 .. 120 C8
Burrell Rd RH16 .... 50 D6
Burrells La TN22 .... 55 A7
Burrells The BN43 .... 161 B6
Burrow Down BN20 .... 184 B5
Burrow Down CI BN20 ...... 184 A5
Burrswood Villas TN3 .... 15 B7
Burry Rd TN37 .... 136 C3
Burslem Rd TN2 .... 9 D8
Burstead CI BN1 .... 143 B3
Burston Gdns RH19 .... 1 C4
Burton Rd BN21 .... 184 E5
Burton Villas BN3 .... 163 D8
Burton Way TN38 .... 159 B6
Burton Wlk BN27 .... 152 B7
Burwash CE Prim Sch TN19 62 B6
Burwash CI
  Eastbourne BN23 .... 174 B4
  Hastings TN34 .... 137 A5
Burwash Lodge **1** BN1 .... 143 C1
Burwash Rd
  Broad Oak TN21 .... 82 C8
  Hove BN3 .... 141 F3
Bush CI
  Telscombe Cliffs BN10 . 167 A1
  Woodingdean BN2 .... 165 D8
Bush Farm Dr BN41 .... 141 C3
Bush Rd BN9 .... 179 B8
Bushbury La TN22 .... 80 A8
Busheyfields BN27 .... 152 A8
Bushy Croft TN39 .... 156 F5
Bushy Gill TN3 .... 7 A3
Butcher's Cross TN7 .... 13 B7
Butcher's La TN35 .... 115 E2
Butcherfield La TN7 .... 13 B6
Bute St BN2 .... 164 D5
Butler's Green Ho RH16 .... 50 B4
Butler's Green Rd RH16 .... 50 C4
Butler's La BN27 .... 130 E3
Butlers Way BN8 .... 124 C5
Butterbox La BN8, RH17 ... 52 D4
Buttercup Wlk BN1 .... 143 B7
Butterfield RH19 .... 1 B3
Butterfly Ctr BN22 .... 185 D4
Buttermere Way BN23 ...... 174 C4
Burton Cl BN2 .... 189 B7
Butts Field BN27 .... 152 C6
Butts La BN20 .... 173 A1
Butts Rd BN42 .... 161 E7
Buttsfield La BN8 .... 105 A5
Buxted CE Prim Sch TN22 . 55 F3
Buxted Ct TN22 .... 56 C3
Buxted Rise TN22 .... 143 B5
Buxted Sta TN22 .... 56 B3
Buxted Wood La TN22 ...... 56 E5
Buxton Dr TN39 .... 157 B6
Buxton Rd Brighton BN1 .. 163 E7
  Eastbourne BN20 .... 188 E8
By Sunte RH19 .... 50 F8

Bydown BN25 .... 181 A4
Bye-law Cotts BN8 .... 101 E6
Byeway The Bexhill TN39 . 156 D5
  Hastings TN34 .... 137 A4
Byeways The BN25 .... 180 F4
Byfields Croft TN39 .... 156 F5
Byland CI BN22 .... 173 E3
Bylands **3** BN22 .... 164 F5
Byng Rd TN4 .... 7 F5
Byron CI **1** RH16 .... 50 E5
Byron Gr **2** RH19 .... 1 C1
Byron St BN3 .... 163 A7
Byron Wlk BN23 .... 174 E3
Byway The BN1 .... 143 E5
Byways TN34 .... 136 D6
Byworth CI Bexhill TN39 .. 156 C6
  Brighton BN2 .... 164 F6

Cabbage Stalk La TN4 .... 7 E2
Caburn Cres BN7 .... 123 A2
Caburn Rd BN3 .... 163 E7
Caburn Way BN27 .... 152 B6
Cackle St TN31 .... 90 A2
Cacklebury CI BN27 .... 152 A6
Cadborough Cliff TN31 ..... 93 A4
Cade St BN22 .... 173 F2
Cadogan CI BN20 .... 175 C4
Cadogan Gdns **6** TN1 ...... 8 B4
Cairngorm CI BN23 .... 174 D3
Cairo Ave BN10 .... 178 A8
Cairo Ave S BN10 .... 178 A7
Caister's CI BN3 .... 163 C8
Caius CI **16** BN43 .... 161 C8
Calbourne RH16 .... 50 D5
Caldbec Ct TN33 .... 112 D5
Caldbec Hill TN33 .... 112 D5
Caldicotts La BN27 .... 128 C4
Caledonian Rd BN1 .... 189 B8
Caley Rd TN1 .... 8 D7
Calgary Rd TN39 .... 157 B7
Calverley Ct TN2 .... 8 C3
Calverley Park Cres **1**
  TN1, TN2 .... 8 B3
Calverley Park Gdns
  TN1, TN2 .... 8 C4
Calverley Pk TN1, TN2 ...... 8 B3
Calverley Rd
  Eastbourne BN21 .... 184 F2
  Royal Tunbridge Wells
  TN1, TN2 .... 8 B3
Calverley St TN1 .... 8 B4
Calverley Wlk BN21 .... 184 F2
Calvert CI TN22 .... 78 A7
Calvert Rd Hastings TN34 160 A6
  Uckfield TN22 .... 78 A7
Camber CI
  Beachlands BN24 .... 175 F6
  Bexhill TN40 .... 157 E6
  Brighton BN2 .... 164 F5
Camber Dr BN24 .... 175 F6
Camber Rd TN31 .... 94 B3
Camber Way BN24 .... 175 F6
Camberlot Rd BN27 .... 128 A2
Cambrian Rd TN4 .... 8 C7
Cambridge Gdns
  Hastings TN34 .... 159 E7
  Royal Tunbridge Wells TN2 8 B2
Cambridge Gr BN3 .... 163 C7
Cambridge Rd
  Bexhill TN39, TN40 ...... 157 C6
  Eastbourne BN22 .... 185 C4
  Hastings TN34 .... 159 E7
  Hove BN3 .... 163 D6
Cambridge St BN2 .... 164 C5
Cambridge Way TN22 ...... 55 C1
Camden Ave TN2 .... 9 C6
Camden Ct Pembury TN2 .. 9 D6
2 Royal Tunbridge Wells
  TN1 .... 8 B4
Camden Hill TN1, TN2 ...... 8 B3
Camden Pk TN2 .... 8 C2
Camden Rd
  Eastbourne BN21 .... 184 F2
  Royal Tunbridge Wells TN1 8 B4
Camden St BN41 .... 162 C6
Camden Terr BN1 .... 189 F6
Camelford St BN2 .... 189 B5
Campbell CI TN22 .... 55 C1
Campbell Cres RH19 .... 1 B1
Campbell Ct TN38 .... 159 A8
Campbell Rd
  Brighton BN1 .... 189 F8
  Royal Tunbridge Wells TN4 8 A6
Camperdown St TN39 ...... 157 B7
Canada CI BN10 .... 167 B1
Canada Way TN39 .... 157 B7
Canadia Rd TN33 .... 112 D8
Canal Bank TN35 .... 139 B7
Canfield CI BN2 .... 143 D1
Canfield Rd BN2 .... 143 D1
Canning St BN2 .... 164 D5

Cannon PI BN1 .... 189 F5
Cansiron La
  Ashurst Wood RH19 ...... 11 F6
  Holtye TN7, TN8 .... 3 E2
Cantelupe Rd
  Bexhill TN40 .... 157 D3
  East Grinstead RH19 ..... 1 F1
Canterbury CI BN22 .... 173 C2
Canterbury Dr **5** BN2 ...... 189 B7
Canterbury Rd TN3 .... 9 E6
Canterbury Rise TN34 ..... 136 E3
Cantercrow Hill BN9 .... 168 F2
Canton **3** RH16 .... 50 D6
Canton PI TN38 .... 158 F8
Cants CI RH15 .... 73 C3
Cants La RH15 .... 73 C3
Canute Dr TN35 .... 137 D3
Canute Rd TN35 .... 137 D3
Capel Ave BN10 .... 178 D7
Capello Path BN27 .... 152 D7
Capenors RH15 .... 72 F1
Caple Ct TN38 .... 159 B8
Caple Gdns TN38 .... 159 B7
Card Hill RH18 .... 11 F1
Carden Ave BN1 .... 143 B6
Carden Ave N BN1 .... 143 A6
Carden Cres BN1 .... 143 A6
Carden Cty Inf Sch BN1 .. 143 B6
Carden Cty Jun Sch BN1 . 143 B6
Carden Hill BN1 .... 143 B5
Cardiff Rd TN38 .... 159 C7
Cardinal Newman Sch
  BN3 .... 163 D8
Cardinals CI TN40 .... 157 F6
Carew Ct **4** BN21 .... 185 A4
Carew Lodge **1** BN21 ..... 184 F4
Carew Rd BN21 .... 184 F4
Carew Views **2** BN21 ...... 184 F4
Carey Down BN10 .... 167 B1
Carfax CI TN39 .... 157 B8
Carinus Gdns TN38 .... 136 A6
Carisbrooke CI BN23 ...... 174 B4
Carisbrooke Rd
  Brighton BN2 .... 164 D7
  Eastbourne BN22 .... 185 B3
  Hastings TN38 .... 159 C7
Carlisle Rd
  Eastbourne BN20, BN21 184 F1
  Hove BN3 .... 162 F6
Carlton CI BN25 .... 180 E4
Carlton Cres TN2 .... 8 C4
Carlton Ct Bexhill TN40 .. 157 D3
  Portslade-by-Sea BN3 .. 162 C8
Carlton Hill BN2 .... 189 B5
Carlton Hill Cty Prim Sch
  BN2 .... 189 B5
Carlton Rd
  Eastbourne BN22 .... 185 C4
  Royal Tunbridge Wells TN2 8 C4
  Seaford BN25 .... 180 D4
Carlton Terr BN3 .... 162 C8
Carlyle Ave BN2 .... 143 D1
Carlyle St BN2 .... 164 C7
Carmel CI TN39 .... 156 D3
Carman Ct BN20 .... 173 B3
Carlisle Rd TN31 .... 142 F6
Caroline CI BN25 .... 180 D5
Carpenter Dr TN38 .... 135 F4
Carpenters Croft BN8 ..... 105 A5
Carpenters Way BN27 ..... 152 A6
Carrier's Path BN27 .... 152 B8
Carriers PI TN3 .... 5 B3
Carroll Wlk BN23 .... 174 E2
Cashman Lodge BN1 .... 143 A5
Caspian CI **8** BN1 .... 189 F7
Caspian Sq BN2 .... 165 F1
Castle Banks **4** BN7 .... 123 C1
Castle CI BN7 .... 123 D2
Castle Ditch La BN7 .... 123 C1
Castle Dr BN24 .... 175 C4
Castle Farm Cotts TN 13 E4
Castle Gate **7** BN7 .... 123 C2
Castle Gdns **10** TN34 ...... 159 F7
Castle Hill TN20 .... 39 A5
Castle Hill Pas TN34 .... 159 F8
Castle Hill Rd TN34 .... 159 F7
Castle Hurst TN32 .... 65 A1
Castle Mount BN20 .... 184 D1
Castle Prec **5** BN7 .... 123 C1
Castle Rd TN4 .... 8 A5
Castle Rise **8** Lewes BN7 123 C1
  Uckfield TN22 .... 78 D4
Castle Sq BN1 .... 189 A5
Castle St Brighton BN1 ... 163 E5
  9 Hastings TN34 .... 159 F7
  2 Royal Tunbridge Wells
  TN1 .... 8 B4
  Winchelsea TN36 .... 117 F7
Castle Terr BN24 .... 175 B6

Castle View Gdns BN24 ... 174 E6
Castle Way TN22 .... 78 D4
Castle Wlk TN5 .... 29 E4
Castledean Sch BN2 .... 143 C2
Castledown Ave TN34 ..... 160 A4
Castledown Cty Prim Sch
  TN34 .... 160 A4
Castledown Terr **7** TN34 160 A4
Castlefields TN7 .... 13 E8
Castleham Rd TN38 .... 135 F5
Castleross Rd BN24 .... 175 C4
Cat St TN7 .... 12 F1
Catherine PI **7** TN1 .... 8 B4
Catherine Vale BN2 .... 165 E8
Catkin Way RH16 .... 51 B4
Catley Ct **2** TN39 .... 157 A4
Catsfield CE Prim Sch
  TN33 .... 133 F8
Catsfield CI TN38 .... 135 D2
Catsfield Place (Wilton
  House Sch) TN33 .... 134 B6
Catsfield Rd TN33 .... 111 E2
Catt's Corner Cotts TN6 .. 27 E1
Catt's Hill TN6 .... 27 E1
Causeway The
  Brighton BN2 .... 164 D6
  5 Seaford BN25 .... 180 E2
Cavalier Way RH19 .... 10 F7
Cavalry Cres BN20 .... 184 B5
Cavell Ave BN10 .... 178 B7
Cavell Ave N BN10 .... 178 C8
Cavendish Ave
  Eastbourne BN22 .... 185 B4
  Hastings TN38 .... 159 A7
Cavendish CI BN10 .... 167 B1
Cavendish Ct TN40 .... 157 D3
Cavendish Dr TN2 .... 8 B3
Cavendish Ho
  12 Brighton BN1 .... 163 E5
  9 Hastings TN37 .... 159 C7
  Peacehaven BN10 .... 167 C1
Cavendish PI
  Brighton BN1 .... 163 E5
  Eastbourne BN21 .... 185 B3
  4 Hastings TN34 .... 160 A4
Cavendish Sch BN1 .... 184 C5
Cavendish St **11** BN2 ...... 189 B5
Cavendish Way BN23 ...... 174 C4
Caveridge La BN8 .... 100 E8
Caverley Rd TN4 .... 8 A6
Caves Rd TN38 .... 159 A6
Cavix Field **7** TN31 .... 67 B7
Caxton Way **13** RH16 ...... 50 E4
Cedar CI Burgess Hill RH15 73 B5
  Eastbourne BN22 .... 173 D2
  Hastings TN37 .... 159 D6
Cedar Ct TN4 .... 8 A5
Cedar Lodge TN4 .... 7 F3
Cedar Ridge TN2 .... 8 B3
Cedar Way RH16 .... 51 B4
Cedars CI TN22 .... 78 C8
Cedars Gdns RH15 .... 142 E3
Cedars The
  1 Brighton BN2 .... 189 B8
  1 Brighton, Withdean
  BN1 .... 142 E3
  Hailsham BN27 .... 129 B1
  Haywards Heath RH16 .. 50 D7
  Mayfield TN20 .... 40 B2
Cedarwell CI BN9 .... 168 B2
Cedarwood **6** BN21 .... 142 E3
Celandine Dr TN38 .... 135 D5
Centenary Ho **9** BN1 .... 142 E2
Centenary Ind Est
  6 BN2 .... 164 B8
Central Ave
  Eastbourne BN20 .... 184 B5
  Polegate BN26 .... 177 E7
  Telscombe Cliffs BN10 . 178 A8
Central Sta TN1 .... 8 A3
Centurion Rd BN1 .... 189 F6
Centurion Rise TN34 .... 137 A4
Ceylon PI BN21, BN22 .... 185 B3
Ceylon Wlk TN39 .... 156 E3
Chadborn CI BN2 .... 164 D5
Chaffinch CI RH15 .... 72 D4
Chaffinch Rd BN23 .... 174 C2
Chaffinch Wlk TN27 .... 78 D5
Chafford Cotts TN3 .... 5 F5
Chafford La TN3 .... 5 F5
Chailey Ave BN2 .... 177 A5
Chailey CI
  Eastbourne BN23 .... 174 E1
  Hastings TN34 .... 136 F5
Chailey Common
  Nature Reserve BN8 ..... 75 D7
Chailey Cres BN2 .... 177 E5
Chailey Ct **2** RH16 .... 50 F3
Chailey Cty Sec Sch BN8 . 100 D7
Chailey Heritage Craft Sch &
  Hospl (New Heritage) BN8 52 E1

Chailey Heritage Craft Sch &
  Hospl (Old Heritage) BN8 . 75 C7
Chailey Heritage Sch &
  Hospl (St George's) BN8 . 75 D7
Chailey La BN8 .... 76 B5
Chailey Rd BN1 .... 143 E4
Chailey St Peter's
  CE Prim Sch BN8 .... 75 E4
Chailey Windmill
  Rural Life Mus BN8 ...... 75 D7
Chain La TN33 .... 112 C5
Chalden PI TN39 .... 156 C6
Chalfont Dr BN3 .... 142 C3
Chalk Farm CI BN20 .... 173 B1
Chalkers La BN6 .... 97 B8
Chalket La TN2 .... 9 C5
Chalkland Rise BN2 .... 165 E8
Chalky Rd BN41 .... 141 A3
Challoners RH17 .... 33 C4
Challoners Cl RH16 .... 50 F2
Challoners Mews BN2 .... 165 F2
Challow CI BN6 .... 97 E4
Chaloner CI RH16 .... 51 B7
Chaloner Rd RH16 .... 51 B7
Chalvington CI
  Brighton BN1 .... 143 E6
  Seaford BN25 .... 180 F6
Chalvington Dr TN37 ...... 136 C6
Chalvington Ho **8** BN21 . 184 D4
Chalvington Rd BN21 ..... 184 C7
Chamberlain Rd BN21 .... 184 C4
Chamberlaines La BN8 ... 124 F6
Chambers Cres TN38 ...... 135 F3
Chambers Rd TN38 .... 135 F3
Chancellor Ho TN4 .... 7 F3
Chancellors Pk BN6 .... 97 F4
Chanctonbury Dr TN34 .. 136 E5
Chanctonbury Rd
  Burgess Hill RH15 .... 73 A1
  Hove BN3 .... 163 E7
Chandler Rd TN39 .... 157 A4
Chandler's Mead BN8 .... 123 A7
Chandos Rd TN1 .... 8 C5
Channel View
  Bexhill TN40 .... 157 C3
  13 Southwick BN42 ..... 161 E7
Channel View E TN40 ..... 157 C3
Channel View Rd
  Eastbourne BN22 .... 185 D5
  Pevensey Bay BN24 ..... 175 E5
  Woodingdean BN2 .... 165 D8
Channel View W TN40 .... 157 C3
Channel Way TN35 .... 138 E3
Channers La BN8 .... 126 D1
Chant La TN6 .... 27 B1
Chantlers CI RH19 .... 1 C2
Chantlers Mead TN8 .... 4 A5
Chantry Ave TN40 .... 157 D6
Chantry Cty Inf Sch TN40 157 C5
Chantry La TN40 .... 157 C5
Chantry The **11** BN21 ..... 184 E4
Chapel Barn CI BN27 ...... 152 C7
Chapel CI
  Burgess Hill RH15 .... 72 F4
  Seaford BN25 .... 180 E3
Chapel Cotts Battle TN33 112 E3
  Mayfield TN20 .... 40 B2
Chapel Field TN31 .... 67 A7
Chapel Gn TN6 .... 25 F2
Chapel Hill
  Crowhurst TN33 .... 134 F4
  Lewes BN7 .... 123 E1
  Sedlescombe TN33 ...... 113 E7
Chapel La
  Ashurst Wood RH19 ...... 11 D6
  Blackboys TN22 .... 80 B7
  East Chiltington BN7 ... 100 A3
  Forest Row RH18 .... 11 F2
  Guestling Green TN35 .. 138 A8
  Horsted Keynes RH17 ... 33 C5
Chapel Mews BN3 .... 163 D5
Chapel Park Rd TN37 ...... 159 C8
Chapel PI
  Portslade-by-Sea BN41 162 B7
  8 Royal Tunbridge Wells
  TN1 .... 8 A2
  Ticehurst TN5 .... 31 E1
Chapel Rd
  Plumpton Green BN7 .... 99 E7
  Southwick BN41 .... 162 A7
Chapel St Brighton BN2 . 189 B5
  Newhaven BN9 .... 179 D7
Chapel Terr **2** BN2 .... 164 D4
Chapman Way TN4 .... 8 C8
Chapman's La
  East Grinstead RH19 ...... 1 B1
  East Grinstead RH19 ...... 1 D1
Charis Ct **16** BN3 .... 163 C7
Charity Farm Way TN6 .... 26 A3
Charles Ave RH15 .... 72 D2
Charles Bennett Ct RH16 . 51 A4

Charles Cl Hove BN3 .... 142 A3
Seaford BN25 .... 180 D5
Charles Ct TN2 .... 8 C3
Charles Moore Ct BN26 ... 173 A7
Charles Rd TN38 .... 159 C8
Charles Rd W TN38 .... 159 B8
Charles St Brighton BN2 ... 189 A4
 Royal Tunbridge Wells TN4 . 8 A8
Charleston Farm BN8 ..... 149 A2
Charleston Manor Gdns
 BN25 .... 182 A6
Charleston Rd BN2 .... 184 D4
Charlesworth Pk RH16 .... 51 C4
Charlotte St BN2 .... 189 B4
Charlston Ave BN9 .... 179 A5
Charlton's Way TN4 .... 7 E1
Charltons The BN1 .... 145 D4
Charlwood Gdns RH15 .... 73 C5
Charlwood Rd RH15 .... 73 D6
Charlwoods Bsns Ctr RH19 . 1 D2
Charlwoods Pl RH19 .... 1 E3
Charlwoods Rd RH19 ...... 1 E3
Charters Ancaster Sch
 TN40 .... 157 F5
Charters Ancaster Sch
 (Jun Dept) TN40 .... 157 E5
Chartfield BN3 .... 142 A2
Chartfield Way BN3 .... 142 B2
Chartres TN40 .... 157 D6
Chartres Cl TN40 .... 157 D6
Chartwell Cl BN25 .... 180 E6
Chartwell Ct BN1 .... 189 F5
Chates Farm Ct BN2 .... 189 B6
Chatfield Cres BN22 ...... 173 C1
Chatfield Rd RH17 .... 50 A6
Chatham Pl Brighton BN1 . 189 F7
12 Seaford BN25 .... 180 E2
Chatham Rd **3** TN37 ..... 136 B2
Chatsfield Cl TN38 .... 135 F4
Chatsworth Ave BN10 .... 167 A1
Chatsworth Cl BN10 ...... 178 A8
Chatsworth Gdns BN10 ... 167 B1
Chatsworth Pk BN10 ...... 167 B1
Chatsworth Rd BN1 .... 163 E8
Chaucer Ave **3** RH19 .... 1 C1
Chaucer Ct **3** RH16 ..... 50 D5
Chaucer Wlk BN23 .... 174 E3
Chawbrook Rd BN22 ..... 185 B4
Cheal Cl BN43 .... 161 A6
Cheapside BN1 .... 189 A6
Cheeleys RH17 .... 33 C5
Chelgates TN39 .... 156 C2
Chelmsford Ct **3** BN20 .. 184 F1
Chelsea Arc RH16 .... 50 E4
Chelsea Cl TN40 .... 157 D4
Chelston Ave BN3 .... 162 D7
Cheltenham Pl BN1 .... 189 A6
Chelwood Cl BN1 .... 143 C6
Chelwood Ct RH15 .... 73 A4
Chelwood Gate Rd TN22 ... 35 B6
Chelworth Rd BN22 ...... 173 D2
Chene Rd BN10 .... 178 F6
Chenies Cl TN2 .... 17 A8
Chepbourne Rd TN40 ..... 157 C4
Chepstow Ct BN1 .... 143 F5
Chequer Grange RH18 .... 11 E1
Chequer Rd RH19 .... 1 E3
Chequers Cl TN6 .... 26 A2
Chequers Way TN6 .... 26 A2
Cherington Cl BN6 .... 97 B5
Cherith Cotts **3** I TN21 ... 82 A6
Cheriton St BN20 .... 184 C4
Cherry Cl RH15 .... 72 E3
Cherry Clack TN21 .... 83 D6
Cherry Cotts TN22 .... 54 F4
Cherry Garden Rd BN20 ... 184 B3
Cherry Gdns
 Heathfield TN21 .... 82 B5
 High Hurstwood TN22 ..... 56 B8
Cherry Side BN27 .... 152 A7
Cherry Tree Cl TN37 ...... 159 D8
Cherry Tree Cl TN21 ...... 106 F7
Cherry Tree Gdns TN40 ... 157 F6
Cherry Tree Rd TN2 .... 7 E1
Cherrywood **5** BN1 ...... 142 E3
Cherwell Cl BN26 .... 173 F5
Cherwell Ct TN21 .... 82 A8
Cherwell Rd TN21 .... 82 A8
Chesham Pl BN2 .... 164 D4
Chesham St BN2 .... 164 D4
Cheshire Ct **8** BN22 .... 185 B4
Chesnut Cl BN27 .... 129 A1
Chester Ave TN2 .... 8 C3
Chester Ct **8** BN3 .... 163 E7
Chester Terr BN1 .... 143 A1
Chesterfield Gdns BN20 .. 188 E8
Chesterfield Rd BN20 ..... 188 E8
Chesterton Ave BN25 ..... 181 B3
Chesterton Cl RH19 .... 10 F7

Chesterton Dr BN25 .... 181 B3
Chestnut Ave TN4 .... 8 B8
Chestnut Cl
 Broad Oak TN31 .... 90 B5
 Burgess Hill RH15 .... 73 B5
 East Grinstead RH19 ...... 2 A1
 Eastbourne BN22 .... 173 E2
 Herstmonceux BN27 ...... 130 E6
 Royal Tunbridge Wells TN4 . 8 A8
Chestnut Cotts
 Fletching TN22 .... 53 F3
 1 Heathfield TN21 ...... 82 A7
Chestnut Dr BN26 .... 173 A6
Chestnut Pl TN8 .... 4 A5
Chestnut Wlk BN27 .... 173 A6
Chestnut Wlk Bexhill TN39 156 C5
 Felcourt RH19 .... 1 C8
Chestnuts Cl RH16 .... 51 A7
Chestnuts The
 Haywards Heath RH16 .... 50 F7
 The Moor TN18 .... 45 F8
Chet Nole RH19 .... 1 D2
Cheviot Cl BN23 .... 174 C3
Cheviots The TN34 .... 137 C4
Cheyne Ct BN43 .... 161 C2
Chichester Cl Bexhill TN39 157 B6
 15 Brighton BN2 .... 164 D4
 Eastbourne BN22 .... 173 E2
 Hove BN3 .... 141 E4
 Peacehaven BN10 .... 178 F7
 Saltdean BN2 .... 177 C5
 Seaford BN25 .... 180 E3
Chichester Ct TN39 .... 156 C3
Chichester Dr E BN2 ...... 177 C5
Chichester Dr W BN2 ..... 177 B5
Chichester Pl BN2 .... 164 D4
Chichester Rd
 Hastings TN38 .... 136 B2
 Seaford BN25 .... 180 E3
Chichester Terr **19** BN2 .. 164 D4
Chichester Way RH15 ..... 73 C5
Chick Hill TN35 .... 139 B8
Chicks La TN17 .... 20 F2
Chiddingly Cl BN2 .... 164 D4
Chiddingly Cty Prim Sch
 BN8 .... 127 E7
Chieveley Dr TN2 .... 8 D1
Chilcomb RH15 .... 73 C1
Chilham Cl BN23 .... 174 D2
Chillies La TN22, TN6 ...... 39 E2
Chilling St RH19 .... 21 D3
Chillis Wood Rd RH16 .... 50 D5
Chilsham La BN27 .... 130 E7
Chilston Cl TN4 .... 8 A5
Chilston Rd TN4 .... 8 A5
Chiltern Cl
 Eastbourne BN23 .... 174 D3
 Shoreham-by-Sea BN43 ... 161 C8
Chiltern Ct BN26 .... 173 A7
Chiltern Dr TN34 .... 137 B3
Chiltern Wlk TN2 .... 8 D2
Chillington Cl
 Burgess Hill RH15 .... 72 F5
 Saltdean BN2 .... 177 C6
Chillington La BN7 .... 100 D3
Chillington Way BN2 ..... 177 C6
Chiswick Pl BN21 .... 185 A2
Chitcombe Rd TN31 .... 89 E5
Chitcombe Rd Wlk TN34 .. 137 A5
Chorley Ave BN2 .... 177 B6
Chown's Hill TN34 .... 137 A6
Chownes Mead La
 RH16, RH17 .... 50 B4
Chrisdory Rd BN41 .... 140 F3
Christ Church Ave **1** TN1 ... 8 A2
Christ Church CE Prim Sch
 TN37 .... 136 C1
Christie Ave BN8 .... 124 D6
Christie Rd BN27 .... 123 A2
Christies RH19 .... 10 D8
Christopher Rd RH19 ...... 1 E1
Church App TN22 .... 79 B5
Church Ave
 Haywards Heath RH16 .... 50 E4
 Westham BN24 .... 175 A6
Church Bailey BN24 ...... 175 A5
Church Bailey Ct BN24 ... 175 A5
Church Cl Brighton BN1 ... 142 F5
 Burgess Hill RH15 .... 73 A3
 Lower Willingdon BN20 ... 173 A4
Church Ct
 3 Haywards Heath RH16 . 50 E4
 Hove BN3 .... 141 F1
Church Farm Cl TN19 ..... 44 C1
Church Gn BN43 .... 161 C7
Church Hill Bexhill TN39 .. 156 D4
 Brighton BN1 .... 142 E7
 Etchingham TN19 .... 44 B2
 Newhaven BN9 .... 179 C7
 Pyecombe BN45 .... 119 C6
 Ringmer BN8 .... 124 D6

Church Hill Ave TN39 ..... 156 D4
Church House Cl BN24 ... 141 C5
Church in the Wood La
 TN38 .... 135 F3
Church La
 Burgess Hill RH16, RH17 .. 73 F6
 Buxted TN22 .... 56 C5
 Catsfield TN33 .... 133 E8
 Clayhill TN31 .... 67 E4
 Danehill RH17 .... 34 A3
 Ditchling BN6 .... 98 D3
 East Grinstead RH19 ...... 1 F1
 1 Eastbourne BN21 ..... 184 D3
 Etchingham TN19 .... 44 C1
 Frant TN3 .... 17 F4
 Guestling Green TN35 .... 116 B1
 Hellingly BN27 .... 129 A6
 Hooe TN33 .... 155 C7
 Horsted Keynes RH17 .... 33 C5
 Jevington BN26 .... 183 C7
 Kingston near Lewes BN7 145 D5
 Lewes, South Malling BN7 123 D3
 Lewes, St Anne's BN7 .... 146 B8
 Ninfield TN33 .... 133 B5
 Northbridge Street TN32 .. 64 C5
 Northiam TN31 .... 67 C6
 Peasmarsh TN31 .... 92 B8
 Pevensey BN24 .... 175 B6
 Pyecombe BN45 .... 119 C6
 Ripe BN27, BN8 .... 149 E8
 Seaford BN25 .... 180 E2
 Southwick BN42, BN43 ... 161 D7
 Westfield TN35 .... 114 E3
Church Marks La BN8 .... 104 F5
Church Mead BN6 .... 98 B3
Church Mews BN20 .... 173 B1
Church Pas **5** TN34 ..... 160 A4
Church Path BN27 .... 129 A5
Church Pl BN2 .... 164 E4
Church Rd Barcombe BN8 . 101 E2
 Burgess Hill RH15 .... 73 A3
 Buxted TN22 .... 56 B4
 Catsfield TN33 .... 133 F7
 Crowborough TN6 .... 25 F2
 Flowers Green BN27 ...... 131 A1
 Hastings TN37 .... 159 D7
 Haywards Heath RH16 .... 50 F4
 Hove BN3 .... 163 B6
 Lamberhurst TN3 .... 20 C6
 Lewes BN7 .... 123 C1
 Mountfield TN32 .... 87 B5
 Newick BN8 .... 76 E6
 Polegate BN26 .... 173 C2
 Portslade-by-Sea BN41 ... 162 B7
 Rotherfield TN6 .... 39 A8
 Royal Tunbridge Wells
 TN1, TN4 .... 8 A3
 Sandhurst Cross TN18 .... 46 F4
 Scaynes Hill RH17 .... 51 F3
Church Sq TN31 .... 93 C5
Church St Bexhill TN40 ... 157 D5
 Brighton BN1 .... 189 A5
 Cowden TN8 .... 4 B5
 Eastbourne BN20, BN21 .. 184 D3
 Hartfield TN7 .... 13 D4
 Hastings TN35 .... 137 C3
 Old Heathfield TN21 ...... 82 B6
 Portslade-by-Sea BN41 ... 162 B7
 Seaford BN25 .... 180 E2
 Ticehurst TN5 .... 31 D1
 Uckfield TN22 .... 78 C7
 Willingdon BN22 .... 173 C2
Church Twitten **15** BN7 .. 123 D1
Church Vale Rd TN40 ...... 157 D5
Church Way **5** BN2 ...... 189 B6
Church Wlk RH15 .... 73 A3
Church Wood Cty Prim Sch
 TN38 .... 135 E4
Church Wood Dr TN38 ... 135 E4
Church Wood Way TN38 .. 135 F2
Churchdale Rd BN22 ..... 185 C6
Churchdale Pl BN22 ...... 185 B6
Churchdale Rd BN22 ..... 185 C6
Churchfield
 East Dean BN20 .... 187 B8
 Westfield TN35 .... 114 D3
Churchfields TN22 .... 35 C4
Churchfields TN35 .... 137 D5
Churchill Cl BN20 .... 184 D3
Churchill Ct TN38 .... 136 B2
Churchill Ho BN3 .... 141 E2
Churchill Rd
 Heathfield TN21 .... 82 B6
 Lewes BN7 .... 123 B3
 Seaford BN25 .... 180 D5
Churchill Sq BN1 .... 189 F5
Churchill Way RH15 ...... 73 C2
Churchland La TN33 ...... 88 E3
Churchsettle La TN5 ...... 42 B7
Churchyard Cotts TN3 .... 7 A8
Chyngton Ave BN25 ...... 181 B4

Chyngton Cl BN23 .... 174 A4
Chyngton Cty Prim Sch
 BN25 .... 181 B4
Chyngton Gdns BN25 .... 181 B4
Chyngton Ho BN25 .... 181 C2
Chyngton La BN25 .... 181 C3
Chyngton La N BN25 ..... 181 C3
Chyngton Pl BN25 .... 181 B2
Chyngton Rd BN25 .... 181 C2
Chyngton Way BN25 ..... 181 C2
Cider House Wlk BN8 .... 105 A5
Cinder Hill Chailey BN8 ... 75 F3
 Cinder Hill RH19 .... 21 B1
Cinderford La BN27 ...... 129 F8
Cinque Ports St TN31 ..... 93 B5
Cinque Ports Way
 Hastings TN38 .... 158 E6
 Seaford BN25 .... 181 C4
Cinquefoil BN10 .... 178 C8
Circus Par BN1 .... 189 A7
Circus St BN2 .... 189 A5
Circus The BN23 .... 185 D8
Cissbury Ave BN10 .... 178 E7
Cissbury Cres BN2 .... 177 E5
Cissbury Rd
 Burgess Hill RH15 .... 72 E4
 Hove BN3 .... 163 E7
Civic Way
 Burgess Hill RH15 .... 73 A3
 Royal Tunbridge Wells TN1 . 8 A2
Clackhams La TN6 .... 38 D7
Clair Ct **1** RH16 .... 50 E5
Clair Rd RH16 .... 50 E5
Clanricarde Gdns **1** TN1 ... 8 A3
Clanricarde Rd **2** TN1 .... 8 A3
Clapham La BN26 .... 182 A8
Claphatch La TN5 .... 31 A5
Clappers The TN32 .... 64 B4
Clare Rd BN7 .... 123 A2
Clare Wlk BN2 .... 164 D5
Claremont **9** TN34 ..... 159 E7
Claremont Cty Prim Sch
 TN2 .... 8 B2
Claremont Gdns TN1, TN2 .. 8 B2
Claremont Rd
 Bexhill TN39 .... 157 B7
 Newhaven BN9 .... 168 F1
 Royal Tunbridge Wells TN1 . 8 B2
 Seaford BN25 .... 180 D3
Claremont Rise TN22 ..... 55 C1
Claremont Sch TN33 ..... 114 B1
Clarence Ct TN37 .... 136 B4
Clarence Dr **2** RH19 .... 10 F7
Clarence Rd
 Eastbourne BN22 .... 185 B4
 Hastings TN37 .... 136 C1
 Royal Tunbridge Wells
 TN1, TN4 .... 8 A3
Clarence Row TN1 .... 8 A3
Clarence Sq BN1 .... 189 F5
Clarendon Ct TN37 .... 136 B4
Clarendon Gdns TN2 ..... 8 A1
Clarendon Ho **2** BN3 .... 163 B7
Clarendon Pl **15**
 Brighton BN2 .... 164 C4
 Portslade-by-Sea BN41 ... 162 C6
Clarendon Rd Hove BN3 ... 163 B7
 Shoreham-by-Sea
 BN42, BN43 .... 161 D8
Clarendon Terr **16** BN2 .. 164 D4
Clarendon Villas BN3 .... 163 B7
Clarendon Way TN2 ...... 8 A1
Claridge TN7 .... 8 A4
Clarke Ave BN3 .... 141 F3
Clarke Ct BN41 .... 162 F6
Clarks Ind Est BN3 .... 163 B8
Claverham Cl TN33 ...... 112 B4
Claverham Com Coll
 TN33 .... 112 A4
Claverham Way TN33 .... 112 B4
Clavering Wlk TN39 ...... 156 B2
Claxton Cl BN21 .... 184 D5
Claxton Rd TN40 .... 158 A5
Clay Corner BN8 .... 101 F6
Clay Hill Rd TN3 .... 19 D6
Clayfields BN10 .... 178 B7
Clays Cl RH19 .... 10 E8
Clayton Ave BN6 .... 97 F3
Clayton Dr RH15 .... 72 F1
Clayton Hill BN45, BN6 ... 119 D7
Clayton Mill Rd BN24 .... 174 B5
Clayton Pk BN6 .... 97 E4
Clayton Rd Brighton BN2 ... 164 D7
 Ditchling BN6 .... 98 C3
Clayton Way BN3 .... 141 F3
Clayton's La TN3 .... 5 E2
Clearwater La RH17 ...... 52 A3
Clearwaters La RH15 ..... 73 D8
Cleavelands BN22 .... 173 B2
Clement Hill Rd TN34 .... 137 B3

Clement La BN26 .... 173 A5
Clementine Ave BN25 .... 180 D5
Clerks Acre Keymer BN6 .... 98 A3
 Keymer BN6 .... 98 A4
Clermont Ct **5** BN1 ..... 142 E2
Clermont Rd BN1 .... 142 E2
Clermont Terr BN1 .... 142 E2
Cleve Cl TN22 .... 79 B5
Cleve Terr BN7 .... 146 B8
Clevedon Rd TN39 .... 157 A6
Clevedown BN7 .... 146 A8
Cleveland TN2 .... 8 D4
Cleveland Cl BN23 .... 174 C3
Cleveland Gdns RH15 .... 73 B2
Cleveland Rd BN1 .... 143 A1
Clevelands RH16 .... 50 E6
Cliff App BN2 .... 164 F4
Cliff Ave BN10 .... 178 E5
Cliff Cl BN25 .... 180 F1
Cliff Ct TN38 .... 158 D6
Cliff End La TN35 .... 139 B7
Cliff Gdns Seaford BN25 ... 180 F1
 Telscombe Cliffs BN10 .... 177 F4
Cliff Park Cl BN10 .... 178 F7
Cliff Rd Brighton BN2 .... 164 F4
 Eastbourne BN20 .... 188 E7
 Seaford BN25 .... 180 F1
Cliff The BN2 .... 164 F4
Cliff Way TN35 .... 138 F5
Cliffe High St BN7 .... 123 D1
Cliffe Ind Est BN7 .... 146 F8
Clifford Ave BN21 .... 184 C6
Clifford Ct **4** Bexhill TN40 157 C4
 Crowborough TN6 .... 25 F2
Clifford Rd **3** TN40 ..... 157 C4
Clifton Cl BN22 .... 184 D8
Clifton Cotts TN1 .... 8 D8
Clifton Ct TN34 .... 159 E8
Clifton Hill BN1 .... 189 F6
Clifton Ho BN22 .... 184 D8
Clifton Mews BN1 .... 189 F6
Clifton Pl Brighton BN1 ... 163 E6
 Royal Tunbridge Wells TN1 . 8 B2
Clifton Rd Brighton BN1 ... 189 F6
 Burgess Hill RH15 .... 72 D5
 Hastings TN37 .... 137 C3
 Newhaven BN9 .... 179 D7
 Royal Tunbridge Wells TN1 . 8 C7
Clifton Rise TN40 .... 157 F5
Clifton St BN1 .... 189 F7
Clifton Terr BN1 .... 189 F6
Clifton Way BN10 .... 178 A8
Cliftonville Ct **6** BN3 .... 163 B7
Cliftonville Rd TN38 ...... 158 D6
Cliftonville Way TN38 .... 158 D6
Climping Cl RH16 .... 50 D3
Clinch Green Ave TN39 ... 156 F7
Clinton Cres TN38 .... 136 B1
Clinton Hill RH7 .... 2 A8
Clinton La **2** BN25 ..... 180 E3
Clinton Pl BN25 .... 180 E3
Clinton Way TN35 .... 138 F5
Clive Ave TN35 .... 160 C6
Clive Villas TN33 .... 112 E3
Cliveden Ct BN23 .... 142 E3
Clock House La TN22 ..... 35 C4
Clock Tower Ct TN39 ..... 157 B3
Clockhouse TN2 .... 8 F6
Cloisters BN9 .... 179 C7
Cloisters The Battle TN33 . 112 D6
 Eastbourne BN22 .... 173 C2
 Hastings TN37 .... 159 D7
Close Eight BN23 .... 174 E3
Close Eighteen BN23 ..... 174 E3
Close Eleven BN23 .... 174 E3
Close Fifteen **6** BN23 .... 174 E2
Close Five BN23 .... 174 E3
Close Four BN23 .... 174 E3
Close Fourteen BN23 ..... 174 E3
Close Nine BN23 .... 174 E3
Close Nineteen BN23 ..... 174 E3
Close One BN23 .... 174 E2
Close Seven BN23 .... 174 E2
Close Seventeen BN23 .... 174 E2
Close Six BN23 .... 174 E3
Close Sixteen BN23 .... 174 E2
Close Ten BN23 .... 174 E2
Close The Blackboys TN22 . 80 B6
 Brighton BN1 .... 142 E5
 Burgess Hill RH15 .... 73 C4
 Crowborough TN6 .... 25 E3
 East Grinstead RH19 ..... 10 D8
 Eastbourne BN20 .... 184 B8
 Fairlight TN35 .... 138 C4
 Friston BN20 .... 183 A1
 Groombridge TN3 .... 15 C6
 Hassocks BN6 .... 97 F4
 Lower Willingdon BN22 ... 173 C3

Close The
Newhaven BN9 .... 168 F2
Rye TN31 .... 93 A6
Seaford BN25 .... 180 F2
Close Three BN23 .... 174 D2
Close Twelve BN23 .... 174 E2
Close Twenty BN23 .... 174 E2
Close Twentyfive BN23 .... 174 D2
Close Twentyfour 4
BN23 .... 174 E2
Close Two BN23 .... 174 D2
Cloudesley Rd TN37 .... 159 C8
Clovelly Ho BN26 .... 173 A7
Clover Ct 2 RH16 .... 50 E4
Clover Way BN41 .... 141 B2
Cloverlea TN34 .... 136 C5
Clovers End BN1 .... 143 B7
Cluny St BN7 .... 146 C8
Clyde Pk BN27 .... 152 C7
Clyde Rd Brighton BN1 ..... 189 A8
Hastings TN37, TN38 ..... 159 C7
Coach and Horses La
RH17 .... 34 C6
Coach & Horses Pas 18
TN2 .... 8 A2
Coach La RH17 .... 34 C6
Coast Rd BN24 .... 176 B7
Coastal Counties Ho 18
BN2 .... 189 B6
Coastguard Cl BN24 .... 176 D8
Coastguard Cotts
Camber TN31 .... 94 D2
Normans' Bay BN24 .... 176 D8
Coastguard La TN35 .... 138 C4
Coastguard Sq
3 Eastbourne BN22 ..... 185 C4
Rye Harbour TN31 .... 94 A3
Coastguards TN35 .... 139 C8
Coates Ct 11 BN42 .... 161 E7
Cobald Rd BN24 .... 175 E5
Cobbett's Ride TN2 .... 7 E1
Cobbetts Mead RH16 .... 51 B3
Cobblers Field TN19 .... 61 A3
Cobbold Ave BN21 .... 184 C5
Cobden Pl 5 BN27 .... 152 C7
Cobden Rd BNC 164 C7
Cobdown La TN22 .... 55 C5
Cobham Towers TN40 .... 157 F4
Cobhams TN3 .... 7 A8
Cobourg Pl 6 TN34 .... 160 A4
Cobton Dr BN3 .... 142 A3
Coburn Ct 12 BN27 .... 123 D1
Cochrane Cl BN23 .... 185 E7
Cockcrow Wood TN37 ...... 136 D5
Cockfield La BN8 .... 76 B3
Cockhaise Cotts RH16 ...... 52 A8
Cockmount La TN5 .... 29 F5
Cockshut Rd BN7 .... 146 C8
Cogger's Cross TN21 .... 106 F3
Cogger's La TN21 .... 106 F4
Coggins Mill La TN20 .... 40 D4
Coghurst Rd TN35 .... 137 C4
Colbourne Ave BN21 .... 143 D2
Colbourne Rd BN3 .... 163 E7
Colchester Vale RH18 .... 11 E2
Colchins RH15 .... 72 F1
Coldean Cty Inf Sch
BN1 .... 143 D6
Coldean Cty Jun Sch
BN1 .... 143 D6
Coldean La BN1 .... 143 E6
Coldharbour Cl TN6 .... 26 A1
Coldharbour La
Newick BN8 .... 76 A7
Rye Foreign TN31 .... 69 E3
Coldharbour Rd
Lower Dicker BN27 .... 128 B2
White Post TN11 .... 5 E8
Coldthorn La BN26, BN27 . 152 A4
Coldwaltham La RH15 .... 73 D2
Colebrook Rd
Brighton BN1 .... 142 D4
Royal Tunbridge Wells TN4 . 8 C8
Southwick BN42 .... 161 F7
Colebrooke Rd TN39 .... 157 A4
Coleman Ave BN3 .... 162 E7
Coleman St BN2 .... 189 B7
Colemans Hatch Rd
RH18, TN7 .... 23 C6
Coleridge St BN3 .... 163 C7
Coleridge Wlk 7 BN23 ..... 174 E2
Coles Ct TN2 .... 8 C3
Colgate Cl BN2 .... 164 F6
Coll of St Barnabas RC 1 F8
Coll of the Holy Child Jesus
TN37 .... 159 D7
College Cl
East Grinstead RH19 ...... 1 F1
College Cl
Portslade-by-Sea BN41 ... 140 F3
College Dr TN2 .... 8 D4
College Gdns BN2 .... 164 C4
College La
East Grinstead RH19 ...... 1 F1
Hurst Wickham BN6 ...... 97 C6
Connaught Rd
6 Eastbourne BN21 ..... 185 A2
Hove BN3 .... 163 A6
Seaford BN25 .... 180 C3
Connaught Terr BN3 .... 163 B7
Connaught Way TN4 .... 7 F5
Connell Dr BN2 .... 164 F1
Conqueror Ind Est TN38 ... 135 F6
Conqueror Rd TN38 .... 158 E7
Conqueror Terr TN33 .... 88 F1
Conquest Hospl TN37 .... 136 D6
Consort Way RH15 .... 72 E2
Constable Rd BN23 .... 174 D1
Constable Way TN40 .... 157 E5
Convent of The
Holy Child Jesus TN20 ... 40 A3
Conway Ct
9 Hastings TN38 .... 159 B6
1 Hove BN3 .... 163 B7
Conway Pl BN3 .... 163 A8
Conway St BN3 .... 163 B8
Cooden Beach Golf Course
TN39 .... 156 A2
Cooden Beach Sta TN39 ... 156 B2
Cooden Cl TN30 .... 156 C3
Cooden Dr TN39 .... 156 E2
Cooden Sea Rd
Bexhill TN39 .... 156 B2
Bexhill TN39 .... 156 C3
Cook Ave BN23 .... 185 E6
Cookham Dene TN40 .... 157 C4
Cooksbridge Rd BN2 .... 164 E6
Cooksbridge Sta BN8 .... 123 A7
Cookstown Cl TN33 .... 132 F6
Coolham Dr BN2 .... 164 E7
Coombe Cl BN27 .... 131 B5
Coombe Hall Sch RH19 .... 10 D6
Coombe Hill Rd RH19 .... 10 D6
Coombe La TN5 .... 41 C7
Coombe Lea 22 BN3 .... 163 C6
Coombe Meadow BN2 ...... 166 E3
Coombe Rd
Brighton BN2 .... 143 D1
Eastbourne BN20 .... 184 C4
Lewes BN7 .... 123 D2
Coombe Rise BN2 .... 166 D3
Coombe Road
Eastbourne BN23 .... 174 C4
Hastings TN34 .... 137 B4
Cotswold Pl 7 BN2 .... 164 F5
Cotswolds The BN42 .... 161 E7
Cottage Cl 2 BN9 .... 168 D1
Cottage Homes BN6 .... 98 E6
Cottage La
Hankham BN24 .... 152 E1
Westfield TN3, TN35 ...... 114 D7
Cottenden Rd TN5 .... 43 A6
Cottesmore St Mary's
RC Prim Sch BN3 .... 163 D8
Coulstock Rd BN6 .... 72 C4
Council Cotts TN32 .... 63 F3
Council Hos
Ginger's Green BN27 ..... 130 C6
Rushlake Green TN21 ..... 83 D1
Countess of Thanet's
Almshouses TN8 .... 3 F3
County Oak Ave BN1 .... 143 B6
Courcels BN2 .... 164 E3
Course The BN7 .... 146 B8
Court Cl Brighton BN1 ...... 142 E7
East Grinstead RH19 ...... 1 F1
Court Cres RH19 .... 1 F1
Court Farm Cl BN9 .... 168 A2
Court Farm Rd
Hove BN3 .... 142 A2
Newhaven BN9 .... 179 C5
Rottingdean BN2 .... 165 F3
Court Meadow TN6 .... 39 B8
Court Meadow Cl TN6 ...... 39 B7
Court Meadow Sch RH17 . 50 A8
Court Ord Cotts BN2 .... 165 F3
Court Ord Rd BN2 .... 165 F3
Court Rd
Eastbourne BN2 .... 173 F2
Lewes BN7 .... 123 D2
Royal Tunbridge Wells TN4 . 7 F4
Court The BN20 .... 173 B1
Courtenwell TN3 .... 6 E4
Courthope Ave TN5 .... 29 F4
Courthope Dr TN39 .... 156 F5
Courthouse St TN34 .... 160 B4
Courtland Rd BN26 .... 173 A5
Courtlands
12 Brighton BN2 .... 189 B6
Cordons BN7 .... 145 D5
Cormorant Cl BN23 .... 174 C2
Corn Ct 7 BN2 .... 164 C6
Cornelius Ave BN9 .... 179 A5
Corner Gn BN8 .... 124 D5
Cornfield Cl BN25 .... 180 F3
Cornfield Gn BN27 .... 129 C1
Cornfield La 6 BN21 .... 185 A2
Cornfield Rd
Eastbourne BN21 .... 185 A2
Seaford BN25 .... 180 F3
Cornfield Terr
11 Eastbourne BN21 ..... 185 A2
Hastings TN37 .... 136 C1
Cornford Cl
Burgess Hill RH15 .... 72 E5
Crowborough TN6 .... 26 A1
Pembury TN2 .... 9 B6
Cornford La TN2 .... 9 B5
Cornford Pk TN2 .... 9 C6
Cornish Cl BN23, BN24 .... 174 B4
Cornmill Gdns BN26 .... 172 E4
Cornwall Ave BN10 .... 178 E6
Cornwall Ct
Eastbourne BN26 .... 184 C5
2 Hove BN3 .... 163 C7
Cornwall Gdns
Brighton BN1 .... 142 E2
5 East Grinstead RH19 ... 10 F8
Cornwall Ho BN1 .... 142 E2
Cornwall Rd TN39 .... 157 B3
Cornwallis Cl BN23 .... 185 F7
Cornwallis Gdns TN34 ...... 159 E8
Cornwallis St 5 TN34 ...... 159 F8
Cornwallis Terr TN34 .... 159 E8
Coronation Cotts
Berner's Hill TN5 .... 31 F2
Burwash TN19 .... 62 A6
Northbridge Street TN2 ... 64 C5
Coronation Gdns
Battle TN33 .... 112 F5
Hurst Green TN19 .... 44 F3
Coronation Rd RH19 .... 10 E7
Coronation St 7 BN2 .... 164 C7
Corseley Rd TN3 .... 15 B5
Corsica Cl BN25 .... 180 F2
Corsica Rd BN25 .... 180 F1
Costells Edge RH17 .... 51 F3
Costume Mus TN40 .... 157 D4
Cotchford Hill TN7 .... 13 D1
Cotchford La TN7 .... 13 C1
Cotswold Cl
Eastbourne BN23 .... 174 C4
Hastings TN34 .... 137 B4
Courtlands
5 Hastings TN38 .... 159 B6
Haywards Heath RH16 ... 50 E3
Newhaven BN9 .... 179 C7
Courtlands Rd BN22 .... 185 A5
Courtney Gate BN3 .... 163 B5
Courtney King Ct 8
BN2 .... 164 C5
Courtney King Ho 1
BN2 .... 164 D4
Courtyard The
East Grinstead RH19 ...... 2 B1
Falmer BN1 .... 144 D6
Hastings TN34 .... 136 E1
Cousley Wood Rd TN5 ...... 30 C7
Coventry Ct BN22 .... 185 D6
Coventry Rd TN37, TN38 .. 136 B3
Coventry St BN1 .... 163 E8
Coverdale Ave TN39 .... 156 C3
Coverdale Ct RH19 .... 1 C3
Covers The BN25 .... 180 F2
Covert The TN39 .... 156 C2
Cow La BN26 .... 181 F8
Cowden Cl TN18 .... 45 E8
Cowden Cross TN8 .... 4 C7
Cowden La TN18 .... 45 E7
Cowden Mews TN8 .... 4 A5
Cowden Rd BN2 .... 177 D4
Cowden Sta TN8 .... 4 D8
Cowden Vlla TN38 .... 136 A2
Cowdens Cl BN3 .... 141 D4
Cowdray Cl TN39 .... 156 D6
Cowdray Ct 1 BN3 .... 163 D7
Cowdray Park Rd TN39 .... 156 C6
Cowfold Rd BN2 .... 164 E5
Cowley Dr BN2 .... 165 F7
Cownwy Ct BN2 .... 165 F1
Cowper St BN3 .... 163 A7
Cox Gr RH15 .... 72 E5
Cox's Cotts BN7 .... 99 E7
Crabtree Ave BN1 .... 143 B5
Crabtree Ho 1 TN38 .... 159 B6
Crackendale Field BN8 ..... 124 E6
Cradle Hill Cty Prim Sch
BN25 .... 181 A5
Cradle Hill Ind Est BN25 .. 181 B5
Cradle Hill Rd BN25 .... 181 B5
Craig Cl TN33 .... 135 A6
Craignair Ave BN1 .... 142 F7
Cranborne Ave BN20 .... 173 B1
Cranbourne St BN1 .... 189 F5
Cranbrook 18 BN2 .... 189 B6
Cranbrook Rd TN37 .... 136 C1
Cranedown BN7 .... 146 B7
Cranfield Rd TN40 .... 157 C4
Cranleigh Ave BN2 .... 177 B5
Cranleigh Cl TN39 .... 157 A4
Cranley Ct BN3 .... 162 D7
Cranmer Ave BN3 .... 141 F1
Cranmer Cl BN7 .... 123 D2
Cranston Ave TN39 .... 157 A4
Cranston Cl TN39 .... 156 F4
Cranston Rd RH19 .... 1 F2
Cranston Rise TN39 .... 156 F4
Cranwell Rd TN4 .... 7 C4
Craven Rd BN2 .... 164 D6
Crawfurd Way RH19 .... 1 F3
Crawley Cres BN22 .... 173 E2
Crawley Rd BN1 .... 143 D6
Crayford Rd BN2 .... 164 C6
Crazy La TN33 .... 113 E7
Crecy Cl TN37, TN38 .... 135 F7
Creek The 11 TN34 .... 160 B4
Crendon Pk TN4 .... 8 A8
Crescent Cl
Burgess Hill RH15 .... 73 B3
Woodingdean BN2 .... 165 E8
Crescent Dr N BN2 .... 165 E8
Crescent Dr S BN2 .... 165 E7
Crescent Mansions BN2 ... 189 B8
Crescent Rd
Brighton BN2 .... 164 C4
East Grinstead RH19 ...... 1 D1
Royal Tunbridge Wells
TN1, TN2 .... 8 B3
Crescent The
Brighton BN2 .... 143 E2
Eastbourne BN20, BN21 .. 184 B5
Felcourt RH19 .... 1 C8
Groombridge TN3 .... 15 C7
Hastings TN37 .... 136 C3
Keymer BN6 .... 98 B3
Lower Willingdon BN20 .. 173 A3
Southwick BN42 .... 161 F8
Westham BN24 .... 173 A3
Crest Rd BN9 .... 168 F1
Crest Way BN41 .... 141 B3
Cresta Cl BN26 .... 173 A7

Cresta Rd BN9 .... 179 A6
Crestway Par **1** BN1 .... 143 C2
Crestway The BN1 .... 143 C2
Cricket Ct RH19 .... 1 E3
Cricketers Field TN32 .... 65 E1
Cricketfield BN8 .... 76 D8
Cricketfield Rd BN25 .... 180 F2
Cricketing La BN27 .... 130 C4
Criers La TN20, TN22 .... 52 E6
Crink Hill BN8 .... 101 F3
Cripland Cl RH16 .... 51 B6
Cripps Ave BN10 .... 167 D1
Crisp Rd BN7 .... 123 A3
Crittle's Ct TN5 .... 29 F4
Crockers Hatch Cnr TN3 ...... 6 D2
Crockers La TN31 .... 67 B8
Crocks Dean BN10 .... 167 D2
Croft Ave BN42 .... 161 F7
Croft Cl BN26 .... 173 A4
Croft Ct
  2 Eastbourne BN22 ..... 185 B3
  6 Seaford BN25 .... 180 E3
Croft Dr BN41 .... 141 A3
Croft La BN25 .... 180 E3
Croft Rd Brighton BN1 ...... 142 D4
  Crowborough TN6 .... 25 F2
  Hastings TN34 .... 160 A4
Croft Terr **2** TN34 .... 160 A4
Croft The Bexhill TN39 ... 157 A4
  Hassocks BN6 .... 97 F5
  Hastings TN34 .... 160 A4
  Lower Dicker BN27 .... 128 B8
  Southwick BN42 .... 161 E8
  Willingdon BN20 .... 173 B1
Croft Works BN27 .... 152 B7
Crofton Park Ave TN39 .... 156 E3
Croham Rd TN6 .... 25 F3
Cromer Way BN27 .... 129 A1
Cromer Wlk **3** TN34 .... 136 F1
Cromleigh Way BN42 .... 140 E2
Cromwell Ct **3** BN3 .... 163 D7
Cromwell Pl **1** RH19 ... 10 F7
Cromwell Rd
  Burgess Hill RH15 .... 72 F3
  Hove BN3 .... 163 C7
  Royal Tunbridge Wells TN2 . 8 C3
Cromwell St BN2 .... 164 C7
Crooked La BN25 .... 180 F2
Cross La TN5 .... 31 D2
Cross Lane Gdns TN5 ...... 31 D1
Cross Levels Way
  BN21, BN22 .... 184 E7
Cross Rd BN3 .... 161 D8
Cross St Brighton BN1 .... 189 A7
  Hastings TN37 .... 159 C2
  Hove BN1, BN3 .... 163 D5
  Polegate BN26 .... 173 A6
Cross Way BN7 .... 123 A2
Cross-in-Hand CE Prim Sch
  TN21 .... 81 F7
Crossbush Rd BN2 .... 164 E6
Crossroad Cl BN42 .... 161 D8
Crossway The
  Brighton BN1 .... 143 B2
  Portslade-by-Sea BN41 .. 141 A2
  Royal Tunbridge Wells TN4 . 7 D2
Crossways Ave RH19 .... 1 C3
Crossways The
  Broad Oak TN21 .... 90 B4
  Hassocks BN6 .... 97 C4
  Stone Cross BN24 .... 174 A6
Crouch Cl BN20 .... 173 B1
Crouch La Linkhill TN18 .... 47 D6
  Lower Street TN33 .... 133 B3
  Seaford BN25 .... 180 E2
Crouchfield Cl **2** BN25 . 180 F2
Crowborough Beacon
  Golf Course TN6 .... 37 C7
Crowborough Hill TN6 ...... 26 D2
Crowborough Rd
  Hastings TN35 .... 137 E4
  Marlpits TN22 .... 35 E6
  Saltdean BN2 .... 177 D4
Crowders La TN33 .... 111 D3
Crowhurst CE Prim Sch
  TN33 .... 134 F5
Crowhurst Cl BN23 .... 174 A4
Crowhurst La TN39 .... 157 C7
Crowhurst Rd
  Brighton BN1 .... 143 C7
  Green Street TN33, TN38 . 135 B3
  Hastings TN38 .... 135 E2
  Crowhurst Sta TN33 ..... 135 A6
Crowmere Ave TN40 .... 157 C5
Crowmere Terr TN40 ...... 157 C5
Crown Cl Hailsham BN27 . 152 A7
  Uckfield TN22 .... 78 C8
Crown Ct **22** TN34 ...... 160 B4
Crown Gdns BN1 .... 189 F5
Crown Hill
  4 Brighton BN2 ...... 164 C6

Crown Hill
  Seaford BN25 .... 180 E7
Crown La TN34 .... 160 B4
Crown Point Ho BN6 .... 97 F4
Crown Rd
  Portslade-by-Sea BN41 .. 162 A8
  Shoreham-by-Sea BN43 . 161 B8
Crown St Brighton BN1 ... 189 F5
  11 Eastbourne BN21 . 184 D4
Crowne Ho **7** BN22 .... 184 E4
Crowden Way BN22 .... 173 D3
Croxton La RH16 .... 51 B6
Crump's Cnr TN22 .... 103 D6
Crunden Rd BN20 .... 184 C4
Cubitt Way TN38 .... 135 E4
Cuckfield Cl TN40 .... 158 A5
Cuckfield Rd
  Burgess Hill RH15, RH17 .. 72 E7
  Goddards' Green
  BN6, RH17 .... 72 A4
Cuckmere Ct BN26 .... 170 F3
Cuckmere Ho BN24 .... 175 E5
Cuckmere House Sch
  BN25 .... 181 C3
Cuckmere House Sch (Tower
  House Annexe) BN25 .... 181 A3
Cuckmere Path TN22 .... 55 E1
Cuckmere Rd
  Newhaven BN9 .... 179 A5
  Seaford BN25 .... 180 E7
Cuckmere Rise TN21 .... 82 B8
Cuckmere Way BN1 .... 143 C5
Cuckmere Wlk BN22 ...... 173 D1
Cuckoo Dr TN21 .... 82 A6
Culpepper RH15 .... 72 E4
Culpepper Cl BN2 .... 143 D2
Culross Ave RH16 .... 50 D5
Culver Cl BN23 .... 174 B4
Culverden Ave TN4 .... 8 A6
Culverden Down TN4 .... 7 F5
Culverden Park Rd TN4 ..... 7 F5
Culverden Pk TN4 .... 7 F5
Culverden Sq TN1, TN4 ..... 8 A6
Culverden St TN1 .... 8 A4
Cumberland Cl
  Bexhill TN40 .... 157 D4
  Eastbourne BN20 .... 184 B6
Cumberland Dr BN1 .... 142 E2
Cumberland Gdns
  Hastings TN38 .... 159 B8
  10 Royal Tunbridge Wells
  TN1 .... 8 A2
Cumberland Lodge
  8 BN1 .... 142 E2
Cumberland Mews **12** TN1 . 8 A2
Cumberland Rd
  Bexhill TN39 .... 157 B7
  Brighton BN1 .... 142 E2
Cumberland Wlk **11** TN1 . 8 A2
Cumnor House Sch RH17 .. 34 B5
Cunningham Cl TN4 .... 8 A7
Cunningham Ct **2** BN21 . 185 E7
Cunningham Dr BN23 ..... 185 E7
Cunningham Ho TN39 ..... 157 B3
Cunningham Rd TN4 .... 8 B7
Curlew Ct
  Hailsham BN27 .... 152 D7
  Hastings TN38 .... 135 E3
Curlews The BN43 .... 141 A8
Curve Rd TN4 .... 8 A5
Curwen Pl BN1 .... 142 E3
Curzon Ho BN2 .... 177 C4
Cuthbert Cl TN39 .... 157 A7
Cuthbert Rd BN2 .... 164 C5
Cutter La TN34 .... 160 A3
Cypress Cl
  Hastings TN38 .... 159 A7
  Shoreham-by-Sea BN43 . 140 A1
Cypress Gr TN2 .... 17 C8
Cyprus Pl TN31 .... 93 B5
Cyprus Rd RH15 .... 73 A3

D'aubigny Rd BN2 .... 164 B8
Dacre Pk BN27 .... 152 D7
Dacre Rd
  Eastbourne BN20, BN21 . 184 C4
  Herstmonceux BN27 ... 130 E6
  Newhaven BN9 .... 179 D7
Dagg La TN32 .... 65 F5
Dakins The RH19 .... 10 E8
Dale Ave Brighton BN1 ... 142 F5
  Keymer BN6 .... 98 A3
Dale Cres BN1 .... 142 F6
Dale Dr BN1 .... 143 A6
Dale Hill BN45 .... 146 A8
Dale Rd Forest Row RH18 . 11 F1
  Lewes BN7 .... 146 A8
Dale St TN1 .... 8 B4
Dale View Gdns BN3 ..... 141 D2

Dale View Gdns BN3 ..... 141 D2
Dalehurst TN6 .... 38 C7
Dalehurst Rd TN39 .... 157 B7
Dales Cl BN27 .... 131 B5
Dalewood Gdns RH15 ..... 73 C2
Dallas La BN8 .... 101 F6
Dallaway Dr BN24 .... 174 B5
Dallaway Gdns RH19 .... 1 E1
Dallington CE Prim Sch
  TN21 .... 84 D3
Dallington Cl TN40 .... 158 A6
Dallington Rd
  Eastbourne BN22 .... 174 A1
  Hove BN3 .... 162 F8
Dalmeny Rd TN39 .... 157 A5
Dalmore Ct TN40 .... 157 C3
Dalton Rd BN20 .... 188 E8
Damian Way BN6 .... 98 B4
Damon Cl BN10 .... 178 C7
Dana Lodge BN10 .... 178 A7
Dane Cl BN25 .... 180 D2
Dane Court Cl TN39 ...... 157 B6
Dane Hts **10** BN25 ..... 180 D2
Dane Rd Hastings TN38 . 159 B8
  Seaford BN25 .... 180 D2
Danehill CE Prim Sch
  RH17 .... 34 B4
Danehill La RH17 .... 33 E5
Danehill Rd BN2 .... 164 F5
Daniel Way TN11 .... 94 F2
Dannfields Ho BN25 ...... 180 E3
Danny Sheldon Ho **14**
  BN2 .... 164 C4
Danum Cl BN27 .... 129 C3
Danworth La BN6 .... 72 B3
Darby's La TN5 .... 30 B2
Darcey Dr BN1 .... 143 A6
Daresbury Cl TN39 .... 157 B6
Darley Rd BN20 .... 188 D7
Dart Ct RH19 .... 2 A3
Dartmouth Cl BN2 .... 143 F1
Dartmouth Cres BN2 ..... 143 F1
Darvel Down TN33 .... 86 B2
Darwall Dr BN25 .... 181 A3
Darwell Cl
  Hastings TN38 .... 135 E1
  Robertsbridge TN32 ...... 64 B3
Darwell Dr BN24, BN26 . 174 A5
Davey Dr BN1 .... 143 B1
Davey's La BN7 .... 123 C2
David Lloyd Club The
  BN23 .... 184 F8
David Salomon's Ho TN3 .... 7 D8
Davids Heights BN21 .... 184 E5
Davigdor Cty Inf Sch
  BN3 .... 163 D6
Davigdor Rd BN3 .... 163 E7
Davis Cl TN39 .... 157 A7
Dawber Bldgs BN27 ...... 152 B7
Dawlish Cl BN2 .... 143 F1
Dawson Terr BN2 .... 164 C6
Daynes Way RH15 .... 72 E1
De Cham Ave TN37 .... 159 D8
De Cham Rd TN37 .... 159 C8
De Chardin Dr TN34 ..... 137 A5
De Courcel Rd BN2 ...... 164 E3
De Grey Cl BN7 .... 123 D2
De La Warr Par TN40 .... 157 E3
De La Warr Rd
  Bexhill TN40 .... 157 E5
  East Grinstead RH19 ...... 1 F1
De Moleyns Cl TN40 ..... 157 D4
De Montfort Rd
  Brighton BN2 .... 164 C7
  Lewes BN7 .... 123 B1
De Roos Rd BN21 .... 184 C5
De Walden Mews BN20 . 188 E8
De Warrenne Rd BN7 .... 123 B1
Deacons Dr BN41 .... 141 C2
Deadman's Cross TN21 ... 83 B5
Deadmans La TN31 .... 93 C6
Deadmantree Hill BN8 .. 101 B3
Deal Ave BN25 .... 181 C5
Deals The TN31 .... 93 B5
Dean Cl BN41 .... 141 C2
Dean Court Rd BN2 ...... 177 A6
Dean Gdns BN41 .... 141 C2
Dean St BN1 .... 163 E5
Dean Wood Cl BN23 ..... 174 A4
Deanery Cl BN7 .... 123 D3
Deans Cl Bexhill TN39 . 157 B6
  Woodingdean BN2 .... 165 E8
Deans Dr TN39 .... 157 A6
Deans Meadow BN6 ..... 101 E5
Deans Rd BN26 .... 170 F3
Deanway BN3 .... 142 B3
Decimus Burton Way **10**
  TN37 .... 159 C8
Decoy Dr BN22, BN21 .. 173 D1
Deepdene TN5 .... 30 A6

Deepdene Gdns
  TN34, TN35 .... 137 C3
Deepdene Sch BN3 ...... 162 D7
Deer Paddock La **7**
  BN27 .... 152 C7
Deerswood La TN39 ..... 156 E5
Deeside The BN1 .... 143 A7
Delavall Wlk BN23 .... 185 F6
Delawarr Dr TN38 .... 135 F6
Delaware Rd BN7 .... 146 A8
Delfryn BN41 .... 140 F3
Dell Cl TN38 .... 136 A1
Dell Dr TN2 .... 8 D4
Dell The
  East Grinstead RH19 ..... 2 B1
  Haywards Heath RH16 .. 50 C5
Dellney Ave RH16 .... 50 F3
Dellsfoot Cotts TN6 ...... 28 A3
Delmonden Rd TN18 ..... 45 C8
Delves Ave TN2 .... 8 C1
Delves Cl BN8 .... 124 D6
Delves Ho BN8 .... 124 D6
Delves Way BN8 .... 124 D6
Den Hill BN20 .... 184 A4
Denbigh Cl TN39 .... 156 E4
Denbigh Rd TN39 .... 8 C7
Dencher Rd BN7 .... 145 E3
Dene Cl BN20 .... 183 B1
Dene Ct BN22 .... 173 C1
Dene Path TN22 .... 55 D1
Dene Side BN20 .... 183 B2
Dene The Hastings TN34 . 137 A5
  Hove BN3 .... 141 D3
  Lower Willingdon BN20 . 173 A3
  Uckfield TN22 .... 55 D1
Dene Vale BN1 .... 142 D5
Dene Way TN3 .... 7 A7
Denecroft BN1 .... 142 D5
Deenehurst Gdns TN34 . 137 A5
Deneside BN1 .... 142 D4
Deneway The BN1 .... 142 D4
Denham Cl TN38 .... 135 E1
Denham Rd BN6, RH15 .. 72 D3
Denham Way TN31 .... 94 E2
Denman's Cl RH16 .... 51 A8
Denman's La
  Haywards Heath RH16 .. 51 A7
  Haywards Heath RH16 .. 51 B7
Denmark Pl TN34 .... 159 F7
Denmark Rd BN41 .... 162 C7
Denmark Terr BN1 .... 163 A5
Denmark Villas BN3 ..... 163 B7
Dennis Hobden Cl BN2 . 143 E1
Denton Cl BN23 .... 93 A6
Denton Cty Prim Sch
  BN9 .... 168 E1
Denton Dr Brighton BN1 . 143 A6
  Newhaven BN9 .... 168 E2
Denton Rd
  Eastbourne BN20 .... 188 D8
  Newhaven BN9 .... 168 E2
Dentons The BN20 ...... 188 D8
Derby Cl **3** BN3 .... 163 E7
Derby Pl **6** BN2 ...... 189 B5
Derek Ave BN3, BN41 .. 162 D6
Derek Ho BN3 .... 162 F6
Derwent Cl BN27 .... 129 A1
Derwent Dr TN4 .... 7 E5
Derwent Lodge Sch TN1 .. 8 B4
Derwent Rd BN20 .... 188 E8
Desmond Rd BN22 ...... 185 D5
Desmond Way BN2 ..... 164 F6
Devil's Dyke Rd
  BN1, BN3, BN41, BN45 .. 141 E7
Devonian Ct BN2 .... 189 B7
Devonshire Cl TN2 ...... 16 B8
Devonshire Cl **1** BN3 . 163 C7
Devonshire Lodge **1**
  BN22 .... 185 C5
Devonshire Pl
  Brighton BN2 .... 189 B5
  Eastbourne BN21 .... 185 A2
Devonshire Rd
  Bexhill TN40 .... 157 C3
  Hastings TN34 .... 159 F8
  Devonshire Sq TN40 ... 157 C3
Dew La TN31 .... 92 A8
Dewe Rd BN2 .... 143 C1
Dewhurst Cotts TN6 ...... 29 B8
Dewlands Hill TN20 .... 38 F2
Dewpond The BN10 ...... 167 B1
Dexter Dr RH19 .... 10 E8
Diana Cl TN40 .... 158 A6
Dickens Cl RH19 .... 2 A2
Dickens Way BN23 ...... 174 E3
Dicklands The BN7 ...... 125 D8
Diggers The BN1 .... 143 B3
Dillingburgh Rd BN20 .. 184 C4

Dillon Way TN1 .... 8 D6
Dinapore Ho **16** BN2 . 189 B6
Diplock Cl BN26 .... 172 F6
Diplocks The BN27 ...... 152 A8
Diplocks The BN27 ...... 152 A8
Diplocks Bldgs BN27 ... 152 A7
Diplocks Wlk BN27 ...... 152 A8
Dirty La RH19 .... 11 E7
Ditchling Bostall BN6 ... 120 D7
Ditchling Common Ctry Pk
  BN6 .... 73 F1
Ditchling Cres BN1 ...... 143 C5
Ditchling Ct **4** BN1 .. 164 B8
Ditchling Dr TN35 .... 137 E4
Ditchling Gdns BN1 ..... 143 B1
Ditchling Mus BN6 .... 98 C3
Ditchling Rd
  Brighton BN1, BN2 ..... 143 B4
  Westmeston BN1, BN6 . 120 D4
Ditchling Rise BN1 ...... 164 A8
Ditchling Way BN27 ..... 152 B6
Ditton's Cnr BN26 .... 173 C6
Ditton's Rd BN26 .... 173 D6
Dittons BN26 .... 173 C6
Dittons Mews TN38 ..... 135 E2
Dittons Rd
  Eastbourne BN21 .... 184 E3
  Stone Cross BN24 ...... 174 B5
Dixter La TN31 .... 67 B8
Dixter Rd TN31 .... 67 A6
Dock The BN8 .... 148 C3
Dodshill TN6 .... 26 A1
Dog Cotts RH19 .... 3 B1
Dog Kennel La TN22 ..... 57 F6
Dogs Hill Rd TN36 ...... 118 B5
Doleham Cotts TN35 ... 115 D5
Doleham Hill TN35 ...... 115 D5
Doleham La TN35 .... 115 B6
Doleham Sta TN35 ...... 115 D5
Dolphin Ct
  Eastbourne BN20 .... 188 E7
  5 Hove BN20 .... 163 A6
Dolphin Ind Est BN43 .. 161 B7
Dolphin L Ctr The RH16 . 50 D5
Dolphin Rd
  Haywards Heath RH16 .. 50 D4
  Shoreham-by-Sea BN43 . 161 B7
Dolphin Way BN43 ...... 161 B7
Donald Hall Rd BN2 .... 164 D5
Donald Way TN36 .... 118 A5
Donkey Mews BN2 ...... 163 D5
Donnington Rd BN2 .... 165 E6
Dorchester TN4 .... 8 B6
Dordrecht Way TN34 ... 136 E1
Dorin Ct TN2 .... 8 C3
Dorking Rd TN1 .... 8 C6
Dorman's Cl RH7 .... 2 A8
Dormans Gdns RH19 ...... 1 E6
Dormans High St RH7 ..... 2 A8
Dormans Park RH19 .... 1 E6
  East Grinstead RH19 .... 1 D3
Dormans Sta RH7 .... 1 F8
Dormans Station Rd RH7 . 1 F8
Dormansland Prim Sch
  RH7 .... 2 A8
Dornden Dr TN3 .... 7 A4
Dorothy Ave BN10 ...... 178 C7
Dorothy Ave N BN10 ... 178 C8
Dorothy Rd BN3 .... 162 D8
Dorothy Stringer Sch
  BN1 .... 142 F3
Dorset Ave RH19 .... 1 C3
Dorset Cotts TN7 .... 14 B4
Dorset Ct **6**
  Eastbourne BN22 .... 185 B3
  Hove BN41 .... 162 C8
Dorset Gdns
  Brighton BN2 .... 189 B5
  East Grinstead RH19 ..... 1 C3
Dorset Pl Brighton BN2 .. 189 B5
  Hastings TN34 .... 159 E7
Dorset Rd Bexhill TN40 . 157 D4
  Bexhill TN40 .... 157 E5
  Lewes BN7 .... 146 D2
  Royal Tunbridge Wells TN2 . 8 D2
Dorset Rd S TN40 .... 157 D4
Dorset St BN2 .... 189 A5
Doubledays RH15 .... 73 B2
Doucegrove TN38 .... 136 A1
Douglas Cl BN27 .... 129 B2
Douglas Rd TN6 .... 27 D1
Dove Ct TN22 .... 78 C8
Dovedale Gdns BN22 .. 173 F2
Dover Cl BN25 .... 181 C5
Dover Rd Brighton BN1 . 143 A2
  Polegate BN26 .... 173 B7
Dower Cl BN2 .... 165 D3

Down Ave TN3 20 A4
Down La TN3 28 C8
Down Rd TN39 157 A5
Down St TN22 54 C5
Down Terr BN2 164 C6
Down The BN3 141 D4
Down's Rd TN34 136 F3
Downash Cl BN2 164 E6
Downash Ct TN5 32 A3
Downash Ho TN5 32 A3
Downes Ct 9 BN43 161 C8
Downey Cl TN37 136 B6
Downland Ave
Peacehaven BN10 178 E6
Southwick BN42 140 E1
Downland Cl
Southwick BN42 140 D1
Woodingdean BN2 165 B8
Downland Copse TN22 78 C8
Downland Cres BN3 141 F3
Downland Ct BN41 141 A2
Downland Dr BN3 141 F3
Downland Rd BN2 165 B8
Downlands Ave TN39 157 B4
Downlands Cl TN39 157 A4
Downlands Sch BN6 97 F3
Downlands Way BN20 183 B1
Downline Cl TN21 106 F7
Downs Ave BN20 184 B6
Downs Cl BN7 123 A2
Downs Cty Inf Sch BN1 189 B8
Downs Cty Jun Sch BN1 143 A1
Downs Park Sch BN41 141 B2
Downs Rd
Burgess Hill RH15 72 E4
Seaford BN25 181 A3
Willingdon BN22 173 B2
Downs Sch The BN20 184 B4
Downs Valley Rd BN2 165 E8
Downs View
Ninfield TN33 133 B5
North Chailey BN8 75 E7
Peacehaven BN10 167 D2
Downs View Cl
East Dean BN20 183 C1
North Chailey BN8 75 E7
Downs View La BN20 183 C1
Downs View Rd BN6 97 F3
Downs View Sch BN2 165 C8
Downs Villas BN9 168 E3
Downs Wlk BN10 167 B2
Downscroft RH15 73 D6
Downside Brighton BN1 142 D5
Hove BN3 142 B3
Lewes BN7 146 A8
Shoreham-by-Sea BN43 140 A1
Downside Cl
Eastbourne BN20 184 C3
Shoreham-by-Sea BN43 140 A1
Downsmeade BN21 184 E3
Downsvalley Rd BN20 173 A4
Downsview
Heathfield TN21 82 B8
Hove BN3 141 D3
Hurstpierpoint BN6 97 A5
Downsview Ave BN2 165 C8
Downsview Cotts BN8 123 A7
Downsview Cres TN22 78 D8
Downsview Dr RH17 74 C4
Downsview Rd
Lower Willingdon BN20 173 A3
Portslade-by-Sea BN41 141 A2
Seaford BN25 181 A3
Downsview Way BN27 152 B7
Downsway Berwick BN26 150 B3
Southwick BN42 140 F1
Woodingdean BN2 144 D1
Draffin La TN31 94 D3
Drake Ave BN23 185 E7
Drake Ct BN25 180 E2
Drapers Way TN38 136 B2
Draxmont Way BN1 142 F3
Drayton Rise TN39 156 D4
Drive Lodge 10 BN3 163 C7
Drive The
Burgess Hill RH15 73 B4
Crowborough TN6 25 D2
Hailsham BN27 152 B6
Hastings TN38 158 F8
Hove BN3 163 C7
Maresfield TN22 55 A5
Maresfield Park TN22 55 A7
Newhaven BN9 179 C5
Royal Tunbridge Wells TN2 8 B1
Southwick BN42 140 E1
Uckfield TN22 78 C8
Drockmill Cl BN26 173 C6
Drove Ave BN2 144 D2
Drove Cres BN41 141 A2
Drove Rd Newhaven BN9 179 D8
Portslade-by-Sea BN41 141 A1
Woodingdean BN2 165 B8
Drove The Brighton BN1 142 D1
Falmer BN1 144 C5
Newhaven BN9 179 E8
Offham BN8 123 A5
Drovers Cl BN41 141 C2
Drovers Way RH15 73 C1
Droveway The
Haywards Heath
RH16, RH17 50 C6
Hove BN3 142 B2
Hove BN3 142 C1
Drummond Cl RH16 50 D4
Drummond Ct RH16 50 D4
Drury La TN38 136 A2
Drusilla's Zoo Park BN26 171 A6
Dryden Wlk BN23 174 E3
Duchess Dr BN25 180 E6
Dudeney Lodge BN1 143 B1
Dudley Inf Sch TN35 160 C5
Dudley Lodge TN2 8 C4
Dudley Rd Brighton BN1 143 B1
Eastbourne BN22 185 B4
Hastings TN35 160 C5
Royal Tunbridge Wells TN1 8 A4
Dudwell Rd BN2 165 E7
Duke Bernard Ct 7 BN22 185 C5
Duke Mews 2 TN37 136 B2
Duke Rd TN37 136 B2
Duke St Bexhill TN39 156 F5
Brighton BN1 189 F5
Hastings TN37 136 B2
Duke Terr TN37 136 B2
Duke's Dr BN20 188 E7
Duke's Mound BN2 164 D4
Dukes Barn Ct RH16 51 B7
Dukes Cl BN25 180 D5
Dukes Hill TN33 112 D6
Dukes La BN1 189 F5
Dukes Rd
Haywards Heath RH16 51 B8
Royal Tunbridge Wells TN1 8 C5
Dulwich Cl BN25 181 B4
Dumb Woman's La TN31 92 D3
Dumbrell Ct BN7 146 B8
Dumbrells Court Rd BN6 98 D4
Dumbrells Ct BN6 98 D4
Dumbrills Cl RH15 73 A5
Dunbar Dr BN27 129 A1
Duncan Ho BN10 167 D1
Dunclutha Rd TN34 136 F4
Duncton Cl RH16 50 D4
Duncton Ho BN6 97 E4
Dundale Rd TN3 9 E1
Dunes Ave TN31 94 F2
Dunning's Rd RH19 10 E7
Dunnings Mill L Complex
RH19 10 E6
Dunorlan Farm Cotts TN2 8 E4
Dunstall Ave RH15 72 E4
Dunstall Farm Rd RH15 72 F4
Dunstan Gr TN4 8 B6
Dunstan Rd TN4 8 B6
Dunstans Croft TN20 40 C3
Dunster Cl BN1 143 B1
Dunvan Cl BN7 123 C3
Durham Cl BN2 144 A1
Durham Ct
Eastbourne BN20 184 B6
Hove BN3 163 B6
Durkins Rd RH19 1 D3
Durrell Cl BN23 174 F2
Dursley Rd BN22 185 A4
Dutchells Way BN22 173 E4
Dyall Cl RH15 72 E4
Dyke Cl BN3 142 B4
Dyke Rd BN1, BN3 163 E7
Dyke Road Ave BN1, BN3 142 C4
Dyke Road Dr BN1 163 F8
Dyke Road Pl BN1, BN3 142 C3
Dymchurch Cl
Polegate BN26 173 C7
Seaford BN25 181 C5
Dymock Cl BN25 181 C4
Dymock's The BN6 98 D3
Dymond Rd TN38 136 A3
Dynevor Rd TN4 8 C7

Eagle Cl TN22 78 E5
Eagle Rd TN31 93 C6
Earl St TN34 159 F8
Earl's Rd TN4 7 F4
Earls Cl BN25 180 C5
Earls Gdn 5 BN7 123 D1
Earwig Cnr BN8 123 E3
East Albany Rd BN25 180 F3
East Ascent TN38 159 C6
East Beach St TN34 160 B3
East Beeches Rd TN6 26 B2
East Bourne St 22 TN34 160 B4
East Brighton Golf Course
BN2 165 B5
East Cl BN26 173 B6
East Cliff TN31 93 C6
East Cliff Rd TN4 8 A6
East Dean Rd BN20 184 B2
East Dean Rise BN25 181 A4
East Dr BN2 164 C5
East Gdns BN6 98 D3
East Grinstead Sta RH19 1 D1
East Hill RH19 1 E6
East Hill Pas 7 TN34 160 B4
East Hoathly CE Prim Sch
BN8 104 F5
East Mascalls Rd RH16 51 E6
East Meadway BN43 161 A6
East Par TN34 160 A3
East Point 6 BN43 161 A6
East St Brighton BN1 189 A4
Coggins Mill TN20 40 D3
Falmer BN1 144 C6
Hastings TN34 160 A4
Lewes BN7 123 D1
Portslade-by-Sea BN41 162 C7
Rye TN31 93 C5
Seaford BN25 180 E3
East Sussex F HQ BN7 123 B2
East Sussex Music Sch
BN7 146 C8
East Sussex Music Sch
(Annexe) BN7 123 D1
East Sussex National
Golf Club TN22 103 C7
East View TN21 82 B6
East View Fields BN7 99 E5
East View Terr TN33 88 F1
East Way BN7 122 F2
East Wick RH16 51 C7
Eastbank BN42 140 F1
Eastbourne Ave BN24 175 D5
Eastbourne Coll BN21 184 F1
Eastbourne Coll of Arts & Tech
Eastbourne BN21 184 E7
Eastbourne, Upperton
BN21 184 E4
Eastbourne, Upperton
BN21 184 F4
Eastbourne Coll of Food &
Fashion BN20 185 A1
Eastbourne District General
Hospl BN21 184 E7
Eastbourne Rd
Brighton BN2 143 D1
Felbridge RH19 1 A5
Halland BN8 104 C6
Lower Willingdon
BN20, BN22, BN26 173 B4
Pevensey Bay BN24 175 C4
Seaford BN25 181 C3
Uckfield TN22 78 F3
Westham BN23, BN24 174 F4
Eastbourne Sta BN21 184 F3
Eastbridge Rd BN9 179 E7
Eastbrook Rd BN41 162 B7
Eastbrook Way BN42 162 A7
Eastdale Rd RH15 73 D4
Eastend La BN6 98 D3
Eastergate TN39 156 D6
Eastergate Rd BN2 143 F4
Eastern Ave
Polegate BN26 173 B7
Shoreham-by-Sea BN43 161 A7
Eastern Cl BN43 161 A7
Eastern Cotts RH16 51 B7
Eastern Pl BN2 164 E4
Eastern Rd Brighton BN2 164 D4
Haywards Heath RH16 50 F3
Haywards Heath, Lindfield
RH16 51 C7
Wivelsfield RH17 74 B4
Eastern Ring Rd BN1 144 C7
Eastern Terr 10 BN2 164 D4
Eastern Terrace Mews 9
BN2 164 D4
Eastfield Cres BN1 143 A4
Eastgate St BN7 123 D1
Eastgate Wharf 9 BN7 123 D1
Easthill Dr BN41 141 B2
Easthill Way BN41 141 B1
Eastlands Cl TN2, TN4 16 E8
Eastlands Rd TN4 7 E1
Eastport La BN7 146 C8
Eastview Cotts BN8 124 E5
Eastway TN39 156 D4
Eastwell Pl BN27 152 B8
Eastwick Cl BN1 143 B7
Eastwood Rd TN39 157 A4
Eatenden La TN32, TN33 87 B3
Eaton Ct 9 BN3 163 B7
Eaton Gardens Mansions 20
BN3 163 C7
Eaton Gate 17 BN3 163 C7
Eaton Gdns BN3 163 C7
Eaton Gr BN3 163 C7
Eaton Hall 19 BN3 163 C7
Eaton Manor 11 BN3 163 C7
Eaton Pl BN2 164 D4
Eaton Rd BN3 163 C7
Eaton Villas BN3 163 B7
Ebden's Hill TN33, TN34 136 B8
Ebenezer Rd TN34 160 B4
Ecclesden 6 BN2 189 B6
Ecmod Rd BN22 185 C6
Edburton Ave BN1 143 A1
Eden Dr TN39 156 F4
Eden Rd TN1 8 A2
Eden Vale
Dormans Park RH19 1 F5
East Grinstead RH19 1 D4
Edenbridge Rd TN7 13 E6
Edensor Rd BN20 188 D7
Edgar Rd TN35 160 C6
Edgehill Cl TN21 81 F7
Edgehill Way BN41 140 F2
Edgeland Terr BN22 173 F1
Edinburgh Ct
Eastbourne BN20 184 C5
Seaford BN25 180 D3
Edinburgh Rd
Bexhill TN40 157 C5
Brighton BN2 164 B8
Hastings TN38 158 E7
Seaford BN25 180 D3
Edinburgh Way RH19 10 F7
Edison Rd BN22, BN23 174 A1
Edith Ave BN10 178 B7
Edith Ave N BN10 178 C8
Edith Rd TN35 137 D3
Edmond Cl BN23 185 F8
Edmonton Rd TN39 157 B7
Edmund Rd TN35 160 C6
Edward Ave Hove BN3 142 A3
Saltdean BN2 166 D3
Edward Cl Hove BN3 142 A3
Seaford BN25 180 A6
Edward Ho BN3 162 F6
Edward Rd
Hastings TN37 159 D7
Haywards Heath RH16 50 E2
Edward St Brighton BN2 189 B5
6 Lewes BN7 123 D1
Royal Tunbridge Wells TN4 7 F8
Rusthall TN4 7 C4
Edward Terr TN38 136 A4
Edward Way RH15 72 D2
Edwin Rd TN35 160 C6
Effingham Cl BN2 177 C6
Effingham Dr TN39 156 D3
Egbert Cl BN23 185 F8
Egerton Rd TN39 157 B3
Egginton Cl BN1 144 A5
Egginton Rd BN1, BN2 144 A5
Egles Gr TN22 78 B8
Egmont Rd BN3 141 D1
Egremont Pl
Brighton BN2 189 B5
Hastings TN34 160 B6
Eight Acre La TN35 115 D1
Eight Bells Cl TN22 56 C4
Eileen Ave BN2 177 B5
Eisenhower Dr TN38 135 F6
Elder Cl BN41 141 B2
Elder Pl BN1 189 A7
Elderwood Cl
Bexhill TN39 157 C7
Eastbourne BN22 173 D2
Eldon Rd BN21 184 C5
Eldred Ave BN1 142 D5
Eleanor Cl Lewes BN7 123 B2
Seaford BN25 180 D5
Eleanor Terr TN35 137 D4
Eley Cres BN2 165 E3
Eley Dr BN2 165 E3
Elford St 3 TN34 159 F8
Elgar Way BN23 174 E3
Elgin Gdns BN25 181 C3
Elim Court Gdns TN6 25 E4
Elim Wlk TN34 136 F2
Eliot Ho 4 RH16 50 E3
Elizabeth Ave BN3 142 A3
Elizabeth Cl Hove BN3 142 A3
Seaford BN25 180 A6
Elizabeth Cres RH19 1 F3
Elizabeth Ct
Eastbourne BN20 184 C5
2 Hailsham BN27 152 C7
7 Hove BN3 163 C7
Polegate BN26 173 A6
Elizabeth Garlick Ct 1
TN1 8 B4
Elizabeth Rd
Hastings TN38 136 A2
Shoreham-by-Sea BN43 161 C8
Elizabethan Cl TN33 132 F2
Ellen Ho 3 BN3 163 B7
Ellen St Hove BN3 163 B7
Portslade-by-Sea BN41 162 C7
Ellenslea Rd TN37 159 C7
Ellenwhorne La TN32 89 A7
Ellerslie La TN39 156 F6
Elliots Way TN21 82 A8
Ellis Gordon Ct BN9 179 B7
Ellis Way TN22 78 A7
Elm Cl Hove BN3 142 C2
Laughton BN8 126 C7
Seaford BN25 181 C3
Elm Cotts
Hailsham BN27 151 A8
Laughton BN8 126 C7
Elm Ct Brighton BN1 163 E8
Newhaven BN9 179 B7
Polegate BN26 173 A6
Portslade-by-Sea BN41 162 B8
Elm Dr
East Grinstead RH19 2 A1
Hove BN3 141 E1
Elm Gn 4 BN27 129 B1
Elm Gr Brighton BN2 164 C7
Eastbourne BN22 173 F1
11 Lewes BN7 146 C8
Elm Grove Cty Prim Sch
BN2 164 C7
Elm Rd BN41 162 B8
Elm Way TN21 82 B6
Elmhurst Ave TN2 9 D8
Elmore Rd BN2 189 B6
Elms Ave BN21 185 B2
Elms La TN35 116 F1
Elms Lea Ave BN1 142 E3
Elms Rd BN21 185 B2
Elms The BN8 124 C5
Elmsdown Pl BN27 152 C7
Elmsmead TN31 70 B4
Elmstead RH19 10 E8
Elmstead Rd TN40 157 E5
Elmwood 9 BN21 184 F4
Elmwood Cl BN23 174 C4
Elmwood Gdns BN23 174 C4
Elphick Rd
Broyle Side BN8 124 F7
Newhaven BN9 179 C8
Elphick's Pl TN2 17 B8
Elphinstone Ave TN34 136 F2
Elphinstone Cty Prim Sch
TN34 160 A6
Elphinstone Gdns TN34 136 F3
Elphinstone Inf Sch TN34 136 F2
Elphinstone Rd TN34 136 F2
Elrington Rd BN3 142 C1
Elsted Cl BN22 174 A1
Elsted Cres BN1 143 C6
Elsted Rd TN39 156 C2
Elven Cl BN20 183 C1
Elven La BN20 183 C1
Elvin Cres BN2 165 E4
Elwood Cl RH15 72 F1
Ely Ct TN2 8 B4
Embassy Ct BN3 163 D5
Emerald Quay BN43 161 A6
Emmanuel Rd TN34 160 A5
Encore Ho TN21 81 F8
Endcliffe Ct BN20 188 E8
Endwell Rd TN40 157 C4
Engalee RH19 1 C2
English Cl BN3 162 E8
English's Pas 10 BN7 123 D1
Enterprise Est BN1 143 C7
Enys Rd BN21 184 F4
Epsom Cl TN38 159 A8
Erica Cl BN23 174 B2
Eridge Cl TN39 157 A4
Eridge Dr TN6 26 A3
Eridge Gdns TN6 26 A3
Eridge Gn BN7 123 B2
Eridge Rd
Boarshead TN3, TN6 26 D7
Crowborough TN6 26 A3
Eastbourne BN21 184 D7
Hove BN3 142 A2
Royal Tunbridge Wells
TN2, TN4 7 E1
Steel Cross TN6 26 C4
Eridge Sta TN3 15 E2
Erin Way RH15 72 E3
Erroll Rd BN3, BN41 162 C6
Ersham Rd BN27 152 B5
Ersham Way BN27 152 B6
Erskine Park Rd TN4 7 C4
Esher Cl BN25 180 F4
Eshton Rd BN22 185 C5
Eskbank Ave BN1 143 A7

Eskdale Cl BN23 .... 174 C4
Esplanade BN25 .... 180 E2
Esplanade The BN10 .... 177 F3
Essenden Rd TN38 .... 159 A7
Essex Cl TN2 .... 16 F8
Essex Ct BN20 .... 184 B6
Essex Pl 3 Brighton BN2 .... 164 C4
  Newhaven BN9 .... 179 C7
Essex Rd TN38 .... 136 A4
Essex St BN2 .... 164 C4
Estate Rd BN9 .... 179 E7
Estcots Cty Prim Sch RH19 ... 2 A1
Estcots Dr RH10 .... 2 A1
Etchingham CE Prim Sch
  TN19 .... 44 D2
Etchingham Rd BN23 .... 174 E1
Etchingham Sta TN19 .... 44 C1
Ethel St BN3 .... 163 B7
Ethelred Cl BN23 .... 185 E8
Etherington Hill TN35 .... 7 C8
Etherton Way BN25 .... 181 A4
Ethnam La TN18 .... 47 E4
Eton Cl BN25 .... 181 A4
Eton Mews 2 BN21 .... 185 A3
Eurythmy Sch RH19 .... 10 E6
Evelyn Ave BN9 .... 179 C7
Evelyn Ct BN41 .... 162 A8
Evelyn Glennie Ct 7 BN2 .... 164 C5
Evelyn Rd BN7 .... 123 B2
Evelyn Terr BN2 .... 164 C5
Everest Ho 2 BN21 .... 162 F7
Eversfield Ct TN37 .... 159 D7
Eversfield Hospl TN38 .... 159 A6
Eversfield Mews N 5
  TN37 .... 159 C7
Eversfield Pl TN37 .... 159 D7
Eversfield Rd BN21 .... 184 F4
Eversley Cl TN37 .... 136 C2
Eversley Cres TN37 .... 136 C2
Eversley Rd Bexhill TN40 .... 157 C3
  Hastings TN37 .... 136 C2
Everton Cotts TN19 .... 62 B6
Evesham TN38 .... 136 A3
Ewart St BN2 .... 189 B6
Ewehurst La TN3 .... 6 F6
Ewell Ct TN40 .... 157 E4
Ewhurst Cl TN34 .... 136 F4
Ewhurst La TN31 .... 66 F4
Ewhurst Rd BN2 .... 143 C1
Excelsior The BN1 .... 142 D4
Exeat Cl Brighton BN2 ...... 164 E6
  Eastbourne BN23 .... 174 B4
Exeter Cl BN22 .... 173 B2
Exeter St BN1 .... 163 E8
Exmouth Pl TN34 .... 160 A4

Factory La BN27 .... 152 A6
Fair La
  Robertsbridge TN32 .... 64 A4
  Robertsbridge TN32 .... 64 C4
Fair Meadow TN31 .... 93 C7
Fair Oak Cl TN21 .... 82 A7
Fair View TN5 .... 30 A6
Fairbanks RH16 .... 50 E4
Fairbridge Way RH15 .... 72 F5
Faircrouch La TN5 .... 29 B5
Fairdene BN42 .... 140 F1
Fairfax Ave TN38 .... 135 F7
Fairfield
  Herstmonceux BN27 .... 130 E6
  Peacehaven BN10 .... 178 B7
Fairfield Ave TN1, TN2 .... 8 B5
Fairfield Chase TN39 .... 156 F4
Fairfield Cl
  Burgess Hill RH15 .... 72 F4
  Shoreham-by-Sea BN43 ... 140 C1
Fairfield Cotts BN26 .... 149 D2
Fairfield Cres BN6 .... 97 A6
Fairfield Gdns
  Burgess Hill RH15 .... 72 F4
  Portslade-by-Sea BN41 ... 141 B1
Fairfield Lodge BN20 .... 188 E8
Fairfield Rd
  Burgess Hill RH15 .... 72 F4
  East Grinstead RH19 ...... 10 F8
  Eastbourne BN20 .... 184 E1
  Hastings TN37 .... 136 C6
Fairfield Way RH16 .... 50 D8
Fairford Cl RH16 .... 50 E5
Fairglen Cotts TN5 .... 29 B4
Fairglen Rd TN5 .... 29 B4
Fairholme 6 BN7 .... 146 C8
Fairholme Rd BN9 .... 168 F1
Fairhurst BN10 .... 177 F3
Fairisle Cl BN27 .... 129 A2
Fairlawn 1 RH16 .... 50 E4
Fairlawn Cres RH19 .... 1 B2
Fairlawn Dr RH19 .... 1 B2
Fairlawns 8 Hove BN3 ...... 163 A6
  Shoreham-by-Sea BN43 ... 161 A8
Fairlawns Dr BN27 .... 130 E6

Fairlea Cl RH15 .... 72 F4
Fairlie Gdns BN1 .... 142 E3
Fairlight TN22 .... 55 E1
Fairlight Ave
  Hastings TN35 .... 137 D3
  Telscombe Cliffs BN10 ... 177 F3
Fairlight Cl Bexhill TN40 ... 158 A5
  Polegate BN26 .... 173 A6
Fairlight Ct BN10 .... 177 F4
Fairlight Cty Prim Sch
  BN2 .... 164 C8
Fairlight Field BN8 .... 124 D5
Fairlight Gdns TN35 .... 138 F4
Fairlight Pl 4 BN2 .... 164 C8
Fairlight Rd
  Eastbourne BN22 .... 185 C5
  Fairlight TN35 .... 138 A4
Fairmile Rd TN2 .... 8 E5
Fairmount Rd TN40 .... 157 D5
Fairplace RH17 .... 74 C4
Fairstone Cl TN35 .... 137 E4
Fairview Cotts TN6 .... 25 E4
Fairview La TN6 .... 25 E4
Fairview Rise BN1 .... 142 D5
Fairway Cl BN20 .... 184 C2
Fairway Cres BN41 .... 141 C2
Fairway The Bexhill TN39 ... 156 F6
  Hastings TN38 .... 158 F8
  Newhaven BN9 .... 179 A7
Fairway Trad Est BN2 ...... 143 E4
Fairways BN1 .... 163 E8
Fairways Cl BN25 .... 181 C2
Fairways Rd BN25 .... 181 B2
Fairways The TN4 .... 8 A7
Falaise Rd
  Hastings TN34, TN37 ..... 159 D7
  Newhaven BN9 .... 168 F1
Falcon Cl BN43 .... 161 C6
Falcon Way BN27 .... 129 B3
Falconbury Dr TN39 .... 156 D3
Falconer Dr TN33 .... 112 F4
Fallowfield Cl BN43 .... 141 F2
Fallowfield Cres BN3 ...... 141 F2
Falls Ct TN38 .... 135 F6
Falmer Ave BN2 .... 177 C6
Falmer Cl BN20 .... 184 B7
Falmer Gdns BN26 .... 165 D8
Falmer Hill BN1 .... 144 B6
Falmer House Rd BN1 .... 144 B6
Falmer Rd
  Woodingdean BN2 .... 144 D1
  Woodingdean BN2, BN1 ... 165 E5
Falmer Sch BN1 .... 144 A5
Falmer Sta BN1 .... 144 B6
Falmouth Cl BN23 .... 185 F8
Faraday Ave RH19 .... 10 F6
Faraday Cl BN22 .... 173 F1
Farlaine Rd BN21 .... 184 C6
Farley Bank TN34, TN35 .... 160 B6
Farley Way TN35 .... 138 E5
Farlington Ave RH16 .... 50 F5
Farlington Cl RH16 .... 50 F5
Farm Cl
  East Grinstead RH19 ...... 11 B8
  Hassocks BN6 .... 97 E4
  Portslade-by-Sea BN41 ... 141 A2
  Seaford BN25 .... 181 B4
Farm Gdns TN31 .... 69 C2
Farm Hill BN2 .... 165 C8
Farm La Camber TN31 .... 94 D3
  Ditchling BN6 .... 98 E3
Farm Mews 8 BN3 .... 163 D6
Farm Rd BN3 .... 163 D6
Farm Trail BN26 .... 151 A4
Farm Way
  Burgess Hill RH15 .... 73 D1
  Southwick BN42 .... 162 A7
Farncombe Cl TN1 .... 8 B2
Farncombe La TN1 .... 8 B2
Farncombe Rd TN1, TN2 ...... 8 C2
Farmland Way BN27 .... 129 C1
Farmlands Ave
  BN26, BN20 .... 172 F4
Farmlands Cl
  Hastings TN37 .... 136 C5
  Lower Willingdon BN26 ... 173 A4
Farmlands Ct BN26 .... 173 A4
Farmlands Way BN26 .... 172 F5
Farmway Cl BN3 .... 141 D2
Farncombe Cl RH17 .... 74 D4
Farncombe Rd 5 BN7 .... 123 E1
Farne Cl BN27 .... 129 A2
Farnham Ave BN6 .... 98 A5
Farnham Beeches TN3 .... 7 A4
Farnham Cl TN3 .... 7 A3
Farnham La TN3 .... 7 A4
Farningham Rd TN6 .... 38 C8
Farnol Ho 4 BN21 .... 184 D4
Farriers Way TN22 .... 78 C6
Farthing Hill TN5 .... 31 E1

Farthing La BN27, TN33 .... 109 E4
Farthings The TN6 .... 26 A3
Faulkners Way RH15 .... 73 A5
Faversham Rd BN23 .... 174 D2
Faygate Cl TN39 .... 157 B8
Faygate Ct BN2 .... 164 E6
Faygate Rd BN22 .... 173 E2
Fayre Meadow TN32 .... 64 C4
Fazan Ct TN5 .... 29 F4
Fearon Rd TN34 .... 136 F2
Felbridge Cl RH19 .... 1 C3
Felbridge Ct RH19 .... 1 A4
Felbridge Ctr The RH19 ..... 1 A3
Felcourt Cotts RH19 .... 1 C8
Felcourt La RH19, RH7 ...... 1 C8
Felcourt Rd RH19, RH7 ...... 1 C7
Fellows Rd TN34 .... 137 B3
Felride RH16 .... 50 E3
Felwater Ct RH19 .... 1 A3
Fennel Wlk BN43 .... 140 B1
Fennell's Cl BN21 .... 184 E5
Ferbies TN3 .... 7 A7
Ferbies Cotts TN3 .... 7 A7
Ferdinand Terr TN3 .... 15 C7
Ferguson Rd TN29 .... 96 D2
Fermor Rd TN6 .... 38 A7
Fermor Row TN6 .... 37 F8
Fermor Way TN6 .... 38 A8
Fern Cl BN23 .... 174 C3
Fern Gn 1 BN27 .... 129 B1
Fern Rd BN25 .... 158 F8
Fernbank Ctr TN6 .... 25 F3
Ferndale TN2 .... 8 D5
Ferndale Cl TN2 .... 8 C4
Ferndale Point TN2 .... 8 C4
Ferndale Rd
  Burgess Hill RH15 .... 73 C2
  Hove BN3 .... 163 D7
Fernhurst Cl BN1 .... 143 B6
Fernhurst Cres BN1 .... 143 B5
Fernlea Cl TN35 .... 114 E4
Ferns The TN1 .... 8 C4
Fernside Ave TN35 .... 135 F1
Fernwood Rise BN1 .... 142 D5
Ferrers Rd BN7 .... 123 B1
Ferring Cl TN31 .... 93 A6
Ferring Ct BN1 .... 143 F5
Ferry Hill TN36 .... 117 E8
Ferry Rd TN31 .... 93 B5
Festival Gdns TN39 .... 157 C7
Feversham Ct BN43 .... 161 B6
Field Cl Burgess Hill RH15 .. 72 F4
  Seaford BN25 .... 181 B2
Field End TN22 .... 55 A4
Field Sch The BN3 .... 162 D7
Field View TN22 .... 64 B3
Field Way TN38 .... 158 E8
Fielden La TN6 .... 25 D1
Fielden Rd TN6 .... 25 D2
Fieldfare Ct BN27 .... 152 D7
Fields End Cl RH16 .... 50 F4
Fieldway
  Broad Oak TN31 .... 90 C5
  Ditchling BN6 .... 98 D3
  Haywards Heath RH16 ..... 50 F8
Fiennes Rd BN27 .... 130 E6
Figg La TN6 .... 37 F8
Filching Cl BN26 .... 172 E3
Filching Ct BN20 .... 184 A5
Filching Manor Motor Mus
  BN26 .... 172 D2
Filching Rd BN20 .... 184 B5
Filder Cl BN22 .... 185 A6
Filsham Dr TN40 .... 158 A6
Filsham Rd TN38 .... 159 A8
Filsham Valley TN38 .... 158 F7
Filsham Valley Sch TN38 ... 158 F7
Finbar Cl BN23 .... 174 D2
Finches Gdns RH16 .... 51 A8
Finches La RH16 .... 51 A8
Finches Park Rd RH16 ...... 51 A8
Finches The Bexhill TN40 ... 157 F4
  2 Hastings TN38 .... 135 A5
  Shoreham-by-Sea BN43 ... 161 A8
Findon Ave BN2 .... 177 B6
Findon Cl Bexhill TN39 ..... 156 E3
  Hove BN3 .... 141 F3
  Seaford BN25 .... 181 C3
Findon Rd BN2 .... 164 F5
Finley Ct TN38 .... 158 F6
Finmere Cl BN22 .... 185 C6
Finmere Rd BN22 .... 185 C6
Finsbury Lodge 1 BN2 ..... 164 C6
Finsbury Rd BN2 .... 164 C6
Fir Cl BN2 .... 165 F7
Fir Grove Rd TN21 .... 81 B6
Fir Toll Cl TN21 .... 39 F2
Fir Toll Rd
  Woolbridge TN20 .... 39 C2
  Woolbridge TN20 .... 39 C2
Fir Tree Cl Bexhill TN39 .... 156 C3
  Hailsham BN27 .... 129 C2

Fir Tree Rd TN4 .... 7 F3
Fir Tree Way BN6 .... 98 A4
Fircroft Cl BN1 .... 142 E3
Firehills Cotts TN35 ...... 138 C3
Firlands RH16 .... 50 F4
Firle Bostal BN8 .... 148 A2
Firle CE Prim Sch BN8 ..... 148 B4
Firle Cl Hastings TN35 .... 137 E4
  Seaford BN25 .... 180 E5
Firle Cres BN7 .... 122 E2
Firle Dr BN25 .... 180 E5
Firle Gn TN22 .... 55 E1
Firle Grange BN25 .... 180 E5
Firle Place BN8 .... 148 C3
Firle Rd Bexhill TN39 ..... 156 D4
  Brighton BN2 .... 164 D6
  Eastbourne BN22 .... 185 B4
  Peacehaven BN10 .... 178 C8
  Seaford BN25 .... 180 E6
Firle Terr BN9 .... 168 D2
Firs Ct TN4 .... 7 F6
First Ave Bexhill TN40 .... 157 F5
  Camber TN31 .... 94 F2
  Hove BN3 .... 163 C6
  Newhaven BN9 .... 179 C7
First St TN3 .... 6 F3
Firtoft Cl RH15 .... 73 B3
Firtree Rd TN34 .... 160 A6
Firwood Cl
  Eastbourne BN22 .... 173 E1
  Heathfield TN21 .... 82 A8
Firwood Rise TN21 .... 82 A8
Fisher Cl BN23 .... 185 F7
Fisher St BN7 .... 123 D1
Fisher's Gate Cotts TN4 ... 14 A1
Fishermen's Mus TN34 ..... 160 B3
Fishersgate Cty Fst Sch
  BN41 .... 162 A7
Fishersgate Sta BN41 ...... 162 C8
Fishersgate Terr
  BN41, BN42 .... 162 A7
Fishmarket Rd TN31 .... 93 C6
Fishponds La TN35 .... 114 E3
Fitch Dr BN2 .... 143 F1
Fitzalan Ho 7 BN21 .... 184 F4
Fitzgerald Ave BN25 .... 180 F2
Fitzgerald Cl BN20 .... 184 F1
Fitzgerald Ho 6 BN25 ..... 180 F2
Fitzgerald Pk BN25 .... 180 F2
Fitzgerald Rd BN7 .... 123 D2
Fitzherbert Dr BN2 .... 164 D8
Fitzjohn Ct BN6 .... 97 F3
Fitzjohns Rd BN7 .... 123 B2
Fitzmaurice Ave BN22 ...... 185 B5
Fitzroy Rd BN7 .... 123 B2
Five Acre Wlk TN34 .... 136 E1
Five Ashes CE Prim Sch
  TN20 .... 58 B6
Five Hos The TN36 .... 117 E8
Five Villages Ho TN36 ..... 116 F6
Fiveways TN1 .... 8 A4
Flag Ct BN3 .... 163 B5
Flamsteed Rd BN27 .... 131 A1
Fleetway Ct TN31 .... 94 F2
Fleming Cl BN23 .... 174 F2
Fletcher Ave TN37, TN38 ... 135 F7
Fletching CE Prim Sch
  TN22 .... 53 F3
Fletching Cl BN2 .... 164 F6
Fletching Rd BN22 .... 173 F1
Fletching St TN20 .... 40 B3
Flimwell Bird Pk TN19 ..... 32 D8
Flimwell Cl Brighton BN2 .. 164 E5
  Eastbourne BN23 .... 174 A4
Flimwell TN5 .... 32 D4
  Hastings TN35 .... 135 D3
Flint Cl
  Portslade-by-Sea BN41 ... 141 B2
  Seaford BN25 .... 180 E6
Flints The BN7 .... 145 E5
Flitterbrook La TN21 ...... 83 C4
Florance La TN3 .... 15 B6
Florence Ave BN3 .... 162 D8
Florence Ct BN1 .... 142 F2
Florence Pl BN1 .... 143 B1
Florence Rd BN1 .... 164 A8
Florida Ct TN38 .... 158 F6
Fold Sch The BN3 .... 162 D7
Folders Cl RH15 .... 73 D1
Folders La BN6, RH15 ...... 73 D1
Foley Cl BN23 .... 185 E7
Folkestone Cl BN25 .... 181 D5
Folkestone Rd TN31 .... 93 F8
Folkington Gdns TN37 ...... 136 C5
Folkington Rd BN26 .... 172 D5
Follett Holt Ho BN8 .... 100 E7
Folly Field BN9 .... 179 C7
Fonthill Rd BN3 .... 163 B8
Fontridge La TN19 .... 62 E3
Fontwell Ave TN35 .... 156 C5
Foords La BN24 .... 174 C7

Foot's La TN19 .... 61 B3
Ford Rd TN38 .... 135 F2
Fordbrook Hill TN6 .... 37 E7
Fordcombe CE Prim Sch
  TN3 .... 6 B5
Fordcombe La TN3 .... 6 C5
Fordcombe Rd TN3 .... 6 C4
Foredown Cl
  Eastbourne BN20 .... 184 C2
  Portslade-by-Sea BN41 ... 141 B2
Foredown Dr BN41 .... 141 C1
Foredown Rd
  Portslade Village BN41 ... 141 B4
  Portslade-by-Sea BN41 ... 141 B2
Forest Dene TN6 .... 26 D1
Forest Fold Cotts TN6 ..... 25 D5
Forest Lodge
  Crowborough Warren TN6 . 37 D8
  2 East Grinstead RH19 ... 10 F8
Forest Pk TN6 .... 25 D2
Forest Pl TN21 .... 80 F6
Forest Rd Brighton BN1 .... 143 E6
  Forest Row RH18 .... 12 B2
  Royal Tunbridge Wells TN2 . 8 C1
Forest Ridge RH19 .... 21 A5
Forest Rise TN6 .... 26 D1
Forest Row Bsns Pk RH18 ... 11 F4
Forest Row CE Inf Sch
  RH18 .... 11 F2
Forest View
  Hailsham BN27 .... 152 A8
  Nutley TN22 .... 35 C3
Forest View Rd RH19 .... 10 E6
Forest Way
  Hastings TN34 .... 136 E1
  Pembury TN2 .... 9 D8
  Royal Tunbridge Wells TN2 . 8 D1
Forewood La TN33 .... 135 A7
Forewood Rise TN33 .... 134 F6
Forge Cl
  Portslade-by-Sea BN41 ... 141 B2
  Staplecross TN32 .... 65 E1
  Uckfield TN22 .... 78 C6
Forge Field TN5 .... 42 F6
Forge La TN32 .... 65 E1
Forge Lane Cotts TN22 ..... 55 A8
Forge Rd TN3, TN6 .... 15 C2
Forge Rise TN22 .... 78 C6
Forge Way
  Burgess Hill RH15 .... 73 A4
  Hastings TN37 .... 136 C5
Forstal The Cobbarn TN3 ... 15 F3
  Pembury TN2 .... 9 E8
Forstall TN3 .... 7 A4
Fort Gate BN9 .... 179 E5
Fort Haven BN43 .... 161 C6
Fort La BN22 .... 185 D6
Fort Newhaven BN9 .... 179 D5
Fort Rd Eastbourne BN22 ... 185 D6
  Newhaven BN9 .... 179 D6
Fort Rise BN9 .... 179 D5
Foster Cl BN25 .... 180 E4
Foundry Ct RH15 .... 73 B3
Foundry La BN7 .... 123 E1
Foundry St BN1 .... 189 A6
Fountains Cl
  Brighton BN1 .... 143 C2
  Eastbourne BN22 .... 173 E3
Founthill Ave BN2 .... 177 B5
Founthill Rd BN2 .... 177 B5
Fourteen Acre La TN35 ..... 115 D4
Fourth Ave BN3 .... 163 B6
Fowey Cl BN43 .... 161 B6
Fowlers Cl TN39 .... 156 E5
Fowly La TN22 .... 56 C7
Fox Cl RH15 .... 72 F1
Fox Hill RH16 .... 50 E1
Fox Hill Cl RH16 .... 50 E1
Fox Hill Village RH16 ..... 50 E1
Fox in the Wood TN5 .... 29 C6
Fox Way BN41 .... 141 B2
Foxcote TN37 .... 136 D5
Foxdown Rd BN2 .... 165 F7
Foxglove Cl BN8 .... 125 A7
Foxglove Rd BN23 .... 174 B3
Foxhill Bexhill TN39 ...... 156 E5
  Peacehaven BN10 .... 167 B1
Foxhill Cl 6 RH16 .... 50 E3
Foxhole La
  Four Throws TN18 .... 46 D8
  Wadhurst TN5 .... 30 B4
Foxhunters Rd BN41 .... 140 F3
Foxwarren RH16 .... 50 C5
Framelle Mount TN22 .... 79 B6
Framfield 11 BN27 .... 164 F5
Framfield CE Prim Sch
  TN22 .... 79 B6
Framfield Cl BN1 .... 143 E6

Framfield Rd Buxted TN22 .. 56 B3
Uckfield TN22 .... 78 D6
Framfield Way BN21 .... 184 D6
Francis Rd RH16 .... 51 B8
Francis St BN1, BN2 .... 189 A7
Francislea RH16 .... 50 E2
Frankfield Rise TN7 .... 8 A1
Franklands Cl RH15 .... 73 B1
Franklands Gdns RH15 ..... 98 A8
Franklands Way RH15 .... 98 A8
Franklin Rd Brighton BN2 .. 164 C7
Portslade-by-Sea BN41 ...... 162 C7
Shoreham-by-Sea BN43 .... 140 D1
Franklin St BN2 .... 164 C8
Franklynn Rd RH16 .... 50 F3
Frankton Ave RH16 .... 51 A3
Frant Ave TN39 .... 156 C5
Frant CE Prim Sch TN3 .... 17 B4
Frant Cl TN39 .... 156 C5
Frant Rd Hove BN3 .... 142 A2
  Royal Tunbridge Wells
  TN2, TN3 .... 17 A7
Frant Sta TN3 .... 17 F5
Frary Wlk TN21 .... 82 A3
Fraser Ave BN23 .... 185 E7
Fraser Ct **2** BN43 .... 161 C8
Freckley Hollow TN33 ...... 111 C1
Fred Emery Ct **10** BN1 .. 163 E5
Freda Gardham
  Cty Prim Sch TN31 .... 93 D6
Frederick Cotts RH16 .... 51 B7
Frederick Gdns BN1 .... 189 A6
Frederick Pl BN1 .... 189 A6
Frederick Rd TN35 .... 137 C3
Frederick St BN1 .... 189 A6
Free Heath Rd TN3, TN5 ..... 19 C3
Freehold Terr **1** BN2 .... 164 C8
Freek's La RH15 .... 73 A5
Freeland Cl BN25 .... 180 A6
Freeman Ave BN22 .... 173 E1
Freemans Rd BN41 .... 162 A8
Freezeland La TN39 .... 134 A2
Fremlin Cl TN4 .... 7 B4
French Gdns RH16 .... 51 A6
Frenches Farm Dr TN21 .... 82 A5
Frenchgate Cl BN22 .... 173 F7
Frenchgate Rd BN22 .... 173 F2
Freshfield Bank RH18 .... 11 E2
Freshfield La RH17 .... 33 E2
Freshfield Pl BN2 .... 164 C5
Freshfield Rd BN2 .... 164 D6
Freshfield St BN2 .... 164 C6
Freshfield Way BN2 .... 164 C5
Freshford Cl BN23 .... 174 D2
Freshwater Ave TN34 ...... 136 E2
Freshwater Sq BN22 .... 173 B3
Freshway BN22 .... 173 C3
Frewen Cl TN31 .... 67 B7
Frewen Coll TN31 .... 67 C5
Frewyn Cl TN38 .... 135 F4
Friar Cl BN1 .... 143 A4
Friar Cres BN1 .... 143 A3
Friar Rd BN1 .... 143 A3
Friar Wlk BN1 .... 142 F4
Friar's Cres TN35 .... 138 B7
Friar's Hill Terr TN35 ...... 138 A7
Friar's Way TN34 .... 136 F4
Friars' Ave BN10 .... 178 E6
Friars Bank TN35 .... 138 B7
Friars Cl BN6 .... 97 E4
Friars Hill TN35 .... 137 F7
Friars Oak Rd BN6 .... 97 E5
Friars Rd TN36 .... 117 F7
Friars Way TN7 .... 8 D6
Friars' Wlk BN7 .... 123 D1
Friday St BN23 .... 174 C3
Fridays The BN20 .... 187 B7
Friezland Rd TN4 .... 7 D1
Frimley Cl BN2 .... 165 F7
Friston Ave BN22 .... 173 C1
Friston Cl Brighton BN2 ... 143 F4
  Friston BN20 .... 183 A1
  Seaford BN25 .... 180 C4
Friston Downs BN20 .... 183 B2
Frith Pk RH19 .... 1 F1
Frith Rd BN3 .... 163 A8
Frobisher Cl BN23 .... 185 F7
Frobisher Ho RH10 .... 167 D1
Frog Hole La TN20 .... 58 C5
Frog La TN1 .... 4 A2
Front Cotts TN5 .... 31 E1
Fruitfields TN5 .... 32 C3
Fry Cres RH15 .... 72 E5
Fryatts Way TN39 .... 156 F6
Fryman's La TN31 .... 89 D2
FTA (Trng Ctr) TN5 .... 29 D6

Fulford Cl TN38 .... 159 A8
Fuller Cl TN5 .... 29 E5
Fuller Rd BN7 .... 123 A3
Fuller's Pas **18** BN7 ..... 123 D1
Fullers La TN31 .... 67 B6
Fullwood Ave BN9 .... 179 B7
Fulmar Cl BN3 .... 142 D1
Fulmar Dr RH19 .... 2 B3
Fulmar Pl **1** TN40 .... 157 C4
Furlongs The BN26 .... 170 F3
Furnace Ave TN3 .... 20 A3
Furnace La
  Beckley Furnace TN31 ..... 90 D7
  Hook Green TN3 .... 19 E4
  Horam TN21 .... 106 D8
  Warbleton TN21 .... 82 E2
Furnace Way TN22 .... 78 E7
Furness Rd BN20, BN21 ... 184 F2
Furnival Ct TN2 .... 16 F8
Furze Croft
  Hastings TN38 .... 159 A8
  Hove BN3 .... 163 D6
Furze Hill BN3 .... 163 D6
Furze Hill Ct BN3 .... 163 E6
Furze Hill Ho BN3 .... 163 E6
Furze La RH19 .... 1 B4
Furzelane BN3 .... 163 D6
Furzefield Ave TN3 .... 7 A8
Furzefield Chase RH19 ...... 1 E6
Furzefield Rd RH19 .... 1 E6
Fyning Pl TN39 .... 156 C5
Fyrsway TN35 .... 138 E4
Fysie La TN19 .... 44 D3

Gableson Ave BN1 .... 142 B4
Gage Ridge RH18 .... 11 E2
Gages The BN27 .... 152 D7
Gainsborough Cres BN23 . 174 D1
Gainsborough Ho **16** BN3 163 C7
Gainsborough La BN26 .... 172 E6
Gainsborough Rd TN40 ... 157 E6
Galley Hill View TN40 ..... 157 E4
Galliers Cl BN1 .... 143 B6
Gallipot Hill TN7 .... 13 C3
Gallops The BN7 .... 123 A1
Gallows Cl BN24 .... 174 E6
Gallows La BN24 .... 174 E6
Galveston Cl BN23 .... 185 F7
Gammons Way TN33 .... 88 E1
Gander Cl RH15 .... 73 A5
Gander Cl RH16 .... 50 F7
Gander Hill RH16 .... 50 F7
Gannet Ho
  5 Eastbourne BN21 ... 185 A2
  Hove BN3 .... 142 B8
Garden Cl Bexhill TN40 .... 157 D4
  East Grinstead RH19 .... 2 B1
  Portslade-by-Sea BN41 ... 162 C8
  Shoreham-by-Sea BN43 .. 140 B1
Garden Cotts **14** TN34 160 E4
Garden Ho The BN1 .... 189 F6
Garden House La RH19 ..... 10 F7
Garden Mews BN20 .... 188 D8
Garden Rd TN1 .... 8 B4
Garden St Lewes BN7 ...... 146 D8
  Royal Tunbridge Wells TN1 . 8 B4
Garden Wood Rd RH19 ..... 10 C8
Gardener St BN41 .... 162 B8
Gardens The
  Southwick BN42 .... 161 F7
Gardner Centre Rd BN1 ... 144 B6
Gardner Cl BN23 .... 185 F7
Gardner Rd BN41, BN42 ... 162 A7
Gardner St Brighton BN1 .. 189 A5
  Herstmonceux BN27 ...... 130 F6
Gardner's Hill TN31 .... 70 B6
Garfield Rd BN27 .... 152 C7
Garland Rd RH19 .... 1 D2
Garnet Dr BN20, BN21 .... 184 C7
Garnet Ho **13** BN2 ...... 164 C4
Garston Pk TN19 .... 62 B6
Garth Cl TN39 .... 157 A5
Gatehouse Cl TN39 .... 157 A5
Gatehouse La
  Burgess Hill BN6, RH15 .. 72 C4
  Framefield TN22 .... 79 C7
Gatelands Dr TN39 .... 157 B6
Gatesmead RH16 .... 50 F8
Gattons Cty Inf Sch The
  RH15 .... 72 E3
Gattons The RH15 .... 72 E3
Gatwick Farm Cotts RH19 ... 3 A4
Gaudick Cl BN20 .... 184 E1
Gaudick Rd BN20 .... 184 C1
Gavin Astor Cl TN40 .... 158 A6
Geary Pl TN5 .... 114 E3
Geering Pk BN27 .... 152 D7
Geering Rd BN24 .... 174 B5
Geers Wood TN21 .... 81 F6
Geerswood Cotts **2** TN21 . 82 A6

Gemma Cl BN27 .... 152 E7
Geneva Rd BN9 .... 179 D6
Genistos The BN6 .... 97 E4
Gensing Rd TN38 .... 159 C7
George Hill TN32 .... 64 B3
George Rainey Sch TN38 . 159 C7
George St Brighton BN2 .. 189 A5
  Hailsham BN27 .... 152 C7
  Hastings TN34 .... 160 A3
  Hove BN3 .... 163 B6
  Portslade-by-Sea BN41 .. 162 C7
  Royal Tunbridge Wells TN2 . 8 C3
  Southwick BN41 .... 162 A7
  Sparrow's Green TN5 ...... 29 F6
Georgian Cl TN40 .... 157 E5
Georgian Wlk TN38 .... 158 F8
Gerald Cl RH15 .... 73 D3
Gerald Rd BN25 .... 180 F1
Gerard St BN1 .... 189 A8
German St TN36 .... 117 E7
Ghyll Rd Crowborough TN6 . 25 E4
  Heathfield TN21 .... 82 A6
Ghyll Side Rd TN31 .... 67 B7
Ghyllside BN2 .... 143 E1
Ghyllside Ave TN34 .... 136 D4
Ghyllside Dr TN34 .... 136 D4
Ghyllside Way TN34 .... 136 D4
Gibb Cl TN40 .... 158 A5
Gibbetts TN3 .... 6 F2
Gibbon Rd BN9 .... 179 C6
Gibraltar Rise TN21 .... 82 A7
Gibson Ct BN7 .... 123 D2
Giffards Cl RH19 .... 1 F1
Gilbert Rd
  Eastbourne BN22 .... 185 B4
  Hastings TN38 .... 159 B8
Gilbert Way BN27 .... 152 B5
Gilberts Dr BN20 .... 187 B8
Gilda Cres RH16 .... 173 A6
Gildredge Rd
  Eastbourne BN21 .... 184 F2
  Seaford BN25 .... 180 F3
Gilham La RH18 .... 11 E2
Gill The TN2 .... 9 E8
Gillham Wood Ave TN39 . 156 D3
Gillham Wood Rd TN39 .. 156 D3
Gilligans The RH15 .... 72 F5
Gillridge Gn TN6 .... 25 F4
Gilman's Dr TN38 .... 135 F1
Gilsman's Hill TN38 .... 136 A1
Gilsman's Pk TN38 .... 135 F1
Gimble Way TN2 .... 9 D8
Gingerbread La TN18 .... 32 F2
Gipps Cross La TN3 .... 6 F3
Girton Ho BN41 .... 162 F6
Githa Rd TN35 .... 160 C6
Glade The Hailsham BN27 . 151 F6
  Mayfield TN20 .... 40 A3
  Uckfield TN22 .... 78 D7
Gladepoint **7** RH16 ...... 50 E5
Glades The Bexhill TN40 .. 157 E6
  East Grinstead RH19 .... 2 B1
Gladstone Bldgs BN6 ..... 101 E4
Gladstone Cl BN22 .... 173 F1
Gladstone Pl BN21 .... 164 C8
Gladstone Rd
  Burgess Hill RH15 .... 73 C4
  Crowborough TN6 .... 25 F1
  Portslade-by-Sea BN41 ... 162 B7
Gladstone Terr BN2 .... 189 B7
Gladys Ave BN10 .... 178 D6
Gladys Rd BN3 .... 142 D1
Glassenbury Dr TN40 ...... 157 F5
Glastonbury Rd BN3 .... 162 D6
Gleave Cl RH19 .... 2 A2
Glebe Cl Bexhill TN40 ..... 157 D3
  Eastbourne BN20 .... 184 D3
  Lewes BN7 .... 146 A8
  Southwick BN42 .... 161 F7
Glebe Cotts TN33 .... 134 C4
Glebe Cty Mid Sch BN42 . 161 D7
Glebe Dr BN25 .... 180 E3
Glebe The Felbridge RH19 . 1 A4
  Hastings TN34 .... 160 B8
  Haywards Heath RH16 ...... 51 A8
  Hurstpierpoint BN6 .... 97 A6
  Pembury TN2 .... 9 D8
  Plumpton TN5 .... 116 F1
Glebe Villas BN3 .... 162 D7
Glebelands Cl BN43 .... 161 B8
Glebelands The TN6 .... 25 F2
Glen Cl BN26 .... 172 F4
Glen Cotts BN26 .... 172 F4
Glen Rise BN1 .... 142 B5
Glen Rise TN22 .... 55 D1
Glen Vue RH19 .... 1 E1
Glencoe TN6 .... 25 F2
Glendale Ave BN21 .... 184 C5

Glendale Ct TN1 .... 8 D6
Glendale Rd
  Burgess Hill RH15 .... 73 B2
  Hove BN3 .... 163 D7
Glendor Rd BN3 .... 162 E6
Glendyne Cl RH19 .... 11 A8
Glendyne Way RH19 .... 11 A8
Gleneagles Cl
  Bexhill TN40 .... 157 E5
  Seaford BN25 .... 180 A6
Gleneagles Ct **13** RH16 . 50 E4
Gleneagles Dr
  Hailsham BN27 .... 152 A8
  Hastings TN38 .... 158 F7
Glenfalls Ave BN1 .... 143 A7
Glengorse TN33 .... 112 F3
Glenham Pl RH19 .... 21 A5
Glenleigh Ave TN39 .... 156 F6
Glenleigh Park Rd TN39 .. 157 A6
Glenleigh Wlk TN32 .... 64 A4
Glenmore Mews **3** BN21 185 A3
Glenmore Pk TN2 .... 16 F8
Glenmore Rd TN6 .... 25 C3
Glenmore Rd E TN6 .... 25 D3
Glenthorn Rd TN39 .... 157 A4
Glenthorne Ho **11** BN21 . 184 F4
Glenview Cl TN35 .... 160 D5
Glessing Rd BN24 .... 174 B6
Gleton Ave BN3 .... 141 D2
Gloucester Ave TN40 ...... 158 A5
Gloucester Cl
  East Grinstead RH19 ..... 11 A8
  Eastbourne BN22 .... 173 C2
Gloucester Cotts **3** TN34 160 A4
Gloucester Ct BN23 .... 174 E1
Gloucester Pas **2** BN1 .. 189 A6
Gloucester Pl BN1 .... 189 A6
Gloucester Rd
  Brighton BN1 .... 189 A6
  Burgess Hill RH15 .... 73 B3
  Sparrow's Green TN5 ...... 29 F6
Gloucester St BN1, BN2 .. 189 A6
Glovers La TN39, TN40 ... 157 C7
Glynde Ave
  Eastbourne BN22 .... 173 E1
  Saltdean BN2 .... 177 D6
Glynde CE Prim Sch BN8 . 147 F7
Glynde Cl BN9 .... 168 D2
Glynde Ct TN39 .... 156 C3
Glynde Ho BN3 .... 163 D6
Glynde Rd BN2 .... 164 D6
Glynde Sta BN8 .... 147 F6
Glyndebourne Ave BN2 .. 177 C6
Glyndebourne Gdns
  TN37 .... 136 C6
Glyndley Manor Cottage Est
  BN24 .... 152 F2
Glyne Ascent TN40 .... 157 F5
Glyne Barn Cl TN40 .... 158 A5
Glyne Dr TN40 .... 158 A5
Glyne Gap Sch TN40 .... 158 A5
Glyne Hall TN40 .... 157 D3
Glynleigh **17** BN2 .... 189 B6
Glynleigh Dr BN26 .... 173 C6
Glynleigh Rd BN24 .... 153 A1
Glynn Rd BN10 .... 167 C1
Glynn Rd W BN10 .... 167 C1
Glynn Rise BN10 .... 167 B1
Goatham La TN31 .... 89 E5
Goddards Green Hospl
  (Cuckfield Hospl Annexe)
  BN6 .... 72 B6
Godden Cl TN31 .... 67 B7
Godden Rd BN6 .... 101 E4
Goddens Gill TN31 .... 67 B7
Godfrey Cl BN7 .... 123 E2
Godwin Rd Hastings TN35 160 C5
  Hove BN3 .... 141 D1
Goffs The BN21 .... 184 E3
Golby Cl BN10 .... 178 A7
Gold La BN10 .... 167 C2
Goldbridge Rd BN8, TN22 .. 76 E7
Goldcrest Dr TN22 .... 78 D5
Golden Cl RH15 .... 73 D3
Golden Miller La BN26 .... 172 F6
Goldhurst Gn TN36 .... 116 E5
Golding Rd BN21 .... 174 F2
Goldsmid Rd BN1, BN3 .. 163 E7
Goldsmith Cl BN23 .... 174 E3
Goldsmiths Ave TN6 .... 25 D3
Goldsmiths L Ctr TN6 .... 25 F4
Goldstone Cl BN3 .... 142 A2
Goldstone Cres BN3 .... 142 B2
Goldstone Cty Jun Sch
  BN3 .... 141 E1
Goldstone Ho **4** BN3 .. 163 B8
Goldstone La BN3 .... 163 B8
Goldstone Rd BN3 .... 163 B7
Goldstone St BN3 .... 163 B7
Goldstone Villas BN3 ...... 163 B7

Goldstone Way BN3 .... 142 A2
Golf Dr BN1 .... 143 B3
Goods Station Rd TN1 .... 8 B4
Goodtrees La TN8 .... 4 B2
Goodwin Cl BN27 .... 129 A2
Goodwins Cl RH19 .... 1 D3
Goodwins The TN2 .... 7 F1
Goodwood Cl
  Bexhill TN40 .... 157 D6
  Willingdon BN20 .... 173 B2
Goodwood Ct **2** BN3 ... 163 D7
Goodwood Way BN2 .... 143 F3
Gooseberry La TN31 .... 67 A3
Gordon Ave BN43 .... 161 A7
Gordon Cl RH16 .... 51 B8
Gordon Ho RH15 .... 73 C4
Gordon Pl TN39 .... 157 B6
Gordon Rd Brighton BN1 . 142 F2
  Burgess Hill RH15 .... 73 C4
  Buxted TN22 .... 56 C3
  Crowborough TN6 .... 25 F2
  Hailsham BN27 .... 152 B7
  Hastings TN34 .... 160 A4
  Haywards Heath RH16 ...... 50 E6
  Portslade-by-Sea BN41 .. 162 C7
  Royal Tunbridge Wells TN4 . 8 C7
  Shoreham-by-Sea BN43 .. 161 A7
  Southwick BN41 .... 162 A7
Gore Park Ave BN21 .... 184 D4
Gore Park Rd BN21 .... 184 D4
Gorham Ave BN2 .... 177 A6
Gorham Cl BN2 .... 177 A6
Gorham Ct BN10 .... 177 E4
Gorham Way BN10 .... 177 E4
Goring Cl BN1 .... 143 F5
Gorringe Cl
  Lower Willingdon BN20 .. 173 A3
  Shoreham-by-Sea BN43 . 161 D7
Gorringe Dr BN20 .... 173 A3
Gorringe Rd BN21, BN22 . 185 A4
Gorringe Valley Rd
  BN20, BN22 .... 173 A3
Gorse Cl Eastbourne BN20 184 B5
  Portslade-by-Sea BN41 .. 140 F4
Gorse Dr BN25 .... 180 F6
Gorse Hill TN21 .... 59 F1
Gorse Rd TN2 .... 8 E5
Gorselands TN33 .... 88 E1
Gorses The TN39 .... 156 C2
Gorsethorn Way TN35 .... 138 E4
Gorseway The TN39 .... 156 C5
Gosford Way BN26 .... 172 F6
Gote La BN8 .... 124 D4
Goudhurst Cl BN23 .... 174 D1
Gower Rd RH16 .... 50 E3
Gows Croft BN7 .... 145 E5
Grace Ct BN6 .... 97 E5
Gradwell End BN8 .... 100 D7
Graffham Cl BN2 .... 164 E6
Grafton St BN2 .... 189 B4
Graham Ave Brighton BN1 142 F5
  Portslade-by-Sea BN41 .. 140 F4
Graham Cl BN41 .... 140 F4
Graham Cres BN41 .... 140 F4
Grampian Cl
  Eastbourne BN23 .... 174 C3
  Royal Tunbridge Wells TN2 . 8 D5
Granary Cotts TN33 .... 112 E4
Grand Ave Bexhill TN40 .. 158 A5
  Hassocks BN6 .... 97 F4
  Hove BN3 .... 163 C6
  Seaford BN25 .... 180 D6
Grand Avenue Mansions **25**
  BN3 .... 163 C6
Grand Cres BN2 .... 177 A5
Grand Ct
  Eastbourne BN21 .... 185 A1
  10 Hastings TN37 ...... 159 C6
Grand Hotel Bldgs BN21 . 185 A1
Grand Junction Rd
  BN1, BN2 .... 189 A4
Grand Par Brighton BN2 .. 189 B5
  Eastbourne BN21 .... 185 B2
  Hastings TN37, TN38 ..... 159 C6
  Polegate BN26 .... 172 F6
Grand Parade Mews BN2 . 189 A5
Grange Ave TN34 .... 136 D4
Grange Cl Brighton BN1 .. 142 E1
  Burgess Hill RH15 .... 73 C5
  Crowborough TN6 .... 25 D1
  Horam TN21 .... 106 F6
Grange Court Dr TN39 .... 157 B6
Grange Ct
  Eastbourne BN21 .... 184 F2
  Lewes BN7 .... 146 C8
  9 Southwick BN42 ..... 161 E7
Grange End BN20 .... 184 F1
Grange Gdns
  Eastbourne BN20 .... 184 F2
  Rusthall TN4 .... 7 D4
Grange Ind Est The BN42 161 D7

Grange Rd
Barcombe Cross BN8 .... 101 D4
Eastbourne BN20, BN21, ... 184 F1
Hastings TN34 .... 136 E5
Hove BN3 .... 162 E8
Lewes BN7 .... 146 C8
Rusthall TN4 .... 7 D4
Southwick BN42 .... 161 E7
Uckfield TN22 .... 78 C7
Grange The
Barcombe Cross BN8 .... 101 D4
Saltdean BN2 .... 177 D4
Uckfield TN22 .... 78 C7
Grangeways BN1 .... 142 E5
Granoon Cotts BN20 .... 187 A4
Grant St BN2 .... 189 B7
Grantham Bank BN8 .... 101 E4
Grantham Cl BN8 .... 100 E7
Grantham Rd BN1 .... 143 A1
Grants Hill Ho TN22 .... 78 C7
Granville Ct
  2 Eastbourne BN20 .... 184 F1
  10 Hove BN3 .... 163 B7
  4 Seaford BN25 .... 180 E2
Granville Rd
  Eastbourne BN20 .... 184 F1
  Hove BN3 .... 163 E7
  Royal Tunbridge Wells TN1 . 8 C5
Graperies The 3 BN2 ...... 164 C5
Grasmere Cl BN23 .... 174 B4
Grassington Rd BN20 ...... 184 F1
Grassmere Ave BN10 .... 177 F4
Grassmere Ct BN10 .... 178 A8
Gratton Ct TN39 .... 157 A3
Gravebury BN27 .... 152 C7
Gravelye Cl RH16 .... 51 B5
Gravelye La
  Haywards Heath RH16 ..... 51 A4
  Haywards Heath RH16 ..... 51 B6
Gravett Ct RH15 .... 72 F2
Graycoats Dr TN6 .... 25 F2
Grays Cotts TN33 .... 112 F3
Grays Cty Inf Sch BN9 .... 179 D6
Graystone La TN35 .... 137 D3
Grazebrook Cl TN39 .... 156 C3
Great Brooms Rd TN4 .... 8 C8
Great Cliffe Rd BN23 ...... 174 E1
Great College St BN2 ..... 164 C4
Great Courtlands TN3 .... 7 A3
Great Dixter TN31 .... 66 F7
Great Footway TN3 .... 6 F3
Great Hall Arc 3 TN1 .... 8 B3
Great Heathmead RH16 .... 50 B6
Great House Ct 4 RH19 ... 10 F8
Great Knelle Farm
  (Childrens Farm) TN31 ... 68 A8
Great Oak TN19 .... 45 A3
Great Rough BN8 .... 76 A6
Great Sanders Ho TN33 .... 88 D4
Great Walstead Sch RH16 ... 51 F6
Great Wilkins BN1 .... 144 B5
Greater Paddock BN8 .... 124 E6
Greatham Ct BN1 .... 142 E6
Grecian Rd TN1 .... 8 B2
Greeba Ct 3 TN38 .... 159 B6
Green Cl Ringmer BN8 ...... 124 D5
  4 Southwick BN42 .... 161 E7
Green Ct 3 BN42 .... 161 E7
Green Field Cl BN42 .... 161 E8
Green Gate BN10 .... 167 C1
Green Gr BN27 .... 152 B8
Green Hedges TN32 .... 63 E4
Green Hedges Ave RH19 .. 1 D2
Green Hedges Cl RH19 .... 1 D2
Green La Bexhill TN39 ..... 156 D5
  Broyle Side BN8 .... 103 B1
  Crowborough TN6 .... 26 B2
  Heathfield TN21 .... 82 B6
  Jevington BN26 .... 172 C1
  Lewes BN7 .... 146 C8
  Seaford BN25 .... 180 E2
  South Chailey BN8 .... 100 E7
  South Street BN8 .... 75 E1
  Woodingdean BN2 .... 165 E6
Green Meadows RH16 ...... 51 B8
Green Park Cnr RH17 .... 74 B4
Green Rd RH17 .... 74 B5
Green Ridge BN1 .... 142 B5
Green Sq TN5 .... 29 F5
Green St BN20, BN21 ...... 184 C4
Green The
  Blackboys TN22 .... 80 A6
  Bodiam TN32 .... 65 E7
  Catsfield TN33 .... 133 E8
  Ewhurst Green TN32 .... 66 B5
  Hastings TN38 .... 159 B8
  Hove BN3 .... 142 C2
  Langton Green TN3 .... 6 E3
  Newick BN8 .... 76 D7
  Ninfield TN33 .... 133 B5
  Ringmer BN8 .... 124 D5

Green The
  Rottingdean BN2 .... 165 F2
  Sedlescombe TN33 .... 113 E8
  Southwick BN42 .... 161 E7
Green View RH15 .... 72 E3
Green Way
  Eastbourne BN20 .... 184 B6
  Royal Tunbridge Wells TN2 . 8 E8
Green Wlk
  Hailsham BN27 .... 129 C1
  Seaford BN25 .... 181 B2
Green Wlk The BN22 .... 173 B3
Greenacres
  Brighton BN1 .... 142 F1
  Peacehaven BN10 .... 167 D2
  Telscombe Cliffs BN10 .... 178 A7
  Westfield TN35 .... 114 E3
Greenacres Dr
  Hailsham BN27 .... 152 C7
  Ringmer BN8 .... 124 D4
Greenacres Way BN27 ..... 152 C8
Greenbank Ave BN2 .... 177 D6
Greene Ct BN7 .... 146 B8
Greenfield Cl
  Brighton BN1 .... 143 A5
  Rusthall TN4 .... 7 C5
Greenfield Cres BN1 .... 142 F5
Greenfield Dr TN22 .... 78 D4
Greenfield Rd
  Burwash TN19 .... 62 C7
  Eastbourne BN21 .... 184 D4
Greenfields BN27 .... 129 A1
Greenfields Cl TN37 .... 136 B6
Greenfields Sch RH18 ..... 11 C1
Greenhill Pk RH16 .... 51 A2
Greenhill Way
  Haywards Heath RH16 .... 51 A2
  Peacehaven BN10 .... 167 C2
Greenlands Cl RH15 .... 98 B8
Greenlands Dr RH15 .... 98 B8
Greenleaf Gdns BN26 ..... 173 A8
Greenlees Hove BN3 .... 141 D2
  Pembury TN2 .... 9 C6
Greenstede Ave RH19 ...... 1 F2
Greenway Ct BN2 .... 177 A5
Greenways Bexhill TN39 .. 156 F7
  Haywards Heath RH16 .... 50 F6
  Ovingdean BN2 .... 165 D3
  Portslade-by-Sea BN41 .. 141 B1
  Southwick BN42 .... 140 F1
Greenways Cnr BN2 .... 165 D4
Greenways Cres BN43 ..... 140 A1
Greenwell Cl BN25 .... 181 B4
Greenwich Rd BN27 .... 152 D7
Greenwich Way BN10 ..... 178 C7
Greenwoods La TN21 ...... 83 D7
Greggs Wood Rd TN1, TN2 . 8 E7
Gregory La BN24 .... 174 F5
Gregory Wlk TN33 .... 113 E8
Grenada TN39 .... 157 A2
Grenada Cl TN39 .... 156 D4
Grenham Ct TN35 .... 137 C3
Grenville Ho BN10 .... 167 D1
Grenville Rd BN24 .... 175 C4
Grenville St BN1 .... 189 F5
Gresham BN27 .... 175 B6
Gresham Cl BN21 .... 184 C6
Gresham Way TN38 .... 159 A8
Gresley Rd TN38 .... 135 F5
Greville Rd TN35 .... 137 C4
Grey Alders RH16 .... 51 B6
Grey Tower Bglws BN24 .. 175 C3
Greyfriars BN3 .... 163 D8
Greyfriars Ct BN7 .... 123 D1
Greyfriars Pl TN36 .... 118 B6
Greyhorses TN39 .... 156 B4
Greys Rd BN20 .... 184 D3
Greystones Ct TN6 .... 25 D4
Grinstead La RH19 .... 21 C7
Grinstead Mount 4 BN2 . 164 F5
Gromenfield TN3 .... 15 C7
Groombridge Hill TN3 .... 6 D1
Groombridge Place TN3 ... 15 C8
Groombridge Place Gdns
  TN3 .... 15 C8
Groombridge Rd TN3 .... 6 A1
Grosvenor Bridge TN1, TN4 . 8 B5
Grosvenor Cres TN38 ..... 159 A6
Grosvenor Cres TN38 ..... 159 A6
Grosvenor Ct BN1 .... 142 E3
Grosvenor Gdns TN38 .... 158 F6
Grosvenor Pk TN1, TN4 .... 8 A4
Grosvenor Rd
  East Grinstead RH19 .... 1 D1
  Royal Tunbridge Wells TN1 . 8 A4
  Seaford BN25 .... 180 E4
Grosvenor St BN2 .... 189 B5
Grosvenor Wlk TN1 .... 8 A4
Grove Ave TN1 .... 8 A2
Grove Bank 8 BN2 .... 189 B6
Grove Ct 5 BN3 .... 163 C6

Grove Hill Brighton BN2 ... 189 B6
  Grove Hill BN27 .... 129 D7
Grove Hill Gdns TN1 .... 8 B2
Grove Hill Rd TN1, TN2 ...... 8 B3
Grove La TN31 .... 70 C4
Grove Park Sch TN6 .... 25 E1
Grove Rd
  Burgess Hill RH15 .... 73 B3
  Eastbourne BN21 .... 184 F2
  Hastings TN35 .... 137 D4
  Seaford BN25 .... 180 F3
Grove Sch The TN38 .... 135 F2
Grove St BN2 .... 189 B6
Grove The Battle TN33 ..... 112 F3
  Bexhill TN39 .... 156 E5
  Crowborough TN6 .... 25 E1
  Eastbourne BN20 .... 184 B7
  Hailsham BN27 .... 152 B6
  Haywards Heath RH16 ..... 51 B3
  Mayfield TN20 .... 40 A2
  Newhaven BN9 .... 168 E2
  Pembury TN2 .... 9 D8
  Rye TN31 .... 93 C6
  Willingdon BN20 .... 172 F3
  Grove Villa 3 BN1 .... 189 F7
Groveland Cl RH15 .... 72 F1
Grovelands Cty Prim Sch
  BN27 .... 129 A1
Grovelands Rd BN27 ...... 129 A1
Grovely La TN1 .... 84 B1
Grover St 3 TN1 .... 8 B4
Growers End BN8 .... 76 D7
Guardian Ct BN26 .... 172 F7
Guardswell Pl BN25 .... 180 F3
Guestling Rd BN22 .... 185 D5
Guestling-Bradshaw
  Prim Sch TN35 .... 138 A8
Guildford Rd 7 TN1, TN2 .. 8 B3
Guildford St BN1 .... 189 F6
Guilford Rd BN1 .... 189 F6
Guinness Ct BN9 .... 168 E1
Guinness Trust
  Holiday Home The BN9 ... 168 E2
Guldeford La TN29, TN31 .. 71 F3
Guldeford Lane Cnr TN31 . 71 D2
Guldeford Rd TN31 .... 93 E7
Gun Rd TN22 .... 80 A6
Gundreda Rd BN7 .... 123 B2
Gunter's La TN39 .... 157 A6
Gurth Rd TN35 .... 160 C5
Gwent Ct 7 BN20 .... 185 C4
Gwydir Mansions 4 BN3 . 163 D6
Gwyneth Gr TN40 .... 157 F7
Gwynne Gdns RH19 .... 1 C2

Hackenden Cl RH19 .... 1 E3
Hackenden La RH19 .... 1 E3
Hackhurst La BN27 .... 128 B4
Hackhurst Lane Ind Est
  BN27 .... 128 B4
Hackwood TN32 .... 63 E4
Haddington Cl BN3 .... 163 B6
Haddington St 11 BN3 .... 163 B7
Hadley Ct Polegate BN26 . 173 A6
  Royal Tunbridge Wells TN4 . 7 F6
Hadley Ho 6 BN21 .... 184 F3
Hadlow Ave BN23 .... 174 B4
Hadlow Cl BN2 .... 164 D6
Hadlow Down Rd TN6 ...... 38 B4
Hadrian Ave BN42 .... 162 A8
Hadrian Gdns TN38 .... 136 A6
Haig Ave BN1 .... 143 D6
Hailsham Ave BN2 .... 166 D3
Hailsham Com Coll BN27 . 152 B8
Hailsham Rd
  Eastbourne BN24 .... 174 B5
  Heathfield TN21 .... 82 A6
  Herstmonceux BN27 ...... 130 E5
  Polegate BN26 .... 172 F7
  Stone Cross BN24, BN26 . 173 F8
Hairpin Croft BN10 .... 167 C1
Half Mile Dro BN8 .... 125 B7
Hall's Grove Rd TN2 .... 8 D2
Hall's Hole Rd TN2 .... 8 E4
Halland Cl BN27 .... 173 D1
Halland Rd BN2 .... 143 F4
Hallett Rd BN2 .... 164 D7
Halley Pk BN27 .... 152 D7
Halley Rd
  Cade Street TN21 .... 82 E8
  Wartling BN27 .... 131 B1
Halls Cotts TN5 .... 29 F5
Hallyburton Rd BN3 .... 162 D8
Halsford Croft RH19 .... 1 B3
Halsford Gn RH19 .... 1 B3
Halsford La RH19 .... 1 C3
Halsford Park Cty Prim Sch
  RH19 .... 1 C2
Halsford Park Rd RH19 .... 1 C2
Halton Cres TN34 .... 160 B6
Halton Hts TN34 .... 160 B6

Halton Pl TN34 .... 160 B6
Halton Rd BN2 .... 185 C4
Halton Shaws BN6 .... 97 B5
Halton Terr TN34 .... 160 B6
Ham Bsns Ctr BN43 .... 161 A7
Ham La Burwash TN19 ..... 62 B6
  Lewes BN7 .... 146 D8
Ringmer BN8 .... 124 C6
Hambleton Cl BN23 .... 174 D3
Hambrook Rd TN5 .... 73 C1
Hamelsham Ct BN27 ...... 152 A8
Hamilton Cl BN41 .... 141 A3
Hamilton Ct
  Brighton BN2 .... 165 A3
  Royal Tunbridge Wells TN4 . 8 A5
Hamilton Gdns TN35 ...... 137 D3
Hamilton Ho
  12 Eastbourne BN21 ...... 184 E4
  Royal Tunbridge Wells TN4 . 8 A5
  Seaford BN25 .... 180 E4
Hamilton Lodge Sch BN2 . 164 B5
Hamilton Mansions BN3 . 163 B5
Hamilton Rd BN1 .... 189 F7
Hamilton Terr TN39 .... 157 A4
Hamlands La BN22 .... 173 B3
Hamlin's Cnr BN6 .... 72 A6
Hammer La BN27, TN21 ... 107 F5
Hammerwood Pk RH19 .... 3 C2
Hammerwood Rd RH19 .... 11 E6
Hammonds Dr
  BN22, BN23 .... 185 C7
Hammonds Ridge RH15 ... 72 F1
Hammy Cl BN43 .... 161 C8
Hammy La BN43 .... 161 B8
Hammy Way BN43 .... 161 B8
Hampden Ave BN22 .... 173 F1
Hampden Cl TN33 .... 112 B4
Hampden Gdns BN9 ...... 168 D2
Hampden Park
  Cty Inf Sch BN22 .... 173 F2
Hampden Park Dr BN22 .. 184 E8
Hampden Park Rd BN22 . 173 E2
Hampden Park Sports Ctr
  BN22 .... 173 D2
Hampden Park Sta BN22 . 173 F1
Hampden Rd BN2 .... 164 C7
Hampden Terr 8 BN2 ..... 185 C4
Hampshire Ct
  Brighton BN2 .... 189 B4
  6 Eastbourne BN23 ...... 174 E1
Hampstead Rd BN1 .... 142 D2
Hampton Pl BN1 .... 163 E5
Hampton Rd BN1 .... 163 E5
Hampton St 14 BN1 .... 163 E5
Hampton Way RH19 .... 10 F7
Hamsey Cl Brighton BN2 . 164 F5
  Eastbourne BN20 .... 184 B6
Hamsey Cres BN7 .... 123 A2
Hamsey Cty Prim Sch
  BN8 .... 123 A8
Hamsey La
  Cooksbridge BN8 .... 123 B7
  Seaford BN25 .... 181 C2
Hamsey Rd Saltdean BN2 . 177 D4
  Sharpthorne RH19 .... 21 A6
Hamshaw Ct BN22 .... 184 F8
Hamsland RH17 .... 33 C4
Hanbury Park Sports Stad
  RH16 .... 51 A5
Hanging Birch La TN21 .... 81 D1
Hangleton Cl BN3 .... 141 D2
Hangleton Cty Inf &
  Jun Sch BN3 .... 141 E2
Hangleton Gdns BN3 ..... 141 D1
Hangleton La
  Hove BN3, BN41 .... 141 D2
  Portslade-by-Sea BN41 .. 141 B2
Hangleton Manor Cl BN3 . 141 E2
Hangleton Rd BN3 .... 141 E2
Hangleton Valley Dr BN3 . 141 D4
Hangleton Way BN3 .... 141 D3
Hankham Cty Prim Sch
  BN24 .... 174 B8
Hankham Hall Rd BN24 ... 174 D7
Hankham Rd BN24 .... 174 B6
Hankham St BN24 .... 174 B8
Hanlye La RH17 .... 50 B8
Hannington Pl BN6 .... 97 A7
Hanover Cl Bexhill TN40 .. 157 C5
  Seaford BN25 .... 180 B6
Hanover Cres BN2 .... 189 B7
Hanover Ct Brighton BN2 . 189 B7
  Eastbourne BN21 .... 184 D5
  Haywards Heath RH16 .... 50 D4
Hanover Mews BN2 .... 189 B7
Hanover Rd
  Eastbourne BN20 .... 184 C6
  Royal Tunbridge Wells TN1 . 8 A4
Hanover St BN2 .... 189 B7

Hanover Terr BN2 .... 189 B7
Hanson Rd BN9 .... 179 C6
Harbour Barn TN36 .... 118 B6
Harbour Ct BN42 .... 161 F7
Harbour Farm TN36 .... 118 B6
Harbour Rd TN31 .... 93 D4
Harbour View Cl BN25 .... 180 B6
Harbour View Rd BN9 .... 179 B5
Harbour Way
  Hastings TN38 .... 135 E7
  Shoreham-by-Sea BN43 . 161 E4
Harbour's Yd TN33 .... 112 E4
Harcourt Cl TN22 .... 78 C6
Harcourt Rd TN22 .... 78 D6
Harding Ave BN22 .... 185 B6
Hardwick Rd
  Eastbourne BN21 .... 185 A2
  Hove BN3 .... 141 E3
Hardwick Way BN3 .... 141 E3
Hardwicke Rd TN34 .... 160 B6
Hardy Dr BN23 .... 185 F6
Hare Way TN37 .... 136 C5
Harebeating Cl BN27 ..... 129 C2
Harebeating Cres BN27 .. 129 C2
Harebeating Dr BN27 .... 129 C2
Harebeating Gdns BN27 . 129 C2
Harebeating La BN27 ..... 129 D1
Harebell Cl BN23 .... 174 C3
Harebell Dr BN41 .... 141 A3
Harecombe Rd TN6 .... 37 F8
Harecombe Rise TN6 ..... 37 F8
Haremere Hall Gdns TN19 . 44 E2
Haremere Hill TN19 .... 44 D2
Harescroft TN2 .... 16 F7
Harewood Cl TN39 .... 157 A3
Harewood Ct 8 BN3 ..... 163 C6
Harfield Cl BN9 .... 168 F2
Hargate Cl TN2 .... 16 F8
Hargreaves Rd BN22 ..... 174 A1
Harison Rd BN25 .... 181 A4
Harkness Dr TN34 .... 137 B5
Harlands Cl RH16, RH17 . 50 C6
Harlands Cty Prim Sch
  Haywards Heath RH16 ... 50 D7
  Uckfield TN22 .... 78 D8
Harlands Rd RH16, RH17 . 50 D6
Harlequin Gdns TN37 ..... 136 A6
Harlequin La TN6 .... 37 E8
Harlequin Pl TN6 .... 37 E8
Harley La TN21 .... 82 A6
Harley Shute Rd TN38 .... 158 E7
Harley Way TN38 .... 158 E6
Harmans Dr RH19 .... 2 B1
Harmans Mead RH19 .... 2 B1
Harmers Hay Rd BN27 .... 129 B1
Harmers Hill BN8 .... 76 C8
Harmony St TN4 .... 7 D4
Harmsworth Cres BN3 .... 141 E3
Harold Cl BN24 .... 175 F7
Harold Dr BN23 .... 185 F8
Harold Mews 2 TN38 .... 159 C6
Harold Pl TN34 .... 159 F7
Harold Rd TN34, TN35 .... 160 C5
Harold Terr TN33 .... 112 F3
Harpers Rd BN9 .... 179 C7
Harrier La TN33 .... 112 F4
Harriers Ct BN27 .... 152 D7
Harries Rd TN1, TN2 .... 8 E7
Harrington Cl 14 BN1 ... 142 E2
Harrington Mansions 7
  BN1 .... 185 A2
Harrington Pl
  Brighton BN2 .... 164 C8
  Eastbourne BN22 .... 185 A2
Hartington Rd BN2 .... 164 C8
Hartington Terr BN2 ...... 164 C8
Hartington Villas BN3 .... 163 B8
Hartwood Lodge 5 TN40 . 157 C4

Harvard Cl BN7 .... 123 C3
Harvard Rd BN8 .... 124 D5
Harvest Cl
  Haywards Heath RH16 ...... 51 B7
  Telscombe Cliffs BN10 .... 167 B2
Harvest Hill RH19 .... 10 E8
Harvest Way TN37 .... 136 C5
Harvesters RH16 .... 50 D2
Harvey Cl TN38 .... 135 F4
Harvey's La BN8, TN22 ..... 103 D4
Harveys Way BN7 .... 123 C1
Harvington Bsns Pk BN22 . 184 F8
Harwood Cl BN23 .... 185 E7
Harwoods Cl **3** RH19 ...... 10 F7
Harwoods La RH19 .... 10 F7
Haslam Cres TN40 .... 157 F6
Hasletts Cl TN4 .... 8 B6
Hassocks Cty Inf Sch BN6 .. 97 F4
Hassocks Lodge BN6 .... 97 F3
Hassocks Rd BN6 .... 97 B5
Hassocks Sta BN6 .... 97 E4
Hastings Ave BN25 .... 181 C5
Hastings Castle TN34 ...... 160 A4
Hastings Cl BN26 .... 173 B7
Hastings Coll of Arts & Tech
  TN38 .... 159 B6
Hastings Mus & Art Gall
  TN34 .... 159 E7
Hastings Mus of Local
  History TN34 .... 160 A4
Hastings Rd Battle TN33 ... 113 B2
  Bexhill TN40 .... 157 E5
  Bexhill TN40 .... 157 F5
  Brighton BN2 .... 164 C8
  Newenden TN17, TN18 ..... 48 C6
  Pembury TN2 .... 9 D6
  Pembury TN2 .... 9 F5
  The Moor TN18 .... 45 F6
Hastings Sea Life Ctr
  TN34 .... 160 B3
Hastings Sports Ctr TN34 159 D8
Hastings Sta TN34 .... 159 D8
Hatch End RH18 .... 11 F2
Hatchgate Cl RH17 .... 50 A6
Hatchgate La RH17 .... 50 A6
Hatfield Cl **16** BN3 .... 163 C6
Hatherley Rd TN37 .... 159 C7
Havelock Rd
  Bexhill TN39, TN40 .... 157 C6
  Brighton BN1 .... 142 F1
  Eastbourne BN22 .... 185 B4
  Hastings TN34 .... 159 F7
Haven Brow BN25 .... 181 A4
Haven Cl
  Beachlands BN24 .... 175 E6
  Lower Willingdon BN22 ... 173 B3
Haven Rd TN38 .... 158 D6
Hawkenbury Cl TN2 .... 8 D2
Hawkenbury Mead TN2 ...... 8 D1
Hawkenbury Rd TN2, TN3 .... 8 E1
Hawkenbury Way BN7 .... 123 A1
Hawkes Farm Cty Prim Sch
  BN27 .... 129 B3
Hawkhurst CE Prim Sch
  TN18 .... 45 F8
Hawkhurst Cl BN23 .... 174 D2
Hawkhurst Pl BN1 .... 143 D6
Hawkhurst Rd
  Brighton BN1 .... 143 D6
  Flimwell TN18, TN19, TN5 .. 32 E2
Hawkhurst Way TN39 .... 156 E3
Hawkins Cl BN43 .... 140 D1
Hawkins Cres BN43 .... 140 D2
Hawkins Rd BN43 .... 140 D1
Hawkins Way BN27 .... 152 B8
Hawks Farm Cl BN27 .... 129 B2
Hawks Rd BN27 .... 129 B2
Hawks Town Cres BN27 .... 129 C2
Hawksbridge Cl BN22 ...... 173 C3
Hawkstown Cl BN27 .... 129 B3
Hawkstown Gdns BN27 ..... 129 B3
Hawkstown View BN27 ..... 129 B3
Hawkswood Dr BN27 .... 129 C3
Hawkswood Rd BN27 .... 129 C3
Hawth Cl BN25 .... 180 C4
Hawth Cl BN25 .... 180 C4
Hawth Cres BN25 .... 180 C4
Hawth Gr BN25 .... 180 C4
Hawth Hill BN25 .... 180 C5
Hawth Park Rd BN25 .... 180 C4
Hawth Pl BN25 .... 180 C4
Hawth Rise BN25 .... 180 C4
Hawth Valley Ct **1** BN25 . 180 C4
Hawth Way BN25 .... 180 D4
Hawthorn Ave TN39 .... 156 D3
Hawthorn Bank BN2 .... 143 F4
Hawthorn Cl
  Burgess Hill RH15 .... 73 D5
  Saltdean BN2 .... 177 C6

Hawthorn Ct BN26 .... 173 B6
Hawthorn Rd
  Eastbourne BN23 .... 185 C7
  Hastings TN35 .... 160 D6
Hawthorn Rise BN9 .... 179 B7
Hawthorn Way BN41 .... 141 A3
Hawthorn Wlk TN2 .... 8 E8
Hawthorne Cl TN21 .... 82 B6
Hawthornes The TN31 .... 90 B4
Hawthorns The
  Burgess Hill RH15 .... 73 A5
  Hailsham BN27 .... 152 A7
Hawthylands Cres BN27 .... 129 B2
Hawthylands Dr BN27 ...... 129 B2
Hawthylands Rd BN27 ...... 129 B2
Haybourne Cl BN2 .... 164 E7
Haybourne Rd BN2 .... 164 E7
Hayes Cl
  Portslade-by-Sea BN41 ... 162 C8
  Ringmer BN8 .... 124 D5
Hayes La TN31 .... 91 C5
Hayes Plat TN31 .... 67 C5
Hayland Gn BN27 .... 129 C1
Haylind Rd RH16 .... 51 B5
Haystoun Cl BN22 .... 173 C2
Haystoun Pk BN22 .... 173 C2
Hayward Rd RH7 .... 123 A3
Haywards Heath Coll
  RH16 .... 50 D6
Haywards Heath Hospl
  RH16 .... 50 C4
Haywards Heath Sta RH16 . 50 E6
Haywards Rd
  Brighton BN1 .... 143 A6
  Haywards Heath RH16 ..... 50 E3
Haywood Way TN34 .... 137 C4
Hazel Bank **3** BN2 .... 189 B7
Hazel Cl Newhaven BN9 ... 179 B7
  Portslade-by-Sea BN41 ... 141 C3
Hazel Court Sch BN23 ..... 174 B3
Hazel Ct TN34 .... 136 F6
Hazel Gr Burgess Hill RH15 . 73 B1
  Lower Willingdon BN20 ... 173 A3
Hazelbank TN3 .... 6 F3
Hazeldene BN25 .... 181 B3
Hazeldene Meads BN1 ..... 142 D2
Hazeldene La BN8 .... 75 F7
Hazelgrove Gdns **8** RH16 . 50 E4
Hazelgrove Rd RH16 .... 50 E4
Hazelwood BN1 .... 142 D3
Hazelwood Ave
  BN22, BN26 .... 173 D4
Hazelwood Cl
  Bexhill TN39 .... 156 C3
  Royal Tunbridge Wells TN2 .. 8 E8
Hazelwood Cotts TN5 .... 31 D1
Hazelwood Gdns TN37 .... 136 D5
Heacham Dr BN23 .... 174 C2
Headland Ave BN25 .... 181 A3
Headlands Cl BN10 .... 178 E7
Heansill La TN18 .... 45 E8
Heath Cl **9** RH16 .... 50 E4
Heath Ct **6** RH16 .... 50 E5
Heath Hill Ave BN2 .... 144 A2
Heath Rd RH16 .... 50 E5
Heath Sq RH16 .... 50 D5
Heathcote Dr RH19 .... 1 C2
Heathdown Cl BN10 .... 167 D2
Heather Bank RH16 .... 50 C5
Heather Cl BN23 .... 174 B3
Heather Ct **9** BN1 .... 163 E6
Heather Way TN35 .... 138 F4
Heather Wlk TN6 .... 26 D1
Heatherdune Rd TN39 ..... 157 A5
Heathfield Ave BN2 .... 177 D6
Heathfield CE Prim Sch
  TN21 .... 82 D6
Heathfield Cl TN34 .... 136 F5
Heathfield Cres BN41 ...... 140 F3
Heathfield Dr BN41 .... 140 F4
Heathfield Gdns TN32 ..... 64 B3
Heathfield L Ctr TN21 ..... 82 D7
Heathfield Rd BN9 .... 168 C4
Heathfield Sch & Com Coll
  TN21 .... 82 E7
Heathfields TN2 .... 8 D4
Heathlands TN35 .... 114 E3
Heathy Brow BN10 .... 167 B1
Heathy Rd RH16 .... 51 B7
Heighton Cl TN39 .... 156 D3
Heighton Cres BN9 .... 168 D2
Heighton Rd BN9 .... 168 E2
Heights The
  Brighton BN1 .... 142 B5
  Hastings TN35 .... 137 E5
Helena Cl **6** Haywards Heath RH16 . 50 E4
Helena Cl BN41 .... 141 C2
Helena Rd BN2 .... 144 C1
Helensdene Wlk TN37 ..... 159 D8

Helenswood Sch (Lower)
  TN37 .... 136 D6
Helenswood Sch (Upper)
  TN34 .... 137 B4
Hellingly Cl BN2 .... 164 F5
Hellingly Cty Prim Sch
  BN27 .... 128 F5
Helvellyn Dr BN23 .... 174 C4
Hempstead Gdns TN22 .... 78 D7
Hempstead La
  Hailsham BN27 .... 128 F1
  Uckfield TN22 .... 78 D7
  Uckfield TN22 .... 78 E8
Hempstead Rd
  Saltdean BN2 .... 166 D3
  Uckfield TN22 .... 78 C7
Hempstead Rise TN22 ...... 78 C7
Hemsley Ho TN21 .... 81 F8
Henderson Cl TN34 .... 136 F3
Hendon St BN2 .... 164 D5
Henfield Cl BN2 .... 164 F6
Henfield Rd BN22 .... 173 E2
Henfield Way'BN3 .... 141 F3
Henge Way BN41 .... 141 B2
Hengist Cl BN23 .... 185 F8
Henleaze BN21 .... 184 E3
Henley Cl
  Royal Tunbridge Wells TN2 . 8 C4
  Rye TN31 .... 93 A6
Henley Cl BN2 .... 164 F4
Henley Rd BN2 .... 164 F4
Henly's Hill BN27 .... 131 F7
Henry Burt Way RH15 ...... 72 F2
Henry Terr **3** TN34 ...... 160 B4
Henwood Green Rd
  TN12, TN2 .... 9 E6
Henwoods Cres TN2 .... 9 D6
Henwoods Mount TN2 ...... 9 E6
Herbert Rd BN1 .... 142 F2
Herbrand Wlk
  TN39, BN24 .... 156 A1
Hereford Ct
  18 Brighton BN2 .... 189 B5
  1 Eastbourne BN23 .... 174 E1
  1 Hove BN3 .... 163 C7
Hereford St BN2 .... 164 E1
Hereward Rd BN23 .... 185 F8
Hereward Way BN7 .... 123 D3
Hermitage La RH19 .... 10 F8
Hermitage Rd RH19 .... 1 D3
Hermitage The TN34 .... 159 E8
Herne Cty Jun Sch TN6 .... 37 F8
Herne Down TN6 .... 38 A7
Herne Rd TN6 .... 37 F8
Heron Cl
  Eastbourne BN23 .... 174 C2
  Hastings TN38 .... 158 E8
  Uckfield TN22 .... 78 D5
Heron Cotts TN18 .... 48 D3
Heron Pl RH19 .... 10 F8
Heron Ridge BN26 .... 173 B6
Heron's Tye BN6 .... 97 F3
Herons Dale Sch BN43 ... 140 C1
Herons The BN43 .... 161 A8
Heronsway TN2 .... 9 B6
Heronsdale Rd BN2 .... 165 F8
Herontye Dr RH19 .... 11 A8
Herring's Rd TN21, TN33 . 109 F8
Herstmonceux Castle Gdns
  BN27 .... 131 A1
Herstmonceux CE Prim Sch
  BN27 .... 131 C1
Herstmonceux Science Ctr
  BN27 .... 131 C1
Hertford Cl TN38 .... 136 A4
Hertford Cty Inf Sch
  BN1 .... 143 B2
Hertford Cty Jun Sch
  BN1 .... 143 C2
Hertford Rd BN1 .... 143 B2
Heskett Pk TN2 .... 9 E6
Hestings Plat **2** TN34 .. 160 B4
Heston Ave BN1 .... 142 F7
Hever Cl BN23 .... 174 D2
Hever Cres TN34 .... 156 F5
Heyworth Cl BN2 .... 165 F5
Heyworth Cty Prim Sch
  RH16 .... 50 F4
Hickling Cl BN23 .... 174 B4
Hickman Way TN34 .... 136 D4
Hickman's Cl RH16 .... 51 B8
Hickman's La RH16 .... 51 A8
Hide Hollow BN23 .... 174 D3
High Bank TN35 .... 137 C3
High Bank Cl TN35 .... 160 C6
High Beech Cl TN35 .... 135 F6
High Beech Country
  Club The TN35 .... 135 F6
High Beech La RH16 ...... 50 F8
High Beeches TN2 .... 8 D6
High Branches TN39 .... 156 E4

High Broom Ind Pk TN4 ..... 8 C8
High Broom La TN6 .... 37 E7
High Broom Rd TN6 .... 37 F7
High Brooms Rd TN4 .... 8 C7
High Brooms Sta TN1 .... 8 C7
High Cl East Dean BN20 . 183 C2
  Portslade-by-Sea BN41 ... 141 A1
High Cross Fields TN6 ..... 25 F3
High Fords TN36 .... 116 E5
High Fords Cl TN36 .... 116 E5
High Hurst Cl BN8 .... 76 D7
High Hurstwood
  CE Prim Sch TN22 .... 37 A1
High Meadow TN1 .... 67 B7
High Park Ave BN3 .... 141 E3
High Pk TN31 .... 67 A7
High Point RH16 .... 51 A3
High Rocks TN3 .... 7 B1
High Rocks La TN3, TN4 ... 7 C1
High Sh Hall The **13**
  BN25 .... 180 E2
High St Alfriston BN26 ... 171 A2
  Barcombe Cross BN8 .... 101 E4
  Battle TN33 .... 112 D4
  Bexhill TN40 .... 157 D5
  Bodiam BN27 .... 189 B5
  Burwash TN19 .... 62 A6
  Buxted TN22 .... 56 C3
  Cowden TN8 .... 4 B5
  Crowborough TN6 .... 25 F3
  Ditchling BN6 .... 98 D3
  East Grinstead RH19 ..... 10 F8
  East Hoathly BN8 .... 105 A5
  Eastbourne BN21 .... 185 A1
  Etchingham TN19 .... 44 C1
  Flimwell TN5 .... 32 C3
  Frant TN3 .... 18 E6
  Hailsham BN27 .... 152 C8
  Hartfield TN7 .... 26 A2
  Hastings TN34 .... 160 B4
  Haywards Heath RH16 .... 51 B8
  Heathfield TN21 .... 82 A8
  Hurstpierpoint BN6 .... 97 B6
  Lamberhurst TN3 .... 20 B5
  Lewes BN7 .... 123 C1
  Maresfield TN22 .... 55 C3
  Mayfield TN20 .... 40 B2
  Newhaven BN9 .... 179 C7
  Newick BN8 .... 76 D7
  Ninfield TN33 .... 133 A6
  Nutley TN22 .... 35 C3
  Pembury TN2 .... 9 C6
  Pevensey BN24 .... 175 A6
  Polegate BN26 .... 173 A6
  Portslade-by-Sea BN41 .. 141 A1
  Robertsbridge TN32 .... 64 B4
  Rotherfield TN6 .... 39 B8
  Rottingdean BN2 .... 165 F1
  Royal Tunbridge Wells TN1 . 8 B2
  Rye TN31 .... 93 C5
  Seaford BN25 .... 180 E2
  Ticehurst TN5 .... 47 A6
  Uckfield TN22 .... 78 A1
  Wadhurst TN5 .... 29 F4
  Westham BN24 .... 175 A6
  Winchelsea TN36 .... 117 F7
High Trees
  3 Eastbourne BN21 .. 184 F4
  Haywards Heath RH16 .... 50 F5
High View TN1 .... 82 B8
High View Rd TN21 .... 143 C2
High Wickham TN35 .... 160 B5
High Woods La TN2 .... 9 B3
Higham Gdns TN35 .... 138 A8
Higham La TN31 .... 67 A7
Highbank BN1 .... 142 C3
Highbridge La BN7 .... 100 B4
Highbrook Cl BN2 .... 143 D3
Highcliff Ct BN2 .... 177 A5
Highcroft Lodge BN1 ..... 142 E1
Highcroft Rd RH19 .... 21 A6
Highcroft Villas BN1, BN3 163 E8
Highden **2** BN2 .... 164 C6
Highdown BN41, BN42 . 140 F1
Highdown Cotts TN17 ...... 20 F3
Highdown Ct BN1 .... 142 E3
Highdown Rd
  Hove BN1, BN3 .... 163 C4
  Lewes BN7 .... 123 A2
Highfield RH17 .... 33 C4
Highfield Cl TN2 .... 8 D8
Highfield Cres BN1 .... 143 A5
Highfield Ct **7** RH16 ... 50 D6
Highfield Cty Jun Sch
  BN22 .... 174 A1
Highfield Dr
  Hastings TN38 .... 135 D3
  Hurstpierpoint BN6 .... 97 C5

Highfield Gdns TN39 ...... 157 C7
Highfield Ind Est N BN22 . 174 A1
Highfield Ind Est S BN23 . 174 A1
Highfield Rd
  East Grinstead RH19 .... 1 D3
  Horam TN21 .... 106 F7
  Royal Tunbridge Wells TN4 . 8 C7
Highfields Brighton BN1 .. 143 E5
  Burwash TN19 .... 62 A6
  Forest Row RH18 .... 11 F2
  Rye TN31 .... 93 B7
Highgate Flats TN6 .... 27 B1
Highgate Rd RH18 .... 11 F1
Highgrove TN2 .... 17 A8
Highland Ct
  Crowborough TN6 .... 25 E3
  Haywards Heath RH16 .... 50 E4
Highland Grange TN6 ...... 25 E3
Highland Lodge BN21 .... 184 F4
Highland Rd RH16 .... 50 F3
Highlands Ave TN22 .... 78 D4
Highlands Cl Bexhill TN39 . 156 F7
  Crowborough TN6 .... 25 E3
  Keymer BN6 .... 98 A3
Highlands Dr
  Burgess Hill RH15 .... 73 A4
  Hastings TN38 .... 159 B7
Highlands Gdns TN38 ..... 159 B7
Highlands Mews **2** TN38 159 B6
Highlands Rd
  Portslade-by-Sea BN41 ... 141 B1
  Seaford BN25 .... 180 F3
Highlands The
  Bexhill TN39 .... 156 F7
  Cuckfield RH17 .... 50 A8
Highlea Cl TN37 .... 136 C5
Highleigh **7** BN2 .... 189 B6
Highsted Pk BN10 .... 167 D2
Highview Ave N BN1 ...... 142 E6
Highview Ave S BN1 ...... 142 E6
Highview Cl
  Hastings TN37 .... 136 D5
  Windmill Hill BN27 .... 131 B5
Highview La BN10 .... 184 F1
Highview La TN22 .... 78 C4
Highview Rd
  Brighton BN1 .... 142 E6
  Telscombe Cliffs BN10 ... 177 F4
Highview Way BN1 .... 142 E6
Highwater View TN38 .... 135 F7
Highway Cl BN2 .... 143 D2
Highway The
  Brighton BN2 .... 143 D2
  Newhaven BN10, BN9 ... 179 A6
  Hastings BN41 .... 141 B2
Highwoods Ave TN39 .... 156 C6
Highwoods Ct TN39 .... 156 E5
Highwoods Golf Course
  TN39 .... 156 D6
Hiham Bglws TN36 .... 117 E7
Hiham Gn TN36 .... 117 F7
Hilary Cl BN26 .... 172 F5
Hilary Lodge **2** BN22 .. 164 C5
Hilbert Cl TN2 .... 8 C5
Hilders Farm Cl TN6 .... 26 E1
Hilgrove Rd BN2 .... 166 D3
Hill Brow BN3 .... 142 B3
Hill Cl TN6 .... 25 E3
Hill Crest
  Dormans Park RH19 .... 1 E6
  Royal Tunbridge Wells TN4 . 8 B7
Hill Crest Ct BN9 .... 179 D6
Hill Crest Rd BN9 .... 179 D6
Hill Dr BN3 .... 142 B3
Hill Farm Way
  BN42, BN43 .... 140 E2
Hill House Prep Sch TN22 . 78 C5
Hill Mead TN22 .... 35 C4
Hill Rd Eastbourne BN20 .. 184 E5
  Fairlight TN35 .... 138 C4
  Lewes BN7 .... 123 B2
  Newhaven BN9 .... 168 F2
  Saltdean BN2 .... 177 B5
Hill Rise Newhaven BN9 .. 168 C5
  Seaford BN25 .... 180 C5
Hill Side BN9 .... 179 D7
Hill St Hastings TN34 ..... 160 A4
  Royal Tunbridge Wells TN1 . 8 B5
Hill Top BN1 .... 142 E8
Hill Top Cl BN41 .... 140 F2
Hill View Way TN4 .... 7 C4
Hillary Cl RH19 .... 2 C1
Hillbank Cl BN41 .... 140 F3
Hillbert Rd TN1, TN2 .... 8 C5
Hillborough Cl TN39 ...... 156 D4
Hillbrow (Brighton Univ)
  BN20 .... 184 E1
Hillbrow Rd BN1 .... 142 D4
Hillbury Gdns TN5 .... 31 D1
Hillcrest Brighton BN1 ... 142 C5
  Rye TN31 .... 93 B7

Hillcrest Ave TN39 .... 157 A6
Hillcrest Cl RH17 .... 51 F3
Hillcrest Ct BN1 .... 142 C5
Hillcrest Dr TN1 .... 8 D7
Hillcrest La RH17 .... 51 F3
Hillcrest Sch TN35 .... 137 E5
Hillcroft BN41 .... 140 F2
Hillgarth TN4 .... 8 A8
Hillrise TN6 .... 26 B2
Hillside Brighton BN2 .... 143 E2
Forest Row RH18 .... 11 E3
Friston BN20 .... 183 B1
Mayfield TN20 .... 40 B2
Portslade-by-Sea BN41 .... 141 C1
Southwick BN42 .... 140 F1
Hillside Ave BN25 .... 181 C5
Hillside Cl RH19 .... 1 E3
Hillside Cotts TN5 .... 30 B8
Hillside Dr TN21 .... 51 A3
Hillside Rd
Bexhill TN39, TN40 .... 157 C5
Hastings, Silverhill Park
TN34 .... 136 E5
Hastings, St Helen's Wood
TN34 .... 136 E3
Hillside Sch BN41 .... 141 B2
Hillside Way
Brighton, Moulsecoomb
BN2 .... 143 E2
Brighton, Westdene BN1 . 142 C4
Hillside Wlk RH17 .... 50 C6
Hilltop Dr TN1 .... 93 B7
Hillview Rd BN2 .... 165 B8
Hillyfield BN7 .... 146 B8
Hillyglen Cl TN34 .... 159 E8
Hindleap Warren
Activity Ctr RH18 .... 22 D5
Hindover Cres BN25 .... 181 A4
Hindover Rd BN25 .... 181 A4
Hinton Cl BN1 .... 143 C2
Hither Chantlers TN3 .... 7 A2
Hoad Rd BN22 .... 185 B4
Hoad's Wood Rd TN34 ...... 137 A3
Hoadleys La TN6 .... 25 D5
Hoadswood Cross TN21 ...... 84 B2
Hoath Hill TN22 .... 87 C5
Hoathdown Ave BN9 .... 179 A7
Hobbs La TN31 .... 68 D6
Hoblands RH16 .... 51 B4
Hobney Rise BN24 .... 174 F5
Hockington La BN20 .... 173 B1
Hodcombe Cl BN23 .... 174 B4
Hoddern Ave BN10 .... 178 B8
Hoddern Cty Jun Sch
BN10 .... 178 B8
Hodshrove La BN2 .... 143 E3
Hodshrove Pl BN2 .... 143 E3
Hodshrove Rd BN2 .... 143 E3
Hoe The TN37 .... 136 B6
Hogarth Ho TN38 .... 159 A8
Hogarth Rd
Eastbourne BN23 .... 174 D1
Hove BN3 .... 162 F7
Hoghole La TN3 .... 19 F2
Hogtrough La TN36 .... 117 E7
Holbrook Cl BN20 .... 188 E8
Holden Park Rd TN4 .... 8 A8
Holdings The
Kingston near Lewes BN7 145 F5
Upper Wellingham BN8 ... 124 B7
Hole Farm Cl TN34 .... 136 E2
Hollamby Pk BN27 .... 157 D2
Holland Ave TN39 .... 156 C4
Holland Mews BN3 .... 163 D5
Holland Rd BN3 .... 163 D6
Holland St BN2 .... 189 B6
Hollands The RH15 .... 73 C4
Hollands Way RH19 .... 2 A4
Hollier's Hill TN40 .... 157 C6
Hollies The TN20 .... 40 A2
Hollin Cl TN4 .... 13 D1
Hollingbourne Ct [8] BN2 .. 164 E4
Hollingbury Copse BN1 .... 143 A4
Hollingbury Cres BN1 .... 143 B2
Hollingbury Ind Est BN1 ... 143 C7
Hollingbury Park Ave
BN1 .... 143 A2
Hollingbury Park
Golf Course BN1 .... 143 B4
Hollingbury Pl BN1 .... 143 B2
Hollingbury Rd BN1 .... 143 B1
Hollingbury Rise BN1 .... 143 B2
Hollingbury Rise W BN1 ... 143 A2
Hollingbury Terr BN1 .... 143 A2
Hollingdean La BN1, BN2 . 164 B8
Hollingdean Rd BN2 .... 164 B8
Hollingdean St BN1 .... 163 B1
Hollingdean Terr BN1 .... 143 B2
Hollinghurst Cl TN37 .... 136 B4
Hollinghurst Rd TN37 ...... 136 B4
Hollington Ct TN38 .... 159 A8

Hollington Cty Inf Sch
TN38 .... 136 A4
Hollington Cty Jun Sch
TN38 .... 136 A4
Hollington Old La TN38 .... 136 A4
Hollington Park Cl TN38 ... 136 A1
Hollington Park Rd TN38 .. 136 A1
Hollow La Blackboys TN22 .. 80 B4
Dormansland RH19, RH7 .... 2 D6
Hollow The RH16 .... 51 B5
Holly Bank [3] BN2 .... 189 B8
Holly Cl Bexhill TN39 .... 156 C6
Brighton BN1 .... 142 E3
Hailsham BN27 .... 152 B6
Heathfield TN21 .... 82 A6
Holly Ct TN6 .... 25 E2
Holly Dr TN21 .... 82 A6
Holly Pl BN22 .... 173 E3
Holly Rd RH16 .... 51 A3
Hollybank Gdns TN38 .... 136 B1
Hollycroft BN7 .... 100 A3
Hollydene Rd TN5 .... 29 F6
Hollyshaw Cl TN2 .... 8 C2
Hollywood Ct [10] RH16 ..... 50 E5
Holm Oak Cl TN39 .... 156 E3
Holmbush Cl
Haywards Heath RH16 ...... 50 E2
Shoreham-by-Sea BN43 .. 140 D2
Holmbush Ct [8] BN43 ..... 161 C8
Holmbush Cty Fst Sch
BN43 .... 140 D1
Holmbush Way
BN42, BN43 .... 140 E1
Holmdale Rd BN9 .... 169 A1
Holmebury Ho [1] TN4 ..... 159 E7
Holmes Ave BN3 .... 141 F1
Holmes Cl BN25 .... 180 A6
Holmes Farm Cotts TN39 . 156 A8
Holmes Hill Cotts BN8 ...... 127 C6
Holmesdale Cl TN5 .... 29 E5
Holmesdale Ct TN34 .... 159 E8
Holmesdale Gdns TN34 .... 159 E8
Holmesdale Rd
Bexhill TN39 .... 157 A4
Burgess Hill RH15 .... 73 A1
Holmewood Ho TN3 .... 7 A2
Holmewood Rd TN4 .... 8 C7
Holmewood Ridge TN3 .... 6 F3
Holmhurst Cl TN4 .... 7 F4
Holmhurst La TN37 .... 136 B5
Holmstead BN2 .... 189 B7
Holmwood Cl BN6 .... 97 F4
Holt Lodge [1] BN2 .... 189 B7
Holt The
Burgess Hill RH15 .... 73 C2
Hailsham BN27 .... 152 A6
Seaford BN25 .... 180 F5
Holters Way BN25 .... 180 F5
Holton Hill BN2 .... 165 E7
Holtview Rd BN2 .... 165 B8
Holtye Ave RH19 .... 2 A3
Holtye Golf Club TN8 .... 3 F3
Holtye Rd RH19 .... 2 B2
Holy Cross CE Prim Sch
TN22 .... 78 C7
Holyrood RH19 .... 11 A8
Holywell Cl BN20 .... 188 E7
Holywell Rd BN20 .... 188 E7
Holywell Wlk BN27 .... 152 B7
Home Farm Bsns Ctr BN1 . 143 D3
Home Farm Ct Frant TN3 ... 17 C4
Horsted Keynes RH17 .... 33 C5
Home Farm La TN2 .... 8 E8
Home Farm Rd BN1 .... 143 D3
Home Platt RH19 .... 21 A6
Home Rd BN1 .... 142 E1
Homebush Ave
Saltdean BN2 .... 177 D5
Telscombe BN2 .... 166 F3
Homecoast Ho BN10 .... 178 B7
Homedane Ho [8] TN34 .... 159 F7
Homedrive Ho BN3 .... 163 C8
Homefield Cl BN25 .... 180 F4
Homefield Rd BN25 .... 180 F4
Homegate Ho [3] BN21 .... 184 F3
Homehall Ho [3] TN40 ...... 188 E8
Homehill Ho [3] TN40 .... 83 D5
Homelands Cl TN39 .... 157 A6
Homelatch Ho [1] BN21 ... 185 A3
Homelawn Ho TN40 .... 157 A5
Homeleaze Ho TN3 .... 17 C4
Homeleigh BN1 .... 142 E5
Homeridge Ho BN2 .... 177 D5
Homestall Rd RH19 .... 11 E8
Homestead The TN1 .... 15 C7
Hometye Ho BN25 .... 180 D3
Homewarr Ho TN40 .... 157 E4
Homewood Cl BN20 .... 188 D3
Homewood Rd TN3 .... 6 F3
Homoeopathic Hospl TN1 .... 8 A3
Honey Croft BN3 .... 141 D4
Honey La BN8 .... 149 D7

Honeycrag Cl BN26 .... 173 A7
Honeypot La BN7, BN8 ...... 100 B7
Honeysuckle Cl
Eastbourne BN23 .... 174 B3
Hailsham BN27 .... 152 B5
Hastings TN37 .... 136 D5
Honeyway Cl BN26 .... 172 F3
Honies Ct TN39 .... 157 C6
Honye Gdns BN20 .... 173 B1
Hoo The BN20 .... 173 B1
Hood Cl BN23 .... 185 E7
Hooe Rd TN33 .... 133 A3
Hook Hill TN5 .... 31 A6
Hookswood Cl TN6 .... 26 A3
Hoopers Cl BN7 .... 123 C3
Hoover Cl TN38 .... 135 F7
Hop Gdn TN22 .... 36 C2
Hope Cotts BN42 .... 161 E8
Hopehouse La TN17, TN18 .. 47 E7
Hopfield Gdns TN22 .... 78 E8
Hopgarden Cl TN34 .... 159 E8
Hoppers Croft La TN19 ...... 62 B6
Hopwood Gdns TN4 .... 8 A6
Horam Park Cl TN21 .... 106 F7
Horebeech La TN21 .... 107 A6
Horizon Cl TN4 .... 8 B4
Horleigh Green Rd TN20 ... 39 C1
Horley Pl BN2 .... 164 E6
Hornbeam TN19 .... 62 B7
Hornblower Cotts TN19 .... 44 C1
Hornbuckles Cl BN8 .... 100 E7
Hornby Pl BN2 .... 144 A1
Hornby Rd BN2 .... 144 A1
Horning Cl BN23 .... 174 B4
Horns Rd TN18 .... 45 D8
Hornshurst Rd TN6 .... 27 B1
Horntye Rd TN37 .... 136 C1
Horsa Cl BN23 .... 185 F8
Horsegrove Ave TN5 .... 31 F1
Horsegrove La TN6 .... 39 B8
Horseshoe Cl TN3 .... 136 B2
Horseshoe La TN31 .... 68 A1
Horsewalk BN27, TN33 .... 154 F7
Horsfield Rd BN7 .... 123 B3
Horsgate Ho RH17 .... 50 A8
Horsham La BN27 .... 155 B6
Horsham Ave N BN10 .... 178 C8
Horsham Ave N BN10 .... 178 C8
Horsham Cl BN23 .... 164 F6
Horsted Ho [1] RH16 .... 50 F3
Horsted Keynes Ind Est
RH17 .... 33 B7
Horsted Keynes Sta RH17 .. 33 A4
Horsted La Danehill RH17 ... 34 A4
Isfield TN22 .... 102 F7
Sharpthorne RH19 .... 21 B3
Horsted Sq TN22 .... 78 A6
Horsye Rd BN22 .... 185 B7
Horton Rd BN1 .... 143 B1
Hoskins Pl RH19 .... 2 A4
Hosmers Field TN6 .... 39 D8
Hospital Villas [5] RH16 ..... 50 F3
Houghton Green La TN31 ... 70 C2
Houghton La TN31 .... 70 C3
Houndean Rise BN7 .... 146 A8
Houndean Rise BN7 .... 145 F8
Hova Villas BN3 .... 163 B6
Hove Bsns Ctr BN3 .... 163 B8
Hove Ent Ctr BN41 .... 162 C6
Hove General Hospl BN3 .. 163 A7
Hove Manor [7] BN3 .... 163 A6
Hove Mus & Art Gall BN3 . 163 A6
Hove Nuffield Hospl BN3 . 162 F7
Hove Park Gdns
Hove BN3 .... 142 B1
Hove BN3 .... 163 B8
Hove Park Rd BN1, BN3 ... 142 C1
Hove Park Sch (Lower)
BN3 .... 141 D2
Hove Park Sch (Upper)
BN3 .... 142 A1
Hove Park Villas BN3 .... 163 B8
Hove Park Way BN3 .... 142 C1
Hove Pl BN3 .... 163 B5
Hove Rd BN3 .... 163 A5
Hove Sta BN3 .... 163 B8
Hovedene BN3 .... 163 B7
How's Cl TN31 .... 90 B5
Howard Ave RH15 .... 72 F4
Howard Cl BN27 .... 152 D6
Howard Ct Hove BN3 .... 142 A2
Peacehaven BN10 .... 178 B7
Howard Gdns TN2 .... 8 B3
Howard Ho Bexhill TN39 .. 156 E4
Peacehaven BN10 .... 167 D1
Howard Pl BN1 .... 189 F7
Howard Rd BN2 .... 165 E6
Howard Sq BN21 .... 185 A2
Howards Cres TN39 .... 156 C4
Howbourne La TN22 .... 56 E5

Howes Cotts TN18 .... 45 F8
Howey Cl BN9 .... 168 F1
Howlett Cl TN38 .... 135 F4
Howlett Dr BN27 .... 129 B2
Howletts Cl BN22 .... 173 F1
Hoyle Rd BN10 .... 178 C7
Hudson Cl BN23 .... 185 G7
Hudson Ct BN22 .... 185 C6
Huggett's La BN20, BN22 . 173 B3
Hughenden Ct [2] TN4 .... 136 F2
Hughenden Pl [1] TN34 ... 136 F2
Hughenden Rd TN34 .... 160 A6
Hughes Rd BN2 .... 164 B8
Hugletts La TN21 .... 83 A7
Humboldt Ct TN2 .... 8 D5
Humphrey Lodge RH15 ...... 73 D3
Humphrey's Gap BN43 ..... 161 A7
Hundred Acre La
BN6, RH17 .... 74 B2
Hundredhouse La TN31 ..... 90 F4
Hungershall Pk TN4 .... 7 E2
Hunloke Ave BN22 .... 185 B6
Hunston Cl BN2 .... 165 F7
Hunt's Gate BN8 .... 52 E3
Hunters Way
Royal Tunbridge Wells TN2 .. 7 F1
Uckfield TN22 .... 78 B8
Hunting Cl TN40 .... 157 C5
Huntingdon Rd TN6 .... 25 F1
Huntingdon Way RH15 ..... 73 D5
Huntley Mill Rd TN5 .... 31 E3
Huntleys Pk TN4 .... 7 F5
Hurdis Rd BN25 .... 180 A6
Hurrell Rd TN34 .... 160 B6
Hurst Cres BN41 .... 162 B8
Hurst Farm Rd RH19 .... 10 D7
Hurst Green CE Sch TN19 .. 45 A2
Hurst Hill BN1 .... 143 C5
Hurst La
Eastbourne BN21 .... 184 D4
Sedlescombe TN33 .... 88 F3
Windmill Hill BN27 .... 131 B5
Hurst Rd
Eastbourne BN21 .... 184 D5
Hassocks BN6 .... 97 D4
Hurst Shaw TN21 .... 107 C8
Hurst The TN2 .... 8 E7
Hurst Way TN34 .... 137 A6
Hurst Wickham Cl BN6 ...... 97 C5
Hurstfield Cl RH16 .... 51 A2
Hurstpierpoint Coll BN6 .... 97 B8
Hurstwood [2] BN2 .... 164 F5
Hurstwood Cl TN40 .... 158 B5
Hurstwood La
Haywards Heath RH16 .... 51 A2
Royal Tunbridge Wells TN4 .. 7 F3
Sharpthorne RH17, RH19 .. 21 D1
Hurstwood Pk TN4 .... 7 F3
Hurstwood Pk Hospl TN2 ... 56 A6
Hurtis Hill TN6 .... 37 E7
Hutton Rd BN1 .... 143 B3
Hyde Cl BN7 .... 145 E5
Hyde Gdns BN21 .... 185 A2
Hyde Rd BN21 .... 184 F2
Hyde The BN2 .... 164 F8
Hyde Tynings Cl BN20 ...... 188 D8
Hydehurst Cl TN6 .... 25 F1
Hydney St BN22 .... 185 C5
Hydneye The BN22 .... 173 F1
Hylden Cl BN2 .... 165 B8
Hyperion Ave BN26 .... 172 E6
Hythe Ave TN38 .... 158 B5
Hythe Cl Polegate BN26 ... 173 C7
Seaford BN25 .... 181 C5
Hythe Cres BN25 .... 181 C4
Hythe Rd BN1 .... 143 A2
Hythe View BN25 .... 181 C4

Ian Cl TN40 .... 157 F7
Icklesham CE Prim Sch
TN36 .... 116 E6
Icklesham Dr TN38 .... 135 D3
Iden Cl BN2 .... 164 E5
Iden Ct TN34 .... 136 D3
Iden Hurst BN6 .... 97 F7
Iden Rd TN31 .... 70 B3
Iden St BN22 .... 174 A2
Iden's La TN21 .... 82 D8
Ifield Cl BN2 .... 177 E6
Ifield Mill Cl BN24 .... 174 B5
Iford Cl BN9 .... 168 D1
Iford & Kingston
CE Prim Sch BN7 .... 145 F5
Ilex Ct RH16 .... 141 A1
Ilex Gn [5] BN27 .... 129 B1
Image Cross Flats RH19 .... 21 A1
Imberhorne La RH19 .... 1 B2
Imberhorne Lower Sch
RH19 .... 1 D3
Imberhorne Sch RH19 .... 1 D3
Imberhorne Way RH19 .... 1 B3

Impala Gdns TN4 .... 8 B6
Imperial Arc BN1 .... 189 F5
Independent Bsns Pk The
RH19 .... 1 A3
Ingham Dr BN1 .... 143 D6
Inglesea Sch TN38 .... 135 F4
Ingleside TN38 .... 135 E4
Ingleside Dr TN6 .... 25 E2
Inglewood Gdns TN38 ...... 135 E4
Ingram Cres E BN3 .... 162 E8
Ingram Cres W BN3 .... 162 E8
Ingram Ct BN3 .... 162 E7
Ingrams Ave TN39 .... 157 C7
Ingrams Way BN27 .... 152 A6
Inholmes Cl RH15 .... 73 C3
Inholmes Park Rd RH15 ..... 73 B3
Ink Pen La RH17 .... 11 E1
Innham's Wood TN6 .... 25 E4
Innings Dr BN24 .... 175 C4
Insley Ct TN39 .... 156 F3
Inverness Rd BN2 .... 164 D8
Inwood Cres BN1 .... 142 E1
Iona Way [12] RH16 .... 50 E4
Irelands La BN7 .... 123 B1
Ironlatch Ave TN38 .... 135 F2
Ironlatch Cl TN38 .... 135 F2
Ironstone Way TN22 .... 78 E7
Ironstones TN3 .... 7 B3
Irving Ho TN1 .... 8 B5
Isaac's La RH16, RH15 ...... 50 A2
Isabel Cl BN25 .... 180 E5
Isabel Cres BN3 .... 162 E8
Isfield Rd Brighton BN1 .... 143 C2
Isfield TN22 .... 102 E5
Isle of Thorns
(Univ of Sussex) RH17 ..... 22 D1
Islingword Pl BN2 .... 164 C6
Islingword Rd BN2 .... 164 C7
Islingword St BN2 .... 189 B6
Ismay Lodge TN39 .... 168 D2
Iveagh Cres BN9 .... 168 D2
Ivor Rd BN2 .... 144 C1
Ivory Pl BN2 .... 189 B6
Ivy Cotts BN8 .... 104 C6
Ivy Dene La RH19 .... 11 D6
Ivy Pl BN1, BN3 .... 163 D5
Ivy Terr BN21 .... 184 F3
Ivyhouse Employment Area
TN34 .... 137 B4
Ivyhouse La TN34, TN35 ... 137 B6
Ivylands Yd TN31 .... 93 B5

Jack O'Dandy Cl BN21 ..... 184 C1
Jackdaws The TN22 .... 78 E4
Jackies La BN8 .... 76 B7
Jacks Hill TN7 .... 13 D2
Jackson Mews BN2 .... 179 C7
Jackson St BN2 .... 189 B7
Jacobs Acre TN40 .... 157 C5
Jacqueline Du Pre Ct [6]
BN2 .... 164 C5
Jane's Ave BN27 .... 130 E6
Jameson Cres TN38 .... 136 A3
Jameson Rd TN40 .... 157 D4
Jane Murray Way
Burgess Hill BN6, RH15 .... 72 D5
Burgess Hill RH15 .... 72 E4
Jane's La RH15 .... 73 E4
Janes Cl RH15 .... 73 C5
Janes La RH15 .... 73 D4
Janeston Ct [4] BN43 ...... 161 C8
Japonica Cl BN43 .... 140 B1
Jardine Ct TN6 .... 25 F2
Jarvis Brook Ctry Pk TN6 ... 38 B8
Jarvis Brook Cty Prim Sch
TN6 .... 38 C7
Jarvisbrook Cl TN39 .... 156 D3
Jasmine Cotts TN3 .... 15 C7
Jasmine Ct BN1 .... 142 F5
Jasmine Gn [2] BN27 ...... 129 B1
Jason Cl BN10 .... 178 C7
Jay Cl BN23 .... 174 C2
Jay Rd BN10 .... 178 E6
Jays The
Burgess Hill RH15 .... 72 E4
Uckfield TN22 .... 78 D4
Jefferies RH17 .... 33 C4
Jefferies Way TN6 .... 25 E4
Jefferson Way TN38 .... 135 F6
Jeffreys Way TN22 .... 55 D1
Jellicoe Cl BN23 .... 185 F7
Jenner's La TN35 .... 137 E6
Jephson Cl BN20 .... 188 F8
Jerome Cl BN23 .... 174 E2
Jersey St BN2 .... 189 B6 *
Jervis Ave BN23 .... 185 E6
Jesmond Cl BN3 .... 162 E7
Jesmond Rd BN3 .... 162 E7

Jesters RH15 .... 73 C7
Jevington Cl TN39 .... 156 D2
Jevington Ct BN43 .... 161 D6
Jevington Dr
　Brighton BN2 .... 143 D1
　Seaford BN25 .... 180 D4
Jevington Gdns BN20 .... 185 A1
Jevington Ho **7** BN21 .... 184 D4
Jevington Rd BN26 .... 172 D2
Jew St BN1 .... 189 A5
Jireh Ct **4** RH16 .... 50 E5
Joan Hughes Ct BN26 .... 173 A6
Joan Nightingale Ho RH16 50 C4
Job's La BN6 .... 72 A6
Joe's La BN27 .... 131 B5
John Dann Cl TN22 .... 80 A6
John Macadam Way TN37 136 A6
John Spare Ct TN4 .... 8 A6
John St Brighton BN2 ...... 189 B6
　Royal Tunbridge Wells TN4 8 A5
John Whittle Lodge **4**
BN2 .... 143 C1
John's Cross Rd TN32 ...... 87 C8
Johns Cl BN10 .... 167 C2
Johnson Bank **4** BN2 .... 164 C7
Johnson Dr RH15 .... 73 D3
Jonas Dr TN5 .... 29 E5
Jonas La TN5 .... 29 E5
Jordan Ct BN3 .... 162 E8
Jordans La BN22 .... 173 D3
Jordans La E BN22 .... 173 D3
Jordans La W BN22 .... 173 C3
Jordans The RH19 .... 10 E8
Joyce Villas TN21 .... 106 E5
Jubilee Cl RH16 .... 51 A4
Jubilee Ct BN22 .... 143 E2
Jubilee Gdns BN25 .... 181 A5
Jubilee Ho BN9 .... 179 C7
Jubilee Rd Bexhill TN39 .. 157 A7
　Burgess Hill RH15 .... 72 E2
　Portslade-by-Sea BN41 .. 162 A8
Jubilee St BN1 .... 189 A6
Judge's Terr RH19 .... 10 E8
Jugg's Rd BN7 .... 146 F7
Juggs Cl BN7 .... 146 B8
Juggs Rd BN7 .... 146 A8
Julian Cl **5** BN43 .... 161 C8
Julian Rd BN3 .... 163 E7
Junction Cl RH15 .... 73 C4
Junction Rd
　Bodiam TN18, TN32 ...... 46 A3
　Brighton BN1 .... 189 F6
　Burgess Hill RH15 .... 65 C5
　Cripp's Corner TN32 .... 8 E2
　Cripp's Corner TN32, TN33 88 D5
　Eastbourne BN21 .... 185 A3
　Hastings TN37 .... 136 B7
　Junction St BN26 .... 173 B6
Juniper Cl
　Hastings TN38 .... 135 E3
　Portslade-by-Sea BN41 .. 141 B3
Juniper Wlk BN43 .... 140 C1
Jury's Gap Coastguard Cotts
TN31 .... 95 E1
Jury's Gap Rd TN29 .... 96 F5

Kammond Ave BN25 ...... 181 B5
Kane Hythe Rd TN33 ...... 111 D6
Karenza Ct BN1 .... 164 A8
Katherine Way BN25 ..... 180 D5
Keats Cl TN38 .... 158 F6
Keats Pl RH19 .... 1 D3
Keats Wlk BN23 .... 174 E3
Kebbell Lodge **12** BN2 .. 189 B5
Kedale Rd RH16 .... 180 E4
Keel Gdns TN4 .... 7 F6
Keere St BN7 .... 146 C8
Keith Wlk BN23 .... 185 F6
Keld Ave TN22 .... 78 D6
Keld Cl TN22 .... 78 D6
Keld Dr TN22 .... 78 D6
Kelly Rd BN3 .... 142 D1
Kelsey Cotts BN8 .... 124 E6
Kelsey Ct RH15 .... 73 D3
Kemble Cl TN2 .... 8 E7
Kemp Cl BN2 .... 164 E4
Kemp St BN1 .... 189 A6
Kemp Town Pl **18** BN2 164 D4
Kemps Farm Rd TN6 ...... 26 B1
Kemps Way TN32 .... 64 C5
Kemptown Mews **11** BN2 . 164 E4
Kendal Cl BN23 .... 179 E7
Kendal Pk TN4 .... 7 E5
Kendal Rd BN3 .... 162 F8
Kenilworth Cl BN23 ...... 174 A2
Kenilworth Rd TN38 ...... 159 B7
Kenmure Ave BN1 .... 143 A7

Kennard Ct RH18 .... 11 E3
Kennedy Ave RH19 .... 1 D3
Kennedy Cl TN21 .... 82 B6
Kennedy Ct TN38 .... 136 B3
Kennedy Rd TN40 .... 157 E4
Kennedy Way BN9 .... 179 B8
Kennel Cl BN8 .... 124 F6
Kennel La TN39 .... 156 C4
Kennett Cl BN26 .... 173 F5
Kenrith Ct TN34 .... 136 E2
Kensington Gdns BN1 .... 189 A6
Kensington Pl BN1 .... 189 A6
Kensington St BN1 .... 189 A6
Kent Cl Bexhill TN40 ...... 158 A5
　Shoreham-by-Sea BN43 .. 161 C7
　Winchelsea TN36 .... 117 E7
Kent Ct BN20 .... 184 B6
Kent & East Sussex Rly
TN17 .... 49 D5
Kent Fields BN7 .... 145 E5
Kent La TN32 .... 85 F6
Kent Rd Hastings TN38 .... 135 F4
　Royal Tunbridge Wells TN4 . 8 A6
Kent St TN33 .... 114 A3
Kent & Sussex Hospl TN4 . 8 A4
Kent's La BN6 .... 99 C7
Kentish Gdns TN2 .... 16 E8
Kenton Cl TN39 .... 157 A5
Kenton Ct BN21 .... 185 A1
Kenton Rd BN3 .... 162 D7
Kents Rd RH16 .... 50 F3
Kenwards BN1 .... 143 D7
Kenwood Cl TN34 .... 137 B4
Kenya Ct **3** BN1 .... 163 E6
Keppel Rd TN34 .... 136 F2
Kepplestone BN20 .... 188 E8
Kerrara Terr BN22 .... 185 B5
Kerrison Mews BN3 .... 163 D5
Kestrel Cl Bexhill TN40 .. 157 E4
　Hove BN3 .... 163 D8
Kestrel Ct BN27 .... 152 D7
Kestrels The
　Hastings TN38 .... 135 F5
　Shoreham-by-Sea BN43 .. 161 A8
Ketcham Cnr BN24 .... 174 E6
Ketche's La RH17,TN22 .... 52 E7
Kevin Gdns BN2 .... 165 E8
Kew St BN1 .... 189 F6
Kewhurst Ave TN39 ...... 156 D3
Keymer Ave BN10 .... 178 D7
Keymer Cl
　Eastbourne BN23 .... 174 E1
　Hastings TN38 .... 158 E6
Keymer Ct RH15 .... 73 B2
Keymer Gdns RH15 .... 73 B1
Keymer Par RH15 .... 73 B2
Keymer Pk BN6 .... 98 B3
Keymer Rd
　Brighton BN1 .... 143 B6
　Burgess Hill RH15 .... 98 B8
　Hassocks BN6 .... 97 F3
Kibbles La TN4 .... 7 E8
Kidbrook RH16 .... 51 B6
Kidbrooke Park
　(Michael Hall Sch) RH18 . 11 D1
Kidbrooke Rise RH18 ...... 11 E2
Kidd's Hill TN22, TN7 ...... 24 A4
Kilbarn Ct RH16 .... 50 D2
Kilbarn Way RH16 .... 50 D2
Kilburn Terr **5** BN21 .... 185 A3
Kilda St **11** BN22 .... 185 A4
Kildare Cl TN34 .... 137 B4
Kildare Ct BN20 .... 184 C3
Kiln Cl TN22 .... 78 D4
Kiln Dr TN31 .... 93 B8
Kiln La
　Haywards Heath RH16 ... 51 B5
　Hooe TN33 .... 155 B7
　Isfield TN22 .... 102 E5
Kiln Rd BN8 .... 125 A8
Kiln The RH15 .... 73 C3
Kilnwood La BN8 .... 100 E7
Kilpatrick Cl BN23 .... 174 D3
Kimberley Rd
　Brighton BN2 .... 143 D1
　Seaford BN25 .... 180 C4
Kindersley Cl RH19 .... 2 B2
Kinfauns Ave BN22 .... 185 B6
King Alfred (Swimming
　Pool & Sports Ctr) BN3 . 163 A5
King Charles Pl **8** BN41 161 A6
King Edward Ave TN37 ... 136 C1
King Edward Cl TN37 .... 136 C3
King Edward's Par

King George VI Mansions
BN3 .... 141 F2
King Henry's Rd BN7 ..... 123 B2
King John Ct **4** BN43 .... 161 A6
King Offa Cty Prim Sch
TN39 .... 157 B5
King Offa Way TN39, TN40 157 C5
King Pl BN1 .... 189 F5
King St Brighton BN1 ..... 189 A5
　East Grinstead RH19 .... 1 E1
King Wood Hill TN31 .... 90 A3
King's Ave
　Eastbourne BN21 .... 184 E5
　Newhaven BN9 .... 168 E1
　Rye TN31 .... 93 D6
King's Bank La TN31 ...... 68 A3
King's Cl BN21 .... 184 E5
King's Dr
　BN20, BN21, BN22 ...... 184 D7
King's Espl BN3 .... 163 A5
King's Gdns BN3 .... 163 B5
King's Hill Rd TN19 .... 62 B3
King's Manor Sch BN43 . 161 D8
King's Mead La BN25 .... 180 D4
King's Rd
　Brighton BN1, BN3 .... 163 E5
　Hastings TN37 .... 159 C7
　Haywards Heath RH16 ... 50 F3
Kingfisher Cl TN22 .... 78 B5
Kingfisher Dr BN27 .... 152 D7
Kingfisher Dr BN23 .... 174 C2
Kingfisher Rise RH19 .... 10 F8
Kings Chase TN6 .... 25 D3
Kings Cl Bexhill TN40 .... 157 C4
　Eastbourne BN21 .... 184 F5
Kings Copse **9** RH19 ... 10 F8
Kings Ct TN6 .... 25 E2
Kings Dr BN3 .... 163 B6
Kings Gate BN3 .... 163 C8
Kings Gdns BN3 .... 163 B6
Kings Par BN1 .... 143 A2
Kings Pk TN2 .... 8 D3
Kings Rd BN42 .... 140 E1
Kings Ride Alfriston BN26 170 F3
　Burgess Hill RH15 .... 73 C1
　Seaford BN25 .... 180 D4
Kings Toll Rd TN2 .... 9 A6
Kings Way RH15 .... 73 D2
Kings Wlk **10** TN4 .... 159 F8
Kingsbury Rd BN1 .... 189 A7
Kingsbury St BN1, BN2 .. 189 A7
Kingscliffe Sch BN2 .... 164 C5
Kingscott Cl TN39 .... 157 B8
Kingsdale Cl Battle TN33 . 112 F3
　Hastings TN37 .... 136 C6
Kingsfield Cl BN42 .... 161 E8
Kingsfield Cotts BN8 ..... 149 E8
Kingsfold **2** BN2 .... 164 F5
Kingsfold Ct **1** BN25 .. 180 F2
Kingsford BN23 .... 185 D7
Kingsland Cl BN43 .... 161 B7
Kingsley Cl TN37 .... 136 A5
Kingsley Rd
　1 Brighton BN1 .... 163 E5
Kingsmarsh Cotts TN20 .. 58 B6
Kingsmead BN25 .... 180 E5
Kingsmead Cl BN25 ...... 180 E4
Kingsmead Way BN25 ... 180 E4
Kingsmead Wlk BN25 .... 180 E4
Kingsmere BN1 .... 142 E2
Kingsmere Ct **2** BN21 . 184 D4
Kingsmere Way BN23 .... 185 F8
Kingsthorpe Rd BN3 ..... 162 F8
Kingston Ave BN25 .... 181 B3
Kingston Bay Rd BN43 .. 161 C6
Kingston Broadway
　BN42, BN43 .... 140 D1
Kingston Cl Brighton BN1 . 143 B6
　Hove BN3 .... 141 E2
　Seaford BN25 .... 180 D5
　Shoreham-by-Sea BN43 .. 161 C8
Kingston Ct **17** BN43 .. 161 C8
Kingston Gn BN25 .... 181 B3
Kingston La
　BN41, BN42, BN43 ...... 161 D7
Kingston Rd
　Eastbourne BN22 .... 173 F2
　Lewes BN7 .... 146 B7
Kingston Ridge BN7 ...... 145 D6
Kingston Villas TN21 .... 106 E5
Kingston Way
　Seaford BN25 .... 181 B3
　Shoreham-by-Sea
　BN42, BN43 .... 140 D1

Kingsway
　Hove BN3, BN41 .... 163 B5
　Seaford BN25 .... 180 D4
Kingsway Ct BN3 .... 163 C5
Kingswood Ave TN39 .... 156 F6
Kingswood Cl TN2 .... 8 C3
Kingswood Flats BN2 .... 189 B5
Kingswood Rd TN2 .... 8 C3
Kingswood St BN2 .... 189 A5
Kinross Ct **3** BN22 ...... 185 A4
Kinsale Ct **5** BN3 .... 163 D7
Kinver La TN40 .... 158 A6
Kipling Ave BN22 .... 165 E7
Kipling Ct
　Bexhill TN40 .... 157 C6
　3 Haywards Heath RH16 . 50 D5
　Rottingdean BN2 .... 177 A5
Kipling Way RH19 .... 1 C1
Kipling Wlk **1** BN23 .... 174 E2
Kirby Dr BN10 .... 167 A1
Kirdford Cl RH15 .... 73 C1
Kirk Way BN20 .... 184 B5
Kirkdale Rd TN1 .... 8 B4
Kirkstall Cl BN22 .... 173 E3
Kitchenour La TN31 .... 68 E5
Kite Cl TN38 .... 158 E8
Kitilear Ct **5** BN3 .... 163 D6
Knebworth Rd TN39 ...... 156 F5
Knelle Rd TN32 .... 64 A4
Knelle View **2** TN31 .... 67 B7
Knepp Cl BN2 .... 143 F2
Knight's Ridge TN2 .... 9 D7
Knights Cl TN2 .... 9 D7
Knights Gate Rd BN1 .... 144 C7
Knights Gdn BN27 .... 152 B6
Knights Meadow TN22 .... 78 E8
Knightsbridge Cl TN4 .... 7 F5
Knole Cl TN40 .... 157 D3
Knole Gr RH19 .... 1 C3
Knole Rd
　Bexhill TN40 .... 157 D3
　Rottingdean BN2 .... 177 A5
Knoll Bsns Ctr The BN3 . 162 D8
Knoll Cl BN3 .... 141 D1
Knoll Cres BN22 .... 174 A1
Knoll Cty Inf Sch BN3 ... 141 D1
Knoll Rd BN22 .... 174 A2
Knoll Rise TN38 .... 159 C7
Knowle Cl
　Crowborough TN6 .... 38 C8
　Langton Green TN3 .... 6 F3
Knowle Cotts TN3 .... 17 E1
Knowle Ct TN38 .... 136 B1
Knowle Hill Bodiam TN32 .. 65 D8
　Mayfield TN20 .... 40 A1
Knowle La BN8 .... 104 A6
Knowle Park Rd TN20 .... 40 A1
Knowle Pk TN6 .... 25 D2
Knowle Rd TN35 .... 138 E5
Knoyle Rd BN1 .... 142 E2
Knyveton Ct RH15 .... 73 B3
Kylemore BN24 .... 175 B6
Kymer Gdns BN6 .... 98 A3

La Marne Ct TN34 .... 136 E2
Laburnam Wlk BN22 ..... 173 D3
Laburnham Ct TN1 .... 8 C7
Laburnum Ave BN3 ...... 141 E1
Laburnum Gdns TN40 ... 157 F6
Laburnum Gr BN1 .... 143 B3
Laburnum Way RH16 .... 51 B4
Lacys Hill BN8 .... 147 F8
Ladies Mile
　Brighton BN1 .... 143 B7
　Withyham TN3 .... 22 B1
Ladies Mile Cl BN1 ...... 142 E6
Ladies' Mile Ct BN1 ..... 142 E6
Ladies' Mile Rd BN1 .... 142 E6
Lady Bee Ind Est BN42 .. 161 E6
Lady Oak La
　TN17, TN18, TN5 .... 32 C7
Lady's Gift Rd TN4 .... 7 F8
Ladycross Ct BN25 .... 181 C3
Ladyfern Ct TN2 .... 8 C4
Ladymead RH15 .... 73 C5
Ladysmith Rd BN2 ...... 164 D8
Lagwood Cl BN6 .... 97 F3
Laine Cl BN1 .... 142 E3
Laines The **2** BN26 .... 170 F3
Lake Dr BN10 .... 178 B8
Lake House Cl TN39 ..... 156 D4
Lake Rd TN4 .... 7 F2
Lake St TN20, TN6 .... 40 D7
Lake View **1** BN2 .... 164 A1
Lake View Rd RH19 .... 1 F5
Lakehurst La TN33 .... 110 B8
Lakelands Cl BN22 .... 174 A1
Lakelands Dr TN39 .... 156 D4
Lakeside Cl 8 E6
Lakeside Ct BN22 .... 174 A1

Laleham Cl
　Eastbourne BN21 .... 184 E4
　Hastings TN37 .... 136 C5
Lamberhurst CE Prim Sch
TN3 .... 20 B6
Lamberhurst Golf Course
TN3 .... 20 C5
Lamberhurst Rd
　TN3, TN12 .... 20 C8
Lamberhurst Vineyard
TN3 .... 20 A4
Lambert Pl BN7 .... 123 D3
Lambert Rd BN23 .... 174 E3
Lamberts Cotts TN33 .... 112 E3
Lamberts Rd TN1, TN2 .... 8 D8
Lambourn Cl RH15 .... 73 B1
Lambourn Way TN2 .... 8 D1
Lambourne Cl BN1 .... 143 C2
Lambourne Rd BN1 ...... 143 C2
Lampington Row TN3 ...... 6 E3
Lampool Cnr TN2 .... 55 A7
Lanark Ct BN20 .... 184 B6
Lancaster Ct **11** BN3 .. 163 A6
Lancaster Dr RH19 .... 2 A3
Lancaster House Rd BN1 . 144 B7
Lancaster Rd
　Brighton BN1 .... 189 F7
　Hastings TN38 .... 135 F5
　Lancaster St BN7 .... 123 D1
Lancing Cl TN34 .... 136 D3
Lancing Ct **5** BN2 ...... 164 F5
Lancing Way BN26 .... 172 F4
Landgate TN31 .... 93 C6
Landport Farm Rd BN7 ... 123 A3
Landport Rd Lewes BN7 . 123 B3
　Lewes BN7 .... 123 C2
Landsdown Rd BN25 .... 181 C5
Landsdowne Way TN40 . 157 E5
Landseer Rd BN3 .... 163 A8
Langdale Cl BN23 .... 174 C4
Langdale Gdns BN3 ...... 162 F6
Langdale Rd BN3 .... 162 F6
Langham Cl
　Hastings TN34 .... 136 F4
　Ringmer BN8 .... 124 D5
Langham Rd
　Hastings TN34 .... 136 F4
　Robertsbridge TN32 ...... 63 F4
Langholm Rd TN3 .... 6 F6
Langley Cl TN39 .... 157 B8
Langley Cres BN2 .... 144 E1
Langley Cty Prim Sch
BN23 .... 174 E1
Langney Gn BN23 .... 185 E8
Langney Rise BN23 ...... 185 E8
Langney Rise BN21, BN22 . 185 B8
Langney Sh Ctr BN23 ... 174 C2
Langridge Dr
　East Grinstead RH19 ..... 10 E8
　Portslade-by-Sea BN41 . 141 B3
Langridge La RH16 .... 51 A5
Langridge Way RH15 ...... 72 E5
Langridges Cl BN8 .... 76 C7
Langton Cl TN33 .... 112 E3
Langton Green Cty Prim Sch
TN3 .... 6 E4
Langton Rd
　Rusthall TN3, TN4 .... 7 C3
　Speldhurst TN3 .... 7 A7
Langton Ridge TN3 .... 7 B3
Langtye La BN26, BN8 ... 149 E6
Lansdown Pl BN7 .... 146 D8
Lansdown Terr TN21 .... 82 B6
Lansdowne Cres BN27 .. 129 A2
Lansdowne Gdns BN27 .. 129 A2
Lansdowne Mews **9** BN3 163 D6
Lansdowne Pl BN3 .... 163 D6
Lansdowne Rd
　Hailsham BN27 .... 129 B2
　Hove BN1, BN3 .... 163 D6
　Royal Tunbridge Wells
　TN1, TN2 .... 8 B4
Lansdowne Sq
　Hove BN1, BN3 .... 163 D5
　8 Royal Tunbridge Wells
TN1 .... 8 B4
Lansdowne St BN3 .... 163 D6
Lansdowne Way BN27 .. 129 B3
Lapierre Rd BN9 .... 179 B7
Lapwing Cl BN23 .... 174 C2
Lapwing Ct BN27 .... 152 D7
Larch Cl Hastings TN38 . 136 A1
　Heathfield TN21 .... 82 B5
　Woodingdean BN2 .... 165 F7
Larch Gdns BN22 .... 173 D3
Larch Way RH16 .... 51 B4
Lark Hill BN3 .... 141 E3
Larke Cl BN43 .... 161 C7
Larkfield Cl TN38 .... 136 A3

Larkfield Way BN1 .... 143 A4
Larkhill TN40 .... 157 C4
Larkspur Dr BN23 .... 174 B3
Larnach Cl TN22 .... 78 D8
Lascelles Terr BN21 .... 185 A1
Lashbrooks Rd TN22 .... 78 B7
Latimer Rd BN22 .... 185 C4
Laton Rd TN34 .... 136 F2
Laughton Cl BN23 .... 174 A4
Laughton Cty Prim Sch
BN8 .... 126 C6
Laughton Lodge Hospl
BN8 .... 126 A8
Laughton Rd
  Broyle Side BN8 .... 125 D6
  Woodingdean BN2 .... 165 F8
Laundry La RH17 .... 22 D1
Laurel 2 RH16 .... 50 D6
Laurel Bank Bexhill TN40 .. 157 E5
  Royal Tunbridge Wells TN4 .. 8 B8
  Wadhurst TN5 .... 30 A4
Laurel Cl RH15 .... 73 D5
Laurel Dene RH19 .... 1 F1
Laurel La TN36 .... 116 F5
Laurel Rd TN1 .... 8 D7
Laurel Way TN1 .... 8 D7
Laurel Wlk TN38 .... 135 E3
Laurels The
  4 Brighton BN2 .... 189 B8
  Uckfield TN22 .... 78 E8
Lauriston Rd BN1 .... 142 E2
Lavant Cl TN39 .... 156 C6
Lavender Cl BN23 .... 174 B3
Lavender Gdns TN5 .... 31 E1
Lavender Hill BN43 .... 140 B1
Lavender Ho BN2 .... 189 B4
Lavender Line TN22 .... 102 E8
Lavender St BN2 .... 189 B4
Lawes Ave BN9 .... 179 C7
Lawes The TN38 .... 159 C7
Lawns Ave BN21 .... 184 D4
Lawns The
  Eastbourne BN22 .... 185 C5
  Hailsham BN27 .... 152 C6
  Willingdon BN20 .... 173 B1
  Willingdon BN22 .... 173 B2
Lawrence Cl BN23 .... 174 D1
Lawrence Ho TN22 .... 78 C7
Lawrence Rd BN3 .... 162 F7
Lawrie La RH16 .... 51 B5
Laylands Cl BN41 .... 162 A7
Laylands Rd BN41 .... 162 A7
Lazanby Ct TN38 .... 159 B8
Le Brun Rd BN21 .... 184 F5
Lea Ave TN31 .... 93 A6
Lea Cl BN9 .... 179 C8
Lea Rd BN10 .... 178 C8
Leach Ct TN22 .... 164 C5
Leaf Hall Rd 10 BN22 ...... 185 B3
Leaf Hospl
  (Univ of Brighton) BN21 .. 184 F4
Leaf Rd BN21 .... 185 A3
Leahurst Court Rd BN1 ..... 142 E3
Leahurst Ct 4 BN1 .... 142 E3
Lealands Cl TN3 .... 15 C6
Lealands Dr TN22 .... 55 C1
Leamland Wlk BN27 .... 152 B7
Leap Cross Small Bsns Ctr
BN27 .... 129 A1
Leas The
  Burgess Hill RH15 .... 72 F4
  Peacehaven Heights BN10 178 F6
  Turner's Green TN5 .... 30 A6
Leasam La TN31 .... 93 B8
Leasingham Gdns TN39 ..... 157 A5
Ledsham Ave TN37 .... 136 B5
Ledsham Cl TN37 .... 136 B5
Ledsham Pk TN37 .... 136 B5
Ledsham Way TN37 .... 136 B5
Lee Rd BN7 .... 123 B2
Lee Way BN9 .... 179 C8
Leeds Ave BN23 .... 185 D7
Leeds Cl TN35 .... 137 D4
Leeds La TN20 .... 58 D6
Leeford Cotts TN33 .... 88 A1
Leeford Vineyard TN33 ...... 88 A1
Leeves Cl TN21 .... 82 A6
Leeves Way TN21 .... 82 A6
Leggs' La TN6 .... 6 E5
Legsheath La RH18, RH19 .. 21 F8
Leicester Cl 5 BN22 .... 185 B4
Leicester Dr TN2 .... 16 E8
Leicester Rd BN7 .... 123 B1
Leicester St BN2 .... 189 B5
Leicester Villas BN3 .... 162 D7
Leighton Cl TN4 .... 8 A7
Leighton Rd
  Horsted Keynes RH17 ...... 33 C5
  Hove BN3 .... 163 A8
Leighton Villas RH17 .... 33 C5
Leneda Dr TN2 .... 16 E8

Lenham Ave BN2 .... 177 B5
Lenham Rd E BN2 .... 177 B5
Lenham Rd W BN2 .... 177 A5
Lennox Cl BN20 .... 184 B5
Lennox Ct TN21 .... 82 B8
Lennox Rd Hove BN3 .... 162 F8
  Shoreham-by-Sea BN43 .. 161 B8
Lennox St BN2 .... 189 B5
Leopold Rd Bexhill TN39 .. 157 B4
  Brighton BN1 .... 189 F6
Lepeland BN27 .... 129 A1
Lesley Cl TN40 .... 157 F7
Leslie St BN22 .... 185 B4
Letheren Pl BN20, BN21 .. 184 D3
Leveller End BN8 .... 76 D7
Leveller Rd BN8 .... 76 D7
Levett Ave BN26 .... 173 C6
Levett Cl BN26 .... 173 C6
Levett Rd BN26 .... 173 C6
Levett Way BN26 .... 173 C6
Levetts La TN32 .... 46 D1
Lewes Bsns Ctr BN7 .... 123 C2
Lewes Cl Bexhill TN39 ...... 157 A6
  Saltdean BN2 .... 177 E5
Lewes Cres BN2 .... 164 E4
Lewes Ct BN7 .... 123 C4
Lewes Golf Course BN7 .... 124 A1
Lewes High Sch BN7 .... 123 B1
Lewes Ho 5 BN21 .... 184 F4
Lewes Rd
  Brighton BN1, BN2 .... 143 E3
  Chelwood Gate
  RH17, RH18 .... 22 C1
  Danehill RH17 .... 34 B3
  Ditchling BN6 .... 98 F2
  Eastbourne BN21 .... 184 F5
  Forest Row RH18 .... 11 E2
  Haywards Heath
  RH16, RH17 .... 51 D4
  Haywards Heath, Lindfield
  RH16 .... 51 B7
  Horsted Keynes RH17 ...... 33 C5
  Isfield TN22 .... 102 E6
  Newhaven BN9 .... 179 C8
  Polegate BN26 .... 172 C6
  Ringmer BN8 .... 124 D6
  Scaynes Hill RH17 .... 51 D4
  Uckfield TN22 .... 78 D4
Lewes St BN2 .... 189 B6
Lewes Sta BN7 .... 146 D8
Lewes Tertiary Coll
  Lewes BN7 .... 123 B1
  Lewes BN7 .... 146 D8
Lewes Tertitary Coll
  (S Bldg) BN7 .... 123 B1
Lewis Ave TN40 .... 158 A5
Lewis Cl BN9 .... 168 F2
Lewis Ct 8 BN2 .... 164 C8
Lewis Rd BN3 .... 163 A3
Lewry Cl BN9 .... 179 B7
Lexden Ct BN25 .... 181 A4
Lexden Dr BN25 .... 181 A5
Lexden Lodge Ind Est TN6 .. 38 D8
Lexden Rd BN25 .... 180 F6
Leybourne Cl BN2 .... 144 A1
Leybourne Gdns TN37 ...... 136 C4
Leybourne Par BN2 .... 144 A1
Leybourne Rd BN2 .... 144 A1
Leyland Rd BN24 .... 175 D4
Leylands Pk RH15 .... 73 B5
Leylands Rd RH15 .... 73 B4
Lichfield Ct 10 BN2 .... 164 F5
Lifeboat Mus BN21 .... 185 A1
Lilac Cl BN22 .... 173 D3
Lillesden Cotts TN18 .... 45 E7
Lillywhite Cl RH15 .... 72 F5
Limden Cl TN5 .... 42 F6
Lime Cl Frant TN3 .... 17 B3
  Hastings TN38 .... 136 B1
  Uckfield TN22 .... 78 D8
Lime Cross BN27 .... 130 F5
Lime Hill Rd TN1 .... 8 A4
Lime Tree Ave TN22 .... 78 D7
Lime Tree Gr RH16 .... 51 C7
Lime Tree Terr TN19 .... 62 A6
Lime Way TN21 .... 82 B6
Limekiln Ct TN6 .... 26 C3
Limes La TN22 .... 56 D3
Limes The
  Dormans Park RH19 .... 1 A5
  13 Eastbourne BN21 ..... 184 E4
Limetree Ave BN22 .... 173 D3
Limney Rd BN2 .... 164 E7
Linchmere BN2 .... 164 E7
Linchmere Ave BN2 .... 177 C5
Lincoln Ave BN10 .... 178 A7
Lincoln Ave S BN10 .... 178 A7
Lincoln Cl
  Eastbourne BN20 .... 188 C8
  2 Hastings TN38 .... 136 A4

Lincoln Cotts BN2 .... 189 B6
Lincoln Ct
  Eastbourne BN20 .... 184 B7
  Hove BN3 .... 163 C8
  Peacehaven BN10 .... 178 A7
Lincoln Rd BN41 .... 162 B7
Lincoln St 3 Mount Sion TN1 .. 8 A2
Lincoln Wood RH16, RH17 . 50 C5
Linden Ave RH19 .... 1 C2
Linden Chase TN22 .... 78 D7
Linden Cl
  Eastbourne BN22 .... 173 E2
  Royal Tunbridge Wells TN2 .. 8 A2
Linden Ct TN22 .... 78 C7
Linden Dr TN22 .... 7 F1
Linden Gr
  Hailsham BN27 .... 129 C3
  Haywards Heath RH16 ...... 51 B7
Linden Park Rd TN2 .... 8 A2
Linden Rd TN40 .... 157 C3
Lindens The 4 BN2 .... 189 B7
Lindfield BN41 .... 141 A1
Lindfield Ave BN25 .... 181 C2
Lindfield Cl BN2 .... 177 B6
Lindfield Ct 2 BN1 .... 143 C2
Lindfield Cty Inf Sch
RH16 .... 51 A7
Lindfield Cty Jun Sch
RH16 .... 51 B7
Lindfield Ent Pk RH16 ...... 51 C6
Lindfield Sch The BN22 ... 173 D2
Lindon Cl BN20 .... 183 B1
Lindsay Cl BN20 .... 184 C2
Lingfield Rd RH19 .... 1 D3
Link Rd BN20 .... 184 D1
Link The Friston BN20 ...... 183 C2
  Rye TN31 .... 93 A5
Link Way TN2 .... 8 E8
Linkden Cotts TN18 .... 45 B7
Links Ave BN10, BN9 .... 179 A7
Links Cl Crowborough TN6 .. 25 D7
  Portslade-by-Sea BN41 .. 162 C8
  Seaford BN25 .... 181 A2
Links Dr TN40 .... 157 E4
Links (Golf Course) The
BN20 .... 184 D2
Links Rd
  Portslade-by-Sea BN41 .. 162 C8
  Seaford BN25 .... 181 A2
Links The Bexhill TN40 .... 157 D3
  Hastings TN38 .... 158 F8
Links Way TN31 .... 94 E2
Linkswood BN21 .... 184 E2
Linkway
  Eastbourne BN20 .... 184 B7
  Westham BN24 .... 174 E6
Linkway The BN1 .... 143 B1
Linley Cl Bexhill TN40 ...... 157 D4
  Hastings TN34 .... 137 A3
Linley Dr TN34 .... 137 A3
Linnet Cl BN23 .... 174 C2
Linnet Gn TN22 .... 78 D7
Linthouse Cl BN10 .... 167 D2
Linton Cres TN34 .... 159 E8
Linton Ct TN34 .... 159 E8
Linton Rd Hastings TN34 .. 159 E8
  Hove BN3 .... 162 F8
Lion Hill BN23, BN24 .... 174 B5
Lion La BN21 .... 185 B3
Lion Mews 4 BN3 .... 162 F7
Lion St TN31 .... 93 C5
Lionel Rd TN40 .... 157 E3
Lions Cl BN21 .... 164 E5
Lions Dene BN1 .... 142 D4
Lions Gdns BN1 .... 142 D2
Lions Pl BN25 .... 180 F2
Liphook Cl BN1 .... 143 C1
Lipscombe Rd TN2 .... 8 D6
Liptraps La TN1, TN2 .... 8 D7
Lismore Rd BN21 .... 185 A2
Lister Ave RH19 .... 10 F6
Lister Rd BN23 .... 174 A1
Litlington Cl 4 BN25 ...... 180 C4
Little Bayham Cotts TN3 ... 18 F4
Little Bentswood RH16 ...... 50 F5
Little Bentswood Cl RH16 .. 50 F5
Little Black Hill RH16 .... 51 B7
Little Common
  Cty Prim Sch TN39 .... 156 D4
  Little Common Rd TN39 .. 156 E5
Little Copse Rd BN6 .... 97 E4
Little Cranbrook BN27 ..... 177 B5
Little East St
  Brighton BN2 .... 189 A4
  Lewes BN7 .... 123 D1
Little Footway TN3 .... 6 F3
Little George St BN2 .... 189 A4
Little Horsted
  CE Prim Sch TN22 .... 78 C1

Little Iridge Farm Cotts
TN19 .... 45 C1
Little King St RH19 .... 1 E1
Little London Rd TN21 ..... 106 F8
Little Mallett TN3 .... 6 F2
Little Mead BN8 .... 123 A7
Little Mount Sion TN1 .... 8 A2
Little Paddock
  Crowborough TN6 .... 25 E1
  Heathfield TN21 .... 82 A7
  Ringmer BN8 .... 124 E6
Little Park Cotts TN33 ...... 112 E5
Little Pk TN5 .... 29 E5
Little Preston St BN1 .... 163 E5
Little Ridge TN35 .... 137 F8
Little Ridge Cty Prim Sch
TN37 .... 136 C5
Little Sherwood Ind Pk
TN36 .... 116 D5
Little Sunnyside TN6 .... 25 F1
Little Trogers La TN20 .... 40 B4
Little Twitten TN39 .... 156 D3
Little Western St 1 BN1 .. 163 E5
Littlemead TN22 .... 35 C3
Littleworth Cl BN2 .... 165 F7
Living World The BN25 .... 181 F4
Livingstone Ho 5 BN3 ..... 163 B7
Livingstone Rd
  Burgess Hill RH15 .... 72 F3
  Hove BN3 .... 163 B7
Livingstone St BN2 .... 164 D5
Lloyd Cl BN3 .... 163 C8
Lloyd Rd BN3 .... 163 C8
Lockitt Way BN7 .... 145 E5
Locks Cres BN41 .... 141 B1
Locks Ct 10 BN42 .... 161 E7
Locks Hill BN41 .... 141 B1
Lockwood Cl BN2 .... 165 F7
Lockwood Cres BN2 .... 165 F7
Loder PI BN1 .... 142 F2
Loder Rd BN1 .... 142 F2
Lodge Ave BN22 .... 173 C1
Lodge Cl
  East Grinstead RH19 .... 1 D1
  Portslade-by-Sea BN41 .. 140 F2
Lodge Hill La BN6 .... 98 C4
Lodge La BN6 .... 98 B2
Lodge Rd TN35 .... 160 C5
Lodge The Brighton BN2 .. 189 B8
  14 Eastbourne BN21 ..... 185 A2
Lodsworth Cl BN2 .... 164 F7
Lomaria Ct TN2 .... 9 A4
Lomas La TN18 .... 47 F5
Lomond Ave BN1 .... 143 B7
London Meed Cty Prim Sch
RH15 .... 73 A1
London Rd
  Bexhill TN39, TN40 .... 157 B5
  Brighton BN1 .... 189 A7
  Brighton, Withdene BN1 .. 142 D4
  Burgess Hill RH15 .... 72 F5
  Crowborough TN6 .... 25 E4
  Danehill RH17 .... 34 C4
  East Grinstead RH19 .... 1 C3
  East Hoathly BN8 .... 105 A5
  Flimwell TN5 .... 32 D3
  Forest Row RH18 .... 11 E2
  Hailsham BN27 .... 129 A2
  Hassocks BN6, RH15 .... 97 E6
  Hastings TN37, TN38 ...... 159 C8
  Hurst Green TN19 .... 45 A3
  John's Cross TN32, TN33 .. 87 D3
  Pyecombe BN1, BN45 ..... 119 C4
  Royal Tunbridge Wells TN4 .. 8 A8
  Royal Tunbridge Wells,
  Mount Sion TN1, TN2, TN4 .. 8 A3
  Uckfield TN22 .... 55 D2
London Road Sta BN1 ...... 164 A8
London Terr BN1 .... 189 A7
Loney Ct 1 BN43 .... 161 C8
Long Acre BN41 .... 184 D5
Long Ave TN40 .... 158 A8
Long Barn Motor Mus
TN21 .... 80 F8
Long Hos TN32 .... 85 D5
Long La TN33 .... 88 E1
Long Man The BN26 .... 171 E3
Long Meads TN3, TN4 .... 7 B4
Long Park Cnr BN6 .... 98 D2
Long Slip TN3 .... 7 A3
Long Wlk RH16 .... 51 B4
Longacre Cl TN37 .... 136 C6
Longfield Rd TN2 .... 8 D8
Longhill Cl BN2 .... 165 E4
Longhill Rd BN2 .... 165 E4
Longhill Sch BN2 .... 165 E4
Longhurst
  9 Brighton BN2 .... 164 E4
  Burgess Hill RH15 .... 72 D2
Longhurst Cotts BN8 .... 75 D7
Longland Rd BN20 .... 184 C4

Longridge Ave BN2 .... 177 D5
Longstone Rd BN21 .... 185 A3
Longview Way TN21 .... 82 A5
Longview Way TN1 .... 8 D7
Lonsdale Gdns TN1, TN2 ..... 8 A3
Lookout The BN10 .... 167 D3
Loose Farm Barns TN33 ... 113 A2
Loose Farm Cotts TN33 ... 113 A2
Lordine La TN32 .... 66 B4
Lords La TN35 .... 137 D3
Lords The BN25 .... 180 E6
Lordsdale Cl BN20 .... 188 D8
Lordswell La TN6 .... 37 E8
Loriners Cl BN3 .... 162 D8
Lorna Rd BN3 .... 163 D7
Lorne Rd BN1 .... 189 A8
Lorraine Ct 7 BN21 .... 163 E7
Lorraine Rd BN9 .... 179 D7
Lossenham La TN18 .... 48 D3
Lottbridge Dr BN22 .... 173 F1
Lottbridge Dro
  Eastbourne BN22, BN23 .. 185 B7
  Eastbourne BN23 .... 185 B7
Lottbridge Rdbt BN22 ...... 185 A8
Lovat Mead TN38 .... 158 E6
Love La Eastbourne BN20 .. 184 D3
  Mayfield TN20 .... 39 F2
  Rye TN31 .... 93 B6
Lovegrove Ct BN3 .... 162 E8
Lovell Cl BN21 .... 184 D5
Lover's Wlk BN1 .... 163 F8
Lowdells Cl RH19 .... 1 C4
Lowdells Dr RH19 .... 1 D4
Lowdells La RH19 .... 1 C3
Lower Bevendean Ave
BN2 .... 143 E1
Lower Chalvington Pl
BN2 .... 164 E5
Lower Church Rd RH15 ..... 72 F3
Lower Cross Cotts TN31 .... 91 E2
Lower Dene BN21 .... 2 A1
Lower Dicker BN27 .... 128 C3
Lower Dr Seaford BN25 ... 180 F5
  Southwick BN42 .... 140 E1
Lower Glen Rd TN37 .... 136 B4
Lower Green Rd
  Pembury TN2 .... 9 D7
  Rusthall TN3, TN4 .... 7 C6
Lower Hazelhurst TN5 .... 31 A4
Lower High St TN5 .... 30 A4
Lower Lake TN33 .... 112 E4
Lower Market St BN3 .... 163 D5
Lower Mere RH16 .... 10 F8
Lower Park Rd TN34 .... 136 E1
Lower Pl BN9 .... 179 C7
Lower Platts TN5 .... 31 F1
Lower Rd
  Eastbourne BN21 .... 184 D4
  Forest Row RH18 .... 11 F3
  Golden Cross BN27 .... 130 E3
  Lower Rock Gdns BN2 .... 189 B4
  Lower Saxonbury TN6 ...... 25 F2
Lower South Rd
  TN37, TN38 .... 136 C1
Lower Sq RH18 .... 11 E3
Loxdale (The Swedish Folk
  High Sch) BN41 .... 141 B1
Loxfield Cl TN20 .... 40 A2
Loxfield Gdns TN6 .... 26 B1
Loxwood Cl Bexhill TN39 .. 156 D5
  Eastbourne BN21 .... 173 C1
Lucas RH17 .... 33 D5
Lucas Cl RH19 .... 2 A1
Lucas Grange RH16 .... 50 D5
Lucas Way RH16 .... 50 C5
Lucastes Ave RH16, RH17 .. 50 C6
Lucastes Rd RH16 .... 50 C5
Lucerne Cl BN41 .... 141 B1
Lucerne Rd BN1 .... 142 E4
Lucinda Way BN25 .... 180 F6
Lucraft Rd BN1, BN2 .... 144 A5
Ludley Hill TN31 .... 91 A6
Ludlow Rise BN2 .... 144 A1
Ludpit La TN19, TN32 .... 63 C6
Luke Lade Ct BN27 .... 152 C7
Lulham Cl BN10 .... 167 B2
Lullington Ave BN3 .... 162 F8

Lullington Cl
Bexhill TN40 .... 158 A6
Eastbourne BN21 .... 184 C7
Seaford BN25 .... 181 B2
Lullington Gdns TN37 ...... 136 C5
Lullington Ho **3** BN21 .... 184 E4
Lunce's Hill RH16, RH17 .... 73 F8
Lundy Wlk BN27 .... 129 A2
Lureland Ct BN10 .... 178 C6
Lurgashall RH15 .... 73 C1
Lushington La BN21 .... 185 A2
Lushington Rd BN21 .... 185 A2
Lustrells Cl BN2 .... 177 B6
Lustrells Cres BN2 .... 177 C6
Lustrells Rd BN2 .... 177 A6
Lustrells Vale BN2 .... 177 C6
Luther St BN2 .... 164 C7
Luton Cl BN21 .... 184 C6
Luxford Cl TN22 .... 78 C7
Luxford Dr TN6 .... 38 A8
Luxford La TN6 .... 38 A8
Luxford Rd
Crowborough TN6 .... 38 A8
Haywards Heath RH16 .... 51 B7
Luxford's La RH19 .... 11 B6
Lychgates Cl TN40 .... 157 D5
Lydd Cl BN23 .... 174 D2
Lydd Rd TN31 .... 95 C1
Lymden La TN5 .... 43 A7
Lyminster Ave BN1 .... 143 A5
Lynchet Cl BN1 .... 143 C3
Lynchet Down BN1 .... 143 C2
Lynchet Wlk BN1 .... 143 C2
Lynchets Cres BN1 .... 141 D3
Lynchets The BN7 .... 123 E3
Lynden Ct **6** BN1 .... 142 E2
Lyndhurst Ave TN34 .... 137 A4
Lyndhurst Ct BN3 .... 163 D7
Lyndhurst Rd BN3 .... 163 D7
Lynholm Rd BN26 .... 173 C6
Lynton Cl
East Grinstead RH19 .... 2 A2
Hurstpierpoint BN6 .... 97 B5
Lynton Park Ave RH19 ...... 2 A2
Lynton St BN2 .... 164 C7
Lynwood TN3 .... 15 C6
Lynwood TN37 .... 136 D5
Lynwood Rd BN2 .... 177 C4
Lyon Cl BN3 .... 163 D7
Lyoth La RH16 .... 51 C4
Lyoth Villas RH16 .... 51 C4
Lytham Ct TN38 .... 158 F8

Mabb's Hill TN5 .... 42 F7
Maberley Rd TN39, TN40 .. 157 C6
Mackerel Hill TN31 .... 68 F4
Mackerel's Rocks BN8 ...... 76 F3
Mackie Ave Brighton BN1 .. 143 A7
Keymer BN6 .... 98 A5
Macmillan Dr BN21 .... 184 C5
Madehurst Cl BN2 .... 164 D5
Madeira Dr BN2 .... 164 C4
Madeira Pk TN1 .... 8 B2
Madeira Pl BN2 .... 189 B4
Madeira Dr TN37 .... 136 C3
Mafeking Rd BN2 .... 143 D1
Magdalen Cl BN23 .... 174 C3
Magdalen Rd
Bexhill TN40 .... 157 D4
Hastings TN37 .... 159 D7
Magna Ct TN40 .... 157 B4
Magnolia Ct TN21 .... 82 B5
Magnolia Dr BN22 .... 173 D2
Magnolia Wlk BN22 .... 173 D2
Magpie Cl Bexhill TN39 .... 156 C6
Hastings TN38 .... 158 E8
Magpie Rd BN23 .... 174 C3
Magreed La TN21 .... 106 B7
Maidstone Rd TN2 .... 9 E8
Main Rd
Icklesham TN35, TN36 .... 116 D5
Westfield TN35 .... 114 E4
Main St Iden TN31 .... 70 B4
Northiam TN31 .... 67 B5
Peasmarsh TN31 .... 69 B2
Mainstone Rd **1** BN3 ..... 162 F7
Maitland Cl TN34 .... 136 E6
Major Cl BN1 .... 143 B1
Major York's Rd TN4 .... 7 F2
Malcolm Gdns BN26 .... 173 A7
Maldon Rd BN1 .... 142 D2
Malines Ave BN10 .... 178 B8
Malines Ave S BN10 .... 178 A7
Mallard Ct BN22 .... 184 F8
Mallard Dr TN22 .... 78 E5
Mallard Pl RH19 .... 10 F8
Mallett Cl **3** BN25 .... 180 E2
Malling Cl BN7 .... 123 D3

Malling Down BN7 .... 123 E3
Malling Hill BN7 .... 123 E2
Malling House
(Sussex Pol HQ) BN7 ..... 123 D3
Malling Ind Est BN7 .... 123 E2
Malling St **1** Lewes BN7 .. 123 E1
Lewes BN7 .... 123 E2
Mallory Rd BN3 .... 142 C2
Malt House Trad Est
BN43 .... 161 B7
Malthouse Bsns Pk The
TN31 .... 69 C2
Malthouse Ct **14** BN2 .... 189 B5
Malthouse La
Burgess Hill BN6, RH15 .... 72 C2
Peasmarsh TN31 .... 69 B2
Peasmarsh TN31 .... 69 D2
Malthouse Trad Est BN43 .. 161 B7
Malthouse Way BN8 .... 123 A7
Maltings Barn The **6** BN7 123 E1
Maltings The
Burgess Hill BN6 .... 72 D4
Peasmarsh TN31 .... 69 B2
Malton Way TN2 .... 8 F7
Malvern Cl BN22 .... 173 E4
Malvern Ho TN39 .... 157 B3
Malvern St **12** BN3 .... 163 B7
Malvern Way TN34 .... 137 B4
Manaton Cl RH16 .... 50 F4
Manchester Rd TN33 .... 133 A6
Manchester St BN2 .... 189 A4
Mandalay Ct BN1 .... 142 D4
Manhattan Ct BN1 .... 142 D4
Manhattan Gdns TN35 .... 137 D4
Manifold Rd BN22 .... 185 B4
Man St TN34 .... 159 FB
Manning Cl RH19 .... 1 D2
Manor Ave BN6 .... 98 A5
Manor Cl Brighton BN2 ... 164 E5
Broyle Side BN8 .... 124 F7
Burgess Hill RH15 .... 73 D4
Horam TN21 .... 106 F7
Icklesham TN36 .... 116 F5
Royal Tunbridge Wells TN4 .. 7 E3
Seaford BN25 .... 181 B3
Southwick BN42 .... 162 A8
Uckfield TN22 .... 78 C8
Willingdon BN20 .... 173 B2
Manor Cotts TN3 .... 20 B5
Manor Cres BN2 .... 164 E5
Manor Ct Seaford BN25 ... 181 B3
Southwick BN42 .... 162 A7
Manor Cty Prim Sch TN22 .. 78 D8
Manor Dr BN10 .... 167 B1
Manor End TN22 .... 78 C8
Manor Gdns BN2 .... 164 E5
Manor Gn BN2 .... 164 E5
Manor Hall Cty Fst Sch
BN42 .... 161 F7
Manor Hall Cty Mid Sch
BN42 .... 161 F8
Manor Hall Rd BN42 .... 161 F8
Manor Lea BN2 .... 164 E6
Manor Paddock BN2 .... 164 E4
Manor Park Cl BN27 .... 129 A3
Manor Park Ct BN26 .... 173 A6
Manor Park Rd BN27 .... 129 A3
Manor Pk TN4 .... 7 E3
Manor Pl BN2 .... 164 E4
Manor Rd Bexhill TN40 .... 157 D4
Brighton BN2 .... 164 E5
Burgess Hill RH15 .... 73 D4
East Grinstead RH19 .... 1 C1
Eastbourne BN22 .... 174 A2
Hastings TN34 .... 160 A5
Horam TN21 .... 106 F8
Portslade-by-Sea BN41 .. 141 B1
Rusthall TN4 .... 7 C4
Seaford BN25 .... 181 B3
Manor Rd N BN25 .... 181 B3
Manor Way Brighton BN2 . 164 E5
Crowborough TN6 .... 37 E8
Eastbourne BN20 .... 184 B8
Polegate BN26 .... 173 B6
Uckfield TN22 .... 78 C8
Mansell Cl TN39 .... 156 C4
Mansell Ct RH15 .... 73 B3
Mansell Rd BN43 .... 161 B8
Mansers La BN27 .... 128 C3
Mansfield Rd BN3 .... 162 E7
Mansion Ct RH15 .... 73 D3
Manston Way TN34 .... 136 E2
Mantell Cl BN7 .... 123 C4
Mantell Ho **2** BN21 ...... 189 B5
Mantell Rd BN23 .... 185 D8
Manton Rd BN2 .... 143 E1
Manvers Rd BN20 .... 184 B3
Maple Ave TN39 .... 156 C6
Maple Cl Bexhill TN39 ..... 156 C3
Burgess Hill RH15 .... 73 B5
Haywards Heath RH16 .... 51 B3

Maple Cl
Maresfield TN22 .... 55 A4
Royal Tunbridge Wells TN2 .. 8 A1
Woodingdean BN2 .... 165 E7
Maple Ct BN27 .... 152 A8
Maple Dr
Burgess Hill RH15 .... 73 A5
East Grinstead RH19 .... 2 A1
Maple Gdns BN3 .... 141 F1
Maple Hts TN37 .... 136 B7
Maple Leaf Cl BN9 .... 179 B7
Maple Rd
Eastbourne BN23 .... 185 D7
Peacehaven Heights BN10 178 F6
Maple Wlk TN39 .... 156 C3
Maplehurst Ct TN37 .... 136 B7
Maplehurst Dr TN37 .... 136 C8
Maplehurst Rd
Eastbourne BN22 .... 173 D2
Hastings TN37 .... 136 C8
Portslade-by-Sea BN41 .. 141 A1
Maplehurst Rise TN37 .... 136 B7
Mapleleaf Gdns BN26 ..... 173 A8
Maples Cotts TN22 .... 80 A6
Maplewood **7** BN1 ...... 142 E3
Marbles Rd BN8 .... 76 D7
Marchants Cl BN6 .... 97 A6
Marchants Dr TN31 .... 94 F2
Marchants Rd BN6 .... 97 A6
Marchants Way RH15 ...... 72 F5
Marcia Cl BN20 .... 184 A8
Marcus Gdns TN38 .... 136 A5
Mardan Ct TN38 .... 159 B7
Marden Cl BN2 .... 144 E1
Marden Ct TN39 .... 157 A3
Marden's Hill TN6 .... 25 B6
Mare Bay Cl TN38 .... 135 E7
Maresfield Bonners
CE Prim Sch TN22 .... 55 B4
Maresfield Dr BN24 .... 175 E6
Maresfield Rd BN2 .... 164 E5
Margaret Ct BN10 .... 178 B7
Margaret St BN2 .... 189 B4
Margery Rd BN3 .... 162 D8
Marina Bexhill TN39, TN40 157 C3
Hastings TN38 .... 159 B6
Marina Court Ave TN40 ... 157 C3
Marina Cl BN9 .... 179 D6
Marina Way BN2 .... 164 D5
Marina Wlk BN23 .... 185 E8
Marine Ave
Beachlands BN24 .... 175 F6
Hove BN3 .... 162 E6
Marine Cl
Beachlands BN24 .... 175 F6
Saltdean BN2 .... 177 B5
Marine Cotts TN31 .... 94 E2
Marine Cres BN25 .... 180 F2
Marine Ct
4 Brighton BN2 .... 189 B5
Telscombe Cliffs BN10 ... 177 F3
Marine Dr
Rottingdean BN2 .... 165 C2
Seaford BN25 .... 180 B5
Marine Gdns BN2 .... 189 B4
Marine Par
Brighton BN2 .... 164 C4
Eastbourne BN21, BN22 .. 185 B3
Hastings TN34 .... 160 A3
Seaford BN25 .... 180 C3
Marine Parade Rd **15**
BN22 .... 185 B3
Marine Rd
Eastbourne BN22 .... 185 B3
Pevensey Bay BN24 .... 175 D5
Marine Sq BN2 .... 164 C4
Marine Terr BN24 .... 175 D5
Marine Terrace Mews **7**
BN2 .... 164 C4
Marine View **3** BN2 ...... 189 B5
Mariners Quay BN2 .... 164 F3
Mariteau Ho TN36 .... 117 E7
Marjoram Pl BN43 .... 140 B1
Mark Cl BN25 .... 181 C2
Mark Cross BN8 .... 126 B2
Mark Cross CE Prim Sch
TN6 .... 28 A3
Mark La BN21 .... 185 A2
Market La **2** BN21 .... 123 D1
Market Pas **6**
Hastings TN34 .... 160 A3
9 Hastings, St Leonards
TN38 .... 159 C6
Market Pl
Burgess Hill RH15 .... 73 A2
Hailsham BN27 .... 152 C7
Hailsham BN27 .... 159 B8
11 Royal Tunbridge
Wells TN2 .... 8 A2
Market Rd Battle TN33 .... 112 C5
Rye TN31 .... 93 C5

Market Sq Battle TN33 .... 112 D5
1 Hailsham BN27 .... 152 C7
Royal Tunbridge Wells TN2 .. 8 A1
Market St Brighton BN1 .. 189 A5
Hastings TN37, TN38 ...... 159 C6
Lewes BN7 .... 123 D1
13 Royal Tunbridge Wells
TN2 .... 8 A2
Rye TN31 .... 93 C5
Market Terr **8** TN38 ..... 159 C6
Markland Way TN22 .... 78 A7
Marklye La TN21 .... 59 B1
Markstakes Cnr BN8 .... 75 F1
Markstakes La BN8 .... 75 F1
Marlborough Cl
Eastbourne BN23 .... 174 D3
Hastings TN38 .... 136 A1
Royal Tunbridge Wells TN4 .. 7 E4
Marlborough Ct
Burgess Hill RH15 .... 72 E3
1 Hove BN3 .... 163 C6
Marlborough Dr RH15 ..... 73 C2
Marlborough Mews BN1 .. 189 F5
Marlborough Pl BN1, BN2 189 A6
Marlborough St BN1 ...... 189 F5
Marle Ave RH15 .... 72 E2
Marle Green Cotts TN21 .. 107 B6
Marley Cl TN33 .... 112 F4
Marley Gdns TN33 .... 112 F4
Marley La TN33 .... 113 B6
Marley Lodge BN2 .... 189 B7
Marley Rd TN31 .... 93 A6
Marley Rise TN33 .... 112 F4
Marline Ave TN38 .... 136 A4
Marline Rd TN38 .... 136 A4
Marlinspike The BN43 .... 161 A6
Marlow Ave BN22 .... 185 B6
Marlow Cl BN2 .... 189 B7
Marlow Dr Hastings TN37 136 C5
Haywards Heath RH16 .... 51 C4
Marlow Rd BN2 .... 164 F4
Marlowes The TN40 .... 157 E5
Marlpit Cl TN40 .... 157 E5
Marlpit Gdns TN5 .... 31 E1
Marlpit Rd RH19 .... 21 A6
Marlpit The TN5 .... 29 E5
Marlpits La TN33 .... 133 A7
Marmion Rd BN3 .... 162 F7
Marsden Rd BN23 .... 174 E1
Marsh Ho **3** BN43 ...... 161 D7
Marsh Quarter La TN18 .... 47 C3
Marshall Ct BN2 .... 173 D1
Marshall La BN9 .... 179 C7
Marshall Rd BN22 .... 185 A8
Marshall Robb BN22 ...... 174 A1
Marshalls Row BN1 .... 189 A7
Marshlands Cty Prim Sch
BN27 .... 152 D8
Marshlands La TN21 .... 82 A7
Marston Ct **6** BN23 ..... 163 E7
Martello Cl
Pevensey Bay BN24 .... 175 C3
1 South Heighton BN9 .. 168 D1
Martello Rd
Eastbourne BN22 .... 185 D6
Seaford BN25 .... 180 E2
Martello Tower Mus BN25 180 E1
Martens Field BN7 .... 146 E1
Martha Gunn Cl BN2 .... 143 E1
Martin Ct BN22 .... 173 D1
Martin Rd BN3 .... 141 D1
Martineau La TN35 .... 137 F5
Martingale Cl TN37 .... 136 C5
Martins The BN10 .... 167 B1
Martlet Ct TN6 .... 25 F1
Martlet Ho Brighton BN1 . 164 A8
Martlet Rd BN27 .... 177 D4
Martlet The BN3 .... 142 C5
Martlets Bexhill TN40 ..... 157 E5
Lower Willingdon BN22 .. 173 B3
Martlets The
Broad Oak TN21 .... 90 C4
Burgess Hill RH15 .... 73 A3
Crowborough TN6 .... 25 F1
Hailsham BN27 .... 152 A7
Lewes BN7 .... 123 D3
South Chailey BN8 .... 100 D7
Martlets The
Burwash Common TN19 .... 60 F3
Ringmer BN8 .... 124 E6
Martyn's Cl BN2 .... 165 E4
Martyns Pl RH19 .... 11 A8
Martyns Way TN38, TN40 . 158 A5
Marwick Ct TN38 .... 159 B8
Marwick Terr TN38 .... 159 B8
Mary Burfield Ct **3** TN21 .. 82 A7
Mary Stamford Gn TN31 .. 94 A3
Maryan Ct BN27 .... 152 B8
Maryland Dr TN2 .... 8 D1
Marylands RH16 .... 50 F5

Maskelyne Rd BN27 .... 131 A1
Mason Cl RH19 .... 1 E2
Mason Rd Rye TN31 .... 93 A5
Seaford BN25 .... 180 F4
Matlock Rd
Brighton BN1, BN3 .... 142 D2
Eastbourne BN20 .... 188 E8
Maudlin Ct TN37 .... 159 C8
Maunsell Rd TN38 .... 135 F5
Maurice Rd BN25 .... 180 F1
Maxfield Cl BN20 .... 184 B5
Maxfield La TN35 .... 115 C3
May Ave BN25 .... 181 B3
May Rd BN2 .... 164 D7
May Tree Gdns TN40 ...... 157 F6
Mayfair Cl BN26 .... 172 F4
Mayfield Ave BN10 .... 178 D6
Mayfield CE Prim Sch
TN20 .... 40 B3
Mayfield Cl
Brighton BN1 .... 143 A5
Mayfield TN20 .... 39 F2
Mayfield Coll TN20 .... 40 C6
Mayfield Cres BN1 .... 142 F5
Mayfield Ct
Broad Oak TN21 .... 59 E1
Burgess Hill RH15 .... 73 B3
Saltdean BN2 .... 177 F5
Mayfield Flat TN21, TN22 .. 81 A8
Mayfield La
Durgates TN5 .... 29 D4
Hastings TN38 .... 135 D2
Mayfield Pk TN5 .... 29 E5
Mayfield Pl BN22 .... 185 A4
Mayfield Rd
Mark Cross TN6 .... 28 A2
Rotherfield TN20 .... 39 A7
Royal Tunbridge Wells TN4 .. 7 F4
Mayfield Way TN40 .... 157 E5
Mayflower Ct
Haywards Heath RH16 .... 50 F4
9 Shoreham-by-Sea
BN43 .... 161 A6
Mayflower Rd RH16 .... 50 F4
Mayflower Sq BN1 .... 189 A7
Mayhew Way BN7 .... 123 D2
Mayhouse Rd RH15 .... 72 F1
Maynard's Green
Cty Prim Sch TN21 .... 82 A2
Mayne Waye TN34 .... 137 B4
Mayo Ct **5** BN2 .... 164 B8
Mayo La TN39 .... 157 A8
Mayo Rd BN2 .... 164 B8
Mayo Rise TN39 .... 157 A8
Maypole Cotts TN22 .... 56 B8
Maypole Rd
Ashurst Wood RH19 .... 11 E6
East Grinstead RH19 .... 1 D2
Maytham Rd TN17 .... 49 C7
Maytree Cotts BN8 .... 100 C7
Maytree Wlk BN1 .... 141 E1
Mayvern Ct TN6 .... 25 F3
Mayview Cl TN1 .... 59 E1
Maywood Ave BN22, BN26 173 E2
Maze Hill TN38 .... 159 B7
Maze Hill Terr TN38 .... 159 B7
McIndoe Rd RH19 .... 1 D3
McWilliam Rd BN2 .... 144 C1
Meachants Cl BN20 .... 173 B2
Meachants La BN20 .... 173 B2
Mead The Bexhill TN39 ... 156 D4
Royal Tunbridge Wells TN2 .. 8 C2
Meadow Bank TN33 .... 112 E4
Meadow Cl
Hailsham BN27 .... 129 B1
Hastings TN38 .... 136 A4
Hove BN3 .... 142 B3
Portslade-by-Sea BN41 .. 141 B2
Rottingdean BN2 .... 165 F3
Southwick BN42 .... 162 A8
Meadow Cres TN39 .... 157 C7
Meadow Dr RH16 .... 51 B6
Meadow Hill Rd **6**
TN1, TN2 .... 8 B3
Meadow Ho BN8 .... 100 E7
Meadow La
Burgess Hill RH15 .... 72 F1
Haywards Heath RH16 .... 51 B6
Meadow Par BN22 .... 165 F3
Meadow Pl TN22 .... 78 C6
Meadow Rd
Groombridge TN3 .... 15 C7
Hailsham BN27 .... 152 A6
Royal Tunbridge Wells TN1 .. 8 A4
Rusthall TN4 .... 7 C4
Meadow The TN2 .... 9 E8
Meadow Vale BN26 .... 165 E5
Meadow View
Rotherfield TN6 .... 39 B7
Westfield TN35 .... 114 E4
Meadow View Cotts TN19 .. 45 A3

Meadow Way
Fairlight Cove TN35 .... 138 E4
Heathfield TN21 .... 82 A6
Seaford BN25 .... 181 B3
Meadowcroft CI RH19 .... 1 C2
Meadowlands Ave BN22 .. 173 D1
Meadows BN6 .... 97 F5
Meadows Rd BN22 .... 173 B2
Meadows The
Crowborough TN6 .... 25 E2
Hastings TN37 .... 136 C5
Hove BN3 .... 141 C3
Lewes BN7 .... 123 E3
Meadowside TN33 .... 88 E1
Meadowside Cotts TN5 .... 31 F1
Meadowview
Brighton BN2 .... 143 E1
Lower Street TN33 .... 133 B5
Meads Ave Bexhill TN39 ... 156 C4
Hove BN3 .... 141 C3
Meads Brow BN20 .... 188 D8
Meads CE Prim Sch BN20 188 D7
Meads CI BN3 .... 141 C3
Meads CI BN20 .... 184 E1
Meads Cty Prim Sch The
RH19 .... 10 E7
Meads Gate BN20 .... 188 E8
Meads Rd Bexhill TN39 .... 156 C4
Eastbourne BN20, BN21 .. 184 E1
Seaford BN25 .... 180 F3
Meads St BN20 .... 188 E8
Meads The Brighton BN1 .. 143 D5
East Grinstead RH19 ...... 10 E7
Meadway Cres BN1 .... 141 F2
Meadway Ct BN42, BN43 .. 161 D8
Meadway The
Brighton BN2 .... 164 F5
Shoreham-by-Sea BN43 ... 161 A6
Mealla CI BN7 .... 123 C3
Medina PI BN3 .... 163 B6
Medina Terr
Hastings TN38 .... 159 A6
Hove BN3 .... 163 B5
Medina Villas BN3 .... 163 B6
Medmerry Hill BN2 .... 143 E2
Medway
Crowborough TN6 .... 26 C1
Hailsham BN27 .... 129 A2
Medway Dr
East Grinstead RH19 ...... 10 D6
Forest Row RH18 .... 11 F2
Forest Row RH18 .... 12 A2
Medway La BN24, BN26 .... 174 A5
Medway Rd TN1 .... 8 B5
Meeching PI BN9 .... 179 C7
Meeching Rd BN9 .... 179 D7
Meeching Rise BN9 .... 179 C7
Meeching Valley
Cty Prim Sch BN9 .... 179 B7
Meeds Rd RH15 .... 73 A2
Meeting House La BN1 .... 189 A5
Megrims Hill TN18 .... 47 A6
Melbourne Rd BN22 .... 185 B4
Melbourne St BN2 .... 164 C8
Melfort Rd TN6 .... 25 D1
Melrose Ave BN41 .... 141 A1
Melrose CI Brighton BN1 .. 143 C2
Hailsham BN27 .... 152 A8
Melvill La BN20 .... 173 B1
Melville Rd BN3 .... 163 E7
Mendip Ave BN23 .... 174 D3
Mendip Gdns TN34 .... 137 B3
Mendip Wlk TN2 .... 8 D5
Menzies Rd TN37, TN38 ... 136 B2
Mercatoria TN38 .... 159 C6
Mercer St TN1 .... 8 B5
Mercers 7 A3
Mercia Ct TN40 .... 157 C5
Mercread Rd BN25 .... 180 F3
Meres La TN20 .... 58 D7
Merevale BN1 .... 143 B2
Merewood Ct BN21 .... 184 E4
Mereworth Rd TN4 .... 8 A6
Meridian Ctr BN10 .... 178 C8
Meridian Cty Prim Sch
BN10 .... 167 C1
Meridian Ind Est The
BN10 .... 178 C7
Meridian L Ctr BN10 ...... 178 C7
Meridian Rd BN7 .... 123 B2
Meridian Way
East Grinstead RH19 ...... 1 F3
Peacehaven BN10 .... 178 C7
Merivale TN34 .... 137 A6
Merlin CI BN3 .... 163 D8
Merlin Ct BN27 .... 152 E7
Merlin Way RH19 .... 2 A3
Merlyn [12] BN21 .... 185 A2
Mermaid Pas TN31 .... 93 B5
Mermaid St TN31 .... 93 B5
Merrimac Ho TN40 .... 157 E4

Merrimede CI TN38 .... 159 A7
Merriments La TN18, TN19 . 45 D5
Merrion CI TN4 .... 8 B7
Merston Way TN4 .... 8 B7
Merton CI BN22 .... 165 E6
Merton Ct TN40 .... 157 E4
Mervyn Ct TN31 .... 93 C5
Metcalfe Ave BN9 .... 179 B8
Metropole Ct
[19] Brighton BN1 .... 163 E5
[1] Eastbourne BN22 ...... 185 B3
Mewetts Ct BN20 .... 173 B3
Mews Ct RH19 .... 10 F6
Mews Rd TN38 .... 159 C6
Mews The Brighton BN1 ... 142 E2
East Hoathly BN8 .... 105 A5
Pembury TN2 .... 9 C6
[5] Royal Tunbridge Wells
TN1 .... 8 B3
Seaford BN25 .... 181 B4
Meyners Ct BN3 .... 141 C3
Michael Fields RH18 ...... 11 E2
Michael Tetley Hall
(Nursery Trng Coll, Dr
Barnardo's Home) TN2 ... 8 B3
Michel CI BN20 .... 183 C1
Michel Dene CI BN20 ...... 183 C1
Michel Dene Rd BN20 ...... 183 C1
Michel Gr BN21 .... 184 E4
Michelbourne CI RH15 .... 72 E1
Michele CI [1] TN38 ...... 136 B1
Michelham CI BN23 .... 174 A4
Michelham Priory BN27 ... 151 B7
Michelham Rd TN22 .... 55 E1
Michelson CI TN38 .... 135 F4
Micklefield Sch BN25 ..... 181 B3
Micklefield Wadhurst Sch
TN5 .... 29 C4
Mid Sussex Golf Club The
.... 99 A5
Middle Dr TN22 .... 55 A6
Middle Field TN2 .... 9 E8
Middle Furlong BN25 ...... 180 F3
Middle Rd
Bells Yew Green TN3 ...... 18 A5
Brighton BN1 .... 142 E1
Hastings TN35 .... 137 D4
Shoreham-by-Sea BN43 ... 161 B7
Middle Row [1] RH19 ...... 10 F8
Middle St Brighton BN1 ... 189 F5
Falmer BN1 .... 144 A4
[8] Hastings TN34 .... 159 F8
Portslade-by-Sea BN41 ... 162 B6
Middle Street Cty Prim Sch
BN1 .... 189 F5
Middle Way
Burgess Hill RH15 .... 73 B3
Lewes BN7 .... 123 A1
Middle Wlk TN2 .... 8 C8
Middleham CI BN8 .... 124 C4
Middlesex Ct [4] BN22 .... 185 B4
Middlesex Rd TN40 .... 157 D3
Middleton Ave BN3 .... 162 D6
Middleton Dr BN23 .... 185 E7
Middleton Rise BN1 .... 142 E5
Middleway BN27 .... 131 B5
Midfields CI RH15 .... 73 B3
Midfields Dr RH15 .... 73 B3
Midfields Wlk RH15 .... 73 B4
Midhurst Rd BN22 .... 173 F2
Midhurst Rise BN1 .... 143 B6
Midhurst Wlk BN3 .... 141 F3
Midway Rd BN2 .... 165 C8
Midway The TN4 .... 7 D2
Mighell St BN2 .... 189 B5
Milchester Ho BN20 .... 188 E8
Milcote Ave BN3 .... 162 F8
Mildenhall Dr TN37 .... 136 B3
Mildmay CI BN8 .... 124 D6
Mildmay Rd BN7 .... 123 A1
Mile End Cotts BN1 .... 142 E6
Mile Oak Cres BN42 ...... 140 F1
Mile Oak Cty Prim Sch
BN41 .... 140 F3
Mile Oak Gdns BN41 ...... 141 A1
Mile Oak Rd
Portslade-by-Sea
BN41, BN42 .... 140 F3
Southwick BN41, BN42 ... 140 F1
Milestones TN21 .... 82 B8
Milfoil Dr BN23 .... 174 B3
Military Rd TN30, TN31 ... 70 F3
Mill Brooks BN8 .... 100 D7
Mill CI
East Grinstead RH19 ...... 10 E7
Friston BN20 .... 183 A1
Hastings TN35 .... 137 E4
Portslade-by-Sea BN41 ... 141 C1
Ringmer BN8 .... 124 E5
South Chailey BN8 .... 100 D7
Tilsmore TN21 .... 81 F7

Mill CI
Wannock BN26 .... 172 F4
Westfield TN35 .... 114 E5
Mill Cnr TN31 .... 67 A3
Mill Cres TN39 .... 156 D5
Mill Ct RH19 .... 10 E7
Mill Cres TN6 .... 25 F3
Mill Dr Crowborough TN6 . 25 F3
Hove BN3 .... 142 A3
Seaford BN25 .... 181 A3
Mill Dro Seaford BN25 .... 180 A5
Uckfield TN22 .... 78 C6
Mill Gap Rd BN21 .... 184 F4
Mill Gdns
Heathfield TN21 .... 82 A5
Ringmer BN8 .... 124 D5
Mill Green Rd RH16 .... 50 E6
Mill Hill CI RH16 .... 50 E7
Mill La Barcombe BN8 ..... 101 D2
Clayton BN45, BN6 .... 119 E7
Crowborough TN6 .... 37 F8
Dormansland RH7 .... 1 F8
East Hoathly BN8 .... 105 A5
Flackley Ash TN31 .... 68 F3
Goddards' Green BN6 ..... 72 A3
Hastings TN35 .... 137 E5
Hellingly BN27 .... 129 A6
Hooe Common TN33 ...... 132 F2
Mark Cross TN6 .... 28 A3
Portslade-by-Sea BN41 ... 141 B1
Rodmell BN7 .... 167 D8
Uckfield TN22 .... 78 C6
Westfield TN35 .... 114 B3
Mill Mead BN8 .... 124 E5
Mill Path BN8 .... 124 E5
Mill Pk RH15 .... 73 C4
Mill Race BN6 .... 97 E8
Mill Rd Brighton BN1 ...... 142 C6
Burgess Hill RH15 .... 73 B3
Eastbourne BN21 .... 184 E5
Hailsham BN27 .... 152 D6
Lewes BN7 .... 123 E3
Ringmer BN8 .... 124 D5
Rye TN31 .... 93 C7
Southwick BN41 .... 162 B7
Tilsmore TN21 .... 81 F7
Winchelsea TN36 .... 117 E8
Mill Rd Ind Est BN41 ...... 162 B7
Mill Rise Brighton BN1 .... 142 C5
Heathfield TN21 .... 82 A8
Robertsbridge TN32 ...... 64 A3
Salehurst BN1 .... 144 C7
Mill Stream Meadow
RH16 .... 50 E6
Mill View BN8 .... 124 C4
Mill View Ct BN24 .... 174 D6
Mill View Rd TN39 .... 157 B7
Mill Way
East Grinstead RH19 ...... 10 E7
Wannock BN26 .... 172 E4
Mill Wood RH15 .... 73 B3
Milland CI TN40 .... 157 C6
Milland Rd BN27 .... 129 B1
Millbank RH15 .... 73 B4
Millberg Rd BN25 .... 181 C4
Millbrook Bsns Pk TN6 .... 38 D8
Millbrook CI TN21 .... 107 A7
Millbrook Gdns BN20 ...... 184 B6
Millbrook Ind Est TN6 .... 38 D8
Millbrook Rd TN6 .... 26 A3
Millcroft BN1 .... 142 C5
Millcroft Ave BN42 .... 140 E1
Millcroft Gdns BN42 ...... 140 E1
Millcross Rd BN41 .... 141 B1
Milldown Rd BN25 .... 180 F3
Miller's Hill TN35 .... 114 E6
Miller's Rd BN1 .... 142 E1
Millers Rise BN27 .... 152 A6
Millers Way RH15 .... 73 B4
Millfield TN33 .... 133 A6
Millfield CI Newick BN8 ... 76 C7
Seaford BN25 .... 181 B4
Millfield Cotts [8] BN2 ... 164 D4
Millfield Rise TN40 .... 157 C4
Millfields BN26 .... 173 A7
Millfields CI BN26 .... 173 A7
Millfields Rd BN41 .... 141 B1
Millington Ct TN22 .... 78 C6
Millrace The BN26 .... 172 F4
Millstream CI TN3 .... 5 D2
Millstream Gdns BN26 .... 172 F4
Millward Rd BN24 .... 175 C3
Millwood CI TN22 .... 55 D4
Millwood CI TN22 .... 55 D4
Millwood Rd TN39 .... 157 A8
Millyard Cres BN2 .... 165 D7
Milner Flats BN2 .... 189 B5
Milner Rd BN2 .... 143 D1
Milnthorpe Gdns BN20 .... 188 E8
Milnthorpe Rd
Eastbourne BN20 .... 188 D8
Hove BN3 .... 162 F8

Milton Cres
East Grinstead RH19 ...... 10 C8
Eastbourne BN21 .... 184 C4
Milton Ct [6] RH16 .... 50 D5
Milton Dr
Royal Tunbridge Wells
TN1, TN2 .... 8 D7
Southwick BN42 .... 161 F8
Milton Rd Brighton BN2 ... 189 B7
Eastbourne BN20, BN21 .. 184 C4
Haywards Heath RH16 .... 50 D6
Milton St BN24 .... 174 B7
Milward Cres TN34 .... 160 A4
Milward Ct [3] BN43 ...... 161 C8
Milward Rd TN34 .... 160 A5
Mimosa CI BN26 .... 173 A7
Mimosa Ct BN1 .... 143 B3
Mindleheim Ave RH19 .... 2 B2
Minnels The BN6 .... 98 A3
Minsted Sq TN39 .... 156 C2
Mint Ct BN26 .... 173 A7
Mint The TN31 .... 93 B5
Mistley CI TN40 .... 158 A6
Mitchelldean BN10 .... 167 C1
Mitre Ho [15] BN1 .... 163 E5
Mitten Rd TN40 .... 157 C4
Moat Croft CI BN21 .... 184 D4
Moat Croft Rd BN21 ...... 184 E4
Moat Farm TN2 .... 17 A7
Moat La Cowden TN8 ...... 4 E7
Waldron TN21, BN8 .... 80 D2
Westfield TN33 .... 114 B3
Moat Rd RH19 .... 1 E2
Mocatta Way RH15 .... 72 D5
Modena Rd BN3 .... 162 F7
Moira House Sch BN20 ... 188 D8
Molesey CI TN22 .... 78 C7
Molesworth St BN3 .... 162 F8
Molyneux Almshouses TN4 . 7 B4
Molyneux Ct TN4 .... 7 F4
Molyneux Park Rd TN4 .... 7 F4
Monarch Gdns
Eastbourne BN23 .... 174 F1
Seaford BN25 .... 181 A5
Monarch Ho BN2 .... 185 E5
Monastery Gdns TN6 ...... 39 B8
Monceux Rd
Eastbourne BN20, BN21 .. 184 C4
Herstmonceux BN27 ...... 130 E6
Monckton Way BN7 .... 145 E5
Monger's Mead BN8 .... 101 E4
Monk CI BN1 .... 143 E6
Monk's House BN7 .... 146 E1
Monks La [8] Lewes BN7 .. 146 C8
Newbury's TN5 .... 30 B8
Monks Way BN7 .... 123 C3
Monks Wlk TN36 .... 117 E7
Monk's Wlk TN36 .... 117 E7
Monmouth St [13] BN3 .... 163 B7
Monson Rd TN1 .... 8 B4
Monson Way [5] TN1 ...... 8 B4
Montacute Gdns TN2 ...... 7 F2
Montacute Rd
Lewes BN7 .... 146 A8
Royal Tunbridge Wells TN2 . 8 A1
Montacute Way TN22 ...... 78 D8
Montague CI BN43 .... 161 D7
Montague Ct
[6] Brighton BN2 .... 164 C4
[2] Shoreham-by-Sea
BN43 .... 161 D7
Montague PI BN2 .... 164 C4
Montague St Brighton BN2 . 164 C4
Montague St [4] BN2 ...... 164 C4
Montague Way BN24 ...... 174 F5
Montagu Way TN6 .... 26 A1
Montefiore Rd BN3 .... 163 E7
Monteith CI TN3 .... 7 A3
Monterey CI BN1 .... 142 E3
Monterey Gdns TN39 ...... 156 E3
Montfort CI BN43 .... 161 D8
Montfort Rd BN24 .... 174 F6
Montfort Rd BN24 .... 174 F6
Montgomery Rd
Hastings TN35 .... 137 D5
Royal Tunbridge Wells TN4 . 8 B7
Montgomery St BN3 .... 163 A7
Montpelier Cres BN1 ...... 163 E6
Montpelier Lodge [8] BN1 163 E6
Montpelier PI [7] BN1 .... 163 E6
Montpelier Rd BN1 .... 163 E5
Montpelier St BN1 .... 163 E6
Montpelier Terr [10] BN1 . 163 E6
Montpelier Villas BN1 ..... 163 E6
Montreal Rd BN2 .... 164 D4
Montserrat TN39 .... 157 A2
Monument View BN2 ...... 164 D6

Moon's La RH19, RH7, TN8 . 2 E8
Moons Hill TN33 .... 133 B6
Moor Hall Dr TN33 .... 132 F6
Moor Hill TN18 .... 45 F8
Moor La
Ashton Green BN8 .... 125 B3
Westfield TN35 .... 114 E3
Moor PI RH19 .... 1 D2
Moor Rd TN35 .... 114 E3
Moor The TN18 .... 45 F8
Moore Pk BN27 .... 152 D7
Moore's La TN31 .... 90 E8
Moorhurst Rd TN34 .... 135 F5
Moorings The
East Grinstead RH19 ...... 1 A3
Eastbourne BN20 .... 188 E8
Shoreham-by-Sea BN43 ... 161 C6
Morangie Rd BN1 .... 129 A2
Morcambe Rd BN1 .... 143 A6
Morestead BN10 .... 167 D1
Morgan CI TN39 .... 157 B8
Morgay Wood La TN35 .... 115 E2
Morlais PI TN36 .... 118 B6
Morlais Ridge TN36 .... 118 B6
Morland Dr TN3 .... 20 B5
Morlands CI TN33 .... 133 B5
Morley CI BN7 .... 146 B7
Morley St BN2 .... 189 B6
Morningside CI BN25 ...... 180 F4
Mornington Cres BN3 ...... 162 D7
Mornington Mansions
BN3 .... 162 D7
Morris Rd BN7 .... 123 E1
Mortain Pk BN27 .... 152 D7
Mortimer Rd BN24 .... 174 F6
Mortimer Gdns BN26 ...... 172 F4
Mortimer Rd
Eastbourne BN22 .... 185 A6
Hove BN3 .... 163 A8
Morton Rd RH19 .... 10 E7
Moscow Rd TN35 .... 137 C3
Motcombe CI TN40 .... 157 D3
Motcombe Cty Inf Sch
BN21 .... 184 C5
Motcombe La BN21 .... 184 D4
Motcombe Rd BN21 .... 184 D4
Motte Field TN7 .... 13 E4
Mottins Hill TN6 .... 38 D8
Moulsecoomb Cty Inf Sch
BN2 .... 143 E3
Moulsecoomb Cty Jun Sch
BN2 .... 143 E3
Moulsecoomb Sta BN2 .... 143 D2
Moulsecoomb Way BN2 ... 143 F4
Mount Caburn Cres BN10 167 C2
Mount CI BN9 .... 179 F8
Mount Dr BN2 .... 177 D6
Mount Edgcumbe Rd TN4 . 8 A3
Mount Ephraim TN1, TN4 . 8 A4
Mount Ephraim Ct TN4 .... 7 F4
Mount Ephraim Rd TN1 ... 8 A4
Mount Harry Rd BN7 ...... 123 A2
Mount Idol View TN39 ..... 157 A8
Mount Joy TN33 .... 112 D5
Mount PI [9] BN7 .... 123 C1
Mount Pleasant
Blackboys TN22 .... 80 A6
Brighton BN2 .... 189 B5
Crowborough TN6 .... 38 B7
[6] Hastings TN38 .... 159 C6
Hook Green TN3 .... 19 E6
Mount Pleasant BN8 ...... 101 E6
Sparrow's Green TN5 ..... 29 E5
The Moor TN18 .... 45 F8
Uckfield TN22 .... 78 C6
Mount Pleasant Ave [2]
.... 8 B3
Mount Pleasant Cres [2]
TN34 .... 136 F1
Mount Pleasant Ct TN34 . 160 A6
Mount Pleasant Hospl
TN35 .... 137 C3
Mount Pleasant Rd
Hastings TN34 .... 160 A6
Royal Tunbridge Wells
TN1, TN2 .... 8 A3
Mount Rd
Eastbourne BN20 .... 188 F8
Hastings TN35 .... 160 C6
Newhaven BN9 .... 179 F8
Mount Sion TN1 .... 8 B3
Mount St Battle TN33 ..... 112 D5
Lewes BN7 .... 146 C8
Mount The
Hailsham BN27 .... 152 C6
Hastings TN38 .... 159 B7
Uckfield TN22 .... 78 C8

Mount View Terr BN27 .... 152 C6
Mount Zion Pl BN1 .... 189 F6
Mountain Ash Cl BN27 .... 152 A8
Mountbatten Cl TN35 .... 137 D5
Mountbatten Ct BN3 .... 162 E8
Mountbatten Dr BN23 .... 185 F7
Mountfield Ct **4** TN1 .... 8 B3
Mountfield Gdns TN2 .... 8 B3
Mountfield La TN32 .... 86 C8
Mountfield Rd
  Eastbourne BN22 .... 173 F1
  Lewes BN7 .... 146 D8
  Royal Tunbridge Wells TN2 .. 8 B3
Mountfield Villas TN2 .... 87 C5
Mountfield & Whatlington
  CE Prim Sch TN32 .... 87 D7
Mountfields BN1 .... 143 C2
Mountney Bridge Bsns Pk
  BN24 .... 174 F4
Mountney Dr BN24 .... 175 F7
Mountney Rd BN21 .... 184 C4
Mountread TN20 .... 58 B7
Mowden Sch BN1 .... 142 D1
Moy Ave BN22 .... 185 B5
Moyne Cl BN3 .... 141 E1
Muirfield Ct **10** RH16 .... 50 E4
Muirfield Rise TN38 .... 158 F8
Mulberry Cl Bexhill TN39 .. 156 C4
  Brighton BN1 .... 142 F3
  Eastbourne BN22, BN26 ... 173 E3
  Shoreham-by-Sea BN43 .. 140 D1
Mulberry Ct BN26 .... 173 A6
Mulberry La BN6 .... 98 D3
Mulberry Way TN21 .... 82 B5
Mulberry Wlk TN37 .... 136 D5
Munns Dr RH15 .... 73 B4
Munster Cotts BN8 .... 101 E4
Munster Gn BN8 .... 101 E4
Murray Ave BN9 .... 179 C7
Museum of Rural Life
  TN32 .... 64 B4
Museum of Shops BN21 ... 185 A2
Musgrave Ave RH19 .... 10 E8
Mushroom Field BN7 .... 145 E5
Muster Ct RH16 .... 50 D4
Muster Gn N RH16 .... 50 D4
Muster Gn S RH16 .... 50 D4
Mutton Hall Hill TN21 .... 82 B8
Mutton Hall La TN21 .... 82 B8
Mutton Hill RH7 .... 2 B7
Myrtle Rd
  Crowborough TN6 .... 25 F1
  Eastbourne BN20 .... 185 D6

Namrik Mews BN3 .... 163 A6
Nan Kemp's Grave BN7 .... 145 E6
Nan Tucks La TN22 .... 56 C2
Nanson Rd BN1 .... 143 D6
Naomi Cl BN20 .... 184 E1
Napier Ho **3** BN2 .... 164 C7
Napier Rd Hastings TN38 .. 135 E4
  Royal Tunbridge Wells TN2 .. 8 B3
Nash La RH17 .... 52 B4
Natal Rd BN2 .... 143 D1
Neale Cl RH19 .... 1 A3
Neath Rd TN29 .... 96 A2
Neaves La BN8 .... 125 A5
Neill's Cl BN9 .... 179 C7
Neills Rd TN4 .... 19 D2
Nellington Ct TN4 .... 7 C4
Nellington Rd TN3, TN4 .... 7 B4
Nelson Dr BN23 .... 185 E6
Nelson Ho TN9 .... 156 E4
Nelson Pl **10** BN2 .... 189 B6
Nelson Rd Hastings TN34 .. 160 A5
  Royal Tunbridge Wells TN2 .. 8 B3
Nelson Row BN2 .... 189 B5
Nesbitt Rd BN2 .... 143 D1
Nestor Ct BN1 .... 142 E1
Nether La TN22 .... 35 C3
Netherfield Ave BN23 .... 174 F2
Netherfield CE Prim Sch
  TN33 .... 86 C2
Netherfield Gn BN2 .... 165 FB
Netherfield Hill TN33 .... 112 B7
Netherfield Hill Cotts
  TN33 .... 112 B7
Netherfield Rd TN33 .... 111 F8
Netherfield Way TN33 .... 86 D2
Netherwood Cl TN34 .... 136 F5
Nettleton Ct TN1 .... 143 B1
Nevill Ave
  Eastbourne BN22 .... 173 E1
  Hove BN3 .... 141 F1
Nevill Cl
  Crowborough Warren TN6 .. 37 C8
  Hove BN3 .... 142 A2
Nevill Cotts BN6 .... 98 D2

Nevill Cres BN7 .... 123 A1
Nevill Ct
  Crowborough Warren TN6 .. 37 C8
  Hove BN3 .... 142 A1
Nevill Gate TN2 .... 8 B1
Nevill Gdns BN3 .... 142 A2
Nevill Gn TN22 .... 55 D1
Nevill Golf Course
  TN2, TN3 .... 17 D7
Nevill Lodge TN2 .... 8 C4
Nevill Pk TN4 .... 7 E3
Nevill Pl BN3 .... 142 A2
Nevill Rd
  Crowborough TN6 .... 25 F3
  Hove BN3 .... 142 A2
  Lewes BN7 .... 123 A2
  Rottingdean BN2 .... 165 F1
  Uckfield TN22 .... 55 D1
Nevill Ridge TN4 .... 7 D7
Nevill St TN1, TN2 .... 8 A2
Nevill Terr TN2 .... 7 F2
Nevill Way BN3 .... 142 A2
Neville Rd
   3 Eastbourne BN22 .... 185 B4
  Peacehaven BN10 .... 178 D6
New Barn Cl
  Hailsham BN27 .... 152 C6
  Portslade-by-Sea BN41 ... 141 B2
  Shoreham-by-Sea BN43 .. 140 B1
New Barn La TN22 .... 78 C5
New Barn Rd
  Rottingdean BN2 .... 165 F3
  Shoreham-by-Sea BN43 .. 140 B1
New Church Rd
  BN3, BN41 .... 162 E7
New College Cl BN23 .... 174 C4
New Cotts
  Crowborough TN6 .... 38 C8
  Five Ashes TN20 .... 58 B6
  Scaynes Hill RH17 .... 51 F1
New Cut Mountfield TN32 .. 87 C5
  Westfield TN35 .... 114 E4
New Dorset St BN1 .... 189 F6
New England Ho BN1 .... 189 A7
New England La
  Rye TN31 .... 93 C8
  Sedlescombe TN33 .... 113 F6
New England Rd
  Brighton BN1 .... 189 F7
  Haywards Heath RH16 ...... 50 F4
  Royal Tunbridge Wells TN2 .. 8 B3
New England Rise BN41 .. 141 A4
New England St BN1 .... 189 A7
New Farthingdale RH7 .... 2 B7
New Forest Lodge TN6 .... 37 C8
New Life Sch RH19 .... 1 D2
New Lydd Rd TN31 .... 94 E2
New Moorsite TN35 .... 114 F3
New Park Ave TN40 .... 157 C4
New Pl Eastbourne BN21 .. 184 D3
  Uckfield TN22 .... 78 C5
New Pond Hill TN21 .... 81 D6
New Rd Brighton BN1 ...... 189 A5
  Crowborough TN6 .... 25 F3
  Eastbourne BN22 .... 185 B4
  Fairlight TN35 .... 138 D4
  Hailsham BN27 .... 129 C4
  Hastings TN35 .... 160 D6
  Keymer BN6 .... 98 B2
  Lewes BN7 .... 123 C1
  Mill Corner TN31 .... 67 B3
  Polegate BN26 .... 173 B6
  Ringmer BN8 .... 124 D3
  Rotherfield TN6 .... 39 C8
  Rye TN31 .... 93 D6
  Saint's Hill TN11 .... 6 A8
  South Heighton BN9 .... 168 D1
  Uckfield TN22 .... 78 D3
New Steine BN2 .... 189 B4
New Steine Mews BN2 ..... 189 B5
New Sussex Hospl BN3 .... 163 E6
New Upperton Rd **6**
  BN21 .... 184 E4
New Way La BN6 .... 97 B2
New Winchelsea Rd
  TN36 .... 93 B3
Newark Pl BN2 .... 189 B6
Newbury Cotts TN5 .... 30 B8
Newbury La TN5 .... 30 C8
Newcomen Rd TN4 .... 8 A5
Newells Cl BN2 .... 144 E1
Newfield La BN9 .... 179 C7
Newfield Rd BN9 .... 179 C7
Newgate Rd TN37 .... 136 C1
Newhaven Harbour Sta
  BN9 .... 179 D6
Newhaven Local &
  Maritime Mus BN9 .... 168 D1
Newhaven Marine Sta
  BN9 .... 179 E6
Newhaven Rd BN25 .... 180 B5

Newhaven Sq BN9 .... 179 D7
Newhaven St BN2 .... 189 B6
Newhaven Town Sta
  BN9 .... 179 D8
Newhaven Wlk TN38 .... 136 A3
Newick CE Prim Sch BN8 .. 76 C6
Newick Cl BN25 .... 181 C2
Newick Dr BN8 .... 76 C7
Newick House Sch RH15 ... 73 C1
Newick La TN20, TN21 .... 59 C5
Newick Rd Brighton BN1 .. 143 E4
  Eastbourne BN20, BN21 .. 184 C6
Newington Ct TN5 .... 31 E1
Newlands TN3 .... 7 A3
Newlands Ave TN39 .... 157 B5
Newlands Cl
  Hastings TN34 .... 136 E5
  Keymer BN6 .... 98 B3
Newlands Cres RH19 .... 1 D2
Newlands Manor Sch
  (Senior) BN25 .... 181 A4
Newlands Park Way BN8 ... 76 C7
Newlands Pl RH18 .... 11 F3
Newlands Rd
  Rottingdean BN2 .... 177 A5
  Royal Tunbridge Wells TN4 .. 8 B7
Newlands Rise TN4 .... 8 A6
Newlands Sch BN25 .... 181 B4
Newlands Way TN4 .... 8 B7
Newmans Way TN35 .... 137 D4
Newmarket Rd BN2 .... 164 C8
Newmarket Terr **8** BN2 .. 164 C8
Newnham Rd TN1, TN2 .... 82 A6
Newnham Way TN21 .... 82 A7
Newport Rd RH15 .... 72 F3
Newport St BN2 .... 189 B7
Newstead **5** BN1 .... 189 F7
Newtimber Dr BN41 .... 141 A1
Newton Ave RH10 .... 10 F6
Newton Cl RH16 .... 51 B7
Newton Ct **3** RH16 .... 50 E5
Newton Pk BN27 .... 152 D7
Newton Rd
  Haywards Heath RH16 ...... 51 C7
  Lewes BN7 .... 123 B2
  Peacehaven BN10 .... 178 C7
  Royal Tunbridge Wells TN1 .. 8 B4
Newton Willows TN3 .... 15 C7
Newton's Hill TN7 .... 13 D3
Newtown Rd BN3 .... 163 BB
Nicholson Ct BN23 .... 174 E1
Nicolson Dr BN43 .... 161 A7
Nightingale Cl
  East Grinstead RH19 .... 10 D7
  Eastbourne BN23 .... 174 C2
Nightingale Cotts TN35 ... 114 D4
Nightingale La RH15 .... 97 F8
Nightingale Rise TN22 ..... 78 D4
Nightingales The
  Royal Tunbridge Wells TN4 .. 8 A5
  Uckfield TN22 .... 78 E5
Nile St BN1 .... 189 A5
Ninfield CE Prim Sch
  TN33 .... 133 B5
Ninfield Pl BN2 .... 164 E7
Ninfield Rd TN39, TN40 .... 157 B7
Nizells Ave BN3 .... 163 E7
Noahs Ark La RH16 .... 51 C7
Nodes La BN27 .... 129 F4
Noel Gn RH15 .... 73 B4
Noel Rise RH15 .... 73 B4
Nolan Rd BN2 .... 165 E7
Nook Cl TN35 .... 137 D3
Norbury Cl TN6 .... 25 E4
Nore Rd BN9 .... 179 B6
Norfolk Bldgs **2** BN1 ..... 163 E5
Norfolk Cl TN39 .... 157 B7
Norfolk Ct **4** BN2 .... 185 C4
Norfolk Dr TN38 .... 135 F5
Norfolk Ho **2** TN37 .... 159 C7
Norfolk Mews **3** BN1 ..... 163 E5
Norfolk Rd Hastings TN34 .. 160 C4
  Royal Tunbridge Wells TN1 .. 8 B2
Norfolk Sq BN1 .... 163 E5
Norfolk St **4** BN1 .... 163 E5
Norfolk Terr BN1 .... 163 E6
Norfolk Way TN22 .... 78 C8
Norlington Cl BN8 .... 124 D6
Norlington Fields BN8 .... 124 D6
Norlington La BN8 .... 124 D7
Norman Cl Battle TN33 ... 112 F4
  Seaford BN25 .... 180 B6
Norman Ct **6** TN34 .... 159 E7
Norman Rd
  Burgess Hill RH15 .... 73 A3
  Hastings TN37, TN38 .... 159 C6
  Hove BN3 .... 162 E6
  Newhaven BN9 .... 179 C7
  Pevensey Bay BN24 .... 175 D4
  Royal Tunbridge Wells TN1 .. 8 B5

Normandale TN39 .... 156 F3
Normandale Ho TN39 ...... 156 F3
Normandy Cl **7** RH19 ..... 10 F8
Normandy Dr TN39 .... 157 B3
Normandy Ho **3** BN2 ..... 163 C6
Normandy Rd TN2 .... 136 C3
Normanhurst **9** BN2 ...... 189 B6
Normans TN39 .... 156 F3
Normans' Bay Sta BN24 .. 176 C8
Normansal Cl BN25 .... 181 A6
Normansal Park Ave
  BN25 .... 181 A6
Normanton La BN27 .... 36 B2
Normanton St **8** BN2 .... 164 C7
Norstead Gdns TN4 .... 8 B7
North Ave BN20 .... 184 B5
North Bank BN6 .... 97 E4
North Barnes La BN7 .... 100 A5
North Beeches Rd TN6 ..... 26 A2
North Camp La BN25 ...... 180 F5
North Cl Polegate BN26 .. 173 B7
  Portslade-by-Sea BN41 ... 141 A2
North Cnr TN21 .... 107 C4
North Common Rd
  BN8, RH17 .... 74 E5
North Crescent Ind Est
  BN27 .... 152 A7
North Ct Hassocks BN6 .... 97 E4
  Lewes BN7 .... 123 E1
North Dr BN2 .... 164 C6
North End BN6 .... 98 D4
North Farm La TN1, TN2 .... 8 D8
North Farm Rd TN1, TN4 .... 8 D8
North Gdns BN1 .... 189 F6
North Heath Cl BN27 .... 129 C2
North La
  Lidham Hill TN35 .... 115 E5
  Portslade-by-Sea BN41 ... 141 A3
North Pl BN1 .... 189 A5
North Point **1** BN43 ...... 161 A6
North Quay Rd BN9 .... 179 D8
North Rd Alfriston BN26 .. 170 F3
  Bexhill TN39 .... 157 C7
  Bodle Street Green BN27 .. 109 C2
  Brighton BN1 .... 189 A6
  Brighton, Preston BN1 .... 142 E1
  Hastings TN37, TN38 .... 136 C1
  Haywards Heath RH16 ...... 51 A7
  Pevensey Bay BN24 .... 175 D5
  Portslade-by-Sea BN41 ... 141 A2
  Ringmer BN8 .... 124 D6
North Road Cotts BN8 .... 124 D6
North Row TN22 .... 78 C8
North Salts TN31 .... 93 C6
North St Alfriston BN26 ... 171 A3
  Brighton BN1 .... 189 A5
  Cowden TN8 .... 4 A6
  Eastbourne BN21 .... 185 B3
  Hailsham BN27 .... 152 BB
  Hastings TN37, TN38 .... 159 C7
  Hellingly BN27 .... 129 A7
  Lewes BN7 .... 123 D2
  Lower Horsebridge
    BN27, TN21 .... 107 A2
  Lower Horsebridge BN27 .. 128 F4
  Mayfield TN20 .... 40 B3
  Portslade-by-Sea BN41 ... 162 C7
  Punnett's Town TN21 .... 83 D6
  Roser's Cross TN21 .... 80 F5
  Rotherfield TN6 .... 39 BB
  Royal Tunbridge Wells TN2 .. 8 B3
  Winchelsea TN36 .... 117 E8
North Terr TN34, TN35 ..... 160 C6
North Trade Rd TN33 .... 112 B4
North Way Lewes BN7 ..... 123 A2
  Newhaven BN9 .... 179 C8
  Seaford BN25 .... 180 F5
North-South Rd BN1 .... 144 B7
Northampton Way **1**
  TN38 .... 136 A4
Northbourne Rd BN22 .... 185 C6
Northbridge St TN32 .... 64 B5
Northcliffe Cl BN25 .... 180 F4
Northcote La BN10 .... 167 A1
Northdown Cl BN9 .... 179 C6
Northdown Rd BN9 .... 179 B6
Northdown Terr RH19 .... 1 D3
Northease Cl BN3 .... 141 D2
Northease Dr BN3 .... 141 D2
Northease Gdns BN3 .... 141 E3
Northerlea BN41 .... 141 A1
Northern Ave TN36 .... 173 B7
Northfield Cl BN25 .... 180 F5
Northfield Ct TN22 .... 102 DB
Northfield Rise
  Hove BN3 .... 141 D4
  Rottingdean BN2 .... 177 A6
Northfield Way TN3 .... 143 A4
Northfields TN3 .... 7 A8
Northfields Bsns Pk BN27 .. 128 A4

Northgate Cl BN2 .... 165 F2
Northiam CE Prim Sch
  TN31 .... 67 B5
Northiam Rd
  Broad Oak TN31 .... 90 A6
  Eastbourne BN20, BN21 .. 184 C4
  Northiam Rise TN38 .... 135 D2
Northiam Sta TN31 .... 48 C2
Northlands Ave RH16 .... 51 B4
Northlands Cotts TN32 ..... 46 C1
Northlands Wood
  Cty Prim Sch RH16 .... 51 B4
Northridge TN31 .... 67 A7
Northumberland Rd TN4 .. 82 A2
Northway RH15 .... 73 C4
Northwood Ave BN2 .... 177 E5
Norton Cl BN3 .... 163 B6
Norton Dr BN2 .... 144 E1
Norton Rd Hove BN3 .... 163 B6
  Newhaven BN9 .... 179 E7
Norton Terr BN9 .... 179 E7
Norway Rd BN22 .... 185 D6
Norway St BN41 .... 162 C7
Norwich Cl BN2 .... 144 A2
Norwich Cres BN2 .... 143 F2
Norwich Dr BN2 .... 144 A2
Norwich House Rd BN1 ... 142 A7
Norwood BN1 .... 143 A4
Nottidge Rd TN4 .... 7 D1
Novington La BN7 .... 100 A2
Nuffield Hospl TN2 .... 8 C3
Nunnery La TN11 .... 5 FB
Nunnery Stables TN2 .... 123 B1
Nursery Cl Hailsham BN27 .. 152 C8
  Haywards Heath RH16 ...... 50 D5
  Polegate BN26 .... 173 B6
  Portslade-by-Sea BN41 ... 140 E4
  Shoreham-by-Sea BN43 .. 161 B8
  Union Street TN5 .... 32 B3
Nursery Field TN22 .... 56 C4
Nursery La
  Maresfield Park TN22 .... 55 B7
  Nutley TN22 .... 35 C4
  Uckfield TN22 .... 78 D4
  Waldron Down TN21, TN22 .. 80 E8
  Windmill Hill BN27 .... 131 B5
Nursery Path BN27 .... 152 B6
Nursery Rd TN4 .... 8 BB
Nursery The RH15 .... 73 C4
Nursery Way TN21 .... 81 E7
Nutbourne Cl BN23 .... 174 E2
Nuthatch Rd BN23 .... 174 C2
Nuthurst Cl BN2 .... 164 F6
Nuthurst Pl BN2 .... 164 F5
Nutley Ave BN2 .... 177 D4
Nutley CE Prim Sch TN22 .. 35 C5
Nutley Cl Hove BN3 .... 141 F3
  Rye TN31 .... 93 A6
Nutley Mill Rd BN24 .... 174 B5
Nye Cl TN6 .... 25 F1
Nye La Ditchling BN6 .... 98 D1
  Westmeston BN6 .... 120 DB
Nye Rd RH15 .... 73 C3
Nyetimber Hill BN2 .... 143 E2
Nym Cl BN8 .... 100 E7

Oak Bank RH16 .... 50 F7
Oak Cl BN1 .... 142 E3
Oak Croft RH19 .... 11 A8
Oak Field The TN35 .... 116 F1
Oak Hall Pk RH15 .... 73 B1
Oak Hall Sch TN21 .... 60 B1
Oak Pas **8** TN34 .... 160 A4
Oak Rd TN1 .... 8 D7
Oak Terr TN31 .... 67 B6
Oak Tree Cl
  Eastbourne BN24 .... 174 C4
  Royal Tunbridge Wells TN1 .. 8 A1
Oak Tree Cotts
  Burgess Hill RH15 .... 73 B3
  Danehill RH17 .... 34 A4
Oak Tree Ct TN22 .... 78 DB
Oak Tree La BN23, BN24 .. 174 C4
Oak Tree Way BN27 .... 129 C2
Oakapple Rd BN42 .... 140 E1
Oakdale Rd
   6 Haywards Heath RH16 .. 50 F3
  Royal Tunbridge Wells TN4 .. 7 F4
Oakdene
  Brighton BN2 .... 143 F4
   7 Haywards Heath RH16 .. 50 D5
Oakdene Ave BN41 .... 140 E3
Oakdene Cl BN41 .... 140 E4
Oakdene Cres BN41 .... 140 E3
Oakdene Gdns BN41 .... 140 E3
Oakdene Rise BN41 .... 140 E4
Oakdene Way BN41 .... 140 E3
Oakdown Ct TN19 .... 61 A4
Oakenfield RH15 .... 73 A5
Oakfield Cl RH15 .... 51 A7
Oakfield Court Rd TN2 ...... 8 C3

Oakfield Rd TN35 .... 137 C3
Oakfield The TN31 .... 93 B8
Oakfield Way
 Bexhill TN39 .... 156 C6
 East Grinstead RH19 .... 1 F3
Oakhill Cotts TN31 .... 68 C4
Oakhill Dr TN31 .... 90 B5
Oakhurst RH16 .... 50 D8
Oakhurst Dr TN34 .... 136 E5
Oakhurst Dr TN6 .... 26 A3
Oakhurst Gdns RH19 .... 1 C2
Oakhurst La RH16 .... 50 D8
Oakhurst Rd TN33 .... 112 D7
Oakland Dr TN32 .... 63 D4
Oakland Villas TN3 .... 15 B7
Oaklands
 Crowborough TN6 .... 26 C1
 South Chailey BN8 .... 100 C7
 Westham BN24 .... 174 D6
Oaklands Ave BN2 .... 177 D5
Oaklands Cl BN26 .... 173 B6
Oaklands Rd
 Groombridge TN3 .... 15 B6
 Haywards Heath RH16 ...... 50 D5
Oaklands Way BN27 .... 152 A6
Oaklea Cl TN37 .... 136 C4
Oaklea Ct TN7 .... 13 D4
Oakley Way TN22 .... 78 C7
Oakleaf Ct BN26 .... 173 A7
Oakleaf Dr BN26 .... 173 A7
Oakleigh Annexe (Queen
 Victoria Hospl) RH19 .... 11 C7
Oakleigh Dr TN21 .... 82 B6
Oakleigh Rd TN39 .... 156 C4
Oakley Cl RH19 .... 11 B7
Oakley Cotts RH19 .... 11 C7
Oakmead Rd RH15 .... 72 F1
Oakmede Way BN8 .... 124 D5
Oakmeeds Com Sch RH15 .. 73 A2
Oakroyd Cl RH15 .... 73 D5
Oaks Cl TN19 .... 63 B8
Oaks Forstal TN18 .... 47 C5
Oaks The
 Burgess Hill BN6 .... 72 C4
 East Grinstead RH19 .... 11 B8
 Hastings TN37 .... 136 D5
 Haywards Heath RH16 ...... 51 A4
 Haywards Heath RH16 ...... 51 A4
 Heathfield TN21 .... 82 B6
Oaktree BN8 .... 101 E4
Oakwood RH16 .... 50 D4
Oakwood Ave TN39 .... 157 B7
Oakwood Cl
 Burgess Hill RH15 .... 73 B2
 Hastings TN34 .... 136 F3
Oakwood Dr TN22 .... 78 E8
Oakwood Pk
 Forest Row RH18 .... 11 F2
 Nutley TN22 .... 35 C4
Oakwood Rd
 Burgess Hill RH15 .... 73 B2
 Haywards Heath RH16 ...... 50 D4
Oakwood Rise TN2 .... 8 E7
Oast Cl TN1 .... 8 D7
Oast House Dr TN31 .... 92 F4
Oast House Field TN36 ...... 116 F6
Oast House Rd TN36 .... 116 F5
Oasthouse Cl TN37 .... 136 D5
Oathall Ave RH16 .... 50 F6
Oathall Com Coll RH16 ...... 50 F6
Oathall Rd RH16 .... 50 E5
Oban Rd TN37 .... 136 B3
Observatory View BN27 ..... 152 D7
Ochiltree Cl TN34 .... 137 A4
Ochiltree Rd TN34 .... 137 A4
Ockenden Way BN6 .... 97 E3
Ockley Hill BN6, RH15 .... 98 B6
Ockley La
 Burgess Hill RH15 .... 98 B7
 Keymer BN6 .... 98 B4
Ockley Way BN6 .... 98 A5
Ocklynge Ave ■ BN21 ...... 184 D4
Ocklynge Cl TN39 .... 156 C5
Ocklynge Cty Jun Sch
 BN21 .... 184 C6
Ocklynge Rd BN21 .... 184 D4
Ockman La TN31 .... 93 C5
Octagon The BN2 .... 164 F3
Offa Ct TN40 .... 157 C4
Offa Rd TN35 .... 137 D3
Offham Cl BN25 .... 180 F5
Offham Ct ■ BN25 .... 180 C4
Offham Rd BN7 .... 123 B2
Okehurst Rd BN20, BN21 .. 184 C3
Old Barn Cl BN20 .... 173 B1
Old Barn Ct RH16 .... 50 D2
Old Barn Way BN42 .... 162 A7
Old Ben Homes BN25 .... 180 F4
Old Boat Cnr BN1 .... 143 C7
Old Boat Wlk BN1 .... 143 B7
Old Brickyard TN31 .... 93 A5

Old Camp Rd BN20 .... 184 C2
Old Church Rd
 Hastings TN37, TN38 ..... 136 A4
 Pembury TN2 .... 9 D8
Old Clergy Ho (NT) BN26 . 171 A2
Old Coastguard Cotts
 BN9 .... 179 D6
Old Coastguards TN35 ...... 139 C7
Old Convent The RH19 ...... 1 E2
Old Court Cl BN1 .... 142 F4
Old Dr BN26 .... 172 F6
Old Dro BN23 .... 174 C3
Old Farm Rd Bexhill TN39 . 157 B6
 Brighton BN1 .... 142 F5
Old Fire Station The ■
 BN22 .... 185 A3
Old Foord Cl BN8 .... 100 D7
Old Forest La TN6 .... 38 E8
Old Forewood La TN33 ..... 134 F7
Old Forge La TN22 .... 36 A1
Old Fort Rd BN43 .... 161 B6
Old Gardens Cl TN2 .... 17 B8
Old Ghyll Rd TN21 .... 82 A5
Old Harrow Rd TN37 .... 136 B4
Old Heath Cl BN8 .... 101 C6
Old Hop Garden The TN31 . 69 C2
Old House Gdns TN34 ...... 136 F4
Old House La TN3 .... 15 F2
Old Humphrey Ave ■
 .... 160 B4
Old La Crowborough,
 Crowborough Warren TN6 25 D3
 Crowborough, Poundfield
 TN6 .... 26 B1
 Mayfield TN20 .... 40 A2
Old London Rd
 Brighton BN1 .... 142 E6
 Hastings TN34, TN35 ..... 160 C6
Old Lydd Rd TN31 .... 94 E2
Old Malling Way BN7 .... 123 C3
Old Manor Cl TN40 .... 157 D4
Old Mansion Cl BN20 ...... 184 A8
Old Mill Cl Brighton BN1 .. 142 E5
 Hailsham BN27 .... 152 A6
 Southwick BN41 .... 162 A7
Old Mill Ct TN6 .... 25 E2
Old Mill La BN26 .... 172 E3
Old Mill Pk TN39 .... 157 A6
Old Mint House BN24 ...... 175 B6
Old Motcombe Mews ■
 BN21 .... 184 D4
Old Orchard Pl BN27 .... 152 B7
Old Orchard Rd BN21 ...... 184 F2
Old Parish La BN2 .... 165 C8
Old Park Cl RH17 .... 50 A6
Old Patcham Mews BN1 ... 142 E6
Old Place Ct BN2 .... 165 F1
Old Rd
 East Grinstead RH19 ...... 1 F1
 Magham Down BN27 ..... 130 A4
Old Rectory Gdns BN43 ... 161 D8
Old Riding School The
 TN3 .... 15 B2
Old River Way TN36 .... 118 B7
Old Roar Rd TN37 .... 136 C5
Old School Cl BN8 .... 124 E6
Old School Cotts BN7 ..... 99 E5
Old School Ho BN27 .... 131 B5
Old School La BN26 .... 173 A7
Old School Pl RH15 .... 72 F2
Old Shoreham Rd
 Portslade-by-Sea
 BN3, BN41 .... 162 C8
 Southwick BN42 .... 140 E1
Old Station Rd TN5 .... 29 E6
Old Steine BN1, BN2 ...... 189 A5
Old Swan La BN27 .... 152 D6
Old Timbers La TN22 ..... 78 C6
Old Top Rd TN35 .... 137 D4
Old Viaduct Ct ■ BN2 ... 164 C8
Old Wardsdown TN5 ...... 32 B3
Old Wickham La RH16 .... 50 E7
Old Willingdon Rd BN20 . 183 B2
Old Wish Rd BN21 .... 184 F1
Old World Cotts TN31 .... 94 F2
Oldaker Rd BN6 .... 76 D7
Olde Place Mews BN1 .... 165 F1
Oldfield Ave BN20 .... 173 A4
Oldfield Cres
 Hailsham BN27 .... 129 B1
 Southwick BN42 .... 161 E8
Oldfield Rd BN20 .... 173 A4
Oldlands Ave BN6 .... 98 A4
Oldlands Hall TN22 ...... 36 D4
Oldlands Hill TN22 .... 36 C2
Olive Rd BN3 .... 162 D8
Oliver Cl Brighton BN2 .. 164 C5
 Crowborough TN6 .... 26 A1
Olives Mdn BN3 .... 163 B5
Olives Meadow TN22 .... 78 D7
Onslow Rd BN3 .... 142 C2

Open Mkt The BN1 .... 189 A7
Orange Row BN1 .... 189 A5
Orchard Ave BN3 .... 142 A1
Orchard Bsns Ctr TN4 .... 8 D8
Orchard Cl Fairwarp TN22 . 36 B2
 Hastings TN34 .... 136 F2
 Haywards Heath RH16 .. 50 D8
 Royal Tunbridge Wells TN1 . 8 D6
 Scaynes Hill RH17 .... 51 F3
 Southwick BN42 .... 161 F8
Orchard Cnr RH16 .... 51 B5
Orchard Cotts TN6 ...... 39 B8
Orchard Gdns BN3 ...... 142 B1
Orchard Gr TN1 .... 8 B5
Orchard La Ditchling BN6 . 98 D4
 Hove BN3 .... 142 C1
Orchard Mews ■ BN9 ... 168 E2
Orchard Rd Brighton BN20 . 173 A3
Orchard Rd Bexhill TN40 . 157 C6
 Hove BN3 .... 142 C1
 Lewes BN7 .... 123 E2
Orchard Rise TN3 .... 15 B8
Orchard The
 Broad Oak TN31 .... 90 B4
 Hassocks BN6 .... 97 F3
 Nutley TN22 .... 35 C4
Orchard Way
 Burgess Hill RH15 ...... 72 F3
 East Grinstead RH19 ... 1 E1
 Haywards Heath RH16 . 50 D8
 Peasmarsh TN31 .... 69 C1
Orchards The
 Brighton BN2 .... 143 E3
 ■ Haywards Heath RH16 . 50 E4
Orchid Cl BN23 .... 174 B3
Orchid Pk RH16 .... 51 C4
Orchid View BN1 ...... 143 C6
Orchidhurst TN2 ...... 8 D8
Ore Sta TN34 .... 160 A6
Oriental Pl BN1 .... 163 E5
Orion Cl BN27 .... 152 D7
Orion Par BN6 .... 97 F7
Ormerod Ave TN38 .. 136 A4
Ormerod Ct ■ RH16 . 50 E5
Ormond Rd BN3 ...... 142 D1
Osborne Cl TN39 .... 156 C3
Osborne Cl TN34 .... 136 E2
Osborne ■ BN43 .... 161 C8
Osborne Ho TN6 .... 38 C8
Osborne Rd Brighton BN1 . 143 A2
 Crowborough TN6 ... 38 C8
 Eastbourne BN20 ... 184 B4
 Osborne Villas BN3 . 162 F4
Osmers Hill TN5 ..... 29 F7
Osmond Rd BN3 .... 163 E7
Osmunda Bank RH19 . 1 E6
Osmunda Ct TN2 ... 8 C4
Osprey Dr TN22 ... 78 E5
Osprey Ho ■ BN1 . 163 E5
Oswald Ct TN40 ... 157 C4
Otham Court La BN26 . 173 B8
Otham Pk BN27 .... 152 D7
Otham Rd BN22 .... 174 A2
Ottafield Ct RH16 . 50 F6
Oulton Cl BN23 .... 174 B3
Our Lady of Lourdes
 RC Prim Sch BN2 . 165 F1
Ousedale Cl BN7 ... 123 B1
Outlook Ave BN10 . 178 F6
Outlook The BN20 . 183 A1
Oval Cl BN10 .... 167 C2
Over St BN1 .... 189 A6
Overdown Rise BN41 . 140 F4
Overhill BN42 ...... 140 E1
Overhill Dr BN1 ... 142 E5
Overhill Gdns BN1 . 142 E5
Overhill Way BN1 . 142 E6
Overton Shaw RH19 . 1 E4
Ovingdean Cl BN2 . 165 D5
Ovingdean Grange Cotts
 BN2 .... 165 D4
Ovingdean Hall Sch BN2 . 165 D4
Ovingdean Rd BN2 . 165 D5
Owen Cl RH15 ..... 72 F1
Owl House Gdns TN3 . 19 E7
Owls Gdns TN5 ... 42 F5
Owlsbury Cross TN21 . 83 B5
Ox Lea TN1 .... 7 A3
Oxbottom Cl BN8 . 76 B6
Oxenbridge La TN19 . 63 C8
Oxenbridge Row TN19 . 63 B8
Oxendean Gdns BN22 . 173 B4
Oxford Cl BN1 .... 189 A7
Oxford Mews BN3 . 163 C7
Oxford Pl BN1 .... 189 A7
Oxford Rd
 ■ Eastbourne BN22 . 185 B4
 Hastings TN38 ...... 136 A3

Oxford St BN1, BN2 ..... 189 A7
Oxford Terr ■ TN34 .... 160 B4
Oxshott Ct TN40 .... 157 F4

Packer Cl RH19 .... 2 A3
Packham Way RH15 ... 72 F4
Paddock Cl Bexhill TN40 . 157 D6
 Fordcombe TN3 .... 6 B5
Paddock Cl BN11 ..... 140 F3
Paddock Gdns
 East Grinstead RH19 . 10 E7
 Polegate BN26 .... 172 F4
Paddock Rd BN21 .... 123 C1
Paddock The
 Eastbourne BN22 ... 173 F2
 Hove BN3 .... 142 C1
 Maresfield TN22 .... 55 A4
 ■ Northiam TN31 ... 67 B7
 Pembury TN2 .... 9 C6
Paddockhall Rd RH16 . 50 D5
Paddocks The
 Cowden TN8 .... 4 A7
 Hailsham BN27 ..... 129 A2
 Plumpton Green BN7 . 99 E6
 Rodmell BN7 .... 167 D8
Padgham Cnr TN21 .. 109 D8
Padgham La TN21 ... 109 D8
Padua Ho BN2 ...... 165 F8
Padua House Flats BN2 . 165 F8
Page's Cotts TN2 ... 82 B8
Pages Ave TN39 ... 156 F2
Pages Cl TN21 .... 81 E7
Pages Hill TN21 .. 81 E7
Pages La TN39 ... 156 E3
Pagets The BN8 .. 76 D7
Pagham Cl BN23 . 174 B4
Pain's Flat RH15, RH17 . 72 D8
Paine's Cnr TN21 . 60 C4
Paines Cotts TN31 . 94 A3
Palace Pl BN1 ... 189 A5
Palesgate La TN6 . 26 C2
Palliser Cl BN23 . 185 E6
Palm Dene BN26 . 173 A7
Palmeira Ave BN3 . 163 D6
Palmeira Ct ■ BN3 . 163 D6
Palmeira Ho ■ BN3 . 163 D7
Palmeira Mansions ■
 BN3 .... 163 D7
Palmeira Pl BN3 . 163 D7
Palmeira Sq BN3 . 163 D6
Palmer Ho BN8 .. 100 E7
Palmers Row BN27 . 152 B7
Palmerston Rd BN9 . 168 F1
Pangdean La BN6 . 72 C4
Pangdene Cl RH15 . 72 F1
Pankhurst Ave BN2 . 164 B8
Pankhurst Cl TN39 . 157 A8
Pankhurst Rise TN39 . 157 A8
Pannel La TN35 .. 116 E2
Pannell Cl RH19 . 1 D1
Pannett RH15 .... 72 E4
Pantiles The
 Royal Tunbridge Wells TN4 . 7 F2
 ■ Royal Tunbridge Wells
 .... 8 A2
Parade The
 Beachlands BN24 ... 175 F6
 Hove BN3 .... 141 E2
 Pevensey Bay BN24 . 175 E5
Paradise Cl BN20 .. 184 D2
Paradise Dr BN20, BN21 . 184 D2
Paradise Family L Pk BN9 . 168 D1
Paragon The BN20 . 172 F3
Parham Cl BN2 ... 164 D5
Park Ave Bexhill TN39 . 157 B3
 Eastbourne BN21, BN22 . 184 D7
 Hastings TN34 ...... 136 D3
 Hove BN3 .... 162 E7
 Keymer BN6 ...... 98 A2
 Shoreham-by-Sea BN43 . 161 A8
 Telscombe Cliffs BN10 . 178 A8
Park Cl Brighton BN1 . 143 E5
 Burgess Hill RH15 . 72 F2
 Eastbourne BN20 . 184 D3
 Hastings TN34 .... 136 D3
 Hove BN3 .... 141 E3
 Hurstpierpoint BN6 . 97 A6
 Portslade-by-Sea BN41 . 141 B1
 Park Coll BN21 ... 184 E7
Park Cres Brighton BN2 . 189 B7
 Crowborough TN6 . 25 F3
 Forest Row RH18 . 12 A2
 Hastings TN34 ... 136 D2
 Portslade-by-Sea BN41 . 162 A8
 Rottingdean BN2 . 165 F1
Park Crescent Pl BN2 . 189 B7

Park Crescent Rd BN2 . 189 B7
Park Crescent Terr BN2 . 189 B7
Park Croft BN26 ...... 173 A5
Park Ct
 Brighton, Patcham BN1 . 142 E6
 Brighton, Preston BN1 . 142 F1
 Burgess Hill RH15 ... 73 A3
 ■ Haywards Heath RH16 . 50 E4
Park Dr TN34 .... 136 D2
Park Drive Cl BN9 . 168 F2
Park Farm Cl TN19 . 63 B8
Park Gate Hailsham BN27 . 129 D3
 Hove BN3 .... 163 D6
Park Gates ■ BN21 . 185 A2
Park Hill BN2 ...... 189 B5
Park La
 Ashurst Wood RH19 . 11 D6
 Table TN33 ...... 112 D4
 Bexhill TN39 .... 157 A6
 Crowborough TN6 . 25 F3
 Eastbourne BN21 . 184 C8
 Portslade-by-Sea BN41 . 141 A1
 Whatlington TN32, TN33 . 88 A5
Park Lodge
 ■ Eastbourne BN21 . 185 A2
 Hove BN3 .... 163 D8
Park Lodge Ct TN38 . 159 B7
Park Manor BN1 ... 142 D4
Park Mead Cty Prim Sch
 BN27 .... 151 A7
Park Rd Bexhill TN39 . 157 B3
 Brighton BN1 ... 143 E5
 Burgess Hill RH15 . 73 A3
 Crowborough TN6 . 25 F3
 Dormans Park RH19 . 1 F6
 East Grinstead RH19 . 1 D1
 Forest Row RH18 . 12 A2
 Hailsham BN27 . 129 B4
 Haywards Heath RH16 . 50 E4
 Heathfield TN21 . 82 B7
 Hove BN3 ...... 82 C6
 Lewes BN7 .... 123 C1
 Peacehaven Heights BN10 . 178 F6
 Rottingdean BN2 . 165 F1
 Royal Tunbridge Wells TN4 . 8 B5
 Seaford BN25 .... 180 D3
 Shoreham-by-Sea BN43 . 161 A8
Park Rise BN3 .... 141 E3
Park Road Terr ■ BN2 . 189 B5
Park Royal BN1 ... 163 E6
Park Shaw TN33 ... 88 E1
Park St Brighton BN2 . 189 B5
 Falmer BN1 ...... 144 C6
 Royal Tunbridge Wells TN2 . 8 C3
Park Terr BN2 .... 165 F1
Park The Crowborough TN6 . 25 F2
 Rottingdean BN2 . 177 A5
Park View Brighton BN1 . 163 E8
 Brighton BN2 .... 164 C6
 Buxted TN22 .... 56 C4
 Hastings TN34 . 136 D2
 Haywards Heath RH16 . 50 E6
 Northiam TN31 . 67 A6
 Peasmarsh TN31 . 69 B2
Park View Cl BN10 . 167 A1
Park View Rd BN3 . 142 B1
Park View Rise BN10 . 178 A8
Park View Terr
 Brighton BN1 .. 163 E8
 Westfield TN35 . 116 E4
Park Village Rd BN1 . 144 B8
Park Village The BN1 . 144 A8
Park Villas TN21 .. 82 B6
Park Way Hastings TN34 . 136 D3
 Southwick BN42 . 161 F8
Park Way Cl BN42 . 161 F8
Park Wood Rd TN34 . 136 F6
Parker Cl BN21 .... 184 E5
Parker Ct BN21 ... 141 B2
Parker Rd TN34 ... 137 A3
Parkfield Ave BN22 . 173 E1
Parkfield Rd TN39, TN40 . 157 C3
Parkland Cty Inf Sch
 BN22 .... 173 E1
Parkland Cty Jun Sch
 BN22 .... 173 D1
Parklands
 Maresfield TN22 . 55 A5
 Royal Tunbridge Wells TN4 . 7 E8
 Shoreham-by-Sea BN43 . 161 C8
Parklands Rd BN6 . 97 F3
Parkmead BN2 ... 189 B7
Parkmore Terr BN1 . 189 F8
Parks Yd TN33 ... 112 D4
Parkside
 Burgess Hill RH15 . 72 F3
 East Grinstead RH19 . 1 C1
 Heathfield TN21 . 82 B6

Parkside
Keymer BN6 .... 98 A4
Portslade-by-Sea BN43 .... 140 A1
Parkside Cty Prim Sch
TN21 .... 82 C5
Parkside Rd BN25 .... 180 F4
Parkstone Par TN34 .... 136 D4
Parkstone Rd TN34 .... 136 D4
Parkview BN6 .... 97 A5
Parkview Rd TN22 .... 55 D1
Parkway BN20 .... 184 B8
Parkwood TN31 .... 70 B4
Parkwood CI TN1 .... 8 C6
Parrock La TN7 .... 12 E2
Parry CI BN23 .... 174 E3
Parsonage CI TN4 .... 7 B5
Parsonage La
Icklesham TN36 .... 116 F6
Lamberhurst TN3 .... 20 B6
Westfield TN33, TN35 .... 114 C4
Parsonage Rd
Eastbourne BN21 .... 184 D4
Rusthall TN4 .... 7 B5
Parsons CI TN38 .... 135 F4
Partridges La TN5, TN6 ..... 28 E6
Pashley Down Cty Inf Sch
BN20 .... 184 B4
Pashley Manor Gdns TN19 . 44 B7
Pashley Rd BN20 .... 184 C2
Paston PI BN2 .... 164 D4
Pasture Hill Rd RH16 .... 50 D6
Patcham By-Pass BN1 ...... 142 E6
Patcham Cty Inf Sch BN1 . 142 E6
Patcham Cty Jun Sch BN1 142 F6
Patcham High Sch BN1 .... 142 F6
Patcham House Sch BN1 . 142 E6
Patcham Mill Rd BN24 .... 174 B5
Patchdean BN1 .... 142 F5
Patching Lodge **5** BN2 .. 164 C5
Paton Rd TN39 .... 157 A8
Paul CI BN27 .... 129 A3
Pavilion Bldgs BN1 .... 189 B5
Pavilion CI BN6 .... 97 E5
Pavilion Ct **11** BN1 .... 163 E7
Pavilion Par BN1 .... 189 A5
Pavilion Rd BN1 .... 144 C7
Pavilion Ret Pk BN2 .... 143 C1
Pavilion St BN2 .... 189 A5
Pavilion Way RH19 .... 10 E8
Paxhill CI TN38 .... 135 E4
Paxhill Park Golf Course
RH16 .... 51 E8
Paygate Rd TN33 .... 113 E7
Payne Ave BN1 .... 162 F8
Payne Terr BN1 .... 143 B1
Paynsbridge Way TN21 .... 107 A7
Paynters Way BN8 .... 76 C7
Paynton Rd TN37 .... 136 B3
Paythorne CI BN42 .... 140 D1
Payton Dr RH15 .... 72 E2
Payton Ho RH15 .... 73 D3
Peace CI BN1 .... 143 C1
Peacehaven Cty Inf Sch
BN10 .... 178 B7
Peacehaven Golf Course
BN9 .... 179 A7
Peacock Ind Est BN3 .... 163 D7
Peacock La BN1 .... 142 E4
Peakdean CI BN20 .... 183 B2
Peakdean La BN20 .... 183 B2
Pearl Ct **3** BN21 .... 185 A2
Pearse PI TN3 .... 20 B5
Peartree CI RH15 .... 72 E3
Peartree Field TN36 .... 116 F6
Peartree Hill TN5 .... 42 E4
Peartree La TN39 .... 156 D6
Peasmarsh CE Prim Sch
TN31 .... 69 B1
Pebble Rd BN24 .... 175 E5
Pebsham Cty Prim Sch
TN40 .... 158 A5
Pebsham Dr TN40 .... 158 A6
Pebsham La TN38, TN40 .. 158 A6
Peckham CI BN7 .... 123 C3
Peel Rd BN2 .... 164 F4
Peelings La BN24 .... 174 D6
Peeps La TN6 .... 39 A6
Pegasus Way RH19 .... 2 B3
Pegler Ave BN9 .... 179 B6
Pegwell CI TN34 .... 136 E2
Pelham Arc **1** TN34 .... 160 A3
Pelham CI
Peacehaven BN10 .... 167 D1
Westham BN24 .... 174 F5
Pelham Cres
Hailsham BN27 .... 152 C6
Hastings TN34 .... 160 A3
Pelham Ct **11** BN25 ..... 180 E2

Pelham PI TN34 .... 160 A3
Pelham Place Cotts RH16 .. 51 A7
Pelham Rd
Haywards Heath RH16 ..... 51 A6
Seaford BN25 .... 180 E2
Pelham Rise BN10 .... 167 D1
Pelham Sq BN1 .... 189 A6
Pelham St Brighton BN1 .. 189 A6
Hastings TN34 .... 159 F7
Pelham Terr Brighton BN1 143 C1
Lewes BN7 .... 123 C2
Pelham Yd **4** BN25 ...... 180 E2
Pell CI TN5 .... 30 A6
Pellbrook Rd BN7 .... 123 B3
Pells CE Prim Sch
Lewes BN7 .... 123 C1
Lewes BN7 .... 123 C2
Pelwood Rd TN31 .... 95 A2
Pembroke Ave BN3 .... 163 A7
Pembroke Ct BN27 .... 129 C3
Pembroke Cres BN3 .... 163 A7
Pembroke Ct **2** BN3 .... 163 A6
Pembroke Gdns BN3 .... 163 A6
Pembury CI
Haywards Heath RH16 ..... 51 B3
Pembury TN2 .... 9 D7
Pembury Cty Prim Sch TN2 . 9 D8
Pembury Gr TN39 .... 157 A7
Pembury Grange TN2 .... 9 A6
Pembury Hospl TN2 .... 9 B7
Pembury Rd
Eastbourne BN23 .... 174 D1
Royal Tunbridge Wells TN2 .. 8 E4
Pendean RH15 .... 73 C1
Pendragon Ct BN3 .... 163 A8
Pendrill PI TN5 .... 29 F5
Penhale Rd BN22 .... 185 D5
Penhurst CI
Eastbourne BN22 .... 174 A1
Hastings TN37 .... 136 D5
Penhurst Dr TN40 .... 158 A6
Penhurst La TN33 .... 110 E6
Penhurst PI BN22 .... 164 F6
Penland CI RH16 .... 50 D7
Penland Ct **10** TN40 ..... 157 E4
Penland Rd Bexhill TN40 .. 157 E5
Haywards Heath
RH16, RH17 .... 50 D7
Penn Cres
Haywards Heath RH16 ..... 51 A5
Ringmer BN8 .... 124 D5
Penn Yd TN2 .... 9 C6
Pennine Rise TN34 .... 137 B4
Pennine Way BN23 .... 174 D3
Pennine Wlk TN2 .... 8 D5
Pennington Ho RH16 ...... 51 A3
Penny La TN40 .... 158 A5
Pennybridge La TN20 ...... 40 D5
Pensford Dr BN23 .... 174 D3
Penshurst Rd TN11, TN3 ... 6 E8
Penstone Ct **4** BN43 ... 161 C8
Pentland CI
Eastbourne BN22 .... 174 E3
Hastings TN37 .... 136 C5
Pentland Rd TN40 .... 158 A6
Penybont TN2 .... 9 E7
Peter Gladwin
Cty Prim Sch BN41 ..... 141 B2
Peter James CI TN31 .... 94 E2
Peter James La TN35 ..... 138 C6
Petersfield TN2 .... 9 E7
Petlands Gdns **4** BN8 ... 52 E3
Petlands Rd RH16 .... 50 E3
Pett CI BN2 .... 164 F6
Pett La TN35, TN36 .... 114 F4
Pett Level Rd TN35, TN36 . 139 B7
Pett Rd TN35 .... 138 C8
Petworth Dr RH15 .... 73 A4
Petworth PI BN22 .... 173 E2
Petworth Rd BN1 .... 143 B6
Pevensey Bay Rd BN23 ... 175 A2
Pevensey Bay Sta BN24 .. 175 C6
Pevensey Castle BN24 .... 175 A6

Pevensey CI BN25 .... 181 B4
Pevensey Ct TN39 .... 157 B3
Pevensey Park Rd BN24 .. 174 F6
Pevensey Rd
3 Brighton BN2 .... 164 C8
Eastbourne BN21, BN22 . 185 B3
Hastings TN37, TN38 .... 159 B7
Newhaven BN9 .... 179 B5
Polegate BN26 .... 173 C6
Pevensey & Westham
CE Prim Sch BN24 ...... 175 A6
Pevensey & Westham Sta
BN24 .... 174 F5
Peverells The BN25 .... 181 A5
Peyton CI BN23 .... 185 F7
Philip Cole CI **16** TN34 . 160 B4
Philip Ct **8** BN3 .... 163 C7
Phoenix Brewery Halls
BN2 .... 189 B7
Phoenix CI BN27 .... 152 E7
Phoenix Cres BN42 .... 161 D8
Phoenix Cswy BN7 .... 123 D1
Phoenix Ct **9** BN2 .... 185 B3
Phoenix Dr RH19 .... 11 E6
Phoenix PI Brighton BN2 . 189 B6
Lewes BN7 .... 123 D1
Phoenix Way BN42 .... 161 D8
Phyllis Ave BN10 .... 178 B8
Picardy CI TN33 .... 112 E4
Piccadilly La TN20 .... 40 C1
Pickers Gn RH16 .... 51 A8
Picketts La TN22 .... 54 D8
Pickforde La TN5 .... 31 D1
Picton St BN2 .... 164 C7
Piddinghoe Ave BN10 .... 178 D6
Piddinghoe CI BN10 ...... 178 D7
Piddinghoe Mead BN9 ... 168 B1
Pilgrim Ct RH16 .... 51 A5
Pilgrims Old Sch BN7 .... 146 A7
Pilgrims Sch BN25 .... 180 E6
Pilmer Rd TN6 .... 25 F4
Pilot Ho **1** BN2 .... 189 B5
Pilot Rd TN34 .... 137 B4
Piltdown Ct Bexhill TN39 . 157 B4
Hastings TN34 .... 136 E1
Piltdown Rd BN2 .... 164 F6
Piltdown Rise TN22 .... 78 D8
Piltdown Way TN22 .... 174 A4
Pinders Rd TN35 .... 160 D6
Pinders Wlk TN35 .... 137 D3
Pine Ave TN34 .... 137 B4
Pine Gr Crowborough TN6 . 25 E3
East Grinstead RH19 .... 1 B3
Pine Tree CI
Hurstpierpoint BN6 .... 97 B5
Newhaven BN9 .... 179 C7
Pine Tree Rd TN21 .... 82 A6
Pine Trees Ct BN6 .... 97 D4
Pine Way BN27 .... 152 A7
Pine Way CI RH19 .... 10 E7
Pine Wlk TN22 .... 78 D8
Pineham Copse RH16 .... 50 F4
Pinehurst RH15 .... 73 A1
Pines The
2 Brighton BN2 .... 189 B7
Haywards Heath RH16 ..... 51 B4
Hove BN3 .... 163 E6
Pinfold TN40 .... 157 D5
Pinnwell Rd BN7 .... 146 D8
Pipe Pas BN7 .... 123 C1
Piper's Gate TN22 .... 78 D4
Pipers CI Bexhill TN40 ... 157 C5
Hove BN3 .... 144 C8
Wadhurst TN5 .... 30 A4
Pipers Field TN22 .... 78 D4
Pipers La TN32 .... 64 B3
Pit Rd BN6 .... 97 A5
Pitreavie Dr BN27 .... 152 A8
Pitt Dr BN25 .... 181 A5
Pitt Gdns BN2 .... 165 D7
Place La BN25 .... 180 E3
Plainfields Ave BN1 .... 143 A7
Plaistow CI BN2 .... 164 F6
Plat The TN31 .... 67 B6
Platt The Dormansland RH7 . 2 A8
Frant TN3 .... 17 B1
Haywards Heath RH16 ..... 51 B5

Plaw Hatch La RH18, RH19 . 21 E5
Playden CI **1** BN2 .... 164 E4
Playden Gdns TN34 .... 137 B4
Playden La TN31 .... 70 C3
Playden St Michael's
CE Prim Sch TN31 ...... 70 C2
Pleasant View Cotts TN6 .. 25 E4
Pleasant View Rd TN6 ..... 25 F4
Plemont Gdns TN39 .... 157 A6
Pleydell Rise TN39 .... 155 F4
Plough La TN37 .... 136 B5
Plover CI BN23 .... 174 C2
Plover Ct Hailsham BN27 . 152 D7
Hastings TN38 .... 135 E3
Plum Tree Cotts TN18 ...... 45 E8
Plumey Feather Cotts TN3 . 14 E3
Plumpton Bostall BN7 .... 121 E6
Plumpton CI Bexhill TN40 . 157 C6
Eastbourne BN23 .... 174 A4
Plumpton Cross BN7 .... 99 E3
Plumpton Crossways
BN7, BN8 .... 74 F1
Plumpton Cty Prim Sch
BN7 .... 99 F5
Plumpton La BN7 .... 99 E3
Plumpton Race Course
BN7 .... 99 E4
Plumpton Rd BN2 .... 164 D6
Plumpton Sta BN7 .... 99 E5
Plymouth Ave BN2 .... 143 F1
Plymouth CI BN23 .... 185 F8
Plynlimmon Rd TN34 ..... 160 A4
Pocock's Rd BN21 .... 184 D5
Pokes Cott TN17 .... 20 F2
Polegate By-Pass BN26 .. 172 F7
Polegate Cty Prim Sch
BN26 .... 173 A7
Polegate Sta BN26 .... 173 A6
Polesden Rd TN7 .... 8 D2
Polley CI TN2 .... 9 D7
Pomper La BN6 .... 72 A2
Pond CI TN31 .... 90 B5
Pond Way RH19 .... 2 B1
Pondcroft Rd RH16 .... 51 B7
Pondsyde Ct BN25 .... 180 F4
Ponswood Rd TN38 .... 136 B2
Pont CI TN21 .... 83 C6
Pook Reed CI TN21 .... 81 F6
Pook Reed La TN21 .... 81 F6
Pool Valley BN2 .... 189 A4
Poona Rd TN1, TN2 .... 8 B2
Poplar Ave BN3 .... 141 E3
Poplar CI Brighton BN1 ... 142 F2
Hove BN3 .... 141 E3
Poplar Wlk BN22 .... 173 D3
Poplars The BN6 .... 98 A3
Poppinghole La TN32 .... 87 E8
Popps La TN39 .... 156 C3
Poppyfield TN31 .... 70 C1
Port Hall Ave BN1 .... 163 E8
Port Hall Mews BN1 ...... 163 E8
Port Hall P! BN1 .... 163 E8
Port Hall Rd BN1 .... 163 E8
Port Hall St BN1 .... 163 E8
Port Rd BN22 .... 174 A1
Porters Way BN26 .... 173 B6
Portfield Ave BN1 .... 143 A6
Portfield TN40 .... 157 D5
Portland Ave BN3 .... 162 E7
Portland CI BN27 .... 129 A1
Portland Cotts **11** TN34 . 159 F8
Portland Gate BN3 .... 162 E7
Portland Ho **5** RH19 ..... 10 F8
Portland PI
10 Brighton BN2 .... 164 C4
11 Hastings TN34 ..... 159 F8
Portland Rd
Burgess Hill RH15 .... 72 F3
East Grinstead RH19 ...... 10 F8
Hove BN3 .... 162 E7

Portsmouth Wood RH16 .... 50 F8
Portsmouth Wood CI RH16 . 50 F8
Posey Cotts BN27 .... 131 B5
Possingworth CI TN21 ...... 80 F8
Post Horn CI RH18 .... 12 B1
Post Horn La RH18 .... 12 B2
Post Office Pas **10** TN34 . 160 A4
Potato La BN8 .... 124 F5
Potman's La TN33, TN39 .. 133 E4
Pottens Mill La TN20 .... 59 F4
Potter's La BN7 .... 146 C8
Potteries Cotts BN27 ..... 128 D3
Potteries The TN22 .... 78 D4
Potters Field BN8 .... 124 D6
Potters La RH15 .... 72 F1
Pottery CI TN31 .... 90 A2
Pottery Cotts BN6 .... 74 A1
Pottery La TN31 .... 90 A2
Pottingfield Rd TN31 .... 93 A6
Potts Marsh Ind Est BN24 174 F4
Pouchlands Dr BN8 .... 100 C7
Pound CI BN23 .... 185 F6
Pound Cnr BN8 .... 101 D4
Pound Gate BN6 .... 97 D3
Pound La Framefield TN22 . 79 F7
Laughton BN8 .... 126 C7
Pound The RH15 .... 72 F4
Poundfield Farm TN6 .... 26 B2
Poundfield Rd
Crowborough TN6 .... 26 B2
Sandhurst TN18 .... 47 B5
Poundsbridge Hill
TN11, TN3 .... 6 D7
Poveys CI RH15 .... 72 D3
Powder Mill La TN4 .... 8 B8
Powdermill CI TN4 .... 8 C8
Powdermill La
Battle TN33 .... 112 C1
Goatham Green
TN31, TN33 .... 89 D3
Powell Gdns BN9 .... 168 D1
Powell Rd BN8 .... 76 D7
Powis Gr BN1 .... 189 F6
Powis Rd BN1 .... 163 E6
Powis Sq BN1 .... 163 E6
Powis Villas BN1 .... 189 F6
Poynings CI BN25 .... 181 C2
Poynings Dr BN3 .... 141 F3
Poynter Rd BN3 .... 162 A6
Pratt's Folly La TN6 .... 25 E1
Prescott Gdns RH15 .... 73 A3
Preston Cir BN1 .... 189 A7
Preston Dro BN1 .... 142 F2
Preston Gr TN22 .... 79 B6
Preston Grange BN1 .... 142 E1
Preston Manor (Mus) BN1 142 E1
Preston Park Ave BN1 ..... 142 F1
Preston Park Sta BN1 ..... 142 D2
Preston Rd Bexhill TN39 . 157 B7
Brighton BN1 .... 163 F8
Preston St BN1 .... 163 E5
Prestonville Ct **1** BN1 ... 189 F7
Prestonville Rd BN1, BN3 . 189 F7
Prideaux Rd BN21 .... 184 E5
Primrose CI BN23 .... 174 B3
Primrose Hill
Bexhill TN39 .... 156 F6
Fairlight Cove TN35 ...... 138 F5
Primrose La RH18 .... 12 A1
Prince Albert St BN1 ...... 189 A5
Prince Charles CI
BN41, BN42 .... 141 A1
Prince Charles Rd BN7 ... 123 E3
Prince Edward's Rd BN7 . 123 B1
Prince Of Wales Ct BN41 . 162 F6
Prince Regent's CI BN2 .. 164 E4
Prince Regent's Ct **2**
BN2 .... 164 E4
Prince William Par
BN22, BN23 .... 185 F6
Prince's Cres BN2 .... 189 B8
Prince's PI BN1 .... 189 A5
Prince's Rd
Brighton BN1, BN2 .... 164 B8
Hastings TN37 .... 159 D7
Prince's St BN2 .... 164 E4
Princes Terr BN2 .... 164 E4
Princes Ave BN3 .... 163 A6
Princes CI Seaford BN25 . 180 E5
Uckfield TN22 .... 78 A7
Princes Cres BN3 .... 163 A6
Princes Ct **6** BN3 .... 163 A6
Princes Field BN26 .... 150 B3
Princes Rd BN23 .... 185 E7
Princes Sq BN3 .... 163 A6
Princess Dr BN25 .... 180 F5
Princess Royal Hospl The
RH16 .... 50 F2
Prinkle La BN27 .... 109 C1
Prinsep Rd BN3 .... 163 A8

Prior's Way TN8 .... 4 A6
Priory Ave TN34 .... 136 E1
Priory Cl Hastings TN34 .... 136 E1
  Pevensey Bay BN24 ...... 175 D5
Priory Cres BN7 .... 146 C8
Priory Ct Brighton BN1 ..... 163 F8
  Eastbourne BN20 .... 184 F1
  Lewes BN7 .... 146 D8
Priory Flats **7** BN7 .... 146 C8
Priory Ho BN7 .... 146 D8
Priory Hts BN30 .... 184 A5
Priory La BN23 .... 174 E3
Priory Meadow Sh Ctr
  TN34 .... 159 F8
Priory Orch **8** BN23 ..... 174 E1
Priory Rd
  Burgess Hill RH15 .... 73 A1
  Eastbourne BN23 .... 174 E2
  Forest Row RH18 .... 11 D2
  Hassocks BN6 .... 97 E5
  Hastings TN34, TN35 .... 160 B8
Priory Sch BN7 .... 146 E8
Priory St Hastings TN34 .. 159 F7
  Lewes BN7 .... 146 C8
Priory The Brighton BN1 .. 142 D5
  Hove BN3 .... 50 F4
Priory Way RH16 .... 50 F4
Promenade BN10 .... 178 C6
Promenade The BN24 ...... 175 D4
Prospect Cotts TN3 .... 20 A3
Prospect Gdns **10** BN21 ... 184 D4
Prospect Pl TN34 .... 159 E7
Prospect Rd
  Heathfield TN21 .... 82 B6
  Royal Tunbridge Wells TN4 .. 7 F8
  Royal Tunbridge Wells
  TN1, TN2 .... 8 C3
Prospect Terr TN21 .... 82 A7
Providence Cotts
  Crowborough TN6 .... 25 D4
  Groombridge TN3 .... 15 C7
Providence Pl BN1 .... 189 A7
Prowting Mead TN39 ...... 156 C4
Pudding Cake La TN22 .... 78 C7
Pulborough Ave BN22 .... 173 E2
Pulborough Cl BN2 .... 164 F7
Pump Ho The BN3 .... 162 D8
Pump La TN22 .... 79 D4
Punnetts Town Cty Prim Sch
  TN21 .... 83 B6
Purbeck Cl BN20 .... 174 C4
Putlands Cres TN39 .... 157 A8
Pyecombe Golf Course
  BN45 .... 119 E6
Pyecombe St BN45 .... 119 A6

Quadrangle The BN8 ...... 105 C5
Quadrant BN1 .... 189 F5
Quadrant The BN6 .... 98 A4
Quail Ct BN27 .... 152 D7
Quakers La RH14 .... 51 A5
Quantock Cl BN23 .... 174 D3
Quantock Gdns TN34 .... 137 B3
Quarry Bank Rd BN1 .... 143 B2
Quarry Cl RH15 .... 73 D3
Quarry Cotts TN5 .... 29 D7
Quarry Cres TN34 .... 160 A5
Quarry Farm TN32 .... 65 D6
Quarry Hill
  Hastings TN38 .... 159 B7
  Haywards Heath RH17 .... 50 D4
Quarry Ho TN38 .... 159 B6
Quarry La BN25 .... 181 A5
Quarry Rd Hastings TN34 .. 160 A5
  Newhaven BN9 .... 179 D5
Quarry Rise RH19 ....'.... 2 A3
Quay Ct BN43 .... 161 B6
Quay Rd TN1 .... 8 B5
Quay The **5** BN43 .... 161 A6
Quebec Cl Bexhill TN39 ... 157 A5
  Eastbourne BN23 .... 185 F7
Quebec Mansions TN38 ... 159 A8
Quebec Rd TN38 .... 136 A4
Quebec St BN2 .... 189 A5
Queen Alexandra Ave
  BN3 .... 142 A3
Queen Anne's Cl BN7 ..... 123 C1
Queen Caroline Cl BN3 .. 142 A3
Queen Elizabeth Ave RH15 .. 73 E2
Queen Mary Ave BN3 ..... 142 A3
Queen Sq BN1 .... 189 F5
Queen Victoria Ave BN3 .. 142 A3
Queen Victoria Hospl The
  RH19 .... 1 F3
Queen's Ave **4** TN34 ... 159 F7
Queen's Cres BN23 .... 185 E7
Queen's Ct RH16 .... 50 F6
Queen's Gdns
  Brighton BN1 .... 189 A6
  Eastbourne BN21, BN22 .. 185 B3

Queen's Gdns
  Hove BN3 .... 163 C5
  Royal Tunbridge Wells TN4 .. 8 B6
Queen's Par
  Eastbourne BN22 .... 173 F1
  Hove BN3 .... 141 E2
Queen's Park Cty Prim Sch
  BN2 .... 164 C5
Queen's Park Rd BN2 ..... 164 C6
Queen's Park Rise BN2 ... 164 C6
Queen's Park Terr BN2 ... 164 C6
Queen's Pl Brighton BN1 .. 189 A7
  Hove BN3 .... 163 C6
Queen's Rd Brighton BN1 .. 189 F6
  East Grinstead RH19 ...... 1 E1
  Eastbourne BN23 .... 185 D7
  Hastings TN34 .... 159 F8
  Lewes BN7 .... 123 D3
  Royal Tunbridge Wells TN4 .. 8 B6
Queens App TN22 .... 55 D1
Queens Cotts TN5 .... 29 E6
Queens Cres RH15 .... 73 A2
Queens Ct TN39 .... 157 B3
Queens Dr Hassocks BN6 .. 97 F4
  Maresfield TN22 .... 54 F4
Queens Park Gdns BN25 .. 180 C4
Queens Rd
  Crowborough TN6 .... 25 F1
  Haywards Heath RH16 ... 50 G6
  Herstmonceux BN27 .... 130 E5
  Southwick BN42 .... 140 E1
Queens Sq TN34 .... 159 F8
Queensbury Mews BN1 ... 163 E5
Queensdown Sch BN1 .... 143 C3
Queensdown School Rd
  BN1, BN2 .... 143 D2
Queensmount TN20 .... 58 B7
Queensway Brighton BN2 .. 164 D6
  East Grinstead RH19 .... 1 E1
  Hastings TN37, TN38 .... 135 E5
  Seaford BN25 .... 181 A6
Querneby Cl BN43 .... 161 D7
Quickbourne La TN31 ...... 67 C7
Quinnell Dr BN27 .... 129 B2
Quintin Cl BN27 .... 152 A5
Quintins The BN27 .... 152 C8

Radcliffe Cl TN37 .... 136 C3
Radinden Dr BN3 .... 142 D1
Radinden Manor Rd BN3 .. 163 D8
Radnor Mews TN38 .... 135 E2
Ragged Dog La TN21 .... 81 B3
Raglan Ct Brighton BN1 ... 189 F5
  Pevensey Bay BN24 ...... 175 C3
Railway App
  East Grinstead RH19 .... 1 E1
  Newhaven BN9 .... 179 D7
Railway Cotts Cowden TN8 .. 4 D8
  Hastings TN38 .... 158 F6
  Horsted Keynes RH19 .... 33 A8
Railway La BN7 .... 123 D1
Railway Rd BN9 .... 179 D7
Railway St BN1 .... 189 F6
Railway View TN6 .... 38 C8
Raleigh Cl BN23 .... 185 E7
Ramsay Way BN23 .... 185 F7
Ramslye Rd TN2, TN4 ...... 16 E8
Ranalah Est BN9 .... 179 D8
Randiddles Cl RH6 .... 97 B4
Randolph La TN31 .... 70 B3
Ranelagh Ct BN23 .... 185 E6
Ranelagh Villas BN3 .... 163 B8
Rangemore Dr BN21 .... 184 D6
Rankine Rd TN1 .... 8 A3
Ranmore Cl TN34 .... 136 E6
Rannoch Rd TN6 .... 25 D2
Rannoch Rd W TN6 .... 25 D2
Ranscombe Hill BN8 .... 147 A6
Ranscombe La BN8 .... 147 D6
Ranworth Cl BN23 .... 174 B4
Raphael Rd BN3 .... 162 F7
Rapson's Rd BN20 .... 173 A3
Rastrick Cl RH15 .... 72 F1
Rattle Rd BN24 .... 174 D6
Ratton Dr BN20 .... 184 B7
Ratton Gdn BN20 .... 184 B7
Ratton La BN20 .... 184 E4
Ratton Sch BN21 .... 184 C7
Ratton Village BN20 ...... 184 B8
Raven Ct Battle TN33 ...... 112 F4
  Hastings TN38 .... 135 E3
Ravens Cl TN39 .... 156 C3
Ravens Croft BN20 .... 188 F8
Ravens Ct BN20 .... 188 F8
Ravenside Ret & L Pk
  TN38 .... 158 A4
Ravenswood BN6 .... 97 E4
Ravenswood Ave TN1, TN2 .. 8 A6
Ravenswood Dr BN2 .... 165 F6
Ravenswood Rd RH15 .... 73 B3
Raving Cl TN34 .... 137 A3

Rayford Cl BN10 .... 178 C7
Rayford Ct Bexhill TN40 ... 157 D4
  6 Seaford BN25 .... 180 E2
Raymond Cl BN25 .... 181 A5
Raystede Ctr for
  Animal Welfare BN8 .... 103 D1
Readers La TN31 .... 69 F5
Reading Rd BN2 .... 164 F4
Reba Ct BN2 .... 177 D4
Rectory Cl Burwash TN19 .. 62 B6
  East Hoathly BN8 .... 105 A5
  Eastbourne BN20 .... 184 D3
  Hastings TN38 .... 136 B2
  Hove BN3 .... 162 D7
  Newhaven BN9 .... 179 C6
  Shoreham-by-Sea BN43 .. 161 D7
Rectory Ct **5** BN43 ..... 161 C8
Rectory Field TN7 .... 13 E4
Rectory La Beckley TN31 ... 67 F4
  Iden TN31 .... 70 B4
  Rye TN31 .... 93 C8
  Winchelsea TN36 .... 117 E7
Rectory Rd
  Newhaven BN9 .... 168 E2
  Shoreham-by-Sea BN43 .. 161 D7
  Rectory Way TN40 .... 157 D5
Red Dyke Cotts BN26 ... 173 F6
Red Lake Cty Prim Sch
  TN35 .... 137 D4
Red Lake Terr TN35 .... 137 D4
Red Oak TN18 .... 45 E8
Red Oast Cotts TN5 .... 32 C3
Redbridge La TN6 .... 37 D5
Redbrook La TN22 .... 56 D4
Redford Cl BN23 .... 174 E1
Redgarth Ct RH19 .... 1 B3
Redgeland Rise TN38 ..... 135 F2
Redgill La BN8 .... 53 B1
Redhill Cl BN1 .... 142 C5
Redhill Dr BN1 .... 142 C5
Redleaf Cl TN2 .... 8 D6
Redman King Rd BN18 .... 125 C1
Redoubt Mus &
  Aquarium The BN22 .... 185 C4
Redoubt Rd BN22 .... 185 C4
Redshank Cl BN27 .... 152 D7
Redvers Rd BN2 .... 143 D1
Redwood Dr RH16 .... 50 D3
Reed Ct BN7 .... 123 D3
Reed Ho BN8 .... 100 F7
Reed Pond Wlk RH16 ...... 51 A4
Reedham Rd BN23 .... 174 B4
Reedswood Rd
  Broad Oak TN21 .... 90 B4
  Hastings TN38 .... 158 E8
Reeves Cl TN3 .... 6 B5
Reeves Hill BN1 .... 143 D5
Reeves Terr TN5 .... 31 E1
Refectory Rd BN1 .... 144 B7
Regal Dr **10** RH19 .... 10 F8
Regency Ct TN22 .... 78 C8
Regency Gdns TN38 .... 159 A8
Regency Hall **15** TN2 ... 8 A2
Regency Mews
  16 Brighton BN1 ...... 163 E5
  Eastbourne BN20 .... 185 A1
Regency Rd BN1 .... 189 F5
Regency Sq BN1 .... 163 C3
Regent Arc BN1 .... 189 A5
Regent Bsns Pk RH15 ...... 72 E2
Regent Hill BN1 .... 189 A6
Regent Pl Hastings TN38 ... 135 F7
  Royal Tunbridge Wells TN2 .. 8 D3
Regent Row BN1 .... 189 F5
Regent Sq TN31 .... 93 C6
Regent St BN1 .... 189 A5
Regents Cl BN25 .... 180 E5
Regina Ct TN4 .... 8 B2
Reginald Rd TN39 .... 157 B4
Regnum Cl BN22 .... 173 E4
Reigate Rd BN1 .... 142 D1
Renfrew Ct BN27 .... 185 D6
Resting Oak Hill BN8 ..... 100 F3
Reynolds Dr TN40 .... 157 E5
Reynolds La TN4 .... 7 F6
Reynolds Rd
  Eastbourne BN23 .... 174 E1
  Hove BN3 .... 162 F7
  Royal Tunbridge Wells TN4 .. 8 A3
Ribbetts Ho BN6 .... 97 A5
Ribbetts The BN6 .... 97 A5
Riccards La TN33 .... 88 A2
Rices Hill RH19 .... 1 F1
Richard Allen Ct **2** BN2 .. 143 C1
Richardson Ct **5** BN3 ... 162 F7
Richardson Rd
  Hove BN3 .... 162 F7
  Royal Tunbridge Wells RH6 .. 97 A3
Richborough Ct TN34 ..... 137 A3
Richington Way BN25 ..... 181 B5
Richland Cl TN35 .... 137 D3

Richmead Gdns TN20 ...... 40 B2
Richmond Ave TN39 .... 156 F3
Richmond Cl TN39 .... 157 A3
Richmond Ct **3** BN3 ..... 163 E7
Richmond Gr TN39 .... 157 A2
Richmond Hts **11** BN2 ... 189 B6
Richmond Par BN2 .... 189 B6
Richmond Pl
  Brighton BN2 .... 189 A6
  Eastbourne BN21 .... 184 F4
Richmond Rd
  Bexhill TN39 .... 157 A3
  Brighton BN2 .... 164 B8
  Pevensey Bay BN24 ...... 175 D5
  Seaford BN25 .... 180 E3
Richmond Sq RH19 .... 1 D2
Richmond St
  Brighton BN2 .... 189 B6
  Hastings TN34, TN35 .... 160 C6
Richmond Terr
  Brighton BN2 .... 189 B7
  1 Seaford BN25 .... 180 E3
Richmond Way RH19 ...... 10 F8
Rickland Cotts TN22 .... 53 B6
Riddens Cl BN7 .... 99 E6
Riddens La BN7 .... 99 E5
Riddens The BN7 .... 99 E5
Riddlesdale Ave TN4 .... 8 A6
Ride The BN1 .... 142 F1
Riders Bolt TN39 .... 156 E5
Ridge Cl Nutley TN22 ...... 35 C5
  Portslade-by-Sea BN41 .. 141 A4
Ridge Rd BN1 .... 144 C7
Ridge The
  Groombridge TN3 .... 15 A6
  Hastings TN34,
  TN35, TN37 .... 136 D6
  Winchelsea Beach TN36 .. 118 C6
Ridge View BN1 .... 143 E5
Ridge W The TN37, TN38 .. 136 A7
Ridge Way RH16 .... 51 B2
Ridgelands Cl BN20 .... 184 C3
Ridgeside Ave BN1 .... 142 E5
Ridgeway
  East Grinstead RH19 ...... 10 E7
  Hurst Green TN19 .... 45 A3
  Pembury TN2 .... 9 F7
  Southwick BN41, BN42 .. 140 F1
  The Moor TN18 .... 45 E8
Ridgeway Cl
  Heathfield TN21 .... 82 A8
  Southwick BN42 .... 140 F1
Ridgeway Gdns BN2 ...... 165 E7
Ridgeway The
  Burgess Hill RH15 .... 73 B4
  Friston BN20 .... 183 B1
  Herstmonceux BN27 .... 130 E6
  Seaford BN25 .... 180 F4
Ridgewood Ave BN2 ...... 166 C3
Ridgewood Cl TN22 .... 78 D4
Ridgewood Gdns TN40 ... 157 E4
Ridgewood Ind Pk TN22 ... 78 E4
Ridgway Cl BN2 .... 165 D8
Ridgway Paddock BN2 ... 145 E6
Ridgway The BN2 .... 165 D8
Ridings The Bexhill TN39 ... 156 F8
  Burgess Hill RH15 .... 73 C2
  Hastings TN37 .... 136 C5
  Newick BN8 .... 76 C7
  Royal Tunbridge Wells TN2 .. 8 F6
  Seaford BN25 .... 180 F5
  Telscombe Cliffs BN10 ... 167 B2
Rigden Rd BN2 .... 142 C1
Riley Rd BN2 .... 143 C1
Rill Wlk RH19 .... 2 B1
Ringle Gn TN18 .... 47 C5
Ringmer Bsns Pk BN8 .... 124 F6
Ringmer Cl BN1 .... 143 A4
Ringmer Com Coll BN8 .. 124 E6
Ringmer Cty Prim Sch
  BN8 .... 124 E5
Ringmer Rd Brighton BN1 .. 143 E4
  Brighton BN1 .... 143 F4
  Newhaven BN9 .... 179 B6
  Seaford BN25 .... 180 F5
Ringmer Way BN23 .... 174 A4
Ringwood Cl BN22 .... 185 B5
Ringwood Ct **5** BN22 ... 185 C5
Ringwood Rd
  Bexhill TN39 .... 157 C7
  Eastbourne BN22 .... 185 B5
Ripe La BN8 .... 126 E2
Ripley Chase BN21 .... 184 E3
Ripsley Cl BN23 .... 174 E2
Risden La TN18 .... 46 D7
Rise Park Gdns BN23 ...... 174 E2
Rise The
  East Grinstead RH19 ...... 10 F8
  Haywards Heath RH16 .... 50 G6
  Portslade-by-Sea BN41 .. 140 F2
Riseden Rd TN5 .... 29 C1

Rising The BN23 .... 174 E2
Rissom Ct BN1 .... 142 E2
River La BN26 .... 171 A3
River Way TN22 .... 78 C6
Riverbourne Ho **16** BN2 .. 185 B4
Riverdale BN7 .... 123 C2
Riverhall Hill TN5 .... 28 E7
Riverside
  Forest Row RH18 .... 11 E3
  Newhaven BN9 .... 179 D6
  Southwick BN42 .... 161 E7
Riverside Ind Est BN7 .... 123 D2
Riverside Rd BN43 .... 161 A6
Rixons Cl RH17 .... 33 C5
Rixons Orch RH17 .... 33 C5
Roadean Cl BN25 .... 181 A4
Robert Lodge BN2 .... 164 F4
Robert Mitchell Sch TN39 .. 157 B7
Robert St BN1 .... 189 A6
Robert Tressell Cl TN34 ... 136 E1
Robert Tressell
  Workshops **7** TN34 ... 159 F8
Robert's Hill TN36 .... 117 E8
Roberts Row TN31 .... 68 C5
Robertsbridge Com Coll
  TN32 .... 63 F4
Robertson Pas TN34 .... 159 F7
Robertson Rd BN1 .... 142 D1
Robertson St TN34 .... 159 F7
Robertson Terr **1** TN34 .. 159 F7
Robertsons Hill TN34 .... 160 B6
Robian Cl TN22 .... 55 A4
Robin Cl
  East Grinstead RH19 .... 1 F2
  Eastbourne BN23 .... 174 C2
Robin Ct TN39 .... 157 A3
Robin Davis Cl BN2 .... 143 E1
Robin Dene BN2 .... 164 E4
Robin Hill TN39 .... 156 D4
Robin Post La BN26 .... 151 B1
Robin Rd BN6 .... 72 D2
Robinia Lodge **1** BN1 ... 142 E2
Robins Row BN8 .... 101 A1
Robinson Rd BN9 .... 179 C8
Robinsons Ct BN22 .... 185 C6
Roborough Cl BN22 .... 185 A4
Robsack Ave TN38 .... 135 E2
Robsack Wood
  Cty Prim Sch TN38 ..... 135 E2
Rochdale Rd TN1 .... 8 C6
Rochester Cl
  Eastbourne BN20 .... 188 C8
  2 Hove BN3 .... 163 D6
Rochester Ct **3** BN3 .... 163 D6
Rochester Gdns BN3 ...... 163 D6
Rochester Ho TN6 .... 26 C1
Rochester Rd **4** TN37 ... 136 B2
Rochester St BN2 .... 164 D5
Rochester Way TN6 .... 26 B1
Rochford Way BN25 .... 180 B6
Rock Channel TN31 .... 93 C5
Rock Channel Quay TN31 .. 93 C5
Rock Cl Hastings TN35 ... 137 D4
  2 Southwick BN42 ... 17 B1
Rock Cotts TN5 .... 17 B1
Rock Gr BN2 .... 164 E4
Rock La TN35 .... 137 D7
Rock Pl BN2 .... 189 A4
Rock St BN2 .... 164 E4
Rock Villa Rd TN1 .... 8 A4
Rock's Hill TN35 .... 114 E7
Rock-A-Nore Par TN34 ... 160 B4
Rock-A-Nore Rd TN34 .... 160 B3
Rockall Dr BN27 .... 129 A2
Rockhurst Dr BN20 .... 184 B6
Rockington Way TN6 .... 38 B8
Rocklands Cotts BN27 .... 131 B5
Rocklands La TN35 .... 160 C5
Rockmead Rd TN35 .... 138 E4
Rocks Hill TN22 .... 64 E6
Rocks La TN22 .... 55 F7
Rocks Park Cty Prim Sch
  TN22 .... 78 B8
Rocks Park Rd TN22 .... 78 B8
Rocks The RH19 .... 11 D6
Rocky La RH16, RH15 ...... 50 D1
Roderick Ave
  Peacehaven BN10 .... 178 B7
  Peacehaven BN10 .... 178 C8
Roderick Ave N BN10 ..... 167 C2
Rodmell Ave BN2 .... 177 D5
Rodmell CE Prim Sch BN7 .. 146 E1
Rodmell Ct **5** BN25 .... 180 C4
Rodmell Pl BN1 .... 143 A6
Rodmell Rd
  Royal Tunbridge Wells TN1 .. 8 A2
  Seaford BN25 .... 181 B2

Rodmill Dr BN21 .... 184 D6
Rodmill Rd BN21 .... 184 D5
Rodney Cl BN23 .... 185 F7
Rodwell TN6 .... 26 C1
Roebuck St **18** TN34 .... 160 B4
Roedale Rd BN1 .... 143 B1
Roedean Cl TN39 .... 157 A5
Roedean Cres BN2 .... 165 A4
Roedean Hts BN2 .... 165 A4
Roedean Path BN2 .... 165 A3
Roedean Rd Brighton BN2 164 F4
Royal Tunbridge Wells
  TN1, TN2 .... 8 A1
Roedean Sch BN2 .... 165 C3
Roedean Terr BN2 .... 165 B3
Roedean Vale BN2 .... 165 B3
Roedean Way BN2 .... 165 B3
Roehaath BN8 .... 75 F4
Roffrey Ave BN22 .... 173 D1
Rolfe Dr RH15 .... 73 D3
Romaine Cl RH15 .... 73 D5
Roman Cl BN25 .... 180 B6
Roman Cres BN42 .... 161 E8
Roman Rd Hove BN3 .... 162 D6
  Southwick BN42 .... 161 E8
Roman Way
  Southwick BN42 .... 161 E8
  Uckfield TN22 .... 78 E7
Romans Way BN24 .... 174 E6
Romany Cl BN41 .... 162 B8
Romford Rd TN2, TN12 .... 9 F7
Romney Cl BN25 .... 181 C4
Romney Rd
  Polegate BN26 .... 173 B7
  Rottingdean BN2 .... 177 A5
Romney St BN2 .... 185 C5
Romsey Cl BN1 .... 143 C2
Rookery Cl BN9 .... 168 E2
Rookery La TN36 .... 117 F7
Rookery The BN23 .... 174 C4
Rookery Way
  Haywards Heath RH16 ..... 50 E1
  Newhaven BN9 .... 168 F2
  Seaford BN25 .... 180 B5
Rookhurst Rd TN40 .... 157 F5
Rookley Cl TN2 .... 8 D2
Rookwood Cl TN22 .... 78 E8
Roopers TN3 .... 7 A4
Roosevelt Cl TN38 .... 136 B3
Rope Wlk Hailsham BN27 . 152 B8
  Rye TN31 .... 93 C6
Rope Wlk The TN18 .... 47 B5
Roper's Gate TN2 .... 7 E1
Rosary Ct RH15 .... 73 D2
Rose Cotts RH17 .... 34 A4
Rose Ct BN6 .... 97 E4
Rose Hill BN2 .... 189 B7
Rose Hill Cl BN1, BN2 ...... 189 A7
Rose Hill Ct BN1 .... 189 A7
Rose Hill Sch TN4 .... 7 E5
Rose Hill Terr BN1 .... 189 A7
Rose Walk Cl BN9 .... 179 C7
Rose Wlk BN25 .... 180 F4
Rose Wlk The BN9 .... 179 C7
Rosebarn Cl RH15 .... 73 C1
Rosebery Ave
  Eastbourne BN22 .... 173 E1
  Woodingdean BN2 .... 165 C8
Rosedale Pl BN22 .... 173 D3
Rosedene Cl BN22 .... 165 E6
Rosefield Cotts TN32 ...... 65 F1
Rosehill Wlk TN1 .... 8 A2
Roselands Bexhill TN39 .. 156 F6
  Sedlescombe TN33 .... 88 E1
Roselands Ave
  Eastbourne BN22 .... 185 C5
  Wellbrook TN20 .... 39 F1
Roselands Ct BN22 .... 185 C5
Roselands City Inf Sch
  BN22 .... 185 B5
Roseleigh Gdns RH17 ...... 51 F3
Rosemary Cl
  Haywards Heath RH17 ...... 50 B4
  Peacehaven BN10 .... 167 C1
Rosemary Dr BN43 .... 140 C1
Rosemary La
  Shellies Green TN35 ...... 138 D6
  Stonecrouch TN5 .... 32 A5
Rosemount Cl BN25 .... 180 A6
Rosetti Rd BN24 .... 175 D4
Roseveare Rd BN22 .... 185 C6
Rossdale TN2 .... 8 D5
Rosslyn Ave BN43 .... 161 A7
Rosslyn Rd BN43 .... 161 A7
Rotary Lodge BN1 .... 143 E6
Rotary Point BN41 .... 141 B1
Rothbury Rd BN3 .... 162 D7

Rother Ave BN26 .... 173 F5
Rother Cl Burwash TN19 ..... 62 B6
  Crowborough TN6 .... 38 A7
Rother Ct TN39 .... 157 B6
Rother Rd BN25 .... 181 A2
Rother View TN19 .... 62 B7
Rotherfield Ave
  Bexhill TN40 .... 157 D4
  Eastbourne BN22, BN23 .. 174 A4
  Hastings TN34 .... 160 B5
Rotherfield Cl BN1 .... 143 B6
Rotherfield Cres BN1 ...... 143 B5
Rotherfield La TN20 .... 39 F4
Rotherfield Rd TN6 .... 38 E8
Rotherhill Rd TN6 .... 38 A7
Rotherhurst La TN6 .... 39 B6
Rothermead TN20 .... 39 F1
Rotherview TN32 .... 64 C5
Rothley Chase RH16 .... 50 F4
Rothsay Rd TN38 .... 159 B7
Rothwell Cl BN9 .... 179 A7
Rotten Row BN7 .... 146 B8
Rottingdean CE Prim Sch
  BN2 .... 177 A6
Rottingdean Pl BN2 .... 165 F4
Rottingdean Rd BN23 ...... 185 D8
Rotyngs The BN2 .... 165 F2
Rough Brow BN25 .... 181 A4
Rough Field RH19 .... 1 D4
Rough The BN8 .... 76 C7
Round Hill Rd **2**
  BN1, BN2 .... 164 B8
Round Hill St **3** BN2 ...... 164 B8
Roundacres Way TN40 ...... 157 E6
Roundel The TN37 .... 136 D5
Roundhay Ave BN10 .... 178 E6
Roundhills Cres BN2 .... 164 B8
Roundhill Rd TN2 .... 8 D1
Roundhouse Cotts TN21 ... 82 D7
Roundway BN1 .... 143 E5
Roundwood La RH16 ...... 50 F8
Roundwood Rd TN37 ...... 136 B5
Rowan Ave
  Eastbourne BN22 .... 173 D3
  Hove BN3 .... 141 E1
Rowan Cl Hastings TN37 .. 136 D6
  Haywards Heath RH16 ..... 51 B4
  Heathfield TN21 .... 82 A5
  Portslade-by-Sea BN41 ... 141 A1
  Seaford BN25 .... 181 C3
Rowan Gdns TN40 .... 157 F6
Rowan Tree Rd TN2 .... 7 F5
Rowan Way BN2 .... 165 E4
Rowan's Ct **1** BN7 ...... 123 C1
Rowandean Ct BN2 .... 177 C4
Rowborns TN33 .... 112 C6
Rowe Ave BN10 .... 178 B7
Rowe Ave N BN10 .... 178 B8
Rowsley Rd BN20 .... 188 D7
Royal Alexandra Hospl for
  Sick Children The BN1 .. 189 F6
Royal Ashdown Forest
  Golf Course BN18 .... 12 A1
Royal Chase TN4, TN1 ...... 7 F4
Royal Cres BN2 .... 164 C4
Royal Crescent Mansions **10**
  BN2 .... 164 C4
Royal Crescent Mews **8**
  BN2 .... 164 C4
Royal Dr BN25 .... 180 E6
Royal George Par BN43 .. 140 C1
Royal George Rd RH15 ..... 72 F3
Royal Mews TN38 .... 159 A6
Royal Military Rd TN36 .. 118 A8
Royal Oak La TN22 .... 56 B8
Royal Par
  Eastbourne BN22 .... 185 C4
  Eastbourne BN22 .... 185 D5
Royal Pavilion BN1 .... 189 A5
Royal Sovereign View
  BN23 .... 185 F6
Royal Sussex Cres BN20 .. 184 B5
Royal Sussex Cty BN7 ...... 146 D8
Royal Sussex Cty Hospl
  (General) BN2 .... 164 D4
Royal Terr **4** BN2 ...... 164 C4
Royal Victoria Place Sh Ctr
  TN2 .... 8 B2
Royles Cl BN2 .... 177 A6
Royston Cl BN20 .... 183 A1
Royston Gdns TN40 .... 157 F6
Rudyard Cl BN2 .... 156 B8
Rudyard Kipling
  Cty Prim Sch BN2 ...... 165 E7
Rudyard Rd BN2 .... 165 E8
Rue De Bayeux TN33 ...... 112 D5
Ruffet Ct TN2 .... 7 E1
Rufus Cl BN2 .... 123 C1
Rugby Cl BN25 .... 181 B4
Rugby **5** BN2 .... 164 E4

Rugby Pl BN2 .... 164 E4
Rugby Rd BN1 .... 143 A1
Rumbolds La RH16 .... 50 D2
Rumsey Ct TN6 .... 25 F1
Rusbridge La **3** BN7 ...... 123 E1
Rush Ct **4** BN22 .... 185 B3
Rushers Cross TN20 .... 40 E5
Rushes The RH16 .... 51 C4
Rushetts TN3 .... 6 F4
Rushey Cl BN8 .... 124 E5
Rushlake Cl BN1 .... 143 B5
Rushlake Cres BN21 .... 184 D6
Rushlake Rd BN1 .... 143 E5
Rushlye Cl TN3 .... 22 C4
Rushmere Rise TN38 ...... 135 E1
Rushwood Cl RH16 .... 51 B4
Ruskin Rd Hove BN3 .... 162 F8
  Willingdon BN20, BN22 ... 173 B1
Rusper Rd Brighton BN1 .. 143 D4
  Eastbourne BN20 .... 184 B6
Ruspers RH15 .... 73 D2
Russell Cotts **4** BN21 ... 184 E4
Russell Cres **2** BN1, BN3 189 F7
Russell Ct **5** TN34 .... 160 A3
Russell Mews **17** BN1 ... 163 E5
Russell Pl BN1 .... 189 F5
Russell Rd BN1 .... 189 F5
Russell Row BN7 .... 123 C3
Russell Sq BN1 .... 189 F5
Russet St TN34 .... 159 F8
Russet Cl BN26 .... 173 C6
Rusthall Grange TN4 .... 7 D4
Rusthall High St TN4 .... 7 C4
Rusthall Pk TN4 .... 7 D4
Rusthall Rd TN4 .... 7 D4
Rustic Cl BN10 .... 167 B1
Rustic Rd BN10 .... 167 B2
Rustington Ct BN20 ...... 188 F8
Rustington Rd BN1 .... 143 A5
Rustlings Cl RH16 .... 51 B5
Rustwick TN4 .... 7 D4
Rutherfords Bsns Pk
  TN33 .... 113 B7
Rutland Cl BN21 .... 184 D3
Rutland Ct
  3 Eastbourne BN23 .. 174 E1
  Hove BN3 .... 162 F6
Rutland Gdns BN3 .... 162 F7
Rutland Rd BN3 .... 163 A7
Rutley Cl TN32 .... 64 C5
Ruxley Ct BN23 .... 174 D2
Rydal Cl TN4 .... 7 E5
Rydal Dr TN4 .... 7 E5
Rydal Way BN21 .... 174 C4
Ryde Cl BN3 .... 141 D1
Ryde Rd BN2 .... 164 D7
Ryders TN3 .... 7 A4
Rye Cl Polegate BN26 ...... 173 C7
  Saltdean BN2 .... 177 F6
  Seaford BN25 .... 181 C4
Rye Golf Links TN31 ...... 94 B2
Rye Harbour Nature Reserve
  TN31 .... 94 B1
Rye Ind Est TN31 .... 93 D4
Rye Rd Four Throws TN18 ... 46 D8
  Hastings TN35 .... 137 D5
  Iden TN30, TN31 .... 70 A8
  Rye Foreign TN31 .... 69 E2
Rye St BN22 .... 185 D6
Rye Sta TN31 .... 93 B6
Ryecroft **12** Brighton BN2 . 164 F5
  Haywards Heath RH16 ..... 50 E3
Ryefield Cl BN21 .... 184 C7
Ryelands Dr BN2 .... 143 D3
Rylstone Rd BN20 .... 185 C4
Rymers Cl TN1 .... 7 E3
Rymill Rd TN38 .... 136 A3
Ryst Wood Rd RH18 .... 12 B1

Sackville Cl
  East Grinstead RH19 ...... 1 C3
  Lewes BN7 .... 123 C1
Sackville Coll RH19 ...... 1 F1
Sackville Ct Bexhill TN40 .. 157 D4
  3 East Grinstead RH19 ... 10 F8
Sackville Gdns
  East Grinstead RH19 ...... 1 C3
  Hove BN3 .... 162 F6
Sackville La RH19 .... 1 C3
Sackville Rd Bexhill TN39 . 157 B3
  Eastbourne BN22 .... 173 F2
  Hailsham BN27 .... 152 C6
  Hove BN3 .... 162 F6
Sackville Sch RH19 .... 2 A1
Sackville Trad Est BN3 ... 163 B8
Sacred Heart RC Prim Sch
  TN35 .... 160 D5
Sacred Heart Sch TN5 ...... 29 D5
Saddler's Ct **6** TN38 ...... 159 B6
Saddlers Cl RH15 .... 73 D1
Sadler Way BN2 .... 164 F6

Sadlers Way BN8 .... 124 D4
Saffron Cl BN43 .... 140 C1
Saffron Gdns BN26 .... 170 F3
Saffrons Ct BN21 .... 184 E2
Saffrons Mead BN20 .... 184 F2
Saffrons Pk BN20 .... 184 E1
Saffrons Rd BN21 .... 184 E1
Saffrons The RH15 .... 72 F5
Saints Hill TN11 .... 6 A8
St Agnes Rd RH19 .... 1 E2
St Andrew's CE Inf Sch
  BN22 .... 185 D6
St Andrew's CE Prim Sch
  BN3 .... 163 B6
St Andrew's Ct BN9 .... 179 B7
St Andrew's Dr BN25 ...... 180 B6
St Andrew's La **11** BN7 ... 123 D1
St Andrews Rd RH15 .... 73 D3
St Ann's Cl **3** BN2 ...... 164 C4
St Anne's Cl TN40 .... 157 D5
St Anne's Cres BN7 ...... 123 B1
St Anne's Ct
  9 Brighton BN2 .... 164 C4
  6 Brighton BN2 .... 189 F7
St Anne's Gdns BN6 .... 98 A1
St Anne's Ho **7** BN1 ...... 189 F7
St Anne's Rd BN21 .... 184 F4
St Anne's Sch BN7 .... 146 B8
St Annes Gn TN19 .... 62 A6
St Anne Rd BN22 .... 173 B3
St Annes Well Ho **7** BN3 163 D6
St Anthony's Ave BN23 ... 185 E8
St Anthonys BN8 .... 124 E6
St Aubyn's Cres BN41 ...... 162 B7
St Aubyn's Mead BN2 ...... 177 A5
St Aubyn's Rd
  Eastbourne BN22 .... 185 B3
  Portslade-by-Sea BN41 ... 162 A7
  Southwick BN41 .... 162 A7
St Aubyns S BN3 .... 163 A5
St Augustine Cl RH17 ...... 51 F3
St Augustine's Cl TN39 .. 156 F3
St Barnabas
  CE Prim Sch TN1 .... 8 B5
St Barnabas' Cl TN1 .... 8 B5
St Bartholomew's
  CE Prim Sch BN1 .... 189 A7
St Bede's Prep Sch BN20 . 188 E7
St Bede's Sch BN27 .... 151 A8
St Bernadette's
  RC Prim Sch BN1 .... 142 E2
St Brelades BN21 .... 185 B2
St Catherine's Cl TN37 ... 159 D8
St Christopher's Rd BN6 .. 97 A6
St Christopher's Sch
  BN3 .... 163 A6
St Christopher's (Trng Coll,
  Dr Barnardo's Home) TN2 8 D4
St Clement's Caves
  TN34 .... 160 A4
St Clement's Ct BN21 ...... 184 D6
St Clements Pl **5** TN38 ... 159 C6
St Crispians BN25 .... 180 D3
St Crispians Ct BN25 ...... 180 D3
St Cuthmans Cl BN20 ...... 164 F6
St David's Ave TN40 .... 157 C5
St David's Ct BN10 .... 178 B8
St David's Rd TN4 .... 8 A6
St Davids Cl BN22 .... 173 D4
St Dominic Cl TN38 .... 159 A8
St Edmund's Rd RH16 ...... 50 F3
St Edward's Cl RH19 .... 1 C1
St Elizabeth's BN25 .... 180 F4
St Francis Chase TN39 ... 157 A5
St Francis Cl RH16 .... 50 F2
St George's La BN6 .... 97 B5
St George's Mews BN1 ... 189 A6
St George's Pk TN2 .... 16 F8
St George's Pl
  Brighton BN1 .... 189 A6
  Hurstpierpoint BN6 ...... 97 B5
St George's Rd
  Bexhill TN39, TN40 ...... 157 C5
  Brighton BN2 .... 164 D4
  Eastbourne BN22 .... 185 B4
  Hastings TN34 .... 160 A5
St George's Sch TN2 .... 9 A5
St George's Terr **5** BN2 .. 164 C4
St Georges Vineyard TN21 . 80 F3
St Giles CE Prim Sch RH17 33 C6

St Giles Cl
  Shoreham-by-Sea BN43 .. 161 B8
  Winchelsea TN36 .... 117 E7
St Gregory Cl BN20 .... 188 E8
St Gregory's Catholic
  Comp Sch TN4 .... 8 A7
St Helen's Ave TN34 ...... 136 E3
St Helen's Cres
  Hastings TN34 .... 136 E2
  Hove BN3 .... 141 D3
St Helen's Ct TN34 ...... 136 E2
St Helen's Down TN34 ... 137 A3
St Helen's Dr BN3 .... 141 D3
St Helen's Park Rd TN34 .. 136 E3
St Helen's Rd
  Brighton BN2 .... 164 D7
  Hastings TN34, TN37 ...... 136 E3
St Helena's Cl **1** BN21 ... 184 E4
St Helens Wood Rd
  TN34 .... 136 E5
St Heliers Ave BN3 .... 162 E7
St James' Ave TN40 .... 157 D6
St James' CE Inf Sch TN2 ... 8 C4
St James' CE Jun Sch TN2 . 8 C4
St James' Cl TN40 .... 157 C7
St James' Cres TN40 ...... 157 D7
St James' Ho **15** BN2 ... 189 B5
St James La TN22 .... 35 C4
St James' Pk TN1, TN2 ...... 8 C5
St James' Rd
  Bexhill TN40 .... 157 C6
St James Rd
  Eastbourne BN22 .... 185 C4
St James' Rd
  Royal Tunbridge Wells
    TN1, TN2 .... 8 C5
St James St BN7 .... 146 C8
St James Wlk BN8 .... 75 E1
St James's Ave BN21 ...... 189 B5
St James's Ct TN1 .... 8 B4
St James's Rd
  East Grinstead RH19 ...... 1 D1
  Hastings TN34 .... 136 F1
St James's St BN2 .... 189 B5
St James's Street Mews
  BN2 .... 189 B5
St John Bank BN8 .... 100 D8
St John St **4** BN7 ...... 123 D1
St John the Baptist
  RC Prim Sch BN2 .... 164 D5
St John's Ave RH15 .... 72 F4
St John's CE Prim Sch
  Crowborough TN6 ...... 25 C4
  Royal Tunbridge Wells TN4 8 A5
St John's Cl
  Crowborough TN6 ...... 25 E3
  East Grinstead RH19 ...... 1 E2
  South Chailey BN8 ...... 100 C7
St John's Dr BN24 .... 174 E6
St John's Hill **2** BN7 ... 123 C1
St John's Ho BN20 .... 188 F8
St John's Mount BN2 ...... 189 B5
St John's Pk TN4 .... 8 A8
St John's Pl Brighton BN2 . 189 B5
  10 Hove BN3 .... 162 F6
St John's Rd Bexhill TN40 . 157 D6
  Crowborough TN6 ...... 25 D4
  East Grinstead RH19 ...... 1 E2
  Eastbourne BN20 .... 188 F8
  Hastings TN37 .... 159 C7
  Haywards Heath RH16 ..... 50 E2
  Hove BN3 .... 162 E6
  Polegate BN26 .... 173 A6
  Royal Tunbridge Wells
    TN1, TN2 .... 8 A6
  Seaford BN25 .... 180 E2
St John's Sch BN2 .... 164 D5
St John's Terr **3** BN7 ... 123 C1
St Johns CE Prim Sch TN4 .. 8 B7
St Johns Cl RH15 .... 73 A3
St Johns Rd RH15 .... 73 A3
St Joseph's Cl BN3 .... 163 A8
St Joseph's
  RC Cty Prim Sch BN2 ... 143 C1
St Joseph's
  RC Prim Sch
    RH16 .... 50 E4
St Joseph's Trad Est BN3 363 A8
St Josephs Way RH16 ...... 50 E4
St Julian's La BN43 .... 161 C7
St Julians CE Prim Sch
  BN6 .... 97 A6
St Keyna Ave BN3, BN41 .. 162 D6
St Kitts TN39 .... 157 A2
St Laurence Cl BN10 ...... 167 A1
St Lawrence CE Prim Sch
  BN6 .... 97 A6
St Lawrence Rd TN39 ...... 157 B7
St Lawrence Way TN6 ...... 97 A7
St Leonard's Ave
  BN3, BN41 .... 162 C7
St Leonard's Gdns
  BN3, BN41 .... 162 C7

St Leonard's Pl BN20 .... 184 C3
St Leonard's Rd
  5 Brighton BN2 .... 164 C8
  Eastbourne BN21 .... 185 A3
  Hove BN3, BN41 .... 162 C7
  Newhaven BN9 .... 168 F2
St Leonards CE Prim Sch
  TN38 .... 159 A7
St Leonards Cl BN9 .... 168 F2
St Leonards Ct TN38 .... 159 A6
St Leonards Pk RH19 .... 1 E1
St Leonards Rd TN40 ...... 157 C3
St Leonards Terr BN26 .... 172 F7
St Leonards (Warrior
  Square) Sta TN38 .... 159 C7
St Louie Cl BN42 .... 162 A8
St Lucia TN39 .... 157 A2
St Luke's CE Inf Sch TN4 .... 8 C7
St Luke's Cty Inf Sch
  BN2 .... 164 C6
St Luke's Cty Jun Sch
  BN2 .... 164 C6
St Luke's La BN9 .... 179 C7
St Luke's Rd
  Brighton BN2 .... 164 C6
  Royal Tunbridge Wells TN4 .. 8 B6
St Luke's Terr BN2 .... 164 C6
St Lukes Ct RH15 .... 73 A3
St Margaret CE Prim Sch
  BN6 .... 98 D3
St Margaret's Ave RH19 ..... 1 F6
St Margaret's Pl BN1 .... 189 F5
St Margaret's Rd
  East Grinstead RH19 .... 1 F3
  Hastings TN37 .... 159 D7
St Margaret's Rise BN25 .. 180 A6
St Margaret's Terr TN37 .. 159 D7
St Margarets BN2 .... 177 A5
St Margarets Cres TN39 .. 156 B8
St Margarets Terr TN31 ... 93 C5
St Mark's CE Prim Sch
  Brighton BN2 .... 164 E5
  Hadlow Down TN22 .... 57 C5
  Royal Tunbridge Wells TN4 .. 7 A3
St Mark's Rd TN2 .... 16 F7
St Mark's St BN2 .... 164 E4
St Marks Cl TN39 .... 156 D5
St Marks Field TN22 .... 57 B5
St Martin's Flats **6** BN2 .. 164 C7
St Martin's La **4** BN7 .... 146 C8
St Martin's Pl BN2 .... 164 C7
St Martin's St BN2 .... 189 B8
St Martins TN33 .... 112 D5
St Martins CE Prim Sch
  BN2 .... 164 C8
St Martins Cres BN9 .... 168 D1
St Martins Rd BN22 .... 173 D3
St Mary Magdalen
  RC Prim Sch BN1 .... 163 E5
St Mary Magdalen's
  RC Prim Sch TN40 .... 157 F6
St Mary Magdalene St
  BN2 .... 189 B8
St Mary Star of the Sea
  RC Prim Sch TN37 .... 159 D8
St Mary the Virgin
  CE Prim Sch TN7 .... 13 D4
St Mary's CE Sch RH19 ...... 1 D2
St Mary's Cl
  Cackle Street TN31 .... 90 A2
  Ticehurst TN5 .... 31 D1
  Willingdon BN22 .... 173 B2
St Mary's Cnr **3** BN21 .. 184 D3
St Mary's Cotts
  Battle TN33 .... 112 E3
  Bexhill TN39 .... 156 F8
  4 Eastbourne BN20 .... 184 D3
St Mary's Ct
  5 Eastbourne BN21 ... 184 D3
  6 Hastings TN37 .... 159 C7
St Mary's Farmhouse
  TN33 .... 112 E3
St Mary's Gdns TN33 ...... 112 E3
St Mary's La
  Bexhill TN39 .... 156 F8
  Speldhurst TN3 .... 7 A8
  Ticehurst TN5 .... 31 D1
St Mary's Pl BN2 .... 189 B5
St Mary's RC Prim Sch
  Crowborough TN6 .... 26 A2
  Portslade-by-Sea BN41 ... 162 B7
St Mary's Rd
  Burgess Hill RH15 .... 72 F2
  Eastbourne BN21 .... 184 D4
  Hastings TN34 .... 160 A5
St Mary's Rd W RH15 ..... 72 E4
St Mary's Sch
  Bexhill TN40 .... 157 E6
  Maynard's Green TN21 .... 82 A1
St Mary's Sq **17** BN22 . 184 D4

St Mary's Terr
  Battle TN33 .... 112 F3
  Hastings TN34 .... 160 A5
St Mary's Villas TN33 ..... 112 E3
St Mary's Wlk BN27 .... 152 C7
St Mary-in-the-Fields
  TN20 .... 40 B2
St Marys TN21 .... 80 E7
St Marys Ave BN27 .... 152 C7
St Marys Garth TN22 ...... 56 C4
St Marys Pl **3** BN43 ... 161 A6
St Matthew's Dr TN38 .... 136 C1
St Matthew's Gdns TN38 . 136 B1
St Matthew's High Brooms
  CE Prim Sch TN4 .... 8 B8
St Matthew's Rd TN38 .... 136 B1
St Matthews Ct BN2 ...... 164 C5
St Mellion CI BN27 .... 151 F8
St Michael's Cty Prim Sch
  TN7 .... 14 B5
St Michael's Pl
  Brighton BN1 .... 163 E6
  8 Hastings TN34 ...... 159 E7
St Michael's Rd
  Portslade-by-Sea BN41 ... 162 B7
  Royal Tunbridge Wells TN4 .. 8 B2
St Michael's Terr BN7 .... 123 D3
St Michaels Cl TN6 .... 38 B8
St Michaels Rd RH19 .... 1 E2
St Nicholas' CE Jun Sch
  BN41 .... 162 B8
St Nicholas Ct RH16 ...... 51 A6
St Nicholas La **13** BN7 . 123 D1
St Nicholas Lodge BN1 ... 189 F5
St Nicholas Pl **2** BN43 . 161 A6
St Nicholas Rd
  Brighton BN1 .... 189 F6
  Portslade-by-Sea BN41 ... 162 B7
St Nicolas CI BN24 .... 175 B6
St Nicolas & St Mary
  CE Sch BN43 .... 161 A8
St Olive's CI TN21 .... 81 C7
St Pancras Gdns BN7 ..... 146 B8
St Pancras Gn BN7 .... 145 E5
St Pancras RC Prim Sch
  BN7 .... 123 B1
St Pancras Rd BN7 .... 146 B8
St Patrick's Cres TN40 ... 157 C5
St Patrick's Rd BN3 .... 163 A7
St Paul's CE Prim Sch
  Brighton BN2 .... 189 F6
St Paul's CE Prim Sch
  Hastings TN37 .... 136 D1
St Paul's Cl RH16 .... 50 F5
St Paul's Ct
  Hastings TN37 .... 159 D8
  Rusthall TN4 .... 7 C4
St Paul's Pl TN37 .... 159 D8
St Paul's RC Sec Sch RH16 . 50 F5
St Paul's Rd TN37 .... 136 C1
St Paul's St Brighton BN2 . 189 B8
  Rusthall TN4 .... 7 C4
St Pauls CE Inf Sch TN4 .... 7 B4
St Pauls CE Jun Sch TN4 .... 7 B4
St Pauls Cl BN22 .... 173 D3
St Peter & St Paul
  CE Prim Sch TN40 .... 157 C4
St Peter's Ave BN10 ...... 178 A8
St Peter's CE Prim Sch TN2 . 8 C3
St Peter's CI Hove BN3 ... 141 F2
St Peter's Cres TN40 ...... 157 D5
St Peter's Cty Inf Sch
  BN41 .... 162 B7
St Peter's Mews TN40 .... 157 D5
St Peter's Pl BN1, BN2 ... 189 A6
St Peter's RC Prim Sch
  BN43 .... 161 A8
St Peter's RC Sch RH19 ..... 1 C1
St Peter's Rd
  Hastings TN37 .... 159 C8
  Portslade-by-Sea BN41 ... 162 B7
  Seaford BN25 .... 180 E5
St Peter's St
  Brighton BN1 .... 189 A7
  Royal Tunbridge Wells TN4 .. 8 B2
St Peters Meadow TN6 ... 39 A7
St Peters Pl BN7 .... 123 C1
St Peters Rd RH15 .... 73 A4
St Peters Row TN3 .... 6 A5
St Philip's Ave BN22 ...... 185 B5
St Philip's RC Prim Sch
  BN22 .... 185 B5
St Philip's Ct TN1 .... 8 D6
St Philips Mews **8** BN3 . 162 F7
St Richard's Ct BN3 .... 141 D1
St Richard's Flats BN41 ... 162 B7
St Richard's RC Sch TN40 . 157 E4
St Richard's Rd BN41 ..... 162 B7
St Richards Ho **3** TN38 . 159 C7

St Richards Rd TN6 .... 38 A7
St Saviour's Rd TN38 ..... 158 F6
St Saviours Ct **1** BN1 ... 164 B8
St Stephens Ct TN1 .... 8 B5
St Swithun's CI RH19 .... 1 F1
St Swithun's La **1** BN7 . 146 C8
St Swithun's Terr **5** BN7 . 146 C8
St Thomas TN39 .... 157 A2
St Thomas a' Becket
  RC Inf Sch BN21 .... 184 F5
St Thomas a' Becket
  RC Jun Sch BN21 .... 184 F5
St Thomas Ct **2** BN7 ... 123 E1
St Thomas of Canterbury Ct
  TN20 .... 40 A2
St Thomas's CE Prim Sch
  TN3 .... 15 D2
St Thomas's Rd TN34 ..... 160 A5
St Thomas's St TN36 ..... 117 F7
St Vincent's Ct BN2 ...... 165 A3
St Vincent's Sch TN38 ... 158 F7
St Vincents Flats TN37 ... 136 B4
St Vincents Pl BN20 .... 184 E1
St Vincents Rd TN38 ...... 158 F7
St Wilfred's Ct **5** RH16 . 50 E4
St Wilfred's Pl BN25 ...... 181 B3
St Wilfreds Rd RH15 .... 73 B4
St Wilfrid's CE Prim Sch
  RH16 .... 50 E4
St Wilfrid's Gn BN27 ...... 152 C8
St Wilfrid's Way RH16 .... 50 E4
St Wilfrids RC Prim Sch
  RH15 .... 50 E4
Salcey CI TN38 .... 135 E2
Salehurst CE Prim Sch
  TN32 .... 64 B4
Salehurst Gdns TN38 ..... 135 D2
Salehurst Rd BN20, BN21 . 184 C4
Salisbury CI BN22 .... 173 C2
Salisbury Rd
  Bexhill TN39, TN40 .... 157 B5
  Eastbourne BN20 .... 188 C8
  Hastings TN37 .... 136 C1
  Hove BN3 .... 163 C6
  Langton Green TN3 .... 6 F3
  Royal Tunbridge Wells TN4 . 8 C8
  Seaford BN25 .... 180 E3
Salisbury Terr TN21 .... 81 B8
Sally Ct **3** BN22 .... 185 B3
Salomons Rd TN4 .... 7 C4
Saltcote Mews TN31 .... 93 C7
Saltdean CI TN39 .... 156 E3
Saltdean Cty Prim Sch
  BN2 .... 177 B6
Saltdean Dr BN2 .... 177 B5
Saltdean Park Rd BN2 .... 177 C5
Saltdean Vale BN2 .... 177 D6
Saltdean Way TN39 .... 156 D3
Salters La TN14 .... 160 B4
Saltwood Rd BN25 .... 181 C4
Salvador CI BN23 .... 185 F7
Salvington Cres TN34 .... 156 F4
San Feliu Ct RH19 .... 2 B2
San Jose CI TN35 .... 160 C6
Sancroft Rd BN20 .... 184 B3
Sanctuary The BN20 ...... 184 B4
Sand Hill La BN8 .... 104 B8
Sand Rd TN3 .... 20 A4
Sandbanks CI BN27 .... 152 A5
Sandbanks Gdns BN27 ... 152 B5
Sandbanks Gr BN27 ...... 152 B6
Sandbanks Rd BN27 ...... 152 A6
Sandbanks Way BN27 .... 152 B6
Sandbrook BN6 .... 97 F3
Sanders Ho BN3 .... 162 E8
Sanderstead **1** BN2 ... 164 F5
Sandfield Rd TN11 .... 6 A7
Sandgate CI BN25 .... 181 A4
Sandgate Rd BN1 .... 143 A2
Sandhaves Hill RH19 .... 2 A4
Sandhill La Boarshead TN6 . 26 E7
  Churches Green
  BN27, TN21 .... 109 B6
Sandhurst Ave Pembury TN2 . 9 B6
  Woodingdean BN2 .... 144 D1
Sandhurst CI
  Royal Tunbridge Wells TN1 . 8 C6
  Sandhurst Cross TN18 ..... 47 A4
Sandhurst Cty Prim Sch
  TN18 .... 47 C5
Sandhurst Gdns TN34 .... 136 F6
Sandhurst Ho TN2 .... 8 D5
Sandhurst La TN39 .... 156 B6
Sandhurst Pk TN1 .... 8 C6
Sandhurst Rd
  TN1, TN2, TN4 .... 8 D6
Sandore CI BN25 .... 181 A4
Sandore Rd BN25 .... 181 A4
Sandown CI
  Eastbourne BN23 .... 174 B4
  Royal Tunbridge Wells TN2 . 8 F6

Sandown Court Com Coll
  TN2 .... 8 F5
Sandown Ct BN3 .... 141 D1
Sandown Cty Prim Sch
  TN35 .... 137 C4
Sandown Gr TN2 .... 8 F6
Sandown Pk TN2 .... 8 F6
Sandown Rd
  Brighton BN2 .... 164 D7
  Hastings TN35 .... 137 C3
  Southwick BN42 .... 161 E8
Sandown Way TN40 .... 157 E6
Sandpiper Wlk BN23 ...... 174 C2
Sandridge TN6 .... 25 F1
Sandringham CI
  East Grinstead RH19 ...... 11 A8
  Hove BN3 .... 142 A3
  Seaford BN25 .... 181 A6
Sandringham Dr BN2 ..... 164 D8
Sandringham Hts TN38 ... 135 D3
Sandringham Lodge **15**
  BN3 .... 163 C6
Sandrock Hall TN34 .... 136 F5
Sandrock Hill TN33 .... 135 A4
Sandrock Ho TN2 .... 8 D4
Sandrock Pk TN34 .... 136 F5
Sandrock Rd TN2 .... 8 C4
Sandrocks Way RH16 ..... 50 E2
Sandwich Dr TN38 .... 158 F8
Sandwich St BN22 .... 185 C6
Sandy CI TN37 .... 136 E5
Sandy Cross Cotts TN21 .. 82 A5
Sandy Cross La TN21 ..... 82 B5
Sandy La
  Coleman's Hatch TN7 ..... 23 D6
  East Grinstead RH19 .... 1 F1
  Framefield TN22 .... 79 A7
  Lions Green TN21 .... 81 E2
Sandy Vale RH16 .... 50 E2
Sanshaw Ct BN21 .... 184 E3
Santa Cruz Dr BN23 ...... 185 F7
Santer Ho TN18 .... 45 E8
Sanyhils Ave BN1 .... 142 F7
Saunders CI
  Hastings TN34 .... 160 A5
  Uckfield TN22 .... 78 A8
Saunders Hill BN1 .... 143 D7
Saunders Park Rise **3**
  BN2 .... 143 C1
Saunders Park View BN2 . 143 C1
Saunders Rd TN4 .... 7 E1
Saunders Way TN31 ...... 95 A2
Savill Rd RH16 .... 51 A8
Sawyard Cotts TN22 ...... 53 C5
Sawyers CI RH15 .... 73 D1
Saxby CI BN23 .... 174 E1
Saxby Rd Bexhill TN39 .. 157 A5
  Burgess Hill RH15 .... 72 D4
Saxon CI BN2 .... 177 D6
Saxon Ct Hastings TN37 . 159 C8
  Hove BN3 .... 162 D6
Saxon La BN25 .... 180 E2
Saxon Mount Sch TN38 . 158 F7
Saxon Pl BN21 .... 184 C6
Saxon Rd Hastings TN35 . 137 D3
  Hove BN3 .... 162 D6
  Newhaven BN9 .... 179 C7
Saxon Rise TN40 .... 157 E4
Saxon St TN37 .... 159 C6
Saxonbury **16** BN22 ... 189 B6
Saxonbury CI TN6 .... 25 F2
Saxonhurst Ct TN37 ..... 136 B4
Saxons TN39 .... 156 F3
Saxonwood Rd TN33 .... 112 C5
Sayerland La BN26 .... 173 A8
Sayerland Rd BN26 ...... 173 A8
Sayers The **5** RH19 ..... 1 C1
Scamps Hill RH16 .... 51 C6
Scanlon CI BN20 .... 184 C2
Scarborough Rd BN1 .... 142 D1
Scarletts Cl TN22 .... 78 B7
Scaynes Hill CE Prim Sch
  RH17 .... 51 F3
Sceptre **2** BN1 .... 142 E2
Schofield Way BN23 ...... 185 F7
School CI
  Burgess Hill RH15 .... 72 F2
  1 Southwick BN42 .... 161 E7
School Cotts
  East Chiltington BN7 .... 100 B3
  Maresfield TN22 .... 55 B4
  School Field BN8 .... 101 E5
School Hill
  Barcombe Cross BN8 .... 101 E4
  Lamberhurst TN3 .... 20 B6
  Maresfield TN22 .... 55 B4
  Old Heathfield TN21 ...... 82 D5
  Winchelsea TN36 .... 117 E8
School La
  Ashurst Wood RH19 ...... 11 E6
  Blackboys TN22 .... 80 A6

School La
  Crowborough, Blackness
  TN6 .... 25 F1
  Crowborough, St John's
  TN6 .... 25 D4
  Danehill RH17 .... 34 B5
  Hadlow Down TN22 .... 57 B5
  Nutley TN22 .... 35 C5
  Peasmarsh TN31 .... 69 B2
  Polegate BN26 .... 173 A7
  Pyecombe BN45 .... 119 C6
  Saltdean BN2 .... 177 C6
School Path BN8 .... 101 D4
School Pl TN40 .... 158 A5
School Rd Hastings TN35 . 137 C3
  Hove BN3 .... 162 F8
School Rise Brighton BN2 . 164 E6
  Royal Tunbridge Wells TN2 . 7 F1
School Terr TN32 .... 64 C5
Schwerte Way **5** TN37 . 159 E7
Science Park Rd BN1 .... 144 B7
Science Park Sq BN1 .... 144 B6
Scotland St BN2 .... 189 B6
Scotney Castle TN3 .... 20 D3
Scotney Castle Gdns TN3 . 20 D3
Scotsford Cl TN21 .... 59 F1
Scotsford Hill TN20 .... 40 E1
Scotsford Rd TN21 .... 59 F2
Scott Rd BN3 .... 162 F7
Scotts Acre TN31 .... 94 E2
Scotts Way TN2 .... 16 E8
Scrace Hill Terr RH16 ..... 73 F8
Scraper's Hill BN8 .... 128 A8
Scrase Lodge RH15 ...... 73 D3
Scutes Cl TN34 .... 137 A3
Sea Ho **10** BN42 ...... 161 E7
Sea Rd Bexhill TN40 ...... 157 D3
  Camber TN31 .... 94 F2
  Fairlight Cove TN35 ..... 139 A5
  Hastings TN38 .... 158 F6
  Pevensey Bay BN24 ..... 175 D5
  Winchelsea Beach TN36 . 118 B7
Seabeach La BN22 .... 185 C5
Seabourne Rd
  Bexhill TN40 .... 158 A6
  Bexhill TN40 .... 158 B5
Seacliffe BN10 .... 177 F3
Seafield Cl BN25 .... 181 B5
Seafield Rd BN3 .... 163 B6
Seaford Cty Prim Sch
  BN25 .... 180 E4
Seaford Head Com Coll
  (Lower) BN25 .... 180 F2
Seaford Head Com Coll
  (Upper) BN25 .... 181 A2
Seaford Rd
  Eastbourne BN20 .... 185 C5
  Hove BN3, BN41 .... 162 C6
  Newhaven BN9, BN25 ... 179 F8
Seaford Sta BN25 .... 180 E3
Seagrave Cl BN25 .... 180 A6
Seagrove Way BN25 ..... 180 F5
Searle Ave BN10 .... 178 E6
Seasaw Way BN2 .... 164 F7
Seaside BN22, BN23 .... 185 C5
Seaside Rd
  Eastbourne BN21, BN22 . 185 B3
  Hastings TN38 .... 158 F6
Seaside Rdbt BN22 ...... 185 D7
Seaside Way TN38 .... 158 F6
Seaview Ave BN10 ...... 178 E6
Seaview Cotts BN27 ..... 129 D3
Seaview Est BN42 .... 161 F7
Seaview Rd
  Newhaven BN9 .... 168 F1
  Peacehaven BN10 .... 178 E6
  Woodingdean BN2 .... 165 B8
Seaview Terr
  Icklesham TN36 .... 116 E5
  Rye TN31 .... 93 C5
Seaville Dr
  Eastbourne BN23 .... 185 D8
  Pevensey Bay BN24 ..... 175 D5
Second Ave Bexhill TN40 . 157 F5
  Camber TN31 .... 94 F2
  Hove BN3 .... 163 C6
  Newhaven BN9 .... 179 C6
Second Rd BN10 .... 178 A7
Sedgebrook Gdns TN34 . 136 E2
Sedgewick Rd TN39, TN40 . 157 C6
Sedlescombe CE Prim Sch
  TN33 .... 88 B3
Sedlescombe Gdns TN38 . 136 B2
Sedlescombe Rd N TN37 . 136 B4
Sedlescombe Rd S TN38 . 136 B1
Sefton Chase TN6 .... 26 A3
Sefton Rd BN41 .... 140 F3
Sefton Way TN6 .... 26 A3

Segrave CI BN7 .... 123 B2
Selba Dr BN2 .... 143 E3
Selborne PI BN3 .... 163 C7
Selborne Rd BN3 .... 163 C6
Selby Ct RH16 .... 50 E3
Selby Gdns TN22 .... 78 D5
Selby Rd
  Eastbourne BN21 .... 184 D5
  Uckfield TN22 .... 78 D6
Selby Rise TN22 .... 78 D5
Selham CI BN1 .... 143 D6
Selham Dr BN1 .... 143 D6
Selham PI BN1 .... 143 D6
Selhurst Rd BN2 .... 165 E6
Sellbourne Pk TN3 .... 17 C4
Selmeston CI TN34 .... 136 D1
Selmeston Ct **2** BN25 ... 180 C4
Selmeston Ho **6** BN21 .. 184 D4
Selmeston Rd BN2 .... 164 F6
Selmeston Rd BN21 .... 184 C7
Selmestone Rd BN2 .... 164 F5
Selsey CI BN1 .... 143 E6
Selsfield CI BN21 .... 184 D6
Selsfield Dr BN2 .... 143 D3
Selwyn Dr BN21 .... 184 E4
Selwyn Ho **9** BN21 ...... 184 E4
Selwyn Park Ct **8** BN21 .. 184 E4
Selwyn Rd BN21 .... 184 E4
Semley Rd Brighton BN1 ... 143 A1
  Hassocks BN6 .... 97 E4
Sempstead La TN31, TN32 .. 66 C4
Senlac Ct TN33 .... 112 D5
Senlac Gdns TN33 .... 112 E4
Senlac Green TN22 .... 78 E8
Senlac PI TN3 .... 15 C7
Senlac Rd BN9 .... 179 D7
Senlac Way TN37 .... 136 C5
Sergison CI RH16 .... 50 D5
Sergison Rd RH16 .... 50 D5
Setfords Field BN8 .... 75 E1
Sevelands CI BN2 .... 164 F7
Seven Acre CI TN37 .... 136 A5
Seven Dials BN1 .... 189 F7
Seven Sisters Ctry Pk
  BN25 .... 182 A2
Seven Sisters Rd BN22 ...... 173 C3
Sevenfields BN6 .... 72 D4
Sevenoaks Rd BN23 .... 174 D2
Seville St BN2 .... 164 D4
Sewell Ave TN40 .... 157 C5
Seymour Ho **5** BN2 ...... 164 D4
Seymour Sq **3** BN2 ...... 164 D4
Seymour St **4** BN2 ...... 164 D4
Shaftesbury Ct TN22 .... 78 C8
Shaftesbury PI BN1 .... 164 A8
Shaftesbury Rd
  Brighton BN1 .... 189 A8
  Royal Tunbridge Wells TN4 .. 8 A5
Shakespeare St BN3 .... 163 A8
Shakespeare Wlk BN23 .... 174 D2
Shalesbrook La RH18 .... 12 A1
Shalfleet CI BN23 .... 174 B3
Shandon CI TN2 .... 8 C4
Shands BN6 .... 97 F3
Shanklin CI BN23 .... 174 B4
Shanklin Ct
  7 Brighton BN2 .... 164 E6
  Hove BN3 .... 141 D1
Shanklin Rd BN2 .... 167 B1
Shannon CI BN10 .... 167 B1
Shannon Way BN23 .... 185 F8
Sharp's Cnr TN21 .... 106 E8
Sharpthorne Cres BN41 ... 141 C1
Sharrow Ct **9** RH16 .... 50 E5
Shaw The TN2 .... 8 C2
Shawcross Ho **10** BN1 .. 142 E2
Shawfield TN6 .... 26 B2
Shaws Cnr **6** TN31 .... 67 B7
Shedden Ct TN21 .... 82 A8
Sheddingdean Bsns Ctr
  RH15 .... 72 F5
Sheddingdean CI RH15 ..... 73 A4
Sheddingdean CI RH15 ..... 72 F4
Sheddingdean Cty Inf Sch
  RH15 .... 73 A5
Sheddingdean Cty Prim Sch
  RH15 .... 73 A5
Sheen Rd BN22 .... 185 B4
Sheep Pen La **3** BN25 .. 181 A3
Sheep Plain TN6 .... 37 D8
Sheep Wlk BN2 .... 165 F1
Sheepbell CI BN41 .... 141 B3
Sheepfair BN7 .... 123 A2
Sheepfold The BN10 .... 167 C1
Sheepsetting La TN21 .... 81 E7
Sheepstreet La TN19, TN5 .. 43 E5
Sheerwater Cres TN34 .... 136 D4
Sheffield Mill La TN22 .... 53 C8

Sheffield Park Gdns TN22 .. 53 D5
Sheffield Park Sta TN22 .... 53 A4
Sheffield Park Way BN22 . 174 A4
Sheiling Rd TN6 .... 25 E3
Shell La **8** TN34 .... 160 A3
Shelldale Ave BN41 .... 162 B7
Shelldale Cres BN41 .... 162 B7
Shelldale Rd BN41 .... 162 B8
Shelley CI BN7 .... 123 B1
Shelley Ct **4** RH16 .... 50 D5
Shelley Pk **4** TN21 .... 82 A7
Shelley Rd
  East Grinstead RH19 .... 1 D1
  Hove BN3 .... 162 F7
  Ringmer BN8 .... 124 D5
Shelley Wood BN6 .... 72 D4
Shelly Wlk **3** BN2 .... 174 E2
Shenfield Way BN1 .... 143 B3
Shenstone RH16 .... 51 B8
Shepham Ave BN2 .... 177 D6
Shepham La BN24, BN26 .. 173 C8
Shepherd St **3**
  TN37, TN38 .... 159 C6
Shepherd's CI TN39 .... 156 D4
Shepherd's Hill TN7 .... 23 D8
Shepherd's Way TN35 ..... 138 E4
Shepherds CI
  Eastbourne BN22, BN26 .. 173 F3
  Piddinghoe BN9 .... 168 B2
  Ringmer BN8 .... 124 E5
Shepherds Cot BN10 .... 167 D2
Shepherds Croft BN1 .... 142 C4
Shepherds Ct TN35 .... 138 E4
Shepherds Mead RH15 .... 72 F4
Shepherds Way
  Ringmer BN8 .... 124 E5
  South Chailey BN8 .... 100 C7
  Uckfield TN22 .... 78 C5
Shepherds Wlk
  Crowborough TN6 .... 26 C1
  Hassocks BN6 .... 97 F5
  Royal Tunbridge Wells TN4 .. 8 D4
Shepherdsgrove La RH19 ... 3 A4
Sheppard Way BN41 .... 141 A3
Sheppey Wlk BN27 .... 129 A3
Sheppeys RH16 .... 50 D2
Shepway The BN25 .... 181 B4
Sheraton Ct BN21 .... 184 F2
Sherborne Ct **3** BN21 .. 184 D4
Sherborne CI Hove BN3 .. 141 D3
Sherborne Tunbridge Wells 7 .. 8 D2
Sherborne Way BN3 .... 141 D3
Sheridan CI RH19 .... 1 C1
Sheridan Mansions BN3 .. 163 A8
Sheridan Terr BN3 .... 163 A8
Sheriff's La TN6 .... 39 D7
Sheringham Ct TN32 .... 65 E2
Sherrington Rd BN2 .... 165 F8
Sherwood CI TN34 .... 136 F1
Sherwood Ho RH16 .... 50 C5
Sherwood Gn BN27 .... 152 B6
Sherwood Park
  Cty Prim Sch TN2 .... 8 D6
Sherwood Rd
  Royal Tunbridge Wells TN4 .. 8 E5
  Seaford BN25 .... 180 F4
Sherwood Rise BN25 .... 180 F4
Sherwood Way TN2 .... 8 D6
Shinewater Ct BN23 .... 174 B3
Shinewater Cty Prim Sch
  BN23 .... 174 A3
Shinewater La BN23 .... 174 B4
Shinewater Rdbt BN23 .... 174 B1
Shingle Ct TN38 .... 135 E7
Shingle Rd BN43 .... 161 A6
Ship St Brighton BN1 ...... 189 F5
  East Grinstead RH19 ...... 10 E8
  Newhaven BN9 .... 179 C8
Ship Street Gdns BN1 ..... 189 F5
Shipley La TN39 .... 156 D3
Shipley Rd BN2 .... 165 E7
Shipwreck Heritage Ctr (Mus)
  TN34 .... 160 B3
Shipyard La TN31 .... 93 C5
Shirlea View TN33 .... 112 E4
Shirley Ave BN3 .... 142 B2
Shirley CI BN43 .... 161 D8
Shirley Dr Hastings TN37 .. 136 B4
  Hove BN3 .... 142 C2
Shirley Gdns TN4 .... 7 C5
Shirley Gr TN4 .... 7 C5
Shirley Rd BN3 .... 163 C8
Shirley St BN3 .... 163 C8
Shirleys BN6 .... 98 E2
Shoreham Beach
  Cty Fst Sch BN43 .... 161 A6
Shoreham By-Pass
  BN41, BN42, BN43, BN15 140 D2
Shoreham Coll BN43 .... 161 D7
Short Brow BN25 .... 181 A4

Short Brow CI BN22 .... 173 B3
Shortdean PI BN21 .... 184 D4
Shortgate Rd BN2 .... 143 F4
Shortlands CI BN22 .... 173 C1
Shotters RH15 .... 72 E1
Shovellstrode La RH19 ..... 11 D8
Showfields Rd TN2 .... 7 F1
Shropshire Ct BN20 .... 184 B7
Shrub La TN19 .... 62 C7
Shrublands Ct TN2 .... 8 C4
Shrublands The TN39 ...... 156 E3
Sicklehatch La TN21 .... 82 B2
Sidcup CI BN23 .... 174 D2
Sidehill Dr BN41 .... 140 F2
Sidley Cty Prim Sch TN39 157 C7
Sidley Gn TN39 .... 157 C6
Sidley Rd BN22 .... 185 C5
Sidley St TN39 .... 157 C7
Sidney CI TN2 .... 16 F8
Silchester Rd TN37, TN38 . 159 C7
Sillwood Ct **7** BN1 ...... 163 E5
Sillwood Hall **6** BN1 ... 163 E5
Sillwood PI **9** BN1 ...... 163 E5
Sillwood Rd **7** BN1 ..... 163 E5
Sillwood St BN1 .... 163 E5
Silva CI TN40 .... 158 A6
Silvan Rd TN38 .... 135 E4
Silver Bank Cotts TN32 .... 64 B8
Silver Birches RH16 .... 51 A4
Silver Hill TN19 .... 45 B1
Silverdale BN6 .... 98 B3
Silverdale Ave BN3 .... 163 D7
Silverdale Ct **7** BN27 .. 152 B8
Silverdale Cty Prim Sch
  TN38 .... 136 B3
Silverdale La TN4 .... 8 B6
Silverdale Rd
  Burgess Hill RH15 .... 73 C2
  Eastbourne BN20 .... 184 F1
  Hove BN3 .... 163 D7
  Royal Tunbridge Wells TN4 .. 8 B6
Silverden Cotts TN18 .... 46 F4
Silverhill Ave TN37 .... 136 C4
Silverlands Rd **1** TN37 .. 136 B2
Silvester Rd TN40 .... 157 C5
Silwood CI TN2 .... 8 E7
Simmonds Ct TN4 .... 7 B4
Simons CI TN6 .... 26 A1
Singleton Rd BN1 .... 143 A6
Singleton Way RH15 .... 73 C1
Sinnock Sq **17** TN34 ... 160 B4
Sir Henry Fermor
  CE Prim Sch TN6 .... 26 A2
Six Bells Mews TN31 .... 67 C5
Skinner's La TN33 .... 133 D8
Skinners' Sch The TN4 .... 8 A6
Skippers Hill Manor
  Prep Sch TN20 .... 58 B7
Skyline View BN10 .... 167 D1
Slade The TN3 .... 20 A3
Sleeches Cross TN3 .... 17 B2
Sleepers Stile Rd TN5 ...... 19 B1
Slider's La TN22 .... 53 A7
Slides The TN38 .... 135 F3
Slimbridge Rd RH15 .... 72 F3
Slindon Ave BN10 .... 178 D6
Slindon Cres BN23 .... 174 E1
Slinford CI BN2 .... 164 D5
Slindon CI La TN21, TN33 . 109 F7
Sloane Ct **4** BN2 .... 164 C5
Sloe La BN26 .... 171 A3
Slonk Hill Rd BN43 .... 140 A1
Slugwash La RH17 .... 74 B7
Smeatons La TN36 .... 118 B5
Smith CI TN33 .... 133 B5
Smithy's CI TN37 .... 136 C5
Smolletts RH19 .... 10 C8
Smugglers CI BN26 .... 170 F3
Smugglers La TN6 .... 25 D5
Smugglers Way TN35 ...... 138 F4
Snape View TN5 .... 29 F4
Snatt's Rd TN22 .... 55 C1
Snednore BN7 .... 145 F5
Snipe CI TN2 .... 9 E8
Snowdon CI BN23 .... 174 D3
Snowdrop La RH16 .... 51 C4
Snowflakes La RH16 .... 51 D6
Soames Ct RH15 .... 72 F4
Solomon's La TN32 .... 87 C4
Solway BN27 .... 129 A2
Solway Ave BN3 .... 142 F7
Somerhill Ave BN3 .... 163 D7
Somerhill Ct **10** BN3 .... 163 D7
Somerhill Cty Jun Sch
  BN3 .... 163 D6
Somerhill Lodge **3** BN3 163 D6
Somerhill Rd BN3 .... 163 D6
Somerset Ct
  Eastbourne BN23 .... 174 E1
  3 Hove BN3 .... 163 C7
Somerset Point **1** BN2 . 164 C4

Somerset Rd TN4 .... 8 A6
Somerset St BN2 .... 164 C5
Somerset Villas TN3 .... 15 C7
Somerville CI BN23 .... 185 E2
Somerville Gdns TN4 .... 7 F4
Sompting CI BN2 .... 164 F7
Sompting Ct **3** BN43 .. 161 B8
Sorrel CI BN23 .... 174 C3
Sorrel Dr BN23 .... 174 C3
South Ave Brighton BN2 .. 164 C5
  Eastbourne BN20 .... 184 B5
  Hurstpierpoint BN6 .... 97 A5
South Bank BN6 .... 97 E3
South Brooks Rd TN29 ..... 96 F2
South CI Beachlands BN24 175 F6
  Burgess Hill RH15 .... 72 E3
  Hailsham BN27 .... 152 B6
South Cliff Bexhill TN39 .. 156 F2
  Eastbourne BN20 .... 188 F8
South Cliff Ave
  Bexhill TN39 .... 156 E2
  Eastbourne BN20 .... 184 F1
South Cliff Tower BN20 ... 188 F8
South Cliffe **7** BN7 ..... 123 E1
South Coast Rd
  Peacehaven BN10, BN9 .. 178 D6
  Telscombe Cliffs
    BN10, BN2 .... 177 E4
South Ct BN7 .... 123 E1
South Downs BN7 .... 99 E5
South Downs Bsns Pk
  BN7 .... 123 E2
South Downs Rd BN7 ...... 123 D2
South Dr RH15 .... 72 E3
South Gr TN1 .... 8 A2
South La Newhaven BN9 .. 179 D7
  Wood's Corner TN32 .... 84 E2
South Lodge **3** BN2 ..... 164 F5
South Lodge CI RH15 .... 72 F4
South Lynn Dr BN21 .... 184 F4
South Malling CE Prim Sch
  BN7 .... 123 D1
South PI **3** BN7 .... 123 D1
South Point **7** BN43 ... 161 A6
South Rd Brighton BN1 ... 142 E1
  Hailsham BN27 .... 152 B6
  Haywards Heath RH16 ..... 50 E4
  Newhaven BN9 .... 179 D7
  Wivelsfield Green RH17 ... 74 D4
  South Rough BN6 .... 76 C7
  South Side TN21 .... 59 E1
  South St Brighton BN1 ... 189 F5
  Crowborough TN6 .... 25 F1
  Ditchling BN6 .... 98 D3
  East Hoathly BN8 .... 104 F4
  Eastbourne BN21 .... 185 A2
  Falmer BN1 .... 144 C6
  Hastings TN37 .... 159 C7
  Lewes BN7 .... 123 E1
  Mayfield TN20 .... 40 B2
  Portslade-by-Sea BN41 .. 141 A1
  Rotherfield TN6 .... 39 B8
  Seaford BN25 .... 180 E2
South Terr
  Broad Oak TN21 .... 59 E1
  Hastings TN34 .... 159 F8
  Westfield TN35 .... 114 E3
South Undercliff TN31 ...... 93 C5
South View Ditchling BN6 .. 98 E5
  10 Eastbourne BN21 . 184 E4
  1 South Heighton BN9 . 168 E2
  South View CI TN19 .... 62 A4
South View Rd
  Crowborough TN6 .... 25 E1
  Royal Tunbridge Wells TN4 .. 8 B8
  Turner's Green TN5 .... 29 F6
  South Way Lewes BN7 .. 123 E1
  Newhaven BN9 .... 179 D7
South Woodlands BN1 .... 142 E5
Southall Ave BN2 .... 143 D2
Southampton CI BN23 .... 185 F8
Southampton St BN2 ..... 189 B6
Southborough CE Prim Schs
  TN4 .... 7 F8
Southborne Rd BN22 ...... 185 C6
Southcourt Ave TN39 ..... 156 F2
Southdown Ave
  Brighton BN1 .... 143 A1
  Hastings TN34 .... 137 B3
  Lewes BN7 .... 146 A8
  Lower Willingdon BN20 ... 173 A3
  Peacehaven BN10 .... 178 E6
  Portslade-by-Sea BN41 .. 162 C8
Southdown CI
  Haywards Heath RH16 ..... 50 D2
  Newhaven BN9 .... 179 B6
  Southdown Cotts BN20 ... 173 B3
Southdown Ct
  3 Hailsham BN27 .... 152 C7
  Eastbourne BN26 .... 172 F6

Southdown Cty Jun Sch
  BN9 .... 179 C7
Southdown Ho **4** BN20 .. 184 F1
Southdown PI BN1 .... 143 A1
Southdown Rd
  Brighton BN1 .... 143 A1
  Eastbourne BN20, BN21 . 184 C7
  Newhaven BN9 .... 179 B6
  Portslade-by-Sea BN41 .. 141 A2
  Seaford BN25 .... 181 A2
  Southwick BN42 .... 161 E7
  Southease Sta BN9 .... 168 A7
Southeast Ct BN27 .... 152 C7
Southern Ave BN26 .... 173 B6
Southern Rd BN22 .... 173 F2
Southern Ring Rd BN1 .... 144 B6
Southfield RH16 .... 172 F5
Southfield Rd
  Royal Tunbridge Wells TN4 .. 8 A6
  Speldhurst TN3 .... 7 A7
Southfields TN5 .... 29 F6
Southfields Ct **5** BN21 . 184 F3
Southfields Rd BN21 .... 184 F3
Southfields Way TN4 .... 8 B8
Southgate TN4 .... 7 F3
Southlands RH19 .... 10 E7
Southlands Dr TN39 .... 157 A7
Southlands Ct **1** BN43 . 161 B8
Southlands General Hospl
  BN43 .... 161 B8
Southlands Rd TN39 .... 157 A7
Southmead CI TN20 .... 40 D3
Southmount BN1 .... 143 B1
Southon CI BN41 .... 140 F3
Southover CE Prim Sch
  BN7 .... 146 C8
Southover High St BN7 .. 146 C8
Southover PI BN2 .... 189 B7
Southover Rd BN7 .... 146 C8
Southover St BN2 .... 189 B6
Southridge Rd TN6 .... 37 E8
Southside Rise TN6 .... 37 E8
Southview RH17 .... 51 F3
Southview CI
  Crowborough TN6 .... 25 E1
  Southwick BN42 .... 140 E1
  Southview Dr TN22 .... 78 D8
Southview Rd
  Peacehaven BN10 .... 178 C8
  Southwater BN42 .... 161 E8
  Southwater CI BN2 .... 164 D6
  Southwater Rd TN37 .... 159 D8
Southway RH15 .... 72 D3
Southway Cty Jun Sch
  RH15 .... 72 D3
Southwick CI RH19 .... 1 D2
Southwick Ho BN42 .... 161 E7
Southwick St BN42 .... 161 E8
Southwick Sta BN42 ...... 161 E7
Southwood Ave TN4 .... 8 A6
Southwood CI TN38 .... 136 A1
Southwood Rd TN4 .... 7 B5
Sovereign CI
  Hastings TN34 .... 137 A4
  Seaford BN25 .... 181 A5
Sovereign Ct BN22 .... 185 C5
Sovereign Ctr BN22 .... 185 E6
Spa Ct BN3 .... 163 B5
Spa Golf Course TN4 .... 7 F2
Spa Ind Est TN2 .... 8 E8
Spa Valley Rly TN4 .... 7 D1
Spaldings The TN38 .... 135 E1
Spanish Ct RH15 .... 73 B4
Sparks Gdns TN33 .... 133 A6
Sparrow Way BN6 .... 72 D3
Sparrows Green Rd TN5 ... 29 F5
Sparrows The BN10 .... 167 D1
Spatham La BN6 .... 98 F4
Speldhurst CE Prim Sch
  TN3 .... 7 A7
Speldhurst Hill TN3 .... 7 B8
Speldhurst Rd
  Langton Green TN3 .... 6 F4
  Royal Tunbridge Wells
    TN3, TN4 .... 8 A8
Spencer Ave BN3 .... 141 D3
Spencer Mews **6** TN1 ... 8 A2
Spencer Rd BN21 .... 185 A2
Spencer's Mews **4** TN1 .. 8 B4
Spences Field BN7 .... 123 E2
Spences La BN7 .... 123 E2
Spicers CI RH15 .... 72 F5
Spindlewood Dr TN39 ... 156 C4
Spinnals Gr BN42 .... 161 D7
Spinney CI BN6 .... 97 D7
Spinney The Battle TN33 . 112 F3
  Bexhill TN39 .... 156 D3
  Burgess Hill RH15 .... 73 B5
  Hassocks BN6 .... 97 F5
  Hastings TN34 .... 136 E1

Spinney The
Haywards Heath
RH16, RH17 .... 50 D8
Hove BN3 .... 142 C3
Robertsbridge TN32 ...... 63 F3
Spinneys The
Heathfield TN21 .... 82 B6
Lewes BN7 .... 123 E2
Spital Rd BN7 .... 123 B1
Spithurst Rd BN8 .... 101 E6
Spode La TN8 .... 4 A7
Sponden La TN18 .... 47 A7
Sportcentre Rd BN1 ... 144 A6
Spotted Cow La TN22 ... 56 E5
Spout Hill TN5 .... 27 D1
Spray Hill TN3 .... 20 B4
Spray's La TN33, TN35 . 114 B4
Spring Cl BN20 .... 173 B1
Spring Copse RH19 ...... 1 D3
Spring Gdns
Brighton BN1 .... 189 A5
Glynde BN8 .... 147 F5
Lewes BN7 .... 123 D1
Rusthall TN4 .... 7 B4
6 Southwick BN42 ...... 161 E7
Spring Hill Northiam TN31 .. 67 B7
Saint's Hill TN11, TN3 ...... 6 A7
Spring Hill Wildfowl Pk
RH18 .... 11 A1
Spring La Bexhill TN39 .. 156 C5
Burwash TN19 .... 61 F6
Clayton BN6 .... 119 E8
Spring Lodge Cl BN23 . 174 E2
Spring Meadow RH18 ... 11 F1
Spring Park TN21 .... 82 A8
Spring St Brighton BN1 163 E5
Hastings TN37 .... 136 C1
Spring Steps TN36 ...... 117 F8
Spring Way RH19 .... 2 A4
Springate Rd BN42 ..... 161 F8
Springett Almshouses
TN18 .... 45 E8
Springett Ave BN8 ...... 124 D5
Springett Cotts BN8 ... 124 D5
Springfield RH19 .... 1 D4
Springfield Ave BN10 . 177 F4
Springfield Cl
Crowborough TN6 .... 26 B2
Westham BN24 .... 174 F6
Springfield Cotts
Cackle Street TN31 ...... 90 A2
Rotherfield TN6 .... 39 B8
Springfield Rd
Bexhill TN40 .... 157 C6
Brighton BN1 .... 164 A8
Eastbourne BN22 .... 185 B4
Groombridge TN3 .... 15 C7
Hastings TN38 .... 136 B1
Springfield Valley Rd
TN38 .... 136 B1
Springfields TN5 .... 31 E1
Springfields Farm Ind Est
RH17 .... 73 F5
Springhead TN2 .... 8 D5
Springhead Way TN6 .... 37 E8
Springside Wlk TN38 .. 135 F1
Springview Apartments
TN1 .... 8 D6
Springwood Rd TN21 .... 82 A8
Spruce Cl BN22 .... 173 D2
Spur Rd BN26 .... 173 B5
Spurway Pk BN26 .... 173 B5
Squab La BN27 .... 130 A5
Square The
Beachlands BN24 .... 175 F6
Brighton BN1 .... 142 E6
Cowden TN8 .... 4 B6
Hailsham BN27 .... 152 A7
Wadhurst TN5 .... 30 A4
Squirrel Cl Bexhill TN39 . 156 E5
Hastings TN38 .... 135 F3
Squirrel Way TN2 .... 8 E5
Stable Ctyd TN2 .... 23 A1
Stable Mews TN7 .... 136 C5
Stabledene Way TN2 ...... 9 D6
Stablefield TN35 .... 114 E4
Stables La **8** BN21 ..... 185 A3
Stacey's Cnr TN21 .... 85 A5
Stafford Ct **2** BN23 ... 174 E1
Stafford Cty Jun Sch
BN22 .... 185 A6
Stafford Ho **8** BN21 .. 184 F3
Stafford House F Ed Ctr
BN6 .... 98 A3
Stafford Rd Brighton BN1 . 163 E8
Royal Tunbridge Wells TN2 . 8 B4
Seaford BN25 .... 180 F3
Stafford Way BN6 .... 98 A3
Stag Rd TN2 .... 8 D8
Stainsby St **1** TN37 .. 159 C7
Stamford **6** RH16 ...... 50 D6

Station Rd
Plumpton Green BN7 ...... 99 E6
Polegate BN26 .... 173 A6
Portslade-by-Sea
BN3, BN41 .... 162 C7
Robertsbridge TN32 ...... 64 B4
Rockrobin TN5 .... 29 C6
Seaford BN25 .... 180 B5
Sharpthorne RH19 .... 21 A6
7 Southwick BN42 .... 161 E7
Stonegate TN5 .... 42 E5
Town Row TN6 .... 27 C1
Winchelsea TN36 .... 92 E1
Withyham TN7 .... 14 B5
Station Road Ind Est
BN27 .... 152 C6
Station St Brighton BN1 . 189 A6
7 Eastbourne BN21 .... 185 A3
Lewes BN7 .... 123 D1
Staveley Rd BN20 .... 188 E8
Steep Hill Brede La TN31 . 89 E2
Steep Rd TN20, TN6 ..... 38 D3
Steine Gdns BN2 .... 189 A5
Steine La BN1, BN2 ..... 189 A5
Steine St BN2 .... 189 A4
Stephen's Rd TN4 .... 8 B6
Stephens Cl BN8 .... 124 D5
Stephens Rd BN1 .... 143 B2
Stephenson Dr RH19 ... 10 F7
Stevens Dr TN39 .... 157 C7
Stevens Ct BN3 .... 162 E7
Stevenson Ct BN23 .... 174 E3
Stevenson Rd
Brighton BN2 .... 164 C5
1 Hastings TN37 ...... 136 B3
Stewards Inn La **3** BN7 . 146 C8
Stewart Rd TN4 .... 8 C7
Steyne Cl **4** BN25 ..... 180 F2
Steyne Cl **9** BN25 ..... 180 E2
Steyne Rd BN25 .... 180 F2
Steyne Villas BN1 ...... 143 B2
Steyne The BN25 .... 180 E2
Steyning Ave Hove BN3 . 141 F3
Peacehaven BN10 ...... 178 C7
Steyning Cl BN25 .... 181 C2
Steyning **7** BN3 .... 163 B7
Steyning Rd
Rottingdean BN2 .... 177 A5
Seaford BN25 .... 181 C2
Stiles The BN27 .... 152 C7
Stirling Cl Brighton BN1 . 189 A5
Seaford BN25 .... 181 C3
Stirling Ct RH15 .... 73 C4
Seaford BN25 .... 181 C3
Stirling Court Rd RH15 . 73 C4
Stirling Ct **5** BN3 ...... 163 C7
Stirling Pl BN3 .... 163 A6
Stirling Rd TN38 .... 135 F5
Stirling Way RH19 .... 2 B3
Stock Dale TN5 .... 138 F4
Stockland Green Rd TN3 . 7 B8
Stockleigh Rd TN38 .... 159 C7
Stocks Meadow TN35 . 133 B5
Stockwell Ct
Burgess Hill RH15 ...... 72 F3
1 Hackwell Rd RH19 .. 50 E3
Stockwell Rd RH19 ...... 10 E6
Stoddards La TN31 ...... 67 F6
Stoke Brunswick Sch RH19 . 11 E7
Stoke Cl BN25 .... 181 B3
Stoke Manor Cl BN25 . 181 B4
Stokes Cotts TN19 ...... 60 F3
Stokes Ho **4** TN39 .... 157 A4
Stone Cotts TN19 .... 19 F4
Stone Court La TN2 .... 9 E8
Stone Cross
Eastbourne BN24 .... 174 B5
Mayfield TN20 .... 39 F2
Stone Cross Cty Prim Sch
BN24 .... 174 B5
Stone Cross Rd
Crowborough TN6 .... 38 A7
Wadhurst TN5 .... 30 A4
Stone Pit La TN18 .... 47 E5
Stone Quarry Rd RH17 .. 34 D7
Stone Row TN6 .... 6 B5
Stone Row Cotts TN5 .... 6 D1
Stone St Brighton BN1 . 163 E5
12 Hastings TN34 ..... 159 F8
Royal Tunbridge Wells TN1 . 8 B4
Stone Works Cotts TN31 . 93 F3
Stonebeach Rise TN38 . 135 F7
Stonecott Cl TN6 .... 37 F8
Stonecroft Cl BN3 ...... 141 E4
Stonecross Rd BN2 .... 143 F4
Stonedene Cl RH18 ..... 12 B2
Stonefield Pl **2** TN34 . 159 F8
Stonefield Rd TN34 .... 159 F8
Stonefield Way RH15 ... 72 F5
Stonegate CE Prim Sch
TN5 .... 42 F5
Stonegate Rd BN23 ... 174 A4

Stonegate Ct TN5 .... 42 F5
Stonegate Rd TN5 ...... 30 C1
Stonegate Sta TN5 ..... 42 D3
Stonegate Way TN21 .. 82 B8
Stoneham Cl BN7 .... 123 C3
Stoneham Rd BN3 ...... 162 F7
Stonehouse Dr
Hastings TN38 .... 136 A2
Hastings, Beauport Park
TN33, TN38 .... 113 F1
Stonehurst Ct BN2 ..... 164 C6
Stonehurst La TN20, TN22 . 57 D7
Stoneleigh Ave BN1 ... 142 F6
Stoneleigh Cl
Brighton BN1 .... 142 F6
East Grinstead RH19 .... 1 F1
Stonelink Cl TN38 ...... 135 F7
Stonepark Dr RH18 ..... 12 A2
Stonepound Crossroads
BN6 .... 97 E4
Stonepound Rd BN6 .... 97 E4
Stonery Cl BN41 .... 141 A2
Stonery Rd BN41 .... 141 A2
Stonestile La TN34, TN35 . 136 F8
Stonewall Park Rd TN3 .. 6 F3
Stonewood Cl BN25 ... 181 C4
Stoney La Hailsham BN27 . 152 C7
Shoreham-by-Sea BN43 . 161 C8
Stoneywish Ctry Pk BN6 . 98 E3
Storrington Cl BN3 ..... 141 E2
Straight Half Mile TN22 . 55 B5
Strand TN31 .... 93 B5
Strand Ct TN31 .... 93 B5
Strand Hill TN36 .... 117 F7
Strand Meadow TN19 ... 62 B7
Strand The BN2 .... 165 A3
Stratford St TN1 .... 8 C5
Strathenden Ct **7** BN25 . 180 E2
Strathfield Cl BN26 ..... 50 F4
Strawberry Cl TN2 .... 16 E7
Strawberry Fields TN31 . 67 A7
Strawberry Way **7** 99 E6
Stream La
Sedlescombe TN33 ..... 88 C2
The Moor TN18 .... 46 A7
Stream Lane Cotts TN18 . 46 A7
Stream Pit La TN18 ...... 47 B6
Stream Pk RH19 .... 1 A3
Streamside Cl TN34 ... 136 E3
Streat Bostall BN6, BN7 . 121 C6
Streat La BN6 .... 99 C4
Streatfield Gdns TN21 .. 81 F8
Streatfield Ho TN22 ..... 78 C8
Streatfield Rd
Tilsmore TN21 .... 81 F8
Uckfield TN22 .... 78 B7
Streele View TN22 ...... 78 E8
Street End La
Broad Oak TN21 .... 59 E1
Broad Oak TN20 .... 59 E5
Street The
Framefield TN22 .... 79 B6
Kingston near Lewes BN7 . 145 E5
Sedlescombe TN33 ..... 88 E1
West Firle BN8 .... 148 B3
Westmeston BN6 .... 120 F8
Streetlands TN33 .... 88 E1
Stringer Way BN1 ...... 142 F3
Stringwalk The BN27 ... 152 C7
Stroma Gdns BN27 .... 128 F2
Strome Ho TN30 .... 157 C7
Strongs Pas **5** TN34 . 160 B4
Stroud Gate RH17 ...... 74 C5
Stroud Rd TN37 .... 136 C2
Stuart Ave BN21 .... 184 C6
Stuart Cl TN2 .... 16 E8
Stuart Way RH19 .... 10 F7
Stubb La TN31 .... 90 D2
Stubbygrove Cotts TN3 . 17 E4
Stud Cotts BN27 .... 151 A8
Studdens La RH17 ...... 108 D1
Sturdee Cl BN23 .... 185 F7
Sturdee Pl TN34 .... 160 A3
Sturton Pl BN27 .... 152 B7
Sudeley Pl BN2 .... 164 D4
Sudeley St BN2 .... 164 D4
Sudeley Terr **6** BN2 ... 164 D4
Suffolk Cl **5** BN22 ..... 185 C4
Suffolk Ho TN39 .... 157 C7
Suffolk St BN3 .... 162 F8
Sugar La RH17 .... 33 C4
Sugworth Cl RH16 ...... 50 D7
Sullington Cl BN2 ...... 143 F4
Sullington Way BN43 .. 161 A8
Sumach Cl BN22 .... 173 E2
Summer Cl BN41 .... 162 A7
Summer Ct BN20 .... 188 D7
Summer Hill TN38 ..... 159 A8
Summer Hill Rd TN39 . 156 F6
Summercourt BN27 ... 152 B8
Summerdale Rd BN3 .. 141 D2

Summerdown Cl BN20 . 184 D3
Summerdown La BN20 . 183 C1
Summerdown Rd BN20 . 184 D3
Summerfields Ave BN27 . 152 A8
Summerfold House Sch
RH15 .... 73 A4
Summerheath Rd BN27 . 152 B8
Summerhill Cl RH16 ..... 50 F7
Summerhill Dr RH16 .... 51 A7
Summerhill Grange RH16 . 50 F7
Summerhill La RH16 ..... 50 F7
Summerlands Rd BN22 . 173 C2
Summersdeane BN42 .. 140 F1
Summervale Rd TN2, TN4 . 7 E1
Sun La **7** TN34 .... 160 A3
Sun St BN7 .... 123 C1
Sunhill Ct TN2 .... 9 C6
Sunningdale Cl
Bexhill TN40 .... 157 E4
Hailsham BN27 .... 129 A1
Seaford BN25 .... 181 A2
Sunningdale Dr TN38 .. 158 F7
Sunninghill Ave BN3 .. 141 F2
Sunninghill Cl BN3 ..... 141 F2
Sunnybank TN5, TN19 .. 32 E3
Sunnybank Cl TN20 ..... 40 B2
Sunnycroft Cl RH17 ..... 51 A2
Sunnydale Ave BN1 .... 143 A6
Sunnydale Cl BN1 ...... 143 A6
Sunnyside Rd TN4 .... 7 C4
Sunnywood Dr RH16 ... 50 D3
Sunset
Beachlands BN24 .... 175 F6
Telscombe Cliffs BN10 . 167 B1
Sunstar La BN20 .... 172 E6
Sunte Ave RH16 .... 50 F7
Sunte Ct RH10 .... 178 D6
Surrenden Cl BN1 ...... 142 F4
Surrenden Cres BN1 ... 142 E4
Surrenden Holt BN1 .... 142 F3
Surrenden Lodge BN1 . 142 F2
Surrenden Pk BN1 ...... 143 A4
Surrenden Rd BN1 ...... 142 F3
Surrey Cl
Royal Tunbridge Wells TN2 . 16 F8
Seaford BN25 .... 180 D4
Surrey Ho **12** BN2 ...... 164 D4
Surrey Rd BN25 .... 180 C4
Surrey St BN1 .... 189 F6
Susan's Rd BN21 .... 185 A3
Susans Cl BN8 .... 105 A5
Sussex Ave BN27 ...... 152 B8
Sussex Chambers 8
TN34 .... 159 F8
Sussex Cl Bexhill TN39 . 156 F5
Hailsham BN27 .... 152 B8
Royal Tunbridge Wells TN2 . 8 C1
Sussex Ct
Eastbourne BN22 .... 185 B5
1 Haywards Heath RH16 . 50 E3
13 Hove BN3 .... 163 C6
Sussex Cty Cricket Gd
BN3 .... 163 C7
Sussex Eye Hospl BN2 . 164 D4
Sussex Gdns
East Dean BN20 .... 183 C1
Haywards Heath RH16 ... 51 B3
6 Eastbourne BN21 ... 185 A2
Telscombe Cliffs BN10 . 167 F3
Sussex House Ind Est BN3 162 F8
Sussex Hts **18** BN1 ... 163 E5
Sussex Mews
4 Brighton BN2 ...... 164 E4
16 Royal Tunbridge Wells
TN2 .... 8 A2
Sussex Nuffield Hospl
BN2 .... 165 C8
Sussex Pl BN2 .... 189 B6
Sussex Rd Hastings TN38 . 159 A6
Haywards Heath RH16 ... 50 E3
Hove BN3 .... 163 B5
Sussex Sq Brighton BN2 . 164 E4
17 Haywards Heath RH16 . 50 E3
Sussex Terr BN2 .... 189 B5
Sussex Toy & Model Mus
BN1 .... 189 A6
Sussex Way
Burgess Hill RH15 .... 72 E5
Telscombe Cliffs BN10 . 177 F3
Sutherland Ave TN39 .. 157 A4
Sutherland Cl **1** TN39 . 157 A4
Sutherland Rd
Brighton BN2 .... 164 C5
Royal Tunbridge Wells
TN1, TN2 .... 8 B3

Sutton Ave
　Peacehaven BN10 ..... 178 B7
　Seaford BN25 ..... 181 A3
Sutton Ave N BN10 ..... 178 B8
Sutton Cl BN2 ..... 144 E1
Sutton Cotts BN7 ..... 146 B3
Sutton Croft La 4 BN25 ..... 180 E3
Sutton Dro BN25 ..... 180 F4
Sutton Park Rd BN25 ..... 180 E3
Sutton Pl TN40 ..... 157 E4
Sutton Rd
　Eastbourne BN21 ..... 185 A3
　Seaford BN25 ..... 181 A3
Suttons Ind Pk TN36 ..... 118 A7
Suttons The Camber TN31 .. 95 A1
　Hastings TN38 ..... 135 F2
Swaine's Pas 6 TN34 ..... 160 B4
Swaines Way TN21 ..... 82 A6
Swainham La TN33 ..... 135 B4
Swainsthorpe Cl RH16 ..... 50 F3
Swallow Bank TN38 ..... 135 F2
Swallow Cl BN23 ..... 174 C2
Swallow Ct TN22 ..... 78 D5
Swallow Dr Battle TN33 .. 112 F4
　Royal Tunbridge Wells TN2 .. 8 F6
Swallows The BN10 ..... 167 B1
Swan Ave 9 TN34 ..... 160 A4
Swan Bsns Ctr BN27 ..... 152 D6
Swan Cl BN8 ..... 100 E7
Swan Rd BN27 ..... 152 D6
Swan Terr TN34 ..... 160 A4
Swanborough Dr BN2 ..... 164 F7
Swanborough Dro BN7 ..... 145 F4
Swanborough Hollow
　BN7 ..... 146 A4
Swanborough Pl BN2 ..... 164 F7
Swanley Cl BN23 ..... 174 D2
Swann Cl RH15 ..... 73 D3
Swannee Cl BN10 ..... 167 D1
Swans Ghyll RH18 ..... 11 E3
Swaylands Ave TN6 ..... 37 F7
Sweda Ct 13 BN2 ..... 164 D4
Sweeps Hill Cl TN2 ..... 9 D7
Sweethaws La TN6 ..... 37 C6
Sweetings La TN3 , TN5 ..... 19 D1
Sweetlands BN6 ..... 98 B5
Swife La TN21 ..... 60 D5
Swift Cl Crowborough TN6 .. 25 F1
　Uckfield TN22 ..... 78 D5
Swiftsden Cotts TN19 ..... 44 F6
Swinburne Ave BN22 ..... 173 C3
Swingate Cross BN27 ..... 129 C5
Swissland Hill RH19, RH7 .. 1 E7
Swynford Dr 1 TN38 ..... 136 A5
Sybron Way TN6 ..... 38 D8
Sycamore Cl Bexhill TN39 . 156 C4
　Eastbourne BN22 ..... 173 D3
　Hastings TN38 ..... 136 A1
　Heathfield TN21 ..... 82 B6
　Portslade-by-Sea BN41 ... 141 C3
　Seaford BN25 ..... 181 C3
　Woodingdean BN2 ..... 165 E8
Sycamore Cotts TN2 ..... 9 C6
Sycamore Ct TN22 ..... 78 D8
Sycamore Dr
　East Grinstead RH19 ..... 2 A1
　Hailsham BN27 ..... 152 B5
Sycamores The BN10 ..... 167 D1
Sydenham Cl TN40 ..... 157 D3
Sydney Cl TN37, TN38 .. 136 B3
Sydney Little Rd TN38 ... 135 D4
Sydney Rd
　Eastbourne BN22 ..... 185 B4
　Haywards Heath RH16 ..... 50 E6
Sydney St BN1 ..... 189 A6
Sydney Tidy Ho 6 BN2 ... 164 C6
Sylvan Cl RH16 ..... 51 B4
Sylvester Way BN3 ..... 141 C3
Symbister Rd BN41 ..... 162 C7
Syresham Gdns RH16 ..... 50 F4

Tackleway TN34 ..... 160 B4
Taddington Ho 2 BN22 .. 185 C4
Taddington Rd 1 BN22 .. 185 C4
Tainter's Brook TN22 ..... 78 E8
Talbot Cres BN11 ..... 143 D6
Talbot Pk TN2 ..... 8 D5
Talbot Rd TN18 ..... 45 F8
Talbot Terr BN7 ..... 123 C1
Tali Ash Dr TN37 ..... 136 C4
Talland Par 18 BN25 ..... 180 E2
Tamarack Cl BN2 ..... 173 D2
Tamerisk Stps 24 TN34 .. 160 B4
Tamworth Rd BN3 ..... 162 F7
Tan Yard Cotts TN36 ..... 117 F8
Tanbridge Rd BN23 ..... 174 F2
Tandridge Rd RH16 ..... 162 E6
Tangier La TN3 ..... 17 B6

Tanglewood Coppice
　TN39 ..... 156 C3
Tangmere Cl TN39 ..... 156 E3
Tangmere Rd BN1 ..... 143 A6
Tanhouse La TN31 ..... 68 F2
Tanners' Brook BN7 ..... 146 D8
Tanners Field RH17 ..... 74 A5
Tanners Way TN6 ..... 26 A1
Tanyard TN18 ..... 47 B5
Tanyard Ave RH19 ..... 11 A8
Tanyard Cotts
　Battle TN33 ..... 112 E3
　Buxted TN22 ..... 56 C1
Tanyard La
　Chelwood Common RH17 .. 34 C4
　Winchelsea TN36 ..... 117 F8
Tapsell's La TN5 ..... 29 D5
Tarner Rd BN2 ..... 189 B6
Tarragon Way BN43 ..... 140 C1
Tarring Cl BN9 ..... 168 D2
Tas Combe Way
　BN20, BN22 ..... 173 B2
Tate Cres RH15 ..... 72 F5
Taunton Gr BN2 ..... 144 A1
Taunton Pl BN2 ..... 144 A1
Taunton Rd BN2 ..... 143 F1
Taunton Way BN2 ..... 144 A1
Tavistock 8 BN21 ..... 185 A2
Tavistock Down BN1 ..... 143 C2
Tavistock & Summerhill Sch
　RH16 ..... 50 F7
Taylor Cl TN38 ..... 135 F4
Taylor St TN4 ..... 8 A8
Tea Garden La TN3, TN4 ..... 7 C2
Teal Cl TN38 ..... 135 E3
Teasley Mead TN3 ..... 5 C4
Tedder Rd TN4 ..... 8 B7
Tedder Terr TN35 ..... 137 D5
Teg Cl BN41 ..... 141 C2
Teknol Ho RH15 ..... 72 E2
Telegraph St 12 BN2 ..... 164 C4
Telford Rd TN38 ..... 136 A5
Telham Cl TN34 ..... 137 A5
Telham La TN33 ..... 112 E1
Telscombe Cliffs
　Cty Prim Sch BN10 ..... 178 A8
Telscombe Cliffs Way
　BN10 ..... 178 A8
Telscombe Pk BN10 ..... 167 C2
Telscombe Rd
　Eastbourne BN23 ..... 174 F2
　Peacehaven BN10 ..... 167 D2
Temple Gdns BN1, BN3 .. 163 E6
Temple Gr RH15 ..... 72 D4
Temple Grove Sch TN22 .. 36 E3
Temple St BN1 ..... 163 E6
Tenantry Down Rd BN2 .. 164 E8
Tenantry Rd BN2 ..... 164 D8
Tennis Cl BN27 ..... 152 B7
Tennis Rd BN3 ..... 162 E6
Tennyson Ct 5 RH16 ..... 50 D5
Tennyson Rise RH19 ..... 10 C8
Tennyson Wlk BN23 ..... 174 E3
Tenterden Cl BN23 ..... 174 D2
Tenterden Rise TN34 ..... 136 E2
Terminus Ave TN39 ..... 157 A3
Terminus Pl
　8 Brighton BN1 ..... 189 F7
　6 Hailsham BN27 ..... 152 C7
Terminus Rd Bexhill TN39 . 157 B3
　Brighton BN1 ..... 189 F7
　Eastbourne BN21 ..... 185 A3
Terminus St BN1 ..... 189 F6
Terrace Rd TN37 ..... 159 C7
Tescombe Grange BN10 .. 177 F3
Teynham Ho BN2 ..... 177 C4
Thackeray Cl BN23 ..... 174 E3
Thakeham Cl TN40 ..... 158 A6
Thalia Ho TN40 ..... 157 B4
Thames Cl BN2 ..... 189 B5
Thanet Way TN34 ..... 136 E2
Thatchers Cl RH15 ..... 73 D1
Thatchings The BN26 ..... 173 A5
Theaklen Dr TN38 ..... 136 B2
Theobalds Gn TN21 ..... 82 A5
Theobalds Rd RH15 ..... 73 D6
Theobold Ho 1 BN1 ..... 189 A6
Theodore Cl TN2 ..... 8 E7
Third Ave Bexhill TN40 ... 157 F6
　Hove BN3 ..... 163 B6
　Newhaven BN9 ..... 179 C6
Third Rd BN10 ..... 178 A7
Third St TN3 ..... 6 F3
Thirlmere Rd TN4 ..... 7 E5
Thomas Brassey Cl TN37 . 136 B5
Thomas Peacocke Com Coll
　TN31 ..... 93 B6
Thomas Peacocke Sch
　TN31 ..... 93 B6
Thomas St Lewes BN7 ..... 123 E2
　Royal Tunbridge Wells TN4 . 8 A5

Thomas Turner Dr BN8 .... 105 A5
Thompson Rd
　Brighton BN1 ..... 143 C1
　Newhaven BN9 ..... 168 F2
Thorn Cotts TN35 ..... 116 A4
Thornbank Cres TN39 .. 156 F3
Thornbush Cres BN41 ... 141 B3
Thorndean Rd BN2 ..... 143 D3
Thornden Cl TN17 ..... 49 A8
Thornden Ct TN17 ..... 49 A8
Thorne Cres TN39 ..... 133 E1
Thornfield Gdns TN2 ..... 8 F5
Thornhill Ave BN1 ..... 143 A7
Thornhill Cl BN1 ..... 141 E2
Thornhill Rise BN41 ..... 141 A4
Thornhill Way BN41 ..... 141 A3
Thorns The TN5 ..... 138 A8
Thornsdale 4 BN2 ..... 189 B6
Thornton Ct 5 BN22 ..... 185 B3
Thornwell Rd BN26 ..... 171 F7
Thornwood Cl BN22 ..... 173 E2
Thorny Cl TN21 ..... 82 A7
Thorpe Works TN4 ..... 7 F8
Three Gables TN22 ..... 35 C4
Three Oaks & Guestling Halt
　TN35 ..... 115 D2
Three Oaks La TN5 ..... 29 D7
Thurrock Cl BN20, BN22 .. 173 B4
Thyme Cl BN43 ..... 140 C1
Thyssel La TN31 ..... 67 B6
Tibbs Mill La TN22, TN6 .... 37 E2
Ticehurst Ave TN39 ..... 155 F5
Ticehurst CE Prim Sch
　TN5 ..... 43 D8
Ticehurst Cl TN39 ..... 155 F4
Ticehurst Rd BN2 ..... 164 F5
Tichborne Cotts RH16 ... 51 C6
Tichborne St BN1 ..... 189 A5
Tickerage La TN22 ..... 79 F6
Tidebrook TN5, TN20 ..... 40 F7
Tidebrook Gdns BN23 ..... 174 F2
Tideswell Rd BN21 ..... 185 A3
Tideway Sch &
　Sixth Form Ctr BN9 .. 179 B6
Tidy St BN1 ..... 189 A6
Tilbury Pl BN2 ..... 189 B5
Tilbury Way BN2 ..... 189 B6
Tile Barn Cl TN21 ..... 102 D8
Tile Barn Rd TN38 ..... 135 F4
Tilehurst Dr BN27 ..... 152 A8
Tilekiln La TN15 ..... 137 E4
Tilers Cl RH15 ..... 73 D3
Tilford Ct TN40 ..... 157 F6
Tilgate Cl Brighton BN2 .. 164 D6
　Eastbourne BN21 ..... 184 D7
Tilgate Dr TN39 ..... 156 D3
Tilley La BN27 ..... 131 E6
Tilling Green Cty Inf Sch
　TN31 ..... 93 A5
Tillingham Ave TN31 ..... 93 B6
Tillingham La TN31 ..... 92 A6
Tillingham View TN31 ..... 90 B5
Tillingham Way BN24 ... 174 A5
Tillington Rd BN2 ..... 164 F7
Tillington Terr TN35 ..... 160 C6
Tillstone Cl BN2 ..... 143 D2
Tillstone St BN2 ..... 189 B5
Tilsmore Cnr TN21 ..... 81 F7
Tilsmore Rd TN21 ..... 81 F7
Timber Yard Cotts BN7 ... 123 E1
Timberlaine Rd BN24 ... 175 C4
Timberley Rd BN27 ..... 173 D1
Timbers Cl BN27 ..... 152 C8
Tindal Cl RH15 ..... 73 C3
Tinker's La TN22 ..... 57 E3
Tinkers La TN5 ..... 31 E3
Tintern Cl Brighton BN1 .. 143 B1
　Eastbourne BN22 ..... 173 E3
Tisbury Rd BN3 ..... 163 C6
Titchfield Cl RH15 ..... 73 D1
Tithe Barn Field TN36 .... 116 F5
Titian Rd BN3 ..... 162 F7
Tiverton Dr TN40 ..... 157 E5
Tivoli 3 BN1 ..... 142 E2
Tivoli Cres BN1 ..... 142 D1
Tivoli Cres N BN1 ..... 142 D2
Tivoli Pl BN1 ..... 142 D2
Tivoli Rd BN1 ..... 142 D2
Tobago TN39 ..... 157 A2
Tobias Sch of Art RH19 ... 10 E6
Tolkien Rd BN2 ..... 174 F2
Toll Wood Rd TN21 ..... 106 F7
Tollgate
　Haywards Heath RH16 .. 51 B8
　Peacehaven BN10 ..... 167 B1
Tollgate Cty Jun Sch
　BN23 ..... 185 D7
Tollgate Gdns BN23 ..... 185 D7
Tollgate Lock TN31 ..... 93 B4
Tollgates TN33 ..... 112 B4
Tollwood Pk TN6 ..... 26 B1

Tollwood Rd TN6 ..... 38 B8
Tompset's Bank RH18 ..... 11 F1
Tonbridge Rd TN2, TN11 ..... 9 A7
Tonbridge Way TN31 ..... 94 E2
Tongdean Ave BN3 ..... 142 C2
Tongdean Ct BN1 ..... 142 D4
Tongdean La
　Brighton BN1, BN3 ..... 142 C4
　Brighton BN1 ..... 142 D4
Tongdean Rd BN3 ..... 142 C3
Tongdean Rise BN1 ..... 142 C4
Top Cross Rd TN40 ..... 158 A7
Top Dr TN22 ..... 55 A6
Top Rd RH19 ..... 21 B5
Tor Rd BN10 ..... 167 C1
Tor Rd W BN10 ..... 167 C2
Torcross Cl BN2 ..... 143 E1
Torfield Cl TN34 ..... 160 B4
Torfield Ct BN21 ..... 184 E4
Torfield Ho TN34 ..... 160 B4
Torfield Rd BN21 ..... 184 E4
Torfield Sch TN34 ..... 160 B5
Toronto Terr
　Brighton BN2 ..... 164 C6
　Lewes BN7 ..... 123 C1
Torrance Cl BN3 ..... 141 F1
Totland Rd BN2 ..... 164 D7
Tott Hill BN6 ..... 97 B5
Tott Yew Rd BN20 ..... 173 A4
Tottington Way BN43 ..... 140 B1
Tovey Cl BN21 ..... 184 D6
Tower Cl
　Beachlands BN24 ..... 175 F7
　East Grinstead RH19 ..... 1 E2
Tower Ct RH19 ..... 1 E2
Tower Ho
　4 Brighton BN1 ..... 142 E2
　Burgess Hill RH15 ..... 73 B2
Tower Mill Pl BN26 ..... 173 A5
Tower Rd Brighton BN2 .. 164 C6
　Hastings TN37, TN38 .. 136 C1
Tower Rd W TN38 ..... 159 B8
Tower Ride Uckfield TN22 .. 55 D1
　Uckfield TN22 ..... 55 E1
Tower St Heathfield TN21 .. 82 B8
　Rye TN31 ..... 93 C6
Tower View TN22 ..... 78 D8
Towergate BN1 ..... 142 E2
Towerscroft Ave TN37 .... 136 C5
Town Hill TN3 ..... 20 A4
Town Place Farm Cotts
　RH17 ..... 52 C7
Towner Art Gall & Mus
　BN21 ..... 184 D3
Townlands Rd TN5 ..... 29 F4
Toy & Model Mus TN3 .. 20 C7
Tozer Ct BN41 ..... 162 B7
Traders Pas TN31 ..... 93 B5
Trafalgar Cl
　Hastings TN38 ..... 135 F7
　Peacehaven BN10 ..... 167 C1
Trafalgar Cotts 8 TN34 .. 160 B4
Trafalgar Ct BN1 ..... 189 A6
Trafalgar Gate BN2 ..... 164 F3
Trafalgar La BN1 ..... 189 A6
Trafalgar Pl BN1 ..... 189 A6
Trafalgar Rd BN41 ..... 162 B8
Trafalgar St BN1 ..... 189 A6
Trafalgar Terr BN1 ..... 189 A6
Tram Rd TN31 ..... 94 A2
Transit Rd BN9 ..... 179 D7
Travellers La TN35 ..... 137 C4
Trebilco Cl TN1 ..... 8 D7
Treblers Rd TN20, TN6 .... 38 E6
Tredcroft Rd BN3 ..... 142 C2
Tree Tops Cl BN2 ..... 165 E8
Treemaines Rd BN23 ..... 174 F2
Treemans Rd RH17 ..... 33 B2
Tremola Ave BN2 ..... 177 C6
Trenches Rd TN6 ..... 25 F1
Trevor Gdns BN8 ..... 147 F6
Treyford Cl BN2 ..... 144 E1
Triangle Rd RH16 ..... 50 E3
Triangle The BN20 ..... 173 B3
Trickland Cotts TN21 ..... 53 C5
Trinity Cl TN2 ..... 8 D4
Trinity Field BN8 ..... 124 E6
Trinity Mews 3 TN34 .... 159 E7
Trinity Pl BN21 ..... 185 B2
Trinity Rd BN6 ..... 97 A6
Trinity St Brighton BN2 .. 189 B7
　10 Hastings TN34 ..... 159 E7
Trinity Trees BN21 ..... 185 A2
Trinity Villas 2 TN34 .... 159 E7
Tristan Gdns TN4 ..... 7 D6
Trojans Platt TN36 ..... 117 E7
Troon Cl BN25 ..... 180 A6
Trossachs Cl BN23 ..... 174 D3
Troy Cl TN6 ..... 26 A1
Truleigh Cl BN2 ..... 165 F7
Truleigh Dr BN41 ..... 141 A4

Truleigh Way BN43 ..... 140 A1
Truman Dr TN38 ..... 135 F6
Tubwell La
　Crowborough TN6 ..... 38 D7
　Maynard's Green TN21 .. 81 F2
Tudor Ave TN38 ..... 159 A7
Tudor Cl
　East Grinstead RH19 ..... 10 F8
　Hove BN3 ..... 141 F2
　Rottingdean BN2 ..... 177 A6
　Seaford BN25 ..... 180 D4
Tudor Ct TN2 ..... 7 E1
Tudor Gdns RH15 ..... 72 F4
Tudor Wlk TN22 ..... 79 B5
Tugwell Rd BN22 ..... 173 F2
Tumulus Rd BN2 ..... 166 C3
Tunbridge Wells Golf Club
　TN4 ..... 7 E3
Tunbridge Wells Gram Sch
　for Boys TN4 ..... 8 A7
Tunbridge Wells Gram Sch
　for Girls TN4 ..... 8 A6
Tunbridge Wells
　Ind Hospl The TN3 ..... 6 B3
Tunbridge Wells Mus TN1 .. 8 B4
Tunbridge Wells Rd
　Argos Hill TN20, TN6 ..... 39 E5
　Mark Cross TN3,TN6 ..... 28 A5
Tunnel Rd TN1 ..... 8 B4
Tuppen Ho BN7 ..... 145 E5
Turkey Cock La TN31 ..... 93 C6
Turkey La RH15 ..... 73 B3
Turkey Rd TN39 ..... 156 F7
Turley Cotts TN3 ..... 7 A8
Turnberry Cl TN38 ..... 158 F7
Turnberry Ct 14 RH16 ... 50 E4
Turnberry Cl BN27 ..... 152 A8
Turner Cl Bexhill TN40 ... 157 E5
　Eastbourne BN23 ..... 174 D1
Turner Ct RH19 ..... 2 A3
Turner's Hill Rd RH19 ... 10 B6
Turners Cotts TN31 ..... 68 C5
Turners Green La TN5 .... 29 F6
Turners Green Rd TN5 .... 29 F6
Turners Mill Cl RH16 .... 50 D7
Turners Mill Rd RH16 .... 50 D6
Turners Way RH15 ..... 72 F4
Turnpike Cl
　Broyle Side BN8 ..... 125 A8
　Peacehaven BN10 ..... 167 C1
Turnpike Piece BN1 ..... 144 B6
Turret Ct RH19 ..... 1 C3
Turton Cl BN2 ..... 164 D5
Tuscan Ct BN10 ..... 177 F3
Tutts Barn La BN22, BN21 . 185 A5
Tuxford Rd TN4 ..... 7 B5
Tweedsmuir Cl BN23 ..... 174 C3
Twineham Cl BN2 ..... 164 F7
Twineham Rd BN1 ..... 184 D7
Twitten Cl 2 BN42 ..... 161 F7
Twitten The Bexhill TN39 . 156 D4
　Burgess Hill RH15 ..... 73 B4
　Crowborough TN6 ..... 25 E1
　Ditchling BN6 ..... 98 D3
　Southwick BN42 ..... 161 E7
Twyford Cres TN37 ..... 136 C4
Twyford Rd BN1 ..... 143 E6
Twyfords TN6 ..... 25 E1
Twyhurst Ct RH19 ..... 1 D3
Twysden Cotts TN18 ..... 47 A4
Tye Cl BN2 ..... 177 D4
Tye Hill Rd BN26 ..... 151 A4
Tye View BN10 ..... 167 A1
Tyedean Rd BN10 ..... 177 F4
Tyler's Gn RH16, RH17 .... 50 B4
Tylers La TN22 ..... 35 E1
Tyndale Ave TN39 ..... 156 C3
Tyson Pl 9 BN2 ..... 189 B5

Uckfield Cl BN2 ..... 164 F6
Uckfield Com Coll TN22 ... 78 D8
Uckfield Com Hospl TN22 .. 78 D6
Uckfield Rd
　Poundgate TN6 ..... 37 B7
　Upper Wellingham BN8 .. 124 B7
Uckfield Sta TN22 ..... 78 C6
Uckham La TN33 ..... 112 E6
Udiam Cotts TN32 ..... 65 C5
Udimore Rd TN31 ..... 91 C3
Under Rd BN27 ..... 130 B3
Undercliff Hastings TN38 .. 159 B6
　Hastings TN38 ..... 159 C6
Undercliff Terr 7 TN38 .. 159 C6
Underdown Rd BN42 ..... 161 E8
Underhill TN22 ..... 55 B5
Underhill La
　Clayton BN45, BN6 ..... 119 E8
　Westmeston BN6 ..... 120 C8
Unicorn Ho 1 TN34 ..... 160 A4
Union Cl BN27 ..... 129 B3
Union Rd BN2 ..... 189 B7

Union Sq **18** TN2 .... 8 A2
Union St Brighton BN1 .... 189 A5
11 Hastings TN34 .... 159 C7
Union Street TN5 .... 32 B3
Univ of Brighton BN1 .... 189 A5
Eastbourne BN20 .... 188 D8
Falmer BN1 .... 144 B6
Univ of Brighton (Belgrave
Street Annexe) BN2 .... 189 B6
Univ of Brighton (Cockcroft/
Watts Annexes) BN2 ...... 143 D2
Univ of Brighton (Finsbury
Road Annexe) BN2 .... 189 B6
Univ of Brighton
(St Peter's Ho) BN2 .... 189 A6
Univ of Sussex BN1 .... 144 A7
Upland Rd BN20 .... 184 C3
Uplands Cl Bexhill TN39 .... 156 F6
Uckfield TN22 .... 55 C1
Uplands Com Coll TN5 .... 30 A4
Uplands Pk TN21 .... 59 E1
Uplands Rd BN1 .... 143 C2
Uplands Sch BN2 .... 143 C2
Uplands TN38 .... 159 B7
Upper Abbey Rd BN2 .... 164 D4
Upper Ave BN21, BN22 .... 185 A4
Upper Bedford St BN2 .... 164 C4
Upper Belgrave Rd BN25 .... 180 F5
Upper Bevendean Ave
BN2 .... 143 E1
Upper Broomgrove Rd
TN34 .... 137 B3
Upper Carlisle Rd BN20 ..... 188 D8
Upper Chalvington Pl
BN2 .... 164 E5
Upper Church Rd TN37 ...... 136 B4
Upper Chyngton Gdns
BN25 .... 181 B4
Upper Cl RH18 .... 11 F2
Upper Clarence Rd TN37 .... 136 C1
Upper Cotts BN2 .... 165 D4
Upper Cumberland Wlk
TN1 .... 8 B1
Upper Dr The BN3 .... 189 A8
Upper Duke's Dr BN20 .... 188 C7
Upper Dunstan Rd TN4 .... 8 B6
Upper Gardner St BN1 .... 189 A6
Upper Glen Rd TN37 .... 136 A5
Upper Gloucester Rd BN1 .. 189 F6
Upper Greenwoods La
TN21 .... 83 C6
Upper Grosvenor Rd
TN1, TN4 .... 8 B6
Upper Hamilton Rd BN1 .... 189 F8
Upper Hollingdean Rd
BN27 .... 143 B1
Upper Horsebridge Rd
BN27 .... 129 A3
Upper King's Dr BN20 .... 173 B1
Upper Kingston La
BN42, BN43 .... 140 D1
Upper Lake TN33 .... 112 E4
Upper Lewes Rd BN2 .... 189 B7
Upper Lodges BN1 .... 143 D8
Upper Market St BN3 .... 163 D5
Upper Maze Hill TN38 .... 159 B7
Upper Nellington TN3 .... 7 A4
Upper North St BN1 .... 189 F5
Upper Park Pl **7** BN2 ...... 189 B5
Upper Park Rd
TN34, TN37 .... 136 C1
Upper Profit TN3 .... 7 A3
Upper Ratton Dr BN20 ...... 184 B8
Upper Rock Gdns BN2 .... 189 B5
Upper Roedale Cotts BN1 . 143 B4
Upper Sea Rd TN40 .... 157 D6
Upper Sherwood Rd
BN25 .... 181 A4
Upper Shoreham Rd
Shoreham-by-Sea BN43 ... 140 B1
Shoreham-by-Sea
BN42, BN43 .... 140 D1
Upper South Rd TN37 .... 136 C1
Upper Sq RH18 .... 11 E3
Upper St East Dean BN20 .. 187 B8
Rusthall TN4 .... 7 D4
Upper St James's St BN2 .. 189 B4
Upper St Johns Rd RH15 ... 73 A4
Upper Station Rd TN21 ...... 82 A7
Upper Stephens TN3 .... 7 A4
Upper Sudeley St **7** BN2 164 D4
Upper Valley Rd BN2 .... 179 B6
Upper Wellington Rd **5**
BN2 .... 164 C7
Upper Winfield Ave BN1 .... 142 F6
Upper Wish Hill BN20 .... 184 B8
Upperton Gdns BN21 .... 184 F3
Upperton La BN21 .... 184 E4
Upperton Rd BN21 .... 184 E4
Upton Ave BN42 .... 140 E1

Upton Quarry TN3 .... 6 F3
Upwick Rd BN20 .... 184 C3

Val Prinseps Rd BN24 .... 175 C4
Vale Brighton BN1 .... 142 E7
Royal Tunbridge Wells TN1 .. 8 A3
Vale Cl BN25 .... 181 B4
Vale Ct BN41 .... 162 B7
Vale Gdns BN41 .... 162 B7
Vale Rd Battle TN33 .... 112 B5
Hastings TN37 .... 136 C2
Haywards Heath RH16 ...... 50 E2
Mayfield TN20 .... 40 B2
Portslade-by-Sea
BN3, BN41 .... 162 C7
Royal Tunbridge Wells TN1 .. 8 A3
Saltdean BN2 .... 166 D3
Seaford BN25 .... 181 A4
Vale The BN2 .... 165 E5
Vale View Rd TN21 .... 82 B6
Valebridge Cl RH15 .... 73 C6
Valebridge Dr RH15 .... 73 C5
Valebridge Rd RH15 .... 73 C6
Valence Rd BN7 .... 123 B1
Valentine Ct
2 Eastbourne BN21 ..... 185 A2
14 Hove BN3 .... 163 C7
Valentine Dr RH15 .... 72 E4
Valerie Cl BN41 .... 141 C2
Vallance Cl RH15 .... 72 E4
Vallance Gdns BN3 .... 163 A6
Vallance Rd BN3 .... 163 A6
Vallensdean Cotts BN41 .... 141 C2
Valley Cl Brighton BN1 ...... 142 C4
Brighton BN1 .... 142 C4
Valley Dene BN9 .... 179 B8
Valley Dr Brighton BN1 ..... 142 C4
Seaford BN25 .... 181 A5
Valley Rd
Crowborough TN6 .... 25 F1
Lewes BN8 .... 146 A8
Newhaven BN9 .... 179 A7
Newhaven BN9 .... 179 B7
Peacehaven BN10 .... 167 C2
Portslade-by-Sea BN41 .... 141 A2
Rusthall TN4 .... 7 D4
Valley Rise BN25 .... 180 F4
Valley Side Rd
TN34, TN35 .... 137 C3
Valley View TN22 .... 53 A8
Valley View Cl TN6 .... 25 F1
Valverde Ho **13** BN3 ..... 163 C7
Vanbrugh Ct **21** BN3 ..... 163 C7
Vantage Wlk TN38 .... 136 B2
Varndean Cl BN1 .... 142 E8
Varndean Coll BN1 .... 142 E3
Varndean Dr BN1 .... 142 E8
Varndean Gdns BN1 .... 142 E3
Varndean Holt BN1 .... 142 E3
Varndean Rd BN1 .... 142 E3
Varndean Sch BN1 .... 143 A3
Vega Cl BN27 .... 152 D7
Ventnor Cl BN23 .... 174 B4
Ventnor Villas BN3 .... 163 B6
Venture Cl TN40 .... 157 F4
Verbania Way RH19 .... 2 B1
Verdant Cl TN34 .... 159 D8
Vere Rd BN1, BN2 .... 189 A8
Veric **12** BN3 .... 163 C7
Vermont Rd TN4 .... 7 C4
Vermont Way TN38 .... 135 F6
Vernon Ave
Peacehaven BN10 .... 178 D6
Woodingdean BN2 .... 165 C8
Vernon Cl BN23 .... 185 E7
Vernon Ct **4** BN1 .... 163 E6
Vernon Lodge **9** BN1 ... 185 A2
Vernon Rd
Royal Tunbridge Wells TN1 .. 8 A6
Uckfield TN22 .... 78 D6
Vernon Terr BN1 .... 163 E7
Vernons Rd BN8 .... 76 C7
Veronica Way BN2 .... 189 B4
Verrall's Wlk **9** BN7 ...... 146 D8
Verulam Pl TN37 .... 159 E7
Viaduct Rd BN1, BN2 .... 189 A7
Vian Ave BN23 .... 185 F7
Vicarage Cl
Newhaven BN9 .... 168 E2
Ringmer BN8 .... 124 D5
Seaford BN25 .... 180 F3
Vicarage Dr BN20 .... 184 D3
Vicarage Field BN27 .... 152 C8
Vicarage La
Burwash Common TN19 ... 61 A4
Eastbourne BN20 .... 184 D3
Hailsham BN27 .... 152 C8
Hellingly BN27 .... 129 A6
Rottingdean BN2 .... 165 F1
Scaynes Hill RH17 .... 51 F3
Westfield TN35 .... 114 D3

Vicarage Rd
Burwash Common TN19 ... 61 A3
Eastbourne BN20, BN21 .. 184 D3
Hailsham BN27 .... 152 C7
Hastings TN34 .... 160 A5
Vicarage Terr BN2 .... 165 F1
Vicarage Way
Hurst Green TN19 .... 45 A3
Ringmer BN8 .... 124 D5
Viceroy Lodge **9** BN3 ... 163 A6
Victor Cl BN25 .... 180 E5
Victoria Ave
Burgess Hill RH15 .... 72 E3
Hastings TN35 .... 137 C4
Peacehaven BN10 .... 178 C7
Victoria Cl
Burgess Hill RH15 .... 72 E3
Hastings TN35 .... 137 C4
Polegate BN26 .... 172 F7
Victoria Cotts TN6 .... 39 C6
Victoria Ct Hastings TN38 . 159 B6
21 Hove BN3 .... 163 C6
Portslade-by-Sea BN41 ... 162 C8
Victoria Dr BN20, BN21 .... 184 C5
Victoria Gdns
Burgess Hill RH15 .... 72 F2
Eastbourne BN20 .... 184 C4
Victoria Gr **9** BN3 .... 163 C6
Victoria Ind Est RH15 .... 72 E2
Victoria Mews BN1 .... 165 F1
Victoria Pl **11** BN1 .... 163 E6
Victoria Rd
Bexhill TN39, TN40 .... 157 B4
Brighton BN1 .... 163 E6
Burgess Hill RH15 .... 72 E2
Crowborough TN6 .... 38 C8
Eastbourne BN20 .... 184 C5
Hailsham BN27 .... 152 C7
Hastings TN37 .... 159 D7
Haywards Heath RH16 ...... 51 A3
Mayfield TN20 .... 40 A3
Polegate BN26 .... 172 F7
Portslade-by-Sea
BN3, BN41 .... 162 C8
Royal Tunbridge Wells TN1 .. 8 B4
Southwick BN41, BN42 ... 161 D7
Windmill Hill BN27 .... 131 B5
Victoria St BN1 .... 163 E6
Victoria Terr TN19 .... 62 A6
Victoria Way
Burgess Hill RH15 .... 72 F2
East Grinstead RH19 .... 10 F7
Winchelsea Beach TN36 .. 118 A5
Victory Mews BN2 .... 165 A3
View Bank TN35 .... 160 D6
View Rd BN10 .... 178 C8
View Terr RH17 .... 2 A8
Views Path RH16 .... 51 B4
Views Wood Path TN22 ...... 55 D1
Viking Cl BN25 .... 180 B6
Viking Way BN23 .... 185 FB
Villa Rd TN37 .... 159 D7
Village Barn The BN1 .... 142 E7
Village Mews TN39 .... 156 C4
Village The BN20 .... 188 D8
Village Way BN1 .... 144 C6
Village Wks BN8 .... 105 A5
Villiers Cl BN23 .... 165 E8
Villiers Ct BN1 .... 189 A6
Vincent Cl BN23 .... 185 F7
Vine Cotts TN6 .... 38 C7
Vine Farm Cotts BN8 .... 104 A5
Vine Pl BN1 .... 189 F6
Vine Sq BN22 .... 185 D6
Vine St BN1 .... 189 A6
Vinehall Cl TN34 .... 137 A5
Vinehall (Prep Sch for Boys)
TN32 .... 87 E9
Vinehall Rd TN32 .... 87 E5
Vineries The
Burgess Hill RH15 .... 73 D3
Eastbourne BN23 .... 174 D2
1 Hove BN3 .... 163 E6
Vines Cross Rd
Brighton BN2 .... 164 F7
Horam TN21 .... 107 B7
Vineyard La TN5 .... 31 C2
Vintry The
Eastbourne BN21 .... 184 C7
Nutley TN22 .... 35 C4
Virgin's Croft TN33 .... 112 D6
Virgin's La TN33 .... 112 D6
Volks Electric Rly
BN1, BN2 .... 164 C4
Vue Gris Nez TN36 .... 118 B5

Wade Cl BN23 .... 185 F7
Wadhurst Bsns Pk TN5 ..... 29 B7
Wadhurst CE Prim Sch TN5 29 F5
Wadhurst Cl
Eastbourne BN22 .... 173 F2

Wadhurst Cl
Hastings TN37 .... 136 B5
Wadhurst La TN33 .... 111 E6
Wadhurst Par TN5 .... 29 F4
Wadhurst Rd TN6 .... 28 C3
Wadhurst Rise BN2 .... 164 F5
Wadhurst Sta TN5 .... 29 C6
Wadlands Brook Rd RH19 ... 1 D5
Wagg Cl RH19 .... 2 A1
Waghorns La BN22 .... 57 C6
Wainwright Cl TN38 .... 135 D3
Wainwright Rd TN39 .... 157 B4
Waite Cl BN7 .... 123 D2
Waites La TN35 .... 138 E5
Wakefield Rd BN2 .... 189 B8
Waldegrave Rd BN1 .... 143 A1
Waldegrave St **4** TN34 . 159 F8
Walden Terr TN33 .... 112 E4
Waldron Cl TN34 .... 136 F2
Waldron Ave BN1 .... 143 D6
Waldron Ct BN22 .... 184 D8
Waldron Ct TN21 .... 82 B8
Waldron Pl BN1 .... 143 D6
Waldron Rd BN8 .... 105 A5
Waldron Thorns TN21 .... 82 A7
Waldshut Rd BN7 .... 123 A3
Wales Farm Cotts BN7 ...... 121 C7
Walesbeech Rd BN2 .... 177 D4
Walker Cl BN23 .... 185 F7
Walks The TN3 .... 15 C8
Wall Hill Rd RH18, RH19 ... 11 E5
Wallace Cl TN2 .... 17 A8
Wallands Cty Prim Sch
BN7 .... 123 A2
Walled Garden The TN22 ... 55 D4
Wallers TN3 .... 7 A8
Wallington Towers TN40 .. 157 F4
Wallis Ave BN23 .... 185 E7
Wallis Cl TN6 .... 26 A1
Wallis Field TN3 .... 15 B6
Wallis Ho RH19 .... 1 E1
Wallis Pl BN23 .... 185 E8
Wallis Way RH15 .... 72 E4
Wallsend Rd BN24 .... 175 C6
Walmer Cres BN2 .... 144 B1
Walmer Rd BN25 .... 181 C4
Walnut Cl Brighton BN1 ... 142 E3
Heathfield TN21 .... 82 B6
Walnut Pk RH16 .... 51 B4
Walnut Tree Wlk BN24 ...... 184 B8
Walnut Wlk BN26 .... 173 A6
Walpole Rd BN2 .... 164 D5
Walpole Terr BN2 .... 164 D5
Walsh Ave TN38 .... 135 F6
Walshes Rd TN6 .... 38 B7
Walsingham Cl BN22 .... 173 D3
Walsingham Rd BN3 .... 162 F6
Walter May Ho **12** BN2 .. 164 F5
Walters Green Rd
TN11, TN3 .... 5 F6
Walton Bank BN1 .... 143 E5
Walton Cl
Eastbourne BN23 .... 174 E3
Hastings TN37 .... 136 C5
Walton Pk TN39 .... 156 F4
Walwers La **14** BN7 ...... 123 D1
Wanderdown Cl BN2 .... 165 E4
Wanderdown Dr BN2 .... 165 E4
Wanderdown Rd BN2 .... 165 D4
Wanderdown Way BN2 ..... 165 E4
Wannock Ave BN20 .... 172 F3
Wannock Cl TN40 .... 158 A6
Wannock Dr BN26 .... 172 F5
Wannock Gdns BN20 .... 172 F3
Wannock La BN20, BN26 .. 172 F3
Wannock Rd
Eastbourne BN22 .... 185 D5
Polegate BN26 .... 172 F5
War Memorial Hospl TN6 .. 25 E1
Warbleton Cl BN2 .... 164 E5
Warburton Cl
East Grinstead RH19 .... 11 A8
Eastbourne BN21 .... 184 C8
Uckfield TN22 .... 78 D8
Ward Cl TN5 .... 29 E5
Ward Way TN39 .... 157 A6
Ward's La TN5 .... 30 E4
Warden Cl RH17 .... 50 A6
Warden Park Sch RH17 ...... 50 A5
Wardrobook Rd TN5 .... 43 D7
Ware Ct RH15 .... 73 D3
Warelands RH15 .... 72 F1
Warenne Rd BN3 .... 141 C4
Wares Field TN22 .... 78 D8
Wares Rd TN22 .... 78 D4
Warleigh Rd BN1, BN2 ...... 189 A8
Warmdene Ave BN1 .... 142 F6
Warmdene Cl BN1 .... 142 F6
Warmdene Rd BN1 .... 142 F6
Warmdene Way BN1 .... 142 F6

Warminster Rd BN24 .... 175 D5
Warner Ct RH15 .... 73 A3
Warnham Ct BN3 .... 163 C5
Warnham Gdns TN39 .... 156 E2
Warnham Rise BN1 .... 143 A5
Warr Gn BN7 .... 123 B3
Warren Ave BN2 .... 165 C8
Warren Cl
Crowborough TN6 .... 25 E2
Eastbourne BN20 .... 188 C8
Friston BN20 .... 183 B1
Hastings TN38 .... 158 E8
Lewes BN7 .... 146 B8
Roser's Cross TN21 .... 81 A6
Woodingdean BN2 .... 165 B8
Warren Cnr TN21 .... 81 A8
Warren Cotts
Mayfield TN20 .... 40 C3
North Chailey BN8 .... 75 F7
Warren Dr BN7 .... 146 A8
Warren Farm La TN3 .... 16 B4
Warren Gdn TN6 .... 25 E2
Warren Hill BN20 .... 184 A1
Warren La
Beacon Down TN21 .... 81 A7
Friston BN20 .... 183 B1
North Chailey BN8 .... 75 E8
Warren Lodge BN10 .... 167 A1
Warren Rd
Crowborough TN6 .... 25 C1
Fairlight TN35 .... 138 C4
Woodingdean BN2 .... 165 B8
Warren Ridge TN3 .... 17 C3
Warren Rise BN2 .... 165 B8
Warren The
Burgess Hill RH15 .... 73 C1
Mayfield TN20 .... 40 C2
Ticehurst TN5 .... 31 E1
Warren Way
North Chailey BN8 .... 75 F8
Telscombe Cliffs BN10 ... 167 A1
Woodingdean BN2 .... 165 D8
Warrenwood BN8 .... 53 A1
Warrior Cl BN41 .... 141 B2
Warrior Gdns TN37 .... 159 C7
Warrior Ho BN20 .... 188 C8
Warrior Sq
6 Eastbourne BN22 .. 185 C4
Hastings TN37 .... 159 D7
Warrs Hill La BN8 .... 75 E8
Wartling Cl TN38 .... 135 F3
Wartling Dr TN39 .... 155 F5
Wartling Rd
Eastbourne BN22 .... 185 D6
Wartling BN27 .... 131 C2
Warwick Ct
4 Eastbourne BN23 .. 174 E1
4 Hove BN3 .... 163 E7
Warwick Mount **2** BN2 .. 164 C4
Warwick Pk TN1, TN2 .... 8 B1
Warwick Rd Bexhill TN39 .. 156 F5
4 Royal Tunbridge Wells
TN1 .... 8 A2
Seaford BN25 .... 180 E3
Washington Ave TN38 ...... 135 F6
Washington Rd RH16 .... 51 A5
Washington St BN2 .... 189 B7
Washwell La TN5 .... 29 F3
Wassall La TN17 .... 48 E7
Watchbell La TN31 .... 93 C5
Watchbell St TN31 .... 93 C5
Waterbury Hill RH17 .... 33 B5
Waterdown Rd TN4 .... 7 F1
Waterdyke Ave BN42 .... 161 E7
Waterfield TN2 .... 17 A7
Waterford Cl BN10 .... 167 C2
Waterfrets Cotts TN6 .... 6 F5
Watergate TN39 .... 157 B8
Watergate La BN7 .... 146 C8
Waterhall Golf Course
BN1 .... 142 A7
Waterhall Rd BN1 .... 142 C6
Waterloo Cl TN37 .... 135 F7
Waterloo Pas **15** TN34 . 160 B4
Waterloo Pl
1 Brighton BN1 .... 189 B6
13 Hastings TN34 .... 160 B4
2 Lewes BN7 .... 123 D1
Waterloo Sq BN26 .... 171 A3
Waterloo St BN3 .... 163 D5
Watermen's Cl TN34 .... 136 F3
Watermill Cl Bexhill TN39 . 157 B7
Lower Willingdon BN20 ..... 173 A5
Watermill Dr TN38 .... 135 F6
Watermill La Clayhill TN31 .. 67 D2
Icklesham TN35, TN36 .... 116 C3
Watermill TN39 .... 134 B2
Waters Cotts TN5 .... 30 A4

Waterside RH19 .... 8 B1
Waterside Cl TN34 .... 137 C3
Waterworks Cotts
  Friston BN20 .... 183 A1
  1 Hastings TN34 .... 159 F8
Waterworks Rd
  Eastbourne BN22 .... 185 A4
  1 Hastings TN34 .... 136 F1
Watling Cl **6** BN42 .... 161 E7
Watling Ct **8** BN42 .... 161 E7
Watling Rd BN42 .... 161 E7
Wattle's Wish TN33 .... 112 C6
Watts Cl TN5 .... 29 F4
Watts La BN21 .... 184 E4
Watts Lodge RH15 .... 73 D3
Watts' Palace La TN31 .... 89 D7
Waverley Cres BN1 .... 143 C1
Waverley Ct **4** TN34 .... 159 E7
Waverley Dr TN2 .... 8 F6
Waverley Gdns BN24 .... 175 D5
Wayfaring Down BN26 .... 172 D3
Wayfield Ave BN3 .... 141 F1
Wayford Cl BN23 .... 174 D2
Wayland Ave BN1 .... 142 C3
Wayside
  Brighton BN1 .... 142 D6
  East Dean BN20 .... 183 B1
Wayside Wlk TN21 .... 81 F6
Weald Ave BN3 .... 162 F8
Weald Cl
  Barcombe Cross BN8 .... 101 E4
  Lewes BN7 .... 123 C2
Weald Rd RH15 .... 72 E3
Weald Rise RH16 .... 50 E1
The Weald RH19 .... 1 F4
Weald View
  Barcombe Cross BN8 .... 101 E4
  Staplecross TN32 .... 65 E2
  Turner's Green TN5 .... 29 F6
Wealden Cl TN6 .... 25 F3
Wealden Cotts TN19 .... 61 C3
Wealden Ind Est TN6 .... 38 C8
Wealden Pk BN22 .... 173 C1
Wealden View TN19 .... 62 B7
Wealden Way
  Bexhill TN39 .... 156 C6
  Haywards Heath RH16 .... 50 D4
Wealdview Rd TN21 .... 81 F7
Weare Rd TN4 .... 8 C8
Weatherby Cl BN21 .... 184 C8
Weavers Cl RH15 .... 73 D1
Wedderburn Rd BN20 .... 173 B1
Week La BN8 .... 124 D2
Weir Wood Resr
  (Nature Reserve) RH19 .... 10 D1
Welbeck Ave
  Hastings TN38 .... 159 A7
  Hove BN3 .... 162 E6
  Royal Tunbridge Wells TN4 . 8 C8
Welbeck Cl
  Burgess Hill RH15 .... 73 D4
  Eastbourne BN22 .... 173 D3
Welbeck Ct **3** BN25 .... 180 E3
Welbeck Dr RH15 .... 73 D4
Welesmere Rd BN2 .... 166 A3
Welkin (Brighton Univ)
  BN20 .... 184 E1
Welkin The RH16 .... 51 B8
Well House Pl BN7 .... 123 C1
Wellcombe Cres BN20 .... 188 D7
Weller Rd TN4 .... 7 C4
Wellesley Cl
  Bexhill TN39 .... 156 D3
  Crowborough TN6 .... 25 D1
Wellesley Ct **10** TN34 ..... 160 B4
Wellesley Rd **6** BN21 ...... 185 A3
Wellfield RH19 .... 11 C7
Wellgreen La BN7 .... 145 F5
Wellhouse La RH15 .... 98 C7
Wellingham La BN8 .... 124 A7
Wellington Ct
  Brighton BN2 .... 165 A3
  3 Eastbourne BN22 ...... 185 C5
Wellington Gdns TN33 .... 112 C5
Wellington Ho **17** TN34 ... 159 F8
Wellington Lodge TN34 ...... 160 A4
Wellington Mews TN34 .... 159 F8
Wellington Pk **1** BN25 ... 181 A3
Wellington Pl
  7 Hastings TN34 .... 159 F7
  Sparrow's Green TN5 .... 29 F5
Wellington Rd
  Brighton BN2 .... 189 B7
  Hastings TN34 .... 160 A4
  Newhaven BN9 .... 168 F2
  Peacehaven BN10 .... 178 E6
  Portslade-by-Sea BN41 .. 162 B6
Wellington Sq TN34 .... 159 F8

Wellington St
  Brighton BN2 .... 164 C7
  1 Lewes BN7 .... 123 D1
Wellington Terr **14** TN34 . 159 F8
Wellington Town Rd RH19 .. 1 D2
Wellingtonia Cl **11** BN1 ... 142 E3
Wellis Ct TN38 .... 159 A8
Wellis Gdns TN38 .... 159 A8
Wellplace Cotts TN36 .... 116 F5
Wells Chase BN7 .... 99 E6
Wells Cl Eastbourne BN20 . 188 C8
  Plumpton Green BN7 .... 99 E6
  Royal Tunbridge Wells TN1 . 8 A3
Wells Lea RH19 .... 2 D3
Wells Meadow RH19 .... 1 D3
Wellsbourne **8** BN2 .... 164 F5
Wendale Dr BN10 .... 167 D2
Wendover Grange **3**
  .... 163 A6
Went Hill Gdns BN22 .... 173 B3
Went Hill Pk BN25 .... 181 A3
Went La BN20 .... 183 C1
Went Way BN20 .... 187 B8
Wenthill Cl BN20 .... 187 B8
Wentworth Cl
  Bexhill TN40 .... 157 F5
  Hailsham BN27 .... 129 A1
Wentworth Dr BN23 .... 185 E6
Wentworth St BN2 .... 189 B4
Wentworth Way TN38 .... 158 F8
West Ascent TN38 .... 159 B6
West Beeches Rd TN6 .... 26 B2
West Blatchington Inf Sch
  .... 141 E4
West Blatchington Jun Sch
  .... 141 E4
West Cl Alfriston BN26 .... 170 F3
  Polegate BN26 .... 173 B7
West Comm RH16 .... 50 F6
West Common Dr RH16 ...... 51 A7
West Dean Rise BN25 .... 181 A4
West Down Rd TN39 .... 157 A5
West Dr BN2 .... 164 C6
West End BN27 .... 130 E6
West End Cotts TN19 .... 60 F3
West Furlong Cl BN6 .... 97 A5
West Furlong La BN6 .... 97 A5
West Gate BN7 .... 99 E6
West Hill
  Dormans Park RH19 .... 1 E6
  East Grinstead RH19 .... 10 D8
West Hill Arc **3** TN34 .... 160 A3
West Hill Cl **3** TN34 ...... 159 B6
West Hill Mews TN38 .... 158 F6
West Hill Pl BN1 .... 189 F6
West Hill Rd Brighton BN1 189 A6
  Hastings TN38 .... 159 A6
West Hill St BN1 .... 189 F7
West Ho **15** BN21 .... 185 A2
West Hoathly Rd RH19 .... 10 D4
West Hove Inf Sch
  BN3 .... 162 F7
West Hove Cty Jun Sch
  BN3 .... 162 F7
West Hove Golf Course
  BN3 .... 141 C5
West Kent Coll of F Ed TN4 . 8 A7
West La RH19 .... 10 D8
West Leigh RH19 .... 10 E7
West Mallion RH16 .... 50 F3
West Par TN39 .... 157 B2
West Park Cres RH15 .... 72 D4
West Rd BN41 .... 162 A7
West Rise Cty Inf Sch
  BN23 .... 174 C2
West Rise Cty Jun Sch
  BN23 .... 174 C2
West St Alfriston BN26 ...... 170 F3
  Brighton BN1 .... 189 F5
  Burgess Hill RH15 .... 72 E4
  Ditchling BN6 .... 98 D3
  Dormansland RH7 .... 2 A8
  East Grinstead RH19 .... 10 E8
  Eastbourne BN21 .... 184 F2
  Hastings TN34 .... 160 A3
  Lewes BN7 .... 123 D1
  Mayfield TN20 .... 40 A2
  Portslade-by-Sea BN41 .. 162 C7
  Rottingdean BN2 .... 165 F1
  Rye TN31 .... 93 C5
  Seaford BN25 .... 180 E2
West St Leonards
  Cty Prim Sch TN38 .... 158 F8
West St Leonards Sta
  TN38 .... 158 F7
West Terr
  Eastbourne BN21 .... 184 F2
  Herstmonceux BN27 ...... 130 E6
West Undercliff TN31 .... 93 A5

West View Hastings TN34 . 160 B6
  Haywards Heath RH16 ...... 51 B6
  Hove BN3 .... 163 C8
  Seaford BN25 .... 180 E2
  Uckfield TN22 .... 55 D1
West View Cotts RH16 .... 51 B6
West View Ct **8** BN25 .... 180 E2
West View Gdns RH19 .... 10 E8
West View Terr BN9 .... 168 D2
West Way BN3 .... 141 D2
Westaway Dr TN39 .... 157 A4
Westbourne TN39 .... 156 C2
Westbourne Gdns BN3 ..... 163 A7
Westbourne Gr BN3 .... 163 A7
Westbourne Pl BN3 .... 163 A6
Westbourne St BN3 .... 163 A7
Westbourne Villas BN3 ..... 162 F6
Westbrook
  Forest Row RH18 .... 11 E3
  Saltdean BN2 .... 177 C6
Westbrook La TN35 .... 114 E5
Westbrook Terr TN2 .... 8 D1
Westbrook Way BN42 .... 161 F7
Westcliff Mansion BN2 ..... 188 F8
Westcombe **1** BN1 .... 163 E7
Westcourt Dr TN39 .... 156 F3
Westdean Ave BN9 .... 179 A5
Westdene Cl TN37 .... 136 C6
Westdene Cty Prim Sch
  BN1 .... 142 C5
Westdene Dr BN1 .... 142 C5
Westdown Ho **4** BN21 . 185 A2
Westdown La TN19 .... 61 A3
Westergate Rd BN2 .... 143 E4
Westerham Rd BN23 .... 174 D1
Westerings The **4** TN21 . 82 A6
Westerleigh Cl TN38 .... 159 A8
Western Ave BN26 .... 173 B7
Western Espl BN3, BN41 .. 162 D6
Western Gdns TN36 .... 38 D8
Western Rd
  Bexhill TN39, TN40 .... 157 C3
  Burgess Hill RH15 .... 72 E3
  Crowborough TN6 .... 38 C7
  Eastbourne BN22 .... 185 B4
  Hailsham BN27 .... 152 B7
  Hastings TN37 .... 159 C7
  Haywards Heath RH16 ...... 50 F4
  Hove BN1, BN3 .... 163 E5
  Hurstpierpoint BN6 .... 97 A7
  Lewes BN7 .... 123 B1
  Newhaven BN9 .... 179 C6
  Newick BN8 .... 76 C7
  Pevensey Bay BN24 .... 175 D4
  Royal Tunbridge Wells TN1 . 8 C5
  Turner's Green TN5 .... 29 F6
Western Road
  Cty Prim Sch BN7 .... 146 C8
Western St BN1 .... 163 D5
Western Terr **5** BN1 ...... 163 E5
Westfield Ave N BN2 .... 166 D3
Westfield Ave S BN2 .... 166 D3
Westfield Cl Brighton BN1 143 A4
  Westfield Cres BN1 .... 143 A5
  Westfield Rd BN21 .... 184 D6
Westfield Cty Prim Sch
  TN35 .... 114 E4
Westfield La TN34, TN35 .. 136 C8
Westfield Rd BN21 .... 184 D6
Westfield Rise BN2 .... 166 E3
Westgate St BN7 .... 123 C1
Westham Cl TN39 .... 156 E3
Westham Dr BN24 .... 175 F6
Westhill Dr RH15 .... 72 E3
Westland Ct BN41 .... 162 A7
Westlands Rd RH16 .... 51 B5
Westmeston Ave BN2 .... 177 B6
Westminster Cl BN22 .... 173 D4
Westminster Cres TN34 .... 137 A4
Westmoreland Ct
  Eastbourne BN20 .... 184 B7
  12 Hove BN3 .... 163 E7
Wickham Dr BN6 .... 97 C5
Westmount Cl
  BN42, BN43 .... 161 D8
Westpoint BN8 .... 76 C7
Westville Rd TN39 .... 157 A4
Westway TN34 .... 159 C7
Westway Gdns BN41 .... 140 E4
Westwood Rd TN4 .... 7 C5
Wharf Rd
  Eastbourne BN21 .... 184 F3
  Hove BN3 .... 162 D6
Whatlington Rd TN33 .... 112 E7
Whatlington Way TN38 .... 135 D2

Wheatfield Ct TN37 .... 136 C5
Wheatfield Way BN2 .... 143 F3
Wheatland Cl BN10 .... 167 B2
Wheatsheaf Cl RH15 .... 72 E5
Wheatsheaf Gdns BN2 ..... 123 C2
Wheatsheaf La RH17 .... 44 A6
Wheel Farm Bsns Pk
  TN35 .... 114 C4
Wheel La TN35 .... 114 D3
Wheelers La TN22 .... 57 D6
Wheelers Lane Cotts TN22 57 D5
Wheelwright Cl BN22 .... 173 D4
Wheelwright La RH15 .... 73 D1
Whichelo Pl BN2 .... 164 C6
Whin Croft Pk TN6 .... 37 D8
Whipping Post La BN2 .... 165 F1
Whippingham Rd BN2 ...... 164 C7
Whippingham St BN2 .... 164 C8
Whistler Ct BN1 .... 142 F1
Whitbread Cl BN23 .... 174 B4
White Bear Pas **3**
  TN1, TN4 .... 8 A2
White Cl BN26 .... 170 F2
White Hill BN7 .... 123 C1
White Hill Ave TN39 .... 156 E4
White Hill Dr TN39 .... 156 E4
White House
  Cty Prim Sch BN27 .... 152 B8
White Lodge Hove BN3 ... 163 C8
  Royal Tunbridge Wells TN1 . 8 C4
White Rock Gdns **7**
  TN34 .... 159 C7
White Rock Pleasure
  Grounds TN34 .... 159 E7
White Rock Rd
  TN34, TN37 .... 159 E7
White St BN2 .... 189 B5
White Way Alfriston BN26 170 F1
  Lewes BN7 .... 146 B1
Whitebread La TN31 .... 67 E8
Whitecross St BN1 .... 189 A6
Whitefield Rd TN4 .... 8 A3
Whitefriars Rd TN34 .... 160 A5
Whitegate Cl TN4 .... 8 A8
Whitegates Cl BN8 .... 100 E7
Whitegates La TN5 .... 29 D8
Whitegates Pk TN35 .... 114 D2
Whitehawk Cl BN2 .... 164 E5
Whitehawk Cres BN2 .... 164 E5
Whitehawk Cty Inf Sch
  BN2 .... 164 E6
Whitehawk Cty Jun Sch
  BN2 .... 164 E6
Whitehawk Hill Rd BN2 .. 164 D5
Whitehawk Rd
  Brighton BN2 .... 164 E6
  Brighton BN2 .... 164 F5
Whitehawk Way BN2 .... 164 E6
Whitehill Cl TN6 .... 25 F1
Whitehill Cty Inf Sch TN6 .. 25 F1
Whitehill Rd TN6 .... 37 F8
Whitehouse Ave TN39 ...... 157 B7
Whitehouse La TN21 .... 81 B4
Whitelot Cl BN42 .... 140 E2
Whitelot Way BN42 .... 140 E2
Whiterock Pl BN42 .... 161 E7
Whitethorn Dr BN1 .... 142 B4
Whiteway Cl BN25 .... 180 E6
Whiteway La BN2 .... 177 E4
Whiteways Cotts BN7 ...... 146 D2
Whitfield La BN8 .... 123 C6
Whitley Rd BN22 .... 185 B5
Whittingehame Gdns
  BN1 .... 142 F3
Whittington Coll RH19 .... 1 A4
Whittington's Way TN34 137 B4
Whittle Dr BN23 .... 174 A1
Whittlewood Cl TN38 ...... 135 E2
Whitworth Rd TN37 .... 136 B7
Whybourne Crest TN2 .... 8 D1
Whydown Hill TN33 .... 133 E6
Whydown Rd TN39 .... 156 B7
Wick Hall BN3 .... 163 D6
Wickets The RH15 .... 72 F5
Wickham Ave TN39 .... 157 B3
Wickham Cl RH16 .... 50 D7
Wickham Dr BN6 .... 97 C5
Wickham Gdns TN4 .... 7 D5
Wickham Hill BN6 .... 97 C4
Wickham La BN7, BN8 .... 100 E3
Wickham Rock La TN36 .. 117 C5
Wickham Way RH16 .... 50 D7
Wickhurst Cl BN41 .... 140 F2
Wickhurst Rd BN41 .... 141 A2
Wickhurst Rise BN41 ...... 140 F3
Wicklands Ave BN2 .... 177 D5
Widbury Cl TN3 .... 6 F2
Widdicombe Way BN2 .... 143 E3
Wigmore Cl BN1 .... 143 B1

Wilbury Ave BN3 .... 163 C8
Wilbury Cres BN3 .... 163 D7
Wilbury Gdns BN3 .... 163 C8
Wilbury Gr BN3 .... 163 C6
Wilbury Lodge **11** BN3 . 163 C6
Wilbury Rd BN3 .... 163 C6
Wilbury Villas BN3 .... 163 C7
Wilby Ave BN42 .... 140 E1
Wild Park Cl BN2 .... 143 E3
Wilderness Gdns **5** TN31 . 67 B7
Wilderness La TN22 .... 57 C3
Wilderness Pk TN6 .... 25 E2
Wilderness Rd BN6 .... 97 A6
Wilderness Rise RH19 .... 2 A6
Wilderness The RH16 .... 51 B8
Wilderness Wood
  (Adventure Pk) TN22 ...... 57 D4
Wilderwick Rd RH19, RH7 . 2 A5
Wilfrid Rd BN3 .... 141 D1
Wilkins Way TN40 .... 157 F6
Wilkinson Cl BN2 .... 165 F3
Wilkinson Way BN25 .... 180 E4
Willard Cl BN22 .... 185 A6
Willetts Cotts TN3 .... 5 C4
Willetts Field BN8 .... 127 E8
Willetts La TN3 .... 5 C4
William Allen La RH16 ...... 51 B6
William Parker Sch
  (Lower) TN34 .... 136 D3
William Parker Sch
  (Upper) TN34 .... 136 D4
William Rd TN38 .... 158 E7
William St Brighton BN2 .. 189 A5
  Royal Tunbridge Wells TN4 . 8 A5
  Southwick BN41 .... 162 B7
William Sutton Ho BN1 .. 189 A5
Williams Ct **7** BN23 .... 174 E1
Williams Rd BN43 .... 161 C8
Willingdon Ave
  Bexhill TN39 .... 157 A4
  Hastings TN38 .... 136 A5
Willingdon Cl
  Hastings TN38 .... 136 A5
  Willingdon BN20 .... 173 B1
Willingdon Ct BN20 .... 173 B3
Willingdon Cty Prim Sch
  BN20 .... 173 A3
Willingdon Dro BN23 ...... 174 B2
Willingdon La BN26 .... 183 C7
Willingdon Park Dr BN22 . 173 D2
Willingdon Rd
  Brighton BN2 .... 143 E1
  Eastbourne BN20, BN21 .. 184 C6
  Willingdon BN20 .... 172 F4
Willingdon Trees
  Cty Prim Sch BN22 .... 173 D3
Willingdon Way
  Hastings TN38 .... 136 A5
  Willingdon BN22 .... 173 B2
Willingford La TN19 .... 61 C2
Willoughby Cres BN22 .... 185 C6
Willow Ave BN27 .... 129 B1
Willow Bank TN32 .... 64 B3
Willow Cl
  East Grinstead RH19 .... 1 D3
  Etchingham TN19 .... 63 B8
  Heathfield TN21 .... 82 B8
  Woodingdean BN2 .... 165 E8
Willow Ct **4** Hove BN3 . 163 D7
  Polegate BN26 .... 173 A6
Willow Dr Bexhill TN39 ... 156 C5
  Polegate BN26 .... 173 A5
  Seaford BN25 .... 181 C3
Willow End TN34 .... 136 F4
Willow Est The BN9 .... 179 E8
Willow Gdns BN6 .... 97 A7
Willow Ho BN6 .... 97 E5
Willow La TN36 .... 118 B6
Willow Mead **8** RH19 ... 10 F8
Willow Mews TN32 .... 64 B3
Willow Pk RH16 .... 51 B4
Willow Stream Cl TN35 ... 115 E3
Willow Tree Rd TN2 .... 7 F1
Willow Way RH17 .... 97 A8
Willow Wlk
  Eastbourne BN22 .... 173 D2
  Newhaven BN9 .... 179 C8
  Royal Tunbridge Wells TN2 . 8 E8
Willowbrook Way BN6 ...... 98 A3
Willowdowne Cl BN26 .... 173 A5
Willowfield Rd BN22 .... 185 B4
Willowfield Sq **7** BN22 . 185 B4
Willowmead TN6 .... 37 E8
Willows The TN22 .... 79 B5
The Willows
  2 Brighton BN2 .... 189 B8
  Burgess Hill RH15 .... 73 C5
  Hassocks BN6 .... 97 E4
  Hastings TN37 .... 136 A6

Wilman Rd TN4 .... 8 B7
Wilmington Cl
Brighton BN1 .... 143 A5
Hassocks BN6 .... 97 F4
Wilmington Gdns BN21 ... 185 A1
Wilmington Par BN1 ...... 142 F5
Wilmington Rd
Hastings TN34 .... 137 A3
Newhaven BN9 .... 179 B6
Seaford BN25 .... 180 D4
Wilmington Sq BN21 ..... 185 A1
Wilmington St BN26 ...... 171 F6
Wilmington Way
Brighton BN1 .... 143 A5
Haywards Heath RH16 ..... 51 A5
Wilmot Ct 6 BN43 .... 161 C8
Wilmot Rd BN43 .... 161 C8
Wilson Ave BN2 .... 164 F6
Wilson Gr TN22 .... 78 A7
Wilson's Cross BN27 ..... 131 F7
Wilton 6 RH16 .... 50 D6
Wilton Ave BN22 .... 173 F2
Wilton Rd TN40 .... 157 C3
Wiltshire Ct BN23 .... 174 E1
Wiltshire Ho 18 BN2 ..... 189 B5
Wiltshire Way TN1 .... 8 D7
Winceby Cl TN39 .... 156 E2
Winchcombe Rd BN22 ... 185 A4
Winchelsea Cl BN25 ..... 181 C5
Winchelsea La
Cock Marling TN31, TN36 ... 92 C1
Hastings TN35 .... 137 E5
Winchelsea Mus TN36 ..... 117 E7
Winchelsea Rd
Eastbourne BN22 .... 185 D6
Guestling Green TN35 ..... 137 F7
Hastings TN35 .... 137 D4
Rye TN31 .... 93 B5
Winchelsea St Thomas
CE Prim Sch TN36 .... 117 F7
Winchelsea Sta TN36 ...... 92 D1
Winchester Ho BN22 ..... 173 E3
Winchester St BN1 .... 189 A8
Winchester Way BN22 ... 173 C2
Wincombe Rd BN1, BN3 ... 142 D1
Windermere Cres BN22 ... 185 C5
Windermere Ct 9 BN2 ... 164 C6
Windermere Rd RH16 .... 50 F4
Windgrove Cotts TN33 ... 112 D6
Windgrove Ho TN33 ..... 112 D6
Winding St 21 TN34 ..... 160 B4
Windlesham Ave
BN1, BN3 .... 163 E6
Windlesham Ct BN41 .... 141 A1
Windlesham Ct 10 BN1 ... 163 E7
Windlesham Gdns
BN1, BN3 .... 163 E7
Windlesham Rd BN1 ..... 163 E6
Windlesham Sch BN1 .... 163 E8
Windmill Ave BN6 .... 97 F3
Windmill Cl
Eastbourne BN21 .... 184 D6
Heathfield TN21 .... 82 B8
Hove BN3 .... 141 F2
Windmill Ct
Royal Tunbridge Wells TN2 .. 8 C3
Winchelsea Beach TN36 .. 118 B6
Windmill Dr Bexhill TN39 .. 157 B6
Brighton BN1 .... 142 D6
Burgess Hill RH15 .... 73 A4
Windmill Gn BN24 .... 174 C5
Windmill La
Ashurst Wood RH19 ...... 11 C7
Cousley Wood TN5 .... 30 C8
Durgates TN5 .... 29 E4
East Grinstead RH19 .... 1 D3

Windmill La
Friston BN20 .... 183 A1
Windmill Par BN42 ...... 140 E1
Windmill Pl BN26 .... 173 A5
Windmill Rd
Hastings TN38 .... 136 B2
Polegate BN26 .... 173 A6
Southwick BN42 .... 140 E1
Windmill St
Brighton BN1 .... 189 B6
Royal Tunbridge Wells TN2 .. 8 C3
Windmill Terr 19 BN2 ... 189 B6
Windmill View BN1 ...... 143 B7
Windmill Way TN36 ..... 118 B7
Windmills Cty Jun Sch
BN6 .... 98 A3
Windover Cres BN7 ..... 123 A2
Windover Way BN22 .... 173 B3
Windsor Cl
Eastbourne BN23 .... 174 C3
Hove BN3 .... 142 A3
Seaford BN25 .... 180 B6
Windsor Ct
Brighton BN1 .... 189 F5
Brighton, Withdean BN1 .. 142 D4
Crowborough TN6 .... 38 C8
8 Eastbourne BN22 .... 185 B3
Polegate BN26 .... 173 A7
Windsor Lodge BN3 ..... 163 B6
Windsor Pl
Crowborough TN6 .... 38 C8
East Grinstead RH19 ...... 11 A8
Hastings TN34 .... 136 E2
Windsor Rd Bexhill TN39 .. 157 B4
Crowborough TN6 .... 38 C8
Hailsham BN27 .... 152 B6
Hastings TN37 .... 136 B3
Windsor St BN1 .... 189 F5
Windsor Way
Polegate BN26 .... 173 A7
Winchelsea Beach TN36 .. 118 A5
Wineham Way TN40 ..... 157 F4
Winfield Ave BN1 .... 142 F6
Winfield Cl Brighton BN1 .. 142 F5
Portslade-by-Sea BN41 .. 141 A3
Wingate Cl TN38 .... 136 A1
Wingle Tye Rd RH15 ..... 98 A8
Winkfield Ct RH16 .... 50 D5
Winkhurst Way RH15 .... 73 D1
Winkney Rd BN22 .... 173 F3
Winnals Pk RH16 .... 50 D5
Winston BN27 .... 152 B7
Winston Cres BN23 ..... 185 D7
Winston Dr TN39 .... 156 F4
Winstone Scott Ave TN1 .. 6 E4
Winterbourne Cl
Hastings TN34 .... 159 D8
Lewes BN7 .... 146 A8
Winterbourne Hollow
BN7 .... 146 B8
Winterbourne La BN7 ... 146 A8
Winterbourne Mews BN7 .. 146 B8
Winterton Way BN43 .... 161 B6
Winton Ave BN2 .... 166 C3
Winton St BN26 .... 171 A4
Wireless Mus RH16 .... 51 B7
Wisden Ave RH15 .... 72 E5
Wiseacre TN3 .... 20 A3
Wish Ct BN3 .... 162 E8
Wish Hill BN20 .... 173 B1
Wish Rd
Eastbourne BN21 .... 185 A2
Hove BN3 .... 162 E6
Wish St TN31 .... 93 B5
Wish Tower Mus BN21 ... 185 A1
Wish Ward TN31 .... 93 B5

Wishing Tree Cl TN38 ...... 135 F2
Wishing Tree La TN38 ..... 135 F1
Wishing Tree Rd TN38 .... 135 F2
Wishing Tree Rd N TN38 .. 136 A4
Wiston Ct 12 BN43 .... 161 C8
Wiston Rd BN2 .... 164 F6
Wiston Way BN2 .... 164 F7
Withdean Ave BN1 .... 142 D2
Withdean Cl BN1 .... 142 D3
Withdean Court Ave BN1 .. 142 D3
Withdean Cres BN1 ...... 142 E3
Withdean Cl 10 BN1 ..... 142 E3
Withdean Hall 3 BN1 .... 142 E3
Withdean Rd BN1 .... 142 D3
Withdean Rise BN1 .... 142 E3
Witherenden Rd TN20 .... 41 A1
Withy Bush RH15 .... 72 E5
Witham Ave BN2 .... 177 C5
Witham Cl BN22 .... 173 F1
Withyham Rd
Bexhill TN39 .... 156 C2
Groombridge TN3 .... 15 A6
Wittersham Rd Iden TN31 .. 70 B7
Potman's Heath
TN17, TN30 .... 49 D4
Wittersham Road Sta
TN17 .... 49 D6
Wivelsfield Cty Prim Sch
RH16 .... 73 F6
Wivelsfield Rd
Haywards Heath RH16 ..... 50 E2
Saltdean BN2 .... 166 C3
Wivelsfield Sta RH15 ..... 73 C4
Woburn Cl BN27 .... 129 A1
Woburn Pl BN1 .... 143 F5
Woburn Way BN22 .... 173 D3
Wolfe Cl TN6 .... 38 A8
Wolseley Rd
Brighton BN1 .... 143 D6
Portslade-by-Sea BN41 .. 162 A8
Royal Tunbridge Wells TN4 .. 8 C7
Wolstead Lodge 3 RH16 .. 50 F3
Wolstonbury Cl BN6 ...... 97 B4
Wolstonbury Ct RH15 .... 73 B2
Wolstonbury Rd BN3 ..... 163 E7
Wolstonbury Way RH15 ... 73 B2
Wolverstone Dr BN1 ..... 143 C2
Wood La BN27 .... 131 D2
Wood Ride RH16 .... 50 D3
Wood Rise Comm TN6 .... 25 F4
Wood St
East Grinstead RH19 .... 1 D1
Royal Tunbridge Wells TN1 .. 8 B4
Wood's Pas 4 TN34 ..... 160 B4
Woodbourne Ave BN1 ... 143 A4
Woodbrook Rd TN34 ..... 136 F2
Woodbury Ave RH19 .... 2 B1
Woodbury Cl
East Grinstead RH19 ...... 11 B8
Royal Tunbridge Wells TN4 .. 8 A5
Woodbury Park Gdns TN4 .. 8 B5
Woodbury Park Rd TN4 .... 8 B5
Woodcombe TN34 .... 136 F4
Woodcote Rd RH18 .... 11 F2
Woodcrest Rd RH15 .... 72 F1
Woodcroft RH15 .... 72 F5
Woodcroft Dr BN21 ...... 184 C7
Woodcutters RH17 .... 51 F3
Woodgate Meadow BN7 .. 99 E7
Woodgate Rd BN22 ...... 185 C5
Woodhams Cl TN33 ...... 112 D5
Woodhill Pk TN2 .... 9 C6
Woodhouse Cl BN3 ...... 162 E7
Woodhouse Rd BN3 ...... 162 E7
Woodingdean Cty Prim Sch
BN2 .... 165 C8

Woodland Ave
Burgess Hill RH15 .... 73 C4
Woodland Ave
Eastbourne BN22, BN21 .. 173 C1
Hove BN3 .... 142 B3
Woodland Cl
Burgess Hill RH15 .... 73 C4
Hove BN3 .... 163 A7
Royal Tunbridge Wells TN4 .. 8 C7
Woodland Cres RH15 ..... 73 C4
Woodland Ct BN3 .... 142 B4
Woodland Dr BN3 .... 142 B3
Woodland Mews TN21 ... 82 B6
Woodland Par BN3 .... 142 B3
Woodland Rd TN4 .... 8 C7
Woodland Rise TN40 ..... 157 E4
Woodland Vale Rd
TN37, TN38 .... 159 C8
Woodland Way
Brighton BN1 .... 142 F4
Crowborough TN6 .... 37 F8
Crowhurst TN33 .... 134 F4
Fairlight Cove TN35 .... 138 E4
Heathfield TN21 .... 82 B6
Woodland Wlk BN2 .... 165 D4
Woodlands Hove BN3 ... 142 C2
Romford TN2 .... 9 F7
Woodlands Cl
Hailsham BN27 .... 129 C2
Heathfield TN21 .... 82 B5
Peacehaven BN10 .... 167 B1
Uckfield TN22 .... 78 D8
Woodlands Rd
East Grinstead RH19 .... 2 A4
Haywards Heath RH16 ..... 50 F4
Woodlands Way TN34 .... 136 E6
Woodleigh Rd RH15 ...... 73 C4
Woodmans Oak TN33 .... 88 A3
Woodpecker Cres BN6 .... 72 D3
Woodpecker Dr BN27 ... 152 A8
Woodpecker Rd BN21 ... 174 B2
Woodridge Cl RH16 .... 51 A3
Woodruff Ave BN3 .... 142 C2
Woods Green Cotts TN5 ... 29 F7
Woods Hill Cl RH19 ...... 11 D6
Woods Hill La RH19 ...... 11 D6
Woods Ho BN3 .... 163 A8
Woodsgate Ave
TN39, TN40 .... 157 C6
Woodsgate Pk TN39 ..... 157 B6
Woodsgate Way TN2 .... 9 B6
Woodside TN6 .... 25 E2
Woodside Cl TN2 .... 9 C6
Woodside Cl TN2 .... 9 C6
Woodside Lodge BN1 .... 142 D2
Woodside Rd
Pembury TN2 .... 9 E6
Rusthall TN4 .... 7 D4
Woodside Terr BN26 ..... 151 F4
Woodside Way BN27 .... 152 A4
Woodslands Cl BN6 .... 97 F4
Woodslands Rd BN6 .... 97 F4
Woodspring Cl TN37 ..... 136 B5
Woodstock RH19 .... 1 C2
Woodstock Rd TN39 ..... 156 C6
Woodview Cl BN1 .... 143 D6
Woodville Rd TN39 .... 157 B3
Woodward Cl BN23 ...... 185 E7
Woodwards Cl RH15 ..... 73 B1
Woolven Cl RH15 .... 72 E1
Worcester Ct
5 Eastbourne BN23 .... 174 E1
2 Hove BN3 .... 163 E6

Worcester Villas BN3 .... 162 C7
Wordsworth Dr BN23 .... 174 E2
Wordsworth Rise 6
RH19 .... 1 C1
Wordsworth St BN3 ...... 163 A7
Workhouse La TN36 ...... 116 F5
Worsham La TN40 .... 157 F7
Worsted La RH19 .... 11 B8
Wray Cl RH19 .... 11 D6
Wren Cl TN21 .... 82 A7
Wren Ct Battle TN33 .... 112 F4
Hastings TN38 .... 135 E3
Wrentham Ho RH15 .... 73 B3
Wrestwood Ave BN22 ... 173 C1
Wrestwood Cl TN40 ..... 157 D6
Wrestwood Rd TN40 ..... 157 D6
Wrotham Cl
Eastbourne BN23 .... 174 D1
Hastings TN34 .... 136 E5
Wroxham Rd BN23 .... 174 B4
Wyatts La RH17 .... 33 D5
Wyberlye Rd RH15 .... 73 A4
Wybourne Rise TN2 ...... 17 B8
Wychperry Rd RH16 .... 50 D5
Wychurst Gdns TN40 .... 157 D6
Wyck St BN41 .... 162 A7
Wykeham Rd TN34 .... 159 E8
Wykeham Terr BN1 ...... 189 F5
Wykeham Way RH15 ..... 73 C2
Wynberg Cotts TN6 .... 39 C6
Wyndham St BN2 .... 189 B4
Wynnes Mews BN3 ...... 163 A7
Wynnstay RH15 .... 73 B2
Wyshe The BN45 .... 119 C6
Wythwood RH16 .... 50 E1

Yardley St BN1 .... 189 A8
Yates Cl TN31 .... 95 A2
Yeomans BN8 .... 125 A7
Yew La RH19 .... 1 B3
Yew Tree Cl
Broyle Side BN8 .... 124 F7
Hastings TN34 .... 136 E6
Heathfield TN21 .... 82 A6
Yew Tree Cotts
Burgess Hill RH15 .... 73 B3
Groombridge TN3 .... 15 F8
Yew Tree Rd TN34 .... 8 B8
Yewtree La TN6 .... 39 E8
Yielding's Cl BN21 .... 184 D5
York Ave
East Grinstead RH19 ...... 11 A8
Hove BN3 .... 163 E6
York Bldgs 6 BN34 ...... 159 F7
York Ct 9 BN3 .... 163 E7
York Gdns 5 TN34 .... 159 F7
York Gr BN1 .... 189 F7
York Hill BN1 .... 189 A7
York Ho BN41 .... 162 B8
York Pl BN1, BN2 .... 189 A6
York Rd Bexhill TN40 ..... 158 A5
Burgess Hill BN6, RH15 ... 72 D2
Eastbourne BN21 .... 184 F2
Hastings TN37 .... 136 C2
Hove BN1, BN3 .... 163 E6
Peacehaven BN10 .... 178 E6
Royal Tunbridge Wells TN1 .. 8 A4
York Villas BN1 .... 189 F7
Yorkshire Ct BN20 .... 184 B7
Youl Grange BN20 .... 184 D1
Youngsmere Cl BN1 ..... 143 C6
Yvonne Robertson Ho
TN40 .... 157 D5

Town and village index

Alciston 170 D8
Alfriston 170 F2
Argos Hill 39 E5
Arlington 150 F4
Ashton Green 125 A5
Ashurst 5 D2
Ashurst Wood 11 E6
Barcombe 101 E2
Barcombe Cross 101 E4
Battle 112 D5
Beachlands 175 F6
Beacon Down 81 A7
Beckley 98 A4
Beckley Furnace 90 D7
Beddingham 147 D4
Bells Yew Green 17 F5
Berner's Hill 32 A2
Berwick 170 F7
Bewlbridge 20 D1
Bexhill 157 A2
Bishopstone 180 C6
Blackboys 80 A5
Blackham 5 A4
Boarshead 26 C6
Bodiam 65 E8
Bodle Street Green 109 C2
Boreham Street 131 F3
Brede 90 B2
Brightling 85 C7
Brighton 164 B4
Brighton 189 A4
Broad Oak
  (nr Heathfield) 59 F1
Broad Oak
  (nr Westfield) 90 C4
Broyle Side 125 A7
Buckland Hill 19 A1
Bullingstone 6* F7
Burgess Hill 73 D2
Burwash 62 B6
Burwash Common 61 A4
Buxted 56 B4
Cade Street 90 A2
Cackle Street 82 E6
Camber 94 F2
Catsfield 133 F8
Chailey 75 A4
Chalvington 150 A7
Chelwood Common 34 D6
Chelwood Gate 34 D8
Churches Green 109 B8
Clayhill 67 D3
Clayton 119 E8
Cliff End 139 B7
Cobbarn 15 F3
Cock Marling 92 A2
Coggins Mill 40 D4
Coghurst 137 C6
Coleman's Hatch 23 E7
Cooksbridge 123 A8
Cooper's Green 55 D4
Cousley Wood 30 C7
Cowbeech 108 C1
Cowden 4 A6
Cripp's Corner 88 D7
Cross-in-Hand 81 C7
Crowborough 26 C1
Crowhurst 134 F6
Cuckfield 50 A6
Dallington 84 D3
Danehill 34 A4
Ditchling 98 D3
Dodd's Hill 35 D2
Dormans Park 1 E6
Dormansland 2 B8
Durgates 29 E5
East Chiltington 100 A3
East Dean 187 B8
East Grinstead 1 E2
East Hoathly 105 B5
Eastbourne 185 B2
Eridge Green 16 B3
Etchingham 44 B1
Etchingwood 56 D1
Ewhurst Green 66 B5
Fairlight 138 C4
Fairlight Cove 138 F5
Fairwarp 36 B2
Falmer 144 D6
Felbridge 1 A6
Felcourt 1 C8
Five Ashes 58 B7
Flackley Ash 68 F3
Fletching 53 F4
Flimwell 32 C3
Flowers Green 130 F3
Folkington 172 B4
Fordcombe 6 B5
Forest Row 11 F3
Four Oaks 68 C5
Four Throws 46 D8
Framfield 79 B6
Frant 17 C3
Friar's Gate 25 B7
Friston 183 A2
Ginger's Green 130 C6
Glynde 147 E7
Goatham Green 89 E5
Goddard's Green 72 A5
Golden Cross
  (nr Hailsham) 127 D6
Golden Cross
  (nr Herstmonceux) ... 130 E3
Green Street 135 B4
Groombridge 15 C7
Grove Hill 107 E1
Guestling Green 138 A8
Guestling Thorn 116 A4
Hadlow Down 57 C5
Hailsham 152 C8
Halland 104 C5
Hammerwood 3 B3
Hamsey 123 C6
Hankham 174 B8
Hartfield 13 D4
Hassocks 97 E4
Hastings 160 B3
Haywards Heath 50 C3
Heathfield 82 B7
Hellingly 129 A5
Henwood Green 9 E6
Heron's Ghyll 36 E3
Herstmonceux 130 E6
High Hurstwood 37 A1
Holtye 3 F3
Hooe 155 D8
Hooe Common 132 F2
Hook Green 19 C4
Horam 106 E7
Horsted Keynes 33 D5
Hove 163 B5
Hurst Green 45 B3
Hurst Wickham 97 C6
Hurstpierpoint 97 B6
Icklesham 116 E6
Iden 70 B4
Iford 146 B3
Isfield 102 E7
Jevington 183 C8
John's Cross 87 C7
Keymer 98 B4
Kilndown 20 F3
Kingston near Lewes ... 145 E5
Lamberhurst 20 B5
Langton Green 6 E3
Laughton 126 C6
Lewes 123 F1
Lidham Hill 115 E6
Linkhill 47 A4
Lions Green 81 B1
Litlington 182 B8
Little Horsted 78 C1
Lower Cousley Wood 30 E8
Lower Dicker 128 D3
Lower Horsebridge 128 F3
Lower Street 133 B5
Lower Willingdon 173 C4
Lunsford Cross 133 E2
Magham Down 129 F4
Maresfield 55 A5
Mark Cross 28 A4
Mayfield 40 A2
Maynard's Green 82 A1
Mill Corner 67 A3
Milton Street 171 D5
Mount Pleasant 101 F6
Mountfield 87 A5
Muddles Green 127 F8
Netherfield 86 C2
Newbury's 30 B8
Newenden 48 D3
Newhaven 179 E6
Newick 76 C8
Ninfield 133 B6
Norman's Bay 176 D8
North Chailey 75 E6
Northbridge Street 64 C6
Northiam 67 B6
Norton 180 C8
Nutley 35 C4
Offham 122 F5
Old Heathfield 82 D5
Ovingdean 165 D3
Oxley's Green 85 E8
Peacehaven 178 D7
Peacehaven Heights ... 178 F5
Peasmarsh 69 B2
Pell Green 30 A7
Pembury 9 C6
Penhurst 110 E6
Pett 138 E8
Pevensey 175 B6
Pevensey Bay 175 E4
Piddinghoe 168 A2
Piltdown 54 C1
Plumpton 121 E8
Plumpton Green 99 E6
Polegate 173 B5
Ponts Green 110 B4
Portslade-by-Sea 162 B5
Potman's Heath 49 E4
Poundgate 37 A6
Poundsbridge 6 D8
Punnett's Town 83 C5
Pyecombe 119 B6
Quaker's Platt 2 A8
Ringmer 124 C6
Ripe 126 D1
Robertsbridge 64 B4
Rockrobin 29 D6
Rodmell 146 D1
Romford 9 F7
Roser's Cross 80 F6
Rotherfield 39 B7
Rottingdean 177 A6
Royal Tunbridge Wells ... 8 D3
Rushlake Green 83 D2
Rusthall 7 C4
Rye 93 B6
Rye Foreign 69 E1
Rye Harbour 93 F2
Saint's Hill 6 A8
Salehurst 64 D5
Saltdean 177 D6
Sandhurst 47 C6
Sandhurst Cross 46 F4
Scaynes Hill 51 E3
Seaford 180 D2
Sedlescombe 88 D1
Selmeston 149 D2
Sharpthorne 21 A6
Sheffield Green 53 C7
Shellies Green 138 C8
Shoreham-by-Sea 161 A5
Shortbridge 77 E8
Shortgate 104 B3
Shover's Green 30 C1
Smart's Hill 6 A8
South Chailey 100 D7
South Heighton 168 E2
South Street 75 E1
Southease 167 E7
Southwick 161 F7
Sparrow's Green 29 F5
Speldhurst 7 B7
Spithurst 101 F7
Standen Street 47 D8
Staplecross 65 E2
Stone Cross
  (nr Eastbourne) 174 C6
Stone Cross
  (nr Royal
  Tunbridge Wells) 6 A2
Stonebridge 29 E6
Stonecrouch 31 F6
Stonegate 42 F6
Streat 99 C3
Tarring Neville 168 D4
Teasley Mead 5 C4
Telscombe 167 B3
Telscombe Cliffs 178 A8
The Moor
  (nr Hurst Green) 45 F8
The Moor
  (nr Westfield) 114 E2
Three Cups Corner 83 F5
Three Leg Cross 31 D3
Three Oaks 115 E2
Ticehurst 31 E1
Tidebrook 41 A8
Town Row 27 C2
Turner's Green 29 F6
Udimore 91 C2
Union Street 32 B3
Upper Dicker 151 A8
Upper Wellingham 124 B8
Vinehall Street 87 C7
Wadhurst 30 A4
Waldron 80 F3
Waldron Down 80 D8
Walter's Green 5 D7
Wannock 172 E4
Warbleton 83 A1
Wartling 154 D7
Watermill 134 B4
Wellbrook 39 E1
West Firle 148 C3
Westdean 182 B4
Westfield 114 F4
Westham 174 E5
Westmeston 120 F8
Whatlington 88 A1
White Post 5 D7
Whitesmith 127 B8
Willingdon 173 A1
Wilmington 171 F5
Winchelsea 117 E7
Winchelsea Beach 118 A5
Windmill Hill 131 B6
Witham 14 A3
Wivelsfield 74 B5
Wivelsfield Green 74 D5
Wood's Corner 84 F3
Woodingdean 165 D7
Woolbridge 39 D2
Wych Cross 22 E5